SCHOLAR Study Guide
Higher English

Authored by:

Unit 1

Andrew Proffitt (Bearsden Academy)

Jenny Simpson (Hutchesons' Grammar School)

Unit 2

Iain Fulton (Glen Urquhart High School)

Nicola McNeil (Wester Hailes Education Centre)

Unit 3

Gary Smith (St. Columba's School)

Reviewed by:

Hugh Murchie (Previously Belmont Academy)

Jim McLaren (Perth Academy)

Heriot-Watt University
Edinburgh EH14 4AS, United Kingdom.

First published 2018 by Heriot-Watt University.

This edition published in 2018 by Heriot-Watt University SCHOLAR.

Copyright © 2018 SCHOLAR Forum.

Members of the SCHOLAR Forum may reproduce this publication in whole or in part for educational purposes within their establishment providing that no profit accrues at any stage, Any other use of the materials is governed by the general copyright statement that follows.

All rights reserved. No part of this publication may be reproduced, stored in a retrieval system or transmitted in any form or by any means, without written permission from the publisher.

Heriot-Watt University accepts no responsibility or liability whatsoever with regard to the information contained in this study guide.

Distributed by the SCHOLAR Forum.

SCHOLAR Study Guide Higher English

Higher English Course Code: C824 76

ISBN 978-1-911057-41-3

Print Production and Fulfilment in UK by Print Trail www.printtrail.com

Acknowledgements

Thanks are due to the members of Heriot-Watt University's SCHOLAR team who planned and created these materials, and to the many colleagues who reviewed the content.

We would like to acknowledge the assistance of the education authorities, colleges, teachers and students who contributed to the SCHOLAR programme and who evaluated these materials.

Grateful acknowledgement is made for permission to use the following material in the SCHOLAR programme:

The Scottish Qualifications Authority for permission to use Past Papers assessments.

The Scottish Government for financial support.

The content of this Study Guide is aligned to the Scottish Qualifications Authority (SQA) curriculum.

All brand names, product names, logos and related devices are used for identification purposes only and are trademarks, registered trademarks or service marks of their respective holders.

Contents

1	Reading for Understanding, Analysis and Evaluation	1
1	Reading	3
2	Understanding	19
3	Analysis	41
4	Evaluation	87
5	The comparison question	95
6	Exam skills	101
7	Practice Papers	111
A	Acknowledgements	129

2	Critical reading	131
1	Scottish Texts: Prose	133
2	Scottish Texts: Drama	157
3	Scottish Texts: Poetry	177
4	Scottish Texts: Exam techniques	219
5	Critical Essay	243
A	Acknowledgements	311

3	Portfolio	313
1	Creative writing	315
2	Discursive writing	411
3	Talking: Tips and techniques	469

Glossary	483
Answers to questions and activities	488

Unit 1: Reading for Understanding, Analysis and Evaluation

1	Reading		3
	1.1	What are U, A & E?	4
	1.2	Sources for reading	5
	1.3	Vocabulary	7
	1.4	Learning points	17
2	Understanding		19
	2.1	Audience and purpose	20
	2.2	Main ideas vs. supporting detail	21
	2.3	Line of thought and line of argument	24
	2.4	Summarising in your own words	33
	2.5	Explaining ideas in your own words	34
	2.6	Explaining in your own words	36
	2.7	Learning points	37
	2.8	End of topic test	38
3	Analysis		41
	3.1	Word Choice	43
	3.2	Imagery	51
	3.3	Sentence structure	60
	3.4	Tone	73
	3.5	Learning points	79
	3.6	End of topic test	80
4	Evaluation		87
	4.1	Evaluating effectiveness	88
	4.2	Evaluating introductions	89
	4.3	Evaluating conclusions	89
	4.4	Evaluating supporting details	90
	4.5	Practising evaluation skills	91
	4.6	Learning points	93
	4.7	End of topic test	94

> **Key point**
>
> Many of the activities and examples in these materials are based upon the 2015 SQA Higher RUAE paper, passages 1 and 2.
>
> 1. Adapted from 'Goodbye birds. Goodbye butterflies. Hello... farmageddon,' by Isabell Oakeshott, taken from The Sunday Times, 19 January 2014.
>
> 2. Adapted from 'Pasture to the Plate' by Audrey Ayton, taken from The Observer supplement, 10 July 1994.
>
> You will find it useful to have a copy of this paper next to you as you work through the resources.

1.1 What are U, A & E?

Whenever you read a text you automatically read for understanding, analysis and evaluation, whether you know it or not. In the exam paper, you slow down that process.

As you will know from National 5:

- understanding is thinking carefully about making sense of the text and the writer's ideas - in other words, you focus on *what* the writer is saying;
- analysis is thinking carefully about the language choices the writer has made when writing the text, such as the vocabulary they choose and how they structure their ideas - in other words, you focus on *how* the writer has expressed their ideas;
- evaluation is thinking carefully about the effectiveness of both ideas and language, making up your own mind about whether the writing convinces us about an opinion or an argument, gets information across well, or succeeds in entertaining us - in other words, you focus on *how well* the writing achieves its purpose.

In addition to these core skills, the Higher RUAE paper also asks you to *compare* two passages on a related topic, identifying similarities and/or differences in the writers' arguments.

This unit will build on everything you learned about RUAE to successfully tackle National 5; it will enhance the skills you have and make you an even more successful reader.

It will focus on the RUAE paper. All the skills you develop here can help you with the Scottish Set Text and you will also be able to transfer your knowledge to your own writing, especially your Portfolio.

1.2 Sources for reading

Now, more than ever, you must make time to read as widely as possible. Candidates with a broad vocabulary and a wide understanding of contemporary issues perform better at Higher.

As at National 5, the RUAE paper is non-fiction. However, at Higher, there are two pieces of journalism from newspapers, magazines or non-fiction books.

They are chosen for their complex and detailed use of language, their strong persuasive line of argument and distinctive style adopted by the writer. In other words, the passages chosen will likely reflect the personality of the writer far more than the passages you will have encountered at National 5. Being familiar with this style of writing, regardless of the topic or argument, is the key to success.

In the past, the SQA has used articles from *The Times*, *The Independent*, *The Observer* and *The Guardian*. So an easy and enjoyable way to prepare for the exam is to regularly read this type of writing. The articles that will be of most use to you are known as *feature, comment, opinion* or *editorial pieces*. They could be on any topic at all —find the ones that interest you the most.

In addition to newspapers and magazines, SQA have also made use of writing taken from websites and blogs. Many leading figures from politics, sport, the arts, science, education, and business blog. These can be interesting reads too. Finally, you may also want to read some book length non-fiction, and useful recommendations can be found on such sites as *London Review of Books*, *Guardian Books*, *Herald Scotland Books* and *New York Times Books*.

Many newspapers and magazines have apps you could download to your device, which will bring quality writing to you, meaning it couldn't be easier to prepare effectively for Higher RUAE. You may also like to follow some of these newspapers, magazines, writers, bloggers and cultural figures on Twitter.

Sources for reading activity Go online

Visit some of the websites listed below and find articles that you are interested in. Add the websites you like best to your bookmarks/favourites. Return regularly to read something new.

BBC News http://www.bbc.co.uk/news
BBC News: Magazine http://www.bbc.co.uk/news/magazine
BBC News: Special Reports http://www.bbc.co.uk/news/special_reports
The Guardian: Comment is Free http://www.theguardian.com/uk/commentisfree
The Guardian: Opinion Weekly Videos http://www.theguardian.com/commentisfree/series/comment-is-free-weekly
The Herald: Opinion http://www.heraldscotland.com/opinion/
The Independent: Voices http://www.independent.co.uk/voices
The New York Times: Opinion Pages http://www.nytimes.com/pages/opinion/index.html
The Observer: The Debate http://www.theguardian.com/theobserver/series/the-debate
The Scotsman http://www.scotsman.com/
The Telegraph: Comment & Analysis http://www.telegraph.co.uk/comment/
The Telegraph: Personal View http://www.telegraph.co.uk/comment/personal-view/
Times Literary Supplement http://www.the-tls.co.uk
New Scientist https://www.newscientist.com/
Sight & Sound http://www.bfi.org.uk/news-opinion/sight-sound-magazine
The Economist:1843 http://www.intelligentlifemagazine.com/
Focus Magazine http://www.sciencefocus.com/
Vanity Fair http://www.vanityfair.com/

Use the following reading log to record the articles you read every week.

TOPIC 1. READING

- Reading quality newspaper articles will help improve your Reading for Understanding, Analysis and Evaluation skills.
- It may also suggest possible topics and arguments for your Writing Folio.
- Use the suggested list of publication websites and sources to find interesting articles to help you complete the log.
- Your teacher might also give you articles to read and log.
- Aim to read at least one article per week.

Title Author Source Date	Purpose(s) inform, persuade, entertain + Audience(s) most likely to be interested in topic	Summary of main points, arguments and ideas (avoid specific details)	Two new or complex words from the article with definitions	Personal response What are your thoughts and opinions on the topic?
Title: 'Lego faces getting angrier, study finds' Author: John Jones Source: The Guardian Date: 12/06/13	Purpose(s): • to inform • ~~to persuade~~ • ~~to entertain~~ Audience(s): • parents • nursery teachers	The number of angry expressions on Lego figures is increasing, happy faces decreasing. May be due to more Lego figures being based on theme/stories involving conflict. Some are concerned this may adversely affect children's development.	1. *Perceived* —past tense of verb 'perceive': to come to realise, understand, see or believe something. 2. *Upshot* —noun: the final result, outcome.	The article made me wonder how appropriate kids' toys are today and if they really have an effect on how children grow up. They probably do, but I think there are more damaging toys out there than angry Lego faces that we should be worried about.

Higher: Non-fiction reading log

1.3 Vocabulary

You should make every effort to expand your vocabulary as widely as possible. However, it is likely that you will come across some words in the Higher RUAE paper that are unfamiliar to you. In such situations remember your strategies for working out the meaning of an unfamiliar word.

© HERIOT-WATT UNIVERSITY

1.3.1 Use the context

Look at the rest of the sentence or the paragraph for clues about the meaning of the word.

Context clues   Go online

There's something calming about cartoon baddies[1]. We can depend on their despicable natures; we can rely on them to be really awful[2], all the time. In a world where everything else is in flux —who are we, where are we, why are we —the villains[3] of our childhood have remained reliably immoral[4]. Whether it's the nefarious Baron Greenback and his henchman Stiletto trying to outsmart Dangermouse, or Dastardly and Muttley trying to overtake the Ant Hill Mob, or even Skeletor causing big trouble for He-man from Castle Greyskull, [5]we know where we are with the depraved[6] and corrupt[7]. Their simplicity reassures us.

Notes:

[1] Idea of 'baddies' suggests stereotypical bad characters or antagonists in stories
[2] Suggests the depth of their bad behaviour
[3] Those who only behave badly
[4] Lacking in any kind of goodness
[5] All examples of classic cartoon bad guys set against their heroic counterparts
[6] Suggests wicked
[7] Suggests a willingness to act dishonestly

Q1: Read the context clues. Then choose the definition of 'nefarious' that best fits the context.

a) Evil
b) Kind-hearted
c) Multifaceted
d) Strong

> As the summer months wore on, there were increasing signs of rapprochement; hostilities all but ceased[1] and my parents began talking again[2]. It was a fragile peace[3], but peace it was; harmony[4] that we had not experienced in that house since my elder brother had left for school. To my relief, my father, not renowned for his warmth, actually seemed both affectionate[5] and relaxed; my mother visibly let go of the tension that had riven her face with lines and bags and wrinkles. Conciliation[6] was their watchword.
>
> Notes:
>
> [1] Suggestion that fighting has come to an end
> [2] Communication has resumed
> [3] No fighting or quarrelling
> [4] Sense of understanding and agreeing with each other
> [5] Being friendly and loving
> [6] Coming together to agree things

Q2: Read the context clues. Then choose the definition of 'rapprochement' that best fits the context.

a) Concern
b) Reconciliation
c) Dissent
d) Compromise

Schwarzenegger's stance has long been gubernatorial. Not only is he still a hulking physical specimen —an apt metaphor for such an approach —but he is absolute, firm and dominating[1] in personality. The move from Hollywood superstar to Californian political[2] aristocracy has been an easy one (no doubt aided by his marriage into the Kennedy[3] clan) and he is both influential and authoritative. Small wonder his nickname has been respun into 'The Governator[4]'.

Notes:

[1] Sense that he is a powerful figure.
[2] Connected to running the country
[3] Well-known American political family
[4] Pun on 'The Terminator' but now connected to his new role in California

Q3: Read the context clues. Then choose the definition of 'gubernatorial' that best fits the context.

a) Controlling
b) Easy-going
c) Popular
d) Confusing

....

TOPIC 1. READING

> There are those, of course, who will always claim that reality TV is vapid. That it's full of personality-less[1] personalities, that it churns out unstimulating telly[2] using tired[3] formats, that it is unimaginative[4] at best, and unpalatable at worse. Think of the TOWIE cast, the Geordie Shorers, the gravel-voiced sales team in Say Yes to the Dress —even reality's own royal family, the Kardashians —and it's not hard to see that reality TV is based on a formula where repetition is key: the same ideas, in the same settings, over and over again.[5]
>
> Notes:
>
> [1] There is nothing remarkable about them
> [2] The TV companies produce low quality boring programmes
> [3] The programmes have been overdone
> [4] Monotonous programmes
> [5] We watch the same things again and again

Q4: Read the context clues. Then choose the definition of 'vapid' that best fits the context.

a) Bland
b) Inspiring
c) Thoughtful
d) Irritating

1.3.2 Make connections to words you know

Look at the word carefully to see if it reminds you of other words you know. The whole word, or the main part of the word (the root), might look familiar.

Connect to words you know — Go online

Colonialism[1] flourished from the 16th century to the 20th century, and led to the rapid growth of many European powers, whose global reach seemingly knew no bounds. But with this speedy expansion came escalating[2] conflict. Not only between proud nations intent on expanding their empires, but also between settlers and the indigenous peoples they sought to displace. Colonialists typically viewed all other cultures as inferior to their own, and took it upon themselves to bestow their superior knowledge and values on those they encountered on their world tour. They saw it as their mission to spread the very best of Western religion, politics and government in less fortunate, more primitive lands. Of course, in reality, European empire-builders rarely played the role of cultural benefactor[3]. History is littered with examples of dictatorial[4] Western powers imposing themselves, uninvited, often by force, upon previously prosperous countries, only to undermine, exploit, and ravage their land, people and culture.

Notes:

[1] looks like 'colony'
[2] looks like 'escalator' and 'scale'
[3] looks like 'benefit'
[4] looks like 'dictator'

Q5: 'Colonialism' means...

a) the travelling of great distances.
b) the sending of settlers to establish control of another country.
c) the establishing of a slave trade.
d) the establishment of a new country by stealing land from another.

....

Q6: 'Escalating' means...

a) rising.
b) moving.
c) unexpected.
d) very large.

TOPIC 1. READING

Q7: 'Benefactor' means...
a) a person who invades another country.
b) a person who gives help.
c) a person who collects things.
d) a person who controls and dominates others.

....

Q8: 'Dictatorial' means...
a) highly ambitious.
b) ruling with absolute power.
c) wealthy and civilised.
d) loud and talkative.

1.3.3 Break down the word

Even if you don't recognise the root of the word, there might be another part of the word - the beginning (prefix) or the end (suffix) - that is familiar.

Common prefixes Go online

Q9: Match the following meanings with the common prefixes.

both	hypo-
two	para-
bad	post-
same	tri-
under, too little	trans-
beside	dys-
around	pseudo-
after	prot-
first, chief	peri-
false	ambi-
across	homo-
three	bi-

....

Q10: For each prefix, write down all the words you can think of that start the same way and share a similar meaning. When you have written down as many as you can, have a look at the answer.

© HERIOT-WATT UNIVERSITY

Common suffixes

Q11: Match the following meanings with the common suffixes.

place for	-eer
state or quality of	-esque
the person affected by an action	-itis
person who does something	-ish
in the style of, resembling	-ulent
practice, system or philosophy	-ling
inflammation of	-arium, -orium
small	-ee
full of	-ism
without, missing	-dom

....

Q12: For each prefix, write down all the words you can think of that start the same way and share a similar meaning. When you have written down as many as you can, have a look at the answer.

1.3.4 Work out the word class

Identifying the word class or 'part of speech' of an unfamiliar word will help you understand its relationship with the words around it, and allow you to make a better educated guess at its meaning.

Identifying the word class

Identify the emboldened word's word class.

Q13: The swimmer was hoping to achieve a new personal best.

a) Noun
b) Adjective
c) Verb
d) Adverb

....

TOPIC 1. READING

Q14: The aim of the game is to best your opponent and emerge victorious.
a) Noun
b) Adjective
c) Verb
d) Adverb

....

Q15: The best solution is not always the most convenient solution.
a) Noun
b) Adjective
c) Verb
d) Adverb

....

Q16: It has always been my belief that I perform best after a good night's sleep.
a) Noun
b) Adjective
c) Verb
d) Adverb

....

Q17: During Ramadan, Muslims fast from dawn to sunset.
a) Noun
b) Adjective
c) Verb
d) Adverb

....

Q18: Lately, buyers are less interested in how fast a car is; they are more concerned with how economical it is.
a) Noun
b) Adjective
c) Verb
d) Adverb

....

Q19: Call an ambulance. This man needs medical help fast!
a) Noun
b) Adjective
c) Verb
d) Adverb

....

© HERIOT-WATT UNIVERSITY

Q20: Twas brillig and the slithy toves did gyre and gimble in the wabe.

a) Noun
b) Adjective
c) Verb
d) Adverb

....

Q21: Twas brillig and the slithy toves did gyre and gimble in the wabe.

a) Noun
b) Adjective
c) Verb
d) Adverb

....

Q22: Twas brillig and the slithy toves did gyre and gimble in the wabe.

a) Noun
b) Adjective
c) Verb
d) Adverb

1.3.5 Try an alternative

Use the clues the context gives you, and any parts of the word that are familiar, to replace the word with another you think means the same thing. See if the sentence still makes sense. Try different alternatives to find a word that fits the context most precisely.

Alternative words Go online

Use the context clues to choose the best word to fill the gap.

Q23: There it was again. A noise. A distinct chime like a knife against the clearest of crystal, like the ring of a ship's bell, like a single note of a piano. I was already _____ from the demands of the day (I had not known, when taking the position, that quite so much of my time would be devoted to chasing an errant ten year old through the countryside, or rising before dawn to comfort a weeping six year old who even now, two years on, could not accept what had happened in this house that night) and I drew the covers even tighter, and snuggled into the nest of quilts and pillows that swathed the bed, trying to ignore the growing sense of unease rising in my chest, and making my mouth taste bitter.

a) enervated
b) nonplussed
c) entranced
d) appalled

....

TOPIC 1. READING

Q24: But deep in the warmth and the familiar comfort of the bed, I felt a little better. Calmer, less perturbed —and my characteristic poise returned: the _____ demeanour they had employed me for. A hush fell, and it was easy to believe I had imagined the noise. The heavy drag of sleep returned to my eyes, and nodding, I imagine I fell into a deep and tranquil sleep.

a) unruffled
b) disturbed
c) elated
d) violent

....

Q25: Again, a chime.
And then, from where I was not yet quite certain, came a scuffling and shuffling of what had to be feet against the worn boards of the hallway. I listened for the squeak I knew would come when he —or she or it —hit the board opposite the nursery, the board that had squeaked every time it was depressed by anything heavier than Millie, the ancient Labrador who prowled, but mostly slept, in the bedroom opposite. _____ in my covers, I believe I held my breath, although I was not conscious of it, and waited for the thing to reach the loose board, knowing that would mean it was directly outside the door.

a) concealed
b) cosseted
c) revealed
d) vulnerable

1.4 Learning points

Summary

- The Higher RUAE exam paper is a non-fiction text and a set of questions which will require you to show you can understand what the text is about, analyse how it is written, and evaluate how well it achieves its purpose.

- The reading skills you develop for the Higher RUAE exam are also used in other areas of the course.

- Regularly reading non-fiction writing is one of the best ways to improve your reading skills and improve your vocabulary.

- You can try to work out the meaning of an unfamiliar word in several ways: use context clues, make connections to words you know, break down prefixes and suffixes, identify the word class, and try an alternative.

Unit 1 Topic 2

Understanding

Contents

2.1 Audience and purpose 20
    2.1.1 Purpose. 20
2.2 Main ideas vs. supporting detail 21
    2.2.1 Supporting detail 23
2.3 Line of thought and line of argument 24
    2.3.1 Linkage of main ideas 27
    2.3.2 Linking sentences 30
2.4 Summarising in your own words 33
2.5 Explaining ideas in your own words 34
    2.5.1 Separating out ideas 34
2.6 Explaining in your own words 36
2.7 Learning points 37
2.8 End of topic test 38

Learning objective

By the end of this topic, you should be able to:

- identify and justify the audience and purpose of a text;
- identify main ideas and supporting detail;
- identify how ideas are structured and linked;
- understand what it means to explain ideas in your own words.

20 UNIT 1. READING FOR UNDERSTANDING, ANALYSIS AND EVALUATION

Questions that test your understanding of the writer's ideas make up the majority of the marks available in a RUAE paper. It is also true to say that they are the most straightforward question types.

You could be asked to *explain*, *identify* or *summarise* the writer's ideas. You could also be questioned on *how ideas are linked together* and *how ideas are developed*. All of these question types will require you to use your own words as far as possible. The reason you are asked to use your own words is that this proves you understand the writer's ideas.

> **Key point**
>
> Many of the activities and examples in these materials are based upon the 2015 SQA Higher RUAE paper, passages 1 and 2.
>
> 1. Adapted from 'Goodbye birds. Goodbye butterflies. Hello... farmageddon,' by Isabell Oakeshott, taken from The Sunday Times, 19 January 2014.
>
> 2. Adapted from 'Pasture to the Plate' by Audrey Ayton, taken from The Observer supplement, 10 July 1994.
>
> You will find it useful to have a copy of this paper next to you as you work through the resources.

2.1 Audience and purpose

A good starting point for understanding a passage in the kind of depth required for Higher English is to think about the possible audiences and purposes of the passage. While there are no direct questions about audience and purpose in the RUAE exam paper, thinking about these aspects will help you better understand the writer's argument.

> Identifying audience and purpose   Go online
>
> Use the reading log from Topic 1 to practise identifying audience and purpose.

2.1.1 Purpose

As you'll be aware from National 5, most texts are written for a purpose: for example, reports inform us, novels entertain us, and opinion pieces persuade us. The texts you encountered during National 5, were probably often 'neutral' in their purpose, or more focused on imparting straightforward information than persuading you of a point of view. This is not the case at Higher, where writers are often selected for their particular perspectives. This means that more often than not the purpose of the writing is to persuade.

© HERIOT-WATT UNIVERSITY

However, you'll also remember that more sophisticated writing —exactly the kind you can expect at Higher —will often have more than one purpose. For example, Charlie Brooker, who writes for The Guardian, generally produces texts that are designed to persuade us to his perspective but there's no denying that his writing is also informative and entertaining. So at different points in a text, the purpose might be different.

Look at the opening paragraph to 'Proms are a terrible, chintzy disappointment —perfect preparation for adulthood' by Jean Hannah Edelstein (The Guardian, 16th June 2016) as follows.

Example

> It might be **17 years since I attended my high-school prom in upstate New York**, but don't think for a moment that the memories aren't still burning bright: [1]the polyester scratch of my don't-stand-near-flames, floor-length frock. The weight of the extravagant corsage that extended from my wrist to my elbow, transforming my arm into a rosy garden border. [2]The inelegant scramble of six formal-wear-clad teenagers as we piled into the back seat of a stretch limousine. **Some may say that the increased popularity of American-style high-school proms in the UK is a bad thing for Britain's youth. I disagree.** Nothing prepares teenagers better for adulthood than the prom, and that's because it's so terrible.[3]
>
> Notes:
>
> [1] The purpose here is to recount personal experience
> [2] Here the writer employs humour to entertain the reader
> [3] Here the writer establishes an argument and counter-argument, designed to persuade the reader

Remember too, that understanding the purpose itself is just a starting point (particularly as you will not be asked a direct question about purpose in the exam). After you understand the writer's purpose, you must begin to establish how that purpose is being pursued by the writer: what are they saying to persuade us (understanding questions will examine this) and how are they saying it (analysis questions will examine this). You might also be asked how well they achieve their purpose (evaluation questions will examine this).

Of course, you will have two passages in which to identify purpose, and the final 5 mark comparative question will ask you to identify the places where the writers' purposes connect (agreement) or contrast (disagreement).

To fully revise identifying possible purposes for a text, visit the SCHOLAR National 5 English pages, Topic 2.1: Audience and purpose.

2.2 Main ideas vs. supporting detail

After you establish the audience and purpose for the text, the next thing to do is to clearly understand the main ideas the writer is putting across, and the details they have selected to support that idea.

22 UNIT 1. READING FOR UNDERSTANDING, ANALYSIS AND EVALUATION

Main ideas

The main idea is the most important point that the writer makes in each paragraph or the most important piece of information.

Main ideas can sometimes be identified by their location in the paragraph. You will already know from your own writing that it is usual to take a new paragraph for a new idea. Therefore, paragraphs often start with a topic sentence that will introduce the new idea that the rest of the paragraph will go on to discuss. Sometimes, however, a topic sentence might come at the end of a paragraph, summing up the main idea after the writer has spent time making a case, laying out facts or building anticipation.

Wherever it appears in a paragraph, the topic sentence is the hook on which all the other details in a paragraph hang.

Which is the topic sentence? Go online

Identify the topic sentence in each paragraph taken from the 2015 Higher RUAE paper, passage 2.

Q1: The aim in confining animals indoors was to cut costs —it succeeded. Indoors, one or two workers can 'look after' hundreds of penned or tethered pigs, or a hundred thousand chickens. Great economies were made and thousands of farm workers lost their jobs. This new policy of cheap meat, eggs and cheese for everyone was completely in tune with the national mood, as Britain ripped up its ration books. It was also in tune with nutritional thinking, as nutritionists at that time thought greater consumption of animal protein would remedy all dietary problems.

....

Q2: So factory farming marched on and became more and more intensive. Where first there were one or two laying hens in a cage, eventually there became five in the same small space. The broiler chicken sheds expanded to cram in vast acres of birds. Many beef cattle were confined in buildings and yards. Until mad cow disease emerged, such animals were fed all kinds of organic matter as cheap food. In the UK dairy cows still spend their summers in the fields, but many of their offspring are reared in the cruelty of intensive veal crate systems.

....

Q3: The aim of those early advocates of intensive farming was 'fast food' - fast from birth to table - and again, they succeeded. Chicken, once an occasional treat, now the most popular meat in Britain, owes its low price largely to the short life of the bird. Today's broiler chicken has become the fastest growing creature on earth: from egg to take-away in seven weeks. Most farm animals now have less than half of their pre-war lifespan. Either they are worn out from overproduction of eggs or milk, or have been bred and fed to reach edible size in a few short weeks or months.

....

© HERIOT-WATT UNIVERSITY

TOPIC 2. UNDERSTANDING

Q4: But meat, eggs and dairy products have indeed become cheap, affordable even to the poor. All of which made nutritionists exceedingly happy until they discovered that their mid-century predecessors had made a mighty blunder. Before intensive farming brought cheap meat and dairy products to our tables, man obtained most of his calories from cereal crops and vegetables. The meat with which he supplemented this diet had a much lower fat content than intensively produced products. Now, however, degenerative diseases like coronary heart disease and several types of cancer have been linked to our increased consumption of fatty foods. War-time Britons, on their measly ration of meat and one ounce of cheese a week, were much healthier.

....

Q5: It is also a scientifically proven fact that intensive farming has caused the loss of hedgerows and wildlife sustained by that habitat, has polluted waterways, decimated rural employment and caused the loss of traditional small farms. We need to act in the interests of human health. We need to show humane concern for animals. We need to preserve what remains of the countryside by condemning the practice of intensive farming. We need to return the animals to the fields, and re-adopt the environmentally friendly, humane and healthy system we had and lost: the small mixed farm.

2.2.1 Supporting detail

Supporting details come in all shapes and sizes at Higher. There are many types of supporting detail, including statistics, facts, quotes, examples, anecdotes and comparisons.

Statistics	Number facts such as dates, quantities, percentages, measurements...
Facts	Evidence that can be tested or proved
Quotes	Something someone has said, usually someone known as an expert on a particular issue or somebody famous
Examples	Specific instances or cases that back up the point being made
Anecdotes	A short description of an event, usually personal, that is often funny or interesting
Comparisons	Looking at the similarities and/or differences between people or ideas or things
Speculation	Put forward a theory or conjecture about what might happen in the future

In the 2015 Higher RUAE paper, passage one, the writer Isabell Oakeshott supported her opinion about intensive farming (and so promoted her purpose: to persuade) using several types of supporting detail.

© HERIOT-WATT UNIVERSITY

Identifying supporting detail	Go online 

Q6: Match the extracts from the text with the type of supporting detail being used.

The writer describes her experience of visiting an enormous orchard in California	Speculation
The writer tells us that bees are hired in, that cows never see grass, and how much chickens sell for.	Statistics
The writer suggests that the British countryside could soon look like the Central Valley, California.	Quotes
The writer repeats the words of Owen Paterson, the UK environment secretary, a man on local radio, and the British Government.	Example
The writer highlights how cheap food has become by telling us 'things that were once delicacies such as smoked salmon, are now as cheap as chips.'	Comparison
The writer tells us that 'the population of tree sparrows has failed 97%'; '50 billion [animals] are kept permanently indoors'; and 'California's bovine population produces as much sewage as 90 million people'	Anecdote
The writer said 'the air can be worse than in Los Angeles'	Facts

2.3 Line of thought and line of argument

In most Higher RUAE passages, the writer pursues their purpose through a line of argument, and it is this organising of points into a complete and convincing argument that should persuade you of their point of view. While there are really any number of ways a skilful writer can create a line of argument, two of the most common are hierarchy of importance and the ripple effect.

Hierarchy of importance: putting the most important or persuasive point at the start, then working through other points in decreasing order of importance or persuasiveness.

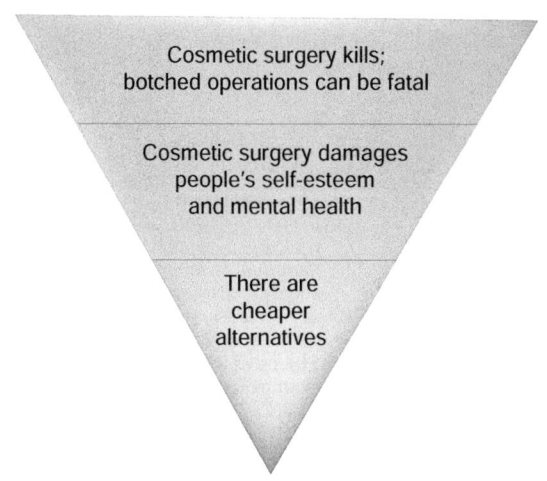

Ripple effect: starting with a small detail (perhaps a seemingly insignificant event or anecdote) then zooming out to show how that fits into a bigger argument or wider issue.

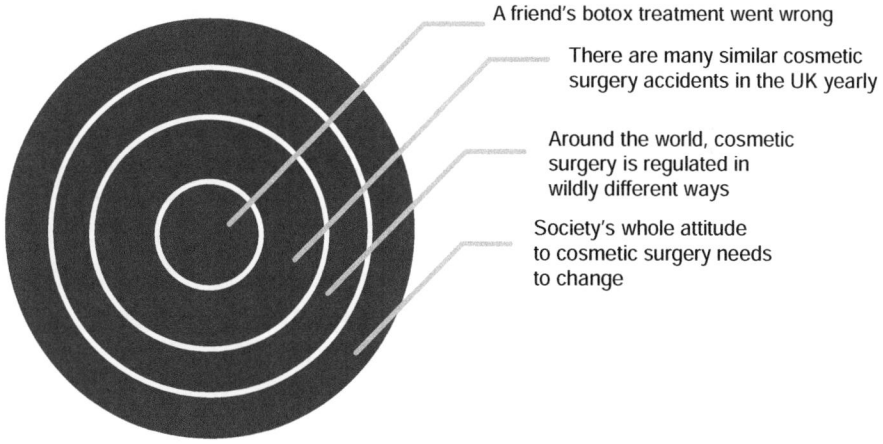

Argument and counterargument: making an argument, offering a counterargument and then dismantling that counterargument forcefully.

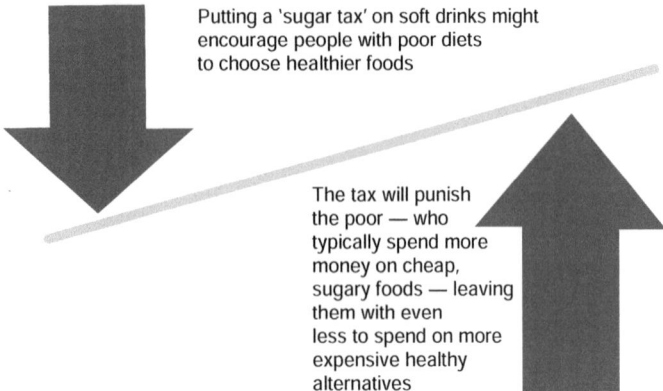

Putting a 'sugar tax' on soft drinks might encourage people with poor diets to choose healthier foods

The tax will punish the poor — who typically spend more money on cheap, sugary foods — leaving them with even less to spend on more expensive healthy alternatives

Circularity: often a writer will use their conclusion to return to an idea, image, example or anecdote used near the start of the article. This can create the feeling of 'closure' - finishing where we began. In the course of the article, however, ideas and arguments will have been explored, which might mean the writer, and/or the reader, now views the opening idea differently.

Whichever pattern they follow, a writer must be focused on the clarity of their argument, the logical structure of their points. Without this, a reader will not be persuaded into agreeing with them.

Take another look at the 2015 Higher RUAE paper, passage one. If you were to work through the line of argument, you might discover this structure:

1. The writer describes the scale and strangeness of the intensive farm in California.
2. She then suggests the British countryside could become like this.
3. She then identifies what might make the British countryside like this.
4. She then discusses the global implications of such farming.
5. She then returns to look more closely at the environmental effects of such processes, specifically again in California.
6. She ends by suggesting these environmental effects pose a danger.

In one respect the writer uses the ripple effect —she begins by focusing on one single anecdotal example in California, and then works out —via the UK —to the global implications of such a model.

TOPIC 2. UNDERSTANDING 27

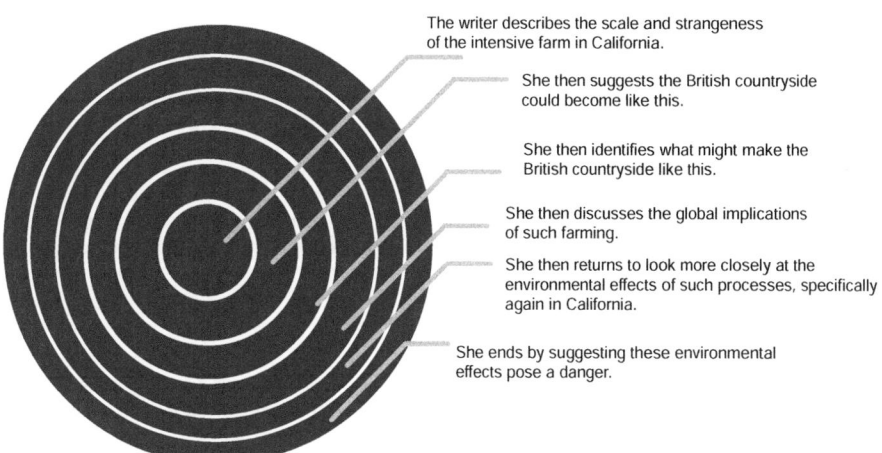

The writer describes the scale and strangeness of the intensive farm in California.

She then suggests the British countryside could become like this.

She then identifies what might make the British countryside like this.

She then discusses the global implications of such farming.

She then returns to look more closely at the environmental effects of such processes, specifically again in California.

She ends by suggesting these environmental effects pose a danger.

However, she doesn't finish there, and like many of the passages selected by SQA, she returns to where she started, her first example of California, and then again returns to speculating on the future of British farming —restating her position forcefully.

Creating a clear line of argument   Go online

Q7: Examine passage two from the 2015 RUAE exam paper. Make notes about the structure of the passage: how the main ideas are sequenced. What patterns are employed by Audrey Eyton?

2.3.1 Linkage of main ideas

The line of thought in a text is not only created by the order of the main ideas; ideas are also linked together.

One way that ideas can be linked together is with 'signpost words' (also known as 'discourse markers' or 'connectives'). Just as a signpost tells you where a road is heading, signpost words show the reader where a line of thought is going.

Signpost words can show that:

- the line of thought will continue in the same direction by *adding* similar ideas;

    Example   Homework takes up time that could be spent together as a family. *Furthermore*, it is often the cause of arguments between parents and children.

© HERIOT-WATT UNIVERSITY

- the line of thought will change direction by *contrasting* an idea with the one before;

    Example Many people assume that the more homework you do, the smarter you'll be. *On the contrary*, research shows that too much homework can in fact be damaging to a child's learning.

- one idea leads to another through *cause and effect*;

    Example There is evidence that homework has no effect on primary school pupils' academic progress. *Consequently*, many primary schools no longer set any homework at all.

- there is an important idea ahead by *emphasising*.

    Example There are many reasons to ban homework: it frustrates parents, adds to teachers' workload but, *most importantly of all*, it sucks the fun out of learning for young children.

- there is an alternative by *qualifying* an idea.

    Example Parents dislike the arguments and stress that homework can cause, *yet* they often feel it is an important part of their child's education.

- there is an example ahead by *illustrating* an idea that came before.

    Example Homework does not always need to involve writing and worksheets. *For instance*, one primary school sets homework tasks that require pupils to photograph a nature walk, record an interview with a local celebrity, and build a website.

- the line of thought is about to come to an end by *summing up*.

    Example *In conclusion*, it seems unlikely that homework will ever disappear completely.

TOPIC 2. UNDERSTANDING

Signpost words Go online

Sort the signpost words into their correct categories in the following questions.

Q8:

Adding	Contrasting

Signpost words: on the other hand, and, as well as, whereas, alternatively, moreover, furthermore, additionally, otherwise, instead of, unlike, also, conversely, too.

....

Q9:

Cause and effect	Emphasising

Signpost words: especially, because, since, in particular, significantly, therefore, above all, consequently, in fact, hence, notably, so, thus, indeed.

....

Q10:

Qualifying	Illustrating	Summing up

Signpost words: illustrated by, in conclusion, to sum up, as long as, however, last of all, such as, as revealed by, although, in the case of, in summary, for example, except, overall, but, for instance, in other words, finally, if, in short, unless.

© HERIOT-WATT UNIVERSITY

Punctuation

In addition to these words and phrases, punctuation can also help you see the development and linkage in the writer's line of argument. The most commonly used punctuation marks for this purpose are shown in the following table.

Colon	Introduces expansions of an idea, including examples, definitions, and explanations
Semi-colon	Links two similar ideas or two contrasting ideas
Dash	Introduces expansions of an idea, including examples, definitions, and explanations
Parenthesis	Inserts additional information to support a point; offers an aside from the writer, often a personal opinion

For a more detailed look at punctuation, see Topic 3 Analysis: 3.3.1

2.3.2 Linking sentences

As you will know from National 5, ideas can be linked together by linking sentences. This is also the case at Higher, although you may also be asked to look at the way full paragraphs form links between ideas.

Remember, that the essential skills are the same: identify the ways in which the lines referenced —whether a single sentence or a paragraph —connect to the idea discussed before and the idea discussed ahead.

> Example On a cold, bright November day I stood among a million almond trees and breathed in the sweet air. I was in Central Valley, California, in an orchard stretching over 700,000 acres. Before me was a vision of how the British countryside may look one day. Beyond the almond orchards were fields of pomegranates, pistachios, grapes and apricots. Somewhere in the distance were almost two million dairy cows, producing six billion dollars' worth of milk a year.
>
> *It may sound like the Garden of Eden but it is a deeply disturbing place.* Among the perfectly aligned rows of trees and cultivated crops are no birds, no butterflies, no beetles or shrubs. There is not a single blade of grass or a hedgerow, and the only bees arrive by lorry, transported across the United States. The bees are hired by the day to fertilise the blossom, part of a multibillion-dollar industry that has sprung up to do a job that nature once did for free.

- 'like the Garden of Eden' refers back to the previous idyllic description of the trees and the air.
- '... but ...' indicates that the idea that follows will qualify the situation by offering a different perspective.
- '... a deeply disturbing place' introduces the paragraph that follows, which highlights the problems concealed beneath such a perfect picture.

| Analysing linking sentences | Go online  |

Identify the parts of each of the following linking sentence that refer back to a previous idea, and link forward to the subsequent idea.

As for the cows, they last only two or three years, ten-to-fifteen years less than their natural life span. Crammed into barren pens on tiny patches of land, they stand around listlessly waiting to be fed, milked or injected with antibiotics. Through a combination of selective breeding, artificial diets and growth hormones designed to maximise milk production, they are pushed so grotesquely beyond their natural limit that they are soon worn out. In their short lives they never see grass.

Could the British countryside ever look like this? If current trends continue, the answer is yes. Farming in Britain is at a crossroads, threatened by a wave of intensification from America. The first mega-dairies and mega-piggeries are already here. Bees are disappearing, with serious implications for harvests. Hedgerows, vital habitats for wildlife, have halved since the Second World War. The countryside is too sterile to support many native birds. In the past forty years the population of tree sparrows has fallen by 97%.

Q11: The link back to the previous idea is:
a) Could
b) British countryside
c) look
d) this

....

Q12: The link forward to the subsequent idea is:
a) Could
b) British countryside
c) look
d) this

....

With an eye to the future, Owen Paterson, the UK environment secretary, has been urging families to buy British food. Choosing to buy fewer imports would reduce the relentless pressure British farmers are under to churn out more for less. Paterson's vision is of a more eco-friendly way of eating, based on locally-produced, seasonal fruit and vegetables and, crucially, British meat.

But, as I discovered when I began looking into the way food is produced, increasingly powerful forces are pulling us in the opposite direction. We have become addicted to cheap meat, fish and dairy products from supply lines that stretch across the globe. On the plus side, it means that supermarkets can sell whole chickens for as little as £3. Things that were once delicacies, such as smoked salmon, are now as cheap as chips. On the downside, cheap chicken and farmed fish are fatty and flaccid. Industrially reared farm animals —50 billion of them a year worldwide —are kept permanently indoors, treated like machines and pumped with drugs.

Q13: The link back to the previous idea is:

a) But
b) I discovered
c) the way food is produced
d) powerful forces are pulling us in the opposite direction

....

Q14: The link forward to the subsequent idea is:

a) But
b) I discovered
c) the way food is produced
d) powerful forces are pulling us in the opposite direction

....

Exploring the area by car, it was not long before I saw my first mega-dairy, an array of towering, open-sided shelters over muddy pens. The stench of manure was overwhelming —not the faintly sweet, earthy smell of cowpats familiar from the British countryside, but a nauseating reek bearing no relation to digested grass. I saw farms every couple of miles, all with several thousand cows surrounded by mud, corrugated iron and concrete.

It may seem hard to imagine such a scene in Britain but it is not far-fetched. Proposals for an 8,000 cow mega-dairy in Lincolnshire, based on the American model, were thrown out after a public outcry. On local radio the man behind the scheme claimed that 'cows do not belong in fields'. It will be the first of many similar fights, because dairies are expanding and moving indoors. The creep of industrial agriculture in Britain has taken place largely unnoticed, perhaps because so much of it happens behind closed doors. The British government calls it 'sustainable intensification'. Without fuss or fanfare, farm animals have slowly disappeared from fields and moved into hangars and barns.

Q15: The link back to the previous idea is:

a) It may seem hard
b) Britain
c) such a scene
d) it is not far-fetched

....

Q16: The link forward to the subsequent idea is:

a) It may seem hard
b) Britain
c) such a scene
d) it is not far-fetched

2.4 Summarising in your own words

You are increasingly likely to be asked to provide summaries in your own words in understanding questions. Summarising with accuracy is perhaps more difficult than you might think: it's easy to fall into the trap of missing the key idea in a summary point, or joining separate points into one, or making the same point twice.

As you'll know from National 5, a summary gives a broad overview of the main ideas or points the writer makes, but ignores supporting detail. Summaries should usually be written in shorter, simpler language than the words used in the passage, and can be bullet pointed. When summarising you are looking at the text from the point of view of the reader, explaining what the writer does or says in the text.

Look at the 2015 Higher RUAE paper, passage one. If you were asked to summarise the key points made by the writer, your answer might look like the following list.

1. Industrialisation has taken over from nature, especially in the USA.
2. British farming is at a point in its development where it too could lose its connection to nature.
3. We are eating and demanding more and more cheaply produced food.
4. The problem is global.
5. Industrial farming is destroying the landscape in the USA.
6. Industrial farming is already happening in Britain and not enough people realise that it is.

As discussed in 2.3, the writer has used the ripple effect —moving from the 'local' example to global issues —and then a circular structure where she returns to her first two points again at the end.

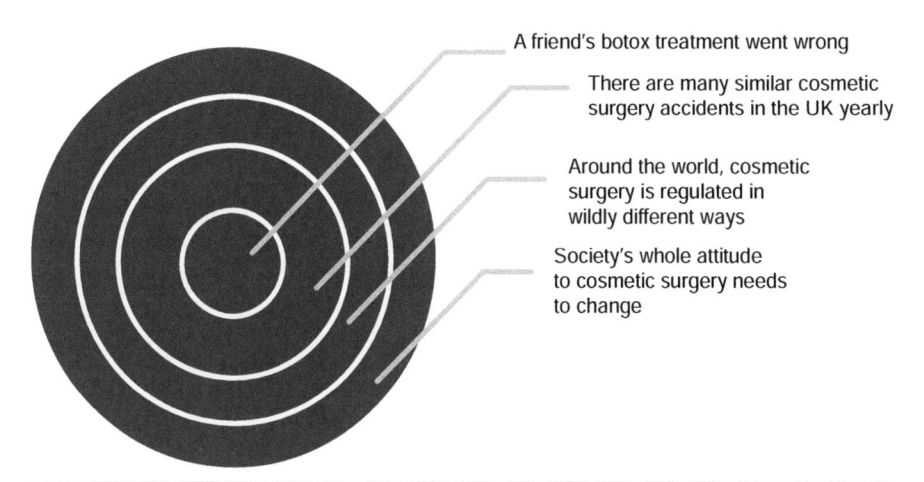

A friend's botox treatment went wrong

There are many similar cosmetic surgery accidents in the UK yearly

Around the world, cosmetic surgery is regulated in wildly different ways

Society's whole attitude to cosmetic surgery needs to change

Q17: Examine passage two from the 2015 RUAE exam paper. Summarise the main idea in each paragraph. When you are finished, compare your answer with the suggested answer.

2.5 Explaining ideas in your own words

In the RUAE exam you will not only be asked to summarise the main ideas of a text; you will also be asked to show your understanding of these ideas by using your own words to explain them. You do not need to discuss or comment on them; instead, you simply find the ideas or points in the section of the text you are directed to, separate them out, and explain them in your own words.

2.5.1 Separating out ideas

In the RUAE exam the question may specify how many separate ideas or points you have to find. If it doesn't, use the number of marks available for the question to guide how many ideas or points you find. It is helpful to bullet point your answer. This will make it easier for you —and the marker —to see how many separate ideas you have identified.

It is useful to take a highlighter into the exam with you. This allows you to highlight the ideas in the passage, before you put them into your own words.

However, it is easy to fall into the habit of highlighting too much. Be careful to pick out separate ideas, even if they are contained in the same paragraph or sentence.

Example

If you were asked why the landscape is unnatural, you might be tempted to highlight most of the following paragraph:

> It may sound like the Garden of Eden but it is a deeply disturbing place. Among the perfectly aligned rows of trees and cultivated crops are no birds, no butterflies, no beetles or shrubs. There is not a single blade of grass or a hedgerow, and the only bees arrive by lorry, transported across the United States. The bees are hired by the day to fertilise the blossom, part of a multibillion-dollar industry that has sprung up to do a job that nature once did for free.

Explaining this in your own words might lead to the answer:

- The landscape is unnatural because there are no native creatures there.

However, there are at least three separate ideas here:

> It may sound like the Garden of Eden but it is a deeply disturbing place. Among the perfectly aligned rows of trees and cultivated crops are no birds, no butterflies, no beetles or shrubs. There is not a single blade of grass or a hedgerow, and the only bees arrive by lorry, transported across the United States. The bees are hired by the day to fertilise the blossom, part of a multibillion-dollar industry that has sprung up to do a job that nature once did for free.

Separating out the ideas makes it easier to explain the two ideas because they have been highlighted separately:

- There are none of the expected fauna.
- There are no natural flora either.
- The only insects —bees —are not native, but imported.

Notice how the ideas are structured by the conjunction 'or', a full stop, and the conjunction 'and'. Remember that signpost words and punctuation can help you to separate out ideas that have been combined together.

Counting main ideas   Go online

Read each of the following extracts and decide how many main ideas are presented.

Q18: The following paragraph describes the impact of on-demand services on our lives. How many criticisms are made?

Streaming and on-demand services have transformed the entertainment landscape forever. Gone are the days when you could be guaranteed to meet colleagues around the water-cooler on a Monday morning to share theories about the latest plot developments in last night's crime drama serial. Gone are the days of gathering with your family around one tv screen to share in the experience of the latest blockbuster or HBO import; instead, every member of the family can now be watching on their own device in their own room, in their own time. Gone too is our self-control. The very notion of waiting a whole seven days to find out what happens to our favourite characters next is anathema to the 'instant' culture in which we all now live; we now binge greedily on all we can watch, only to be left with a twinge of guilt when we realise we will have nothing to talk to our families and colleagues about for the next month or two. Until, that is, the next boxed-set series is uploaded and we can start the inevitable process all over again.
....

Q19: The following paragraph describes the author's experience of being the only male in a ballet class. How many emotions are conveyed?

Stepping into a ballet class, the only male in a room thronging with twenty, thirty young girls, I became acutely aware of everything that marked me out as different: my height, my seemingly gargantuan feet, my hulking frame... All of which was intensified by the mirrored walls, in which my reflection seemed impossible to avoid. For several months I tried desperately not to look at myself. Yet, as time passed, I came to appreciate that my individuality was an asset. I grew proud of my strength and dexterity, would no longer blush when asked to dance in front of others, and felt a strange glow of satisfaction when visitors passing the studio would halt in their tracks to watch me - the lone male dancer in a sea of tutus - as I rehearsed my routines, my eyes trained firmly on my own reflection.

2.6 Explaining in your own words

To show that you understand them, you should always explain ideas from the text in your own words, unless you are specifically asked to quote. Once you have found the answer in the passage and highlighted the appropriate words, you should aim to explain the writer's idea in your own way. You do not need to write in full sentences and you do not have to repeat the words of the question.

Changing individual words

Some words will not need to be changed. This includes the names of specific people and places, also known as proper nouns, or words for which there is no straightforward alternative. There is also no need to change very commonly used words, because doing so does not show your understanding of the writer's idea (and remember that's the point of this type of question). It may also change the meaning of the sentence.

Example

Farming in Britain is at a crossroads, threatened by a wave of intensification from America

could be rewritten as

Farming in Britain has reached a crucial point, and is at risk of becoming just like American industrial agriculture.

In your own words (1) Go online

Put the following idea into your own words. Remember not to change very common words, proper nouns, or words for which there is no straightforward alternative.

Q20: There is not a single blade of grass or a hedgerow, and the only bees arrive by lorry, transported across the United States.

Grouping ideas together

When explaining in your own words, it is sometimes a good idea to group similar ideas together.

Example

Beyond the almond orchards were fields of pomegranates, pistachios, grapes and apricots

could be rewritten as

she could see a great expanse of fields growing fruit and nuts.

TOPIC 2. UNDERSTANDING

> **In your own words (2)**   Go online
>
> Put the following idea into your own words, grouping together similar ideas as appropriate.
>
> **Q21:** Among the perfectly aligned rows of trees and cultivated crops are no birds, no butterflies, no beetles or shrubs.

Generalising specific examples

Writers often provide more than one example to support their main idea. There is no need, when explaining in your own words, to look at each one individually. Instead, make a general statement.

Example

    On the downside, cheap chicken and farmed fish are fatty and flaccid

could be rewritten as

    the quality of low-cost produce is poor.

> **In your own words (3)**   Go online
>
> Put the following idea into your own words, generalising specific examples.
>
> **Q22:** The countryside is too sterile to support many native birds. In the past forty years the population of tree sparrows has fallen by 97%.

2.7 Learning points

Summary

- The three main purposes of a text are to inform, to persuade, to entertain.
- Some texts may have multiple purposes.
- Main ideas are often found in topic sentences, at the start or end of a paragraph.
- Main ideas can be supported by various types of supporting detail.
- Adding words, sequencing words and punctuation can help you find the different ideas that make up the line of thought.
- Answer all understanding questions using your own words to show you understand the writer's ideas.
- When explaining in your own words, avoid word by word translation.
- When explaining in your own words, group and generalise similar ideas.

© HERIOT-WATT UNIVERSITY

2.8 End of topic test

End of Topic 2 test 1 — Go online

Proms are a terrible, chintzy disappointment —perfect preparation for adulthood

Jean Hannah Edelstein
The Guardian
16 June 2015

It might be 17 years since I attended my high-school prom in upstate New York, but don't think for a moment that the memories aren't still burning bright: the polyester scratch of my don't-stand-near-flames, floor-length frock. The weight of the extravagant corsage that extended from my wrist to my elbow, transforming my arm into a rosy garden border. The inelegant scramble of six formal-wear-clad teenagers as we piled into the back seat of a stretch limousine. Some may say that the increased popularity of American-style high-school proms in the UK is a bad thing for Britain's youth. I disagree. Nothing prepares teenagers better for adulthood than the prom, and that's because it's so terrible.

My mother, an expat Scot with little patience for pointless American rituals, was indulgent in allowing me to attend my high-school prom (and funding it), but was resolute in her insistence on referring to the event as 'the practice wedding'. At the time, I found this insulting; in retrospect, I see its acuity. What is a prom but an early opportunity to celebrate heterosexual gender stereotypes through the ritualistic spending of money on anachronistic things that are completely absent from everyday life? Ballgowns, fancy cars, chicken breasts prepared to be served to 300 people simultaneously: so rare are the occasions when they make sense, we must create and perpetuate rituals around them.

What better way to herald a child's passing from parental dependence to full-time servant of capitalism than an occasion that promises glamour in proportion to expenditure, but which manifests itself as a night with the unglamorous people they see every day? Unglamorous people in uncomfortable outfits, some rented, emitting a chintzy glow under the light of a moon that was made of papier-mache by the kids in third-period art class? The promise of prom is spectacle; the reality is disappointment. Could anything prepare children better for the gruelling realities of human existence? I think not.

Some may say that the Kardashian-inspired scale of today's proms is excessive. But if children are to learn that money can't buy happiness, could there be any better lesson than that given when arriving by helicopter to your school prom only to realise that you still have bad skin and that your math teacher is your chaperone? More is more, I say, when it comes to helping impressionable young people understand that no amount of expense on taffeta frocks and sequined handbags will alleviate the terrible ennui of adult life.

Would we rather that our children wait until they are in their late 20s to get to grips with the fact that a loveless relationship cannot be saved by extravagant expense? No, we wouldn't, for that is the innocence that leads to £75,000 weddings between people who file for divorce before they've reached their one-year anniversary. Much better that a girl should know early on the heartbreak of a boyfriend turning up in a tie that doesn't match her dress. Far more helpful that a young man's fancy should be smashed at the sight of his girlfriend doing a sultry electric slide with her physics lab partner.

TOPIC 2. UNDERSTANDING

The prom is a microcosm of adulthood: stupid conventions and rules, established by long-gone arbiters of taste. Slut-shaming of women. Relationships modelled according to a socially acceptable script rather than the reality of two individuals and how they feel about each other. Go for it, kids! One might even say it's the night of your lives.

©*The Guardian*

True or false?

Q23: The writer has tried hard to forget her prom experience.

a) True
b) False

....

Q24: The writer believes the increased popularity of American-style high-school proms in the UK is a bad thing for Britain's youth.

a) True
b) False

....

Q25: The writer thinks proms are a good preparation for the realities of adult life.

a) True
b) False

....

Q26: The writer's mother did not let the writer go to her high-school prom.

a) True
b) False

....

Q27: The writer now agrees with her mother that proms are like practice weddings.

a) True
b) False

....

Q28: The writer has a pessimistic view of adult life after high-school.

a) True
b) False

Throughout the article, the writer uses details (often listed) to support her purpose: to persuade the reader that 'proms are a terrible, chintzy disappointment.' Identify the point being supported by the following details.

© HERIOT-WATT UNIVERSITY

40 UNIT 1. READING FOR UNDERSTANDING, ANALYSIS AND EVALUATION

Q29: ...the polyester scratch of my don't-stand-near-flames, floor-length frock. The weight of the extravagant corsage that extended from my wrist to my elbow, transforming my arm into a rosy garden border. The inelegant scramble of six formal-wear-clad teenagers as we piled into the back seat of a stretch limousine.

a) She can recall every little detail of her prom
b) Proms are glamorous
c) Proms are very popular

....

Q30: Unglamorous people in uncomfortable outfits, some rented, emitting a chintzy glow under the light of a moon that was made of papier-mache by the kids in third-period art class?

a) It takes a lot of work to stage a prom
b) People enjoy getting dressed up for prom
c) Proms are always a let down

....

Q31: Stupid conventions and rules, established by long-gone arbiters of taste. Slut-shaming of women. Relationships modelled according to a socially acceptable script rather than the reality of two individuals and how they feel about each other.

a) Proms are sexist
b) Proms are dangerous
c) Proms are outdated and artificial

End of Topic 2 test 2	Go online

Explain the following ideas using your own words. Avoid trying to translate word by word; instead, focus on the point the writer is making.

Q32: What is a prom but an early opportunity to celebrate heterosexual gender stereotypes through the ritualistic spending of money on anachronistic things that are completely absent from everyday life?

....

Q33: The promise of prom is spectacle; the reality is disappointment

....

Q34: More is more, I say, when it comes to helping impressionable young people understand that no amount of expense on taffeta frocks and sequined handbags will alleviate the terrible ennui of adult life.

....

Q35: The prom is a microcosm of adulthood: stupid conventions and rules, established by long-gone arbiters of taste.

Unit 1 Topic 3

Analysis

Contents

- 3.1 Word Choice 43
    - 3.1.1 Connotations 44
    - 3.1.2 Connecting connotations to the writer's purpose 47
    - 3.1.3 Emotive language and euphemism 50
- 3.2 Imagery 51
    - 3.2.1 Types of imagery 52
    - 3.2.2 Extended imagery 52
    - 3.2.3 The literal and the figurative 53
    - 3.2.4 Choosing the right qualities 56
    - 3.2.5 Connecting imagery to the writer's purpose 59
- 3.3 Sentence structure 60
    - 3.3.1 Punctuation marks 60
    - 3.3.2 Sentence types 61
    - 3.3.3 Sentence patterns 64
    - 3.3.4 Connecting sentence structure to the writer's purpose 69
- 3.4 Tone 73
    - 3.4.1 Register 74
    - 3.4.2 Positive and negative tones 74
    - 3.4.3 Identifying tone 76
    - 3.4.4 Explaining how tone is created 77
- 3.5 Learning points 79
- 3.6 End of topic test 80

Learning objective

By the end of this topic, you should be able to:

- understand words have connotations which can be positive, negative or neutral;
- comment on subtle differences in connotations;
- analyse how a writer's word choice helps them achieve their purpose;
- identify similes, metaphors, personification and extended images;
- understand how images are constructed;
- analyse how writers' use of imagery helps them achieve their purpose
- identify sentence types: statement, exclamation, command, question, rhetorical question, minor sentence, short sentence, long sentence;
- identify sentence patterns: repetition, list, climax, anticlimax, parallel structure, alliteration, antithesis, inversion, polysyndetic list, asyndetic list;
- identify and explain the function of punctuation: inverted commas, parenthesis, colon, semi-colon, dash, ellipsis;
- understand that tone is created by language techniques;
- identify different tones;
- explain how language features create tone.

TOPIC 3. ANALYSIS

As you'll know from National 5, questions about the writer's use of particular language features —word choice, imagery, sentence structure, tone —are 'analysis' questions.

These question types require you to interrogate fully the effect of the writer's language choices and the ways in which these choices develop and enhance the writer's argument. At Higher, this can be a complex business; the writer's language will be sophisticated, erudite and thoughtfully selected. You will also find a much greater number of possible answers for each analysis question than you did at National 5.

Of course, the way you structurally tackle these questions remains the same as it was at National 5 —you must select evidence from the passage, and then fully analyse why it has been used, and what effect it has. Remember, though, that your analysis is expected to be more detailed than at National 5, and that you do not get credit or marks for your quotations from the passage.

> **Key point**
>
> Many of the activities and examples in these materials are based upon the 2015 SQA Higher RUAE paper, passages 1 and 2.
>
> 1. Adapted from 'Goodbye birds. Goodbye butterflies. Hello... farmageddon,' by Isabel Oakeshott, taken from The Sunday Times, 19 January 2014.
>
> 2. Adapted from 'Pasture to the Plate' by Audrey Ayton, taken from The Observer supplement, 10 July 1994.
>
> You will find it useful to have a copy of this paper next to you as you work through the resources.

3.1 Word Choice

There are approximately a million words in the English language. This allows writers to deliberately choose exactly the right words to help them achieve their purpose. The words a writer chooses can reveal much to the reader; we gain an insight into their passions and attitudes, into their opinions and emotions.

Look at the 2015 Higher RUAE paper, passage one. If you have worked through Topic 2: Understanding, you'll already know that the writer, Isabel Oakeshott, is opposed to intensive farming. In paragraph 3, her use of language makes this opposition very clear. In this paragraph alone, she makes a number of significant word choices to ensure that you too share her horror at the conditions the cows are kept in.

> As for the cows, they last only two or three years, ten-to-fifteen years less than their natural life span. *Crammed* into *barren* pens on *tiny patches* of land, they stand around *listlessly* waiting to be fed, milked or injected with antibiotics. Through a combination of selective breeding, *artificial* diets and growth hormones designed to maximise milk production, they are *pushed* so *grotesquely* beyond their natural limit that they are soon *worn out*. In their short lives they never see grass.

Each word is loaded with connotations, and collectively they demonstrate the power of her argument.

3.1.1 Connotations

Every word has a denotation —the definition you would find if you looked the word up in the dictionary. But words also have connotations —the feelings or ideas associated with a word. It is the connotations of a word that create its emotional impact on the reader; we intuitively decode the connotations every time we read:

Taking the same example from the 2015 Higher RUAE paper, we can examine the connotations closely.

Example

As for the cows, they last only two or three years, ten-to-fifteen years less than their natural life span. Crammed[1] into barren[2] pens on tiny patches[3] of land, they stand around listlessly[4] waiting to be fed, milked or injected with antibiotics. Through a combination of selective breeding, artificial[5] diets and growth hormones designed to maximise milk production, they are pushed[6] so grotesquely[7] beyond their natural limit that they are soon worn out[8]. In their short lives they never see grass.

Notes:

[1] packed in, barely any room to move or to breathe, sense of being on top of one another
[2] empty and bare; bereft of any feature or comfort
[3] incredibly small and limited
[4] without any life or energy, no spirit, no hope
[5] unnatural, not what they should be eating, foreign, bad for them
[6] controlled by someone else, no self-determination
[7] unnaturally, like monsters, something you can't bear to see
[8] exhausted, sense of being ground down

Identify the correct connotations   Go online

Read the following extracts taken from the 2015 Higher RUAE paper, passage one, and identify the words and phrases from the connotations.

It may sound like the Garden of Eden but it is a deeply disturbing place. Among the perfectly aligned rows of trees and cultivated crops are no birds, no butterflies, no beetles or shrubs. There is not a single blade of grass or a hedgerow, and the only bees arrive by lorry, transported across the United States. The bees are hired by the day to fertilise the blossom, part of a multibillion-dollar industry that has sprung up to do a job that nature once did for free.

Q1: Which word/phrase carries the connotations: unnaturally straight, geometric, manufactured?

....

TOPIC 3. ANALYSIS 45

Q2: Which word/phrase carries the connotations: unnerving, ominous, unsettling?

....

Could the British countryside ever look like this? If current trends continue, the answer is yes. Farming in Britain is at a crossroads, threatened by a wave of intensification from America. The first mega-dairies and mega-piggeries are already here. Bees are disappearing, with serious implications for harvests. Hedgerows, vital habitats for wildlife, have halved since the Second World War. The countryside is too sterile to support many native birds. In the past forty years the population of tree sparrows has fallen by 97%.

Q3: Which word/phrase carries the connotations: drained, bare, barren?

....

Q4: Which word/phrase carries the connotations: fundamentally important, necessary for?

....

But, as I discovered when I began looking into the way food is produced, increasingly powerful forces are pulling us in the opposite direction. We have become addicted to cheap meat, fish and dairy products from supply lines that stretch across the globe. On the plus side, it means that supermarkets can sell whole chickens for as little as £3. Things that were once delicacies, such as smoked salmon, are now as cheap as chips. On the downside, cheap chicken and farmed fish are fatty and flaccid. Industrially reared farm animals —50 billion of them a year worldwide —are kept permanently indoors, treated like machines and pumped with drugs.

Q5: Which word/phrase carries the connotations: limp, unappealing, flabby?

....

Q6: Which word/phrase carries the connotations: treats, refined, rarely had?

....

My journey to expose the truth, to investigate the dirty secret about the way cheap food is produced, took me from the first mega-dairies and piggeries in Britain to factory farms in France, China, Mexico, and North and South America. I talked to people on the front line of the global food industry: treadmill farmers trying to produce more with less. I also talked to their neighbours —people experiencing the side effects of industrial farms. Many had stories about their homes plummeting in value, the desecration of lovely countryside, the disappearance of wildlife and serious health problems linked to pollution.

Q7: Which word/phrase carries the connotations: large scale, mechanised, profit-led?

....

Q8: Which word/phrase carries the connotations: destruction of something special, damage, vandalism?

....

© HERIOT-WATT UNIVERSITY

46 UNIT 1. READING FOR UNDERSTANDING, ANALYSIS AND EVALUATION

I wanted to challenge the widespread assumption that factory farming is the only way to produce food that everyone can afford. My investigation started in Central Valley, California, because it demonstrates the worst-case scenario —a nightmarish vision of the future for parts of Britain if current practices continue unchecked. It is a five-hour drive south of San Francisco and I knew I was getting close when I saw a strange yellowish-grey smog on the horizon.

Q9: Which word/phrase carries the connotations: pervasive, inescapable, persistent?

....

Q10: Which word/phrase carries the connotations: frightening, surreal, distressing?

....

Exploring the area by car, it was not long before I saw my first mega-dairy, an array of towering, open-sided shelters over muddy pens. The stench of manure was overwhelming —not the faintly sweet, earthy smell of cowpats familiar from the British countryside, but a nauseating reek bearing no relation to digested grass. I saw farms every couple of miles, all with several thousand cows surrounded by mud, corrugated iron and concrete.

Q11: Which word/phrase carries the connotations: stomach-turning, repellent, highly off-putting?

....

Q12: Which word/phrase carries the connotations: imposing, looming, threatening?

It's also important to consider subtle shades of meaning —differences between words that have the same or similar denotations, but different connotations. You may also wish to consider if the writer is deliberately formal or informal, and if they employ jargon.

To recap all these issues, look at the SCHOLAR National 5 pages, 3.1 Word Choice for more practice working with connotations.

© HERIOT-WATT UNIVERSITY

3.1.2 Connecting connotations to the writer's purpose

In isolation, though, connotations mean little; it's not enough just to be able to spot them and write down three possible connotations to demonstrate you understand the word. You must be able to demonstrate you understand why the writer has used that particular word and how it develops the argument. In other words, you have to link it to the writer's purpose.

In a neutral text —something that is focussed on providing information in a non-biased manner —language is used to impart fact, without drama or colour.

Example

> Campaigners have expressed concern[1] about the health implications[2] of a diet primarily based on ready meals and fast food[3].
>
> Notes:
>
> [1] No emotion; simply factual
> [2] Doesn't say whether the implications are good or bad
> [3] Factual descriptions of the type of food

In a persuasive text, language is a tool the writer uses to manipulate the reader, to make them feel sympathetic or angry about an issue; writers might also persuade by using negative connotations to criticise, or positive connotations to praise.

Example

> Activists[1] have been screaming[2] from the rooftops about the deadly impact[3] of junk food[4].
>
> Notes:
>
> [1] Suggests people who are passionate about a real cause; on the side of truth
> [2] Has emotional connotations of panic or desperation; suggests the issue is very important and they must be heard
> [3] Shows the writer thinks the effect on health couldn't be more serious: it is a life or death situation
> [4] Connotations of rubbish, something that should be thrown away because it has no nutritional worth

One way of developing your own writing skills, as well as helping you understand how professional writers make language suit their purpose, is to turn neutral statements into persuasive statements.

Examples

1. Praise

Neutral

Preliminary estimates indicate that the proportion of people living on less than $1.25 per day fell in 2010 to less than half the 1990 rate and during the same period over two billion people gained access to improved drinking water sources. The share of slum dwellers in urban areas declined from 39 per cent in 2000 to 33 per cent in 2012, improving the lives of at least 100 million people.

Persuasive

There's no doubt we are winning the war against poverty, winning the war against deprivation. The number of people around the world living on less than $1.25 a day has been cut in half —while over two billion people —that's around one quarter of the world's total population —now have access to clean, fresh and free drinking water.

....

2. Criticise

Neutral

Research suggests sea levels worldwide have been rising at a rate of 3.5 millimetres per year since the early 1990s. This increase has been linked to global warming, and puts thousands of coastal cities, like Venice, and whole islands at risk.

Persuasive

Terrifying statistics tell us that sea levels are rising; year on year the water level surges higher. And it's not a problem that's limited to one area of the planet either; all over the world vulnerable communities are at considerable risk of flooding, or even being consumed whole by the sea.

Praising and criticising

Now have a go at producing persuasive statements yourself from neutral sources.

Praise

1. Since 2010, roughly £220m has been spent on improving British sea water quality, with more investments planned in the years to 2020. In all, 633 British bathing waters were monitored this year, of which 377, or 60%, were judged excellent, and 599 sites were sufficient for bathing.

2. Positive figures emerged from Europe recently with the news that recycling levels for PET bottles across the EU last year were up 9.4% to 1.59 million tonnes compared to the previous year; the collection of PET bottles in Europe is now a 51%.

Criticise

1. Obesity rates have risen over the past eight years —in 1993 13% of men and 16% of women were obese —in 2011 this rose to 24% for men and 26% for women. The NHS has not yet fully responded to this increase.
2. 47% of adult inmates in UK prisons are reconvicted within one year of release. For those serving sentences of less than 12 months this increases to 58%. Nearly three quarters (73%) of under 18 year olds are reconvicted within a year of release.

Example : Neutral language

Persuasive

So factory farming marched on. And became more and more intensive. Where first there were one or two laying hens in a cage, eventually there became five in the same small space. The broiler chicken sheds expanded to cram in vast acres of birds. Many beef cattle were confined in buildings and yards. Until mad cow disease emerged, such animals were fed all kinds of organic matter as cheap food. In the UK dairy cows still spend their summers in the fields, but many of their offspring are reared in the cruelty of intensive veal crate systems.

Neutral

Factory farming has developed, with increasing numbers of hens per unit. Larger spaces were designed to hold bigger numbers of birds. Additionally, beef cattle were also housed in units, and fed cost-effectively on organic matter. In the UK, cattle used for diary often live outside in the summer, with their young being kept in veal crates.

Neutral language

Using the following persuasive extracts from the 2015 Higher RUAE paper, passage two, and eliminate the critical word choice, creating instead a neutral tone.

1. With this knowledge, the only possible moral justification for intensive farming of animals collapses. The cheap animal production policy doesn't help the poor. It kills them. In addition, the chronic suffering endured by animals in many intensive systems is not just a sentimental concern of the soft-hearted. It is a scientifically proven fact. Cracks are beginning to show in our long-practised animal apartheid system, in which we have convinced ourselves, against all evidence, that the animals we eat are less intelligent, less in need of space and exercise than are those we pat, ride or watch.

2. But meat, eggs and dairy products have indeed become cheap, affordable even to the poor. All of which made nutritionists exceedingly happy —until they discovered that their mid-century predecessors had made a mighty blunder. Before intensive farming brought cheap meat and dairy products to our tables, man obtained most of his calories from cereal crops and vegetables. The meat with which he supplemented this diet had a much lower fat content than intensively produced products. Now, however, degenerative diseases like coronary heart disease and several types of cancer have been linked to our increased consumption of fatty foods. War-time Britons, on their measly ration of meat and one ounce of cheese a week, were much healthier.

3.1.3 Emotive language and euphemism

Words chosen to either convey the writer's emotion, or to stir up the reader's feelings, are called emotive language. Such words often carry very strong positive or negative connotations.

Matching neutral and emotive terms Go online

Q13: Match the neutral terms with their emotive counterparts.

government	main
economic savings	banged up
changing	jails
freedom fighter	abolish
injure	regime
kill	blinkered
detained	crash
correctional centre	laughter
economic downturn	manipulating
focused	terrorist
remove	cuts

Writers can also soften unpalatable ideas by using mild and indirect language - known as euphemisms - for words considered too blunt or shocking.

TOPIC 3. ANALYSIS

Matching emotive words and euphemisms   Go online

Q14: Match the emotive terms with their euphemistic counterparts.

cuts	big boned
war	sex
poor	tired and emotional
torture	military intervention
lied	downsizing
drunk	enhanced interrogation
died	underprivileged
accidental deaths	between job
fat	misspoke
the birds and the bees	collateral damage
unemployed	spassed away

3.2 Imagery

Images create pictures in the mind; that's why we call them 'images'. A writer uses imagery so you can imagine a picture of the idea in your head. Images are used to emphasise the writer's attitude, or to make an idea more vivid, or to entertain the reader —and, often, all three of these.

An image is a comparison —where the writer compares something that is being described to something else. By understanding the comparison, we can transfer qualities from one thing to the other. This can make the description more vivid in our minds, help us to understand more about the thing being described, and can show the writer's attitude towards it.

For example, a writer might suggest that there is a 'mountain of homework to be done'; 'mountains' and 'homework' are usually unrelated. It is not literally true that the homework is the size of a mountain. Instead, the reader understands what a mountain is like —huge and hard to climb —and creates a mental picture of a towering pile of homework. The reader can then transfer this knowledge and understand that the writer is suggesting that there is a lot of work that needs to be completed, and that doing so will be hard work and challenging.

The reader can also work out what the writer's attitude to the homework is: the writer feels intimidated by the amount of work they have to do.

© Heriot-Watt University

3.2.1 Types of imagery

As you'll be aware, there are three types of image addressed in RUAE: similes, metaphors and personification. Similes suggest that one thing is 'like' or 'as' another; metaphors suggest one thing actually 'is' another; personification transfers human qualities to inanimate objects.

You can fully revise the differences between these types of imagery by visiting the SCHOLAR National 5 pages, 3.2.1.

In the Higher RUAE exam, it is likely there will be questions that require you to identify and analyse an image. This means you must be able to find images on your own. Remember that you are looking for ideas that are not literally true —when the writer describes the farm as a 'Garden of Eden', she is simply comparing the view to the idealised concept of 'Eden.' The clue words 'like' and 'as' will help you find similes, but all types of imagery can be identified by finding comparisons that are not literally true.

> **Identifying images**   Go online
>
> Q15: Make sure you have a copy of the 2015 Higher RUAE paper, passage one, next to you. Using a highlighter, read the passage very carefully and highlight all the images you can find before comparing them with the suggested answers.

3.2.2 Extended imagery

Sometimes, a writer will develop a single comparison over a number of linked images. While you can analyse each image separately, it is useful to recognise when writers use extended images as the more images you have, the easier it will be to explain their combined effect, and to understand the powerful argument the writer is presenting.

In this example, the writer compares the boy's anger to fire.

> Example
>
> The boy's eyes *blazed* and *burned*. His cheeks *glowed like coals* as the reality of the situation sank in. When he spoke, it was *as if hot sparks were exploding* from his lips, threatening to *set alight* the listener. At any minute, it seemed that his fury would *erupt like a volcano* and *swallow the room in hot lava*. I shrank back from him, terrified I would be *burned* by a passionate word or a vindictive exclamation.
>
> There are seven separate images used to convey just how upset the boy is. Each one individually helps the reader to recognise that the boy is angry, but taken together they emphasise the extreme ferocity and danger of his temper.

TOPIC 3. ANALYSIS

Finding extended images

Highlight all the images that form the extended image in the following paragraphs.

Q16: There are 6 parts of this extended image to find.

Often the House of Commons more resembles a three ring circus than a place of serious debate. While the Speaker tries to exert ringmaster-like pressure on the assembled acts, behaviour regularly descends into chaos. Those in the cheap seats jeer and yell, waving papers in the air, and clowning around. The front benches —the party leaders and cabinet ministers —are often seen clapping like performing seals.
....

Q17: There are 5 parts to this extended image to find.

Scotland has long had a reputation as the sickman of Europe. While countries like Denmark, the Netherlands and Iceland are recognised around the world as healthy Northern European countries, Scotland continues to wheeze and creak. And that's with a national health service —usually a marker of a healthy society. It's about time we were written a straight-talking prescription telling us to put down the deep fried Mars Bar, slip on our trainers][and get out into the fresh air. Without fundamental change, delivered quickly, Scotland will continue to hobble along behind our contemporaries, coughing and spitting.
....

Q18: There are 5 parts of this extended image to find.

For months afterwards, public opinion on the matter was regularly stoked by inflammatory stories in newspapers and dangerous sparks let loose on social media. Those close to the celebrity tried to extinguish the rumours, denying any inappropriate behaviour. Despite this, they kept reigniting.

3.2.3 The literal and the figurative

All images —whether they are similes, metaphors or personification —are made up of two parts: the literal idea the writer wants the reader to understand and the figurative, which is the comparison that hopefully further illuminates the idea for the reader.

Deconstructing images

Practise identifying which is the literal and which is the figurative using these examples from the 2015 Higher RUAE paper, passage one. Make sure you have the paper next to you as you answer the questions.

It may sound like the Garden of Eden but it is a deeply disturbing place.

Q19: What type of image is this?

a) Simile
b) Metaphor
c) Personification

© HERIOT-WATT UNIVERSITY

Q20: What is literally being described in this image?

a) An orchard
b) A disturbance
c) Eden

Q21: What is the figurative (imagined) part of this image?

a) An orchard
b) A disturbance
c) Eden

... threatened by a *wave of intensification* from America.

Q22: What type of image is this?

a) Simile
b) Metaphor
c) Personification

Q23: What is literally being described in this image?

a) Intensive farming
b) America
c) A wave

Q24: What is the figurative (imagined) part of this image?

a) Intensive farming
b) America
c) A wave

... treadmill farmers trying to produce more with less

Q25: What type of image is this?

a) Simile
b) Metaphor
c) Personification

TOPIC 3. ANALYSIS

Q26: What is literally being described in this image?

a) Treadmills
b) Farmers
c) Production lines

....

Q27: What is the figurative (imagined) part of this image?

a) Treadmills
b) Farmers
c) Production lines

> Many had stories about their homes plummeting in value...

Q28: What type of image is this?

a) Simile
b) Metaphor
c) Personification

....

Q29: What is literally being described in this image?

a) Stories
b) Something falling
c) Homes

....

Q30: What is the figurative (imagined) part of this image?

a) Stories
b) Something falling
c) Homes

3.2.4 Choosing the right qualities

Of course, simply spotting and dismantling the image is not enough to gain you any marks at Higher; what's important is that you are able to select the appropriate qualities of the figurative part of the image, e.g, in the metaphor 'public opinion on the matter was regularly stoked by inflammatory stories', it is the idea that public opinion is being fuelled and stirred up by stories, not that stoking involves a metal rod, physical contact or coal.

Choose the right qualities for the image Go online

Decide if the following qualities are relevant to the comparison being made.

It may sound *like the Garden of Eden* but it is a deeply disturbing place

Q31: Eden is beautiful.

a) Relevant
b) Not Relevant

....

Q32: Eden is peaceful.

a) Relevant
b) Not Relevant

....

Q33: Eden is full of snakes.

a) Relevant
b) Not Relevant

....

Q34: Eden is rural.

a) Relevant
b) Not Relevant

....

Q35: Eden has two people living in it.

a) Relevant
b) Not Relevant

... threatened by a *wave of intensification* from America.

Q36: Waves are wet.

a) Relevant
b) Not Relevant

TOPIC 3. ANALYSIS

Q37: Waves are powerful.

a) Relevant
b) Not Relevant

Q38: Waves are vast.

a) Relevant
b) Not Relevant

Q39: Waves are noisy.

a) Relevant
b) Not Relevant

Q40: Waves rush forward.

a) Relevant
b) Not Relevant

... *treadmill farmers* trying to produce more with less

Q41: A treadmill is a conveyor belt.

a) Relevant
b) Not Relevant

Q42: A treadmill is never-ending.

a) Relevant
b) Not Relevant

Q43: A treadmill requires a lot of energy.

a) Relevant
b) Not Relevant

Q44: A treadmill makes no progress.

a) Relevant
b) Not Relevant

Q45: A treadmill has a large wheel.

a) Relevant
b) Not Relevant

Many had stories about their *homes plummeting in value* ...

Q46: Something plummeting gets lower.

a) Relevant
b) Not Relevant

Q47: Something plummeting moves very quickly.

a) Relevant
b) Not Relevant

Q48: Something plummeting tumbles over.

a) Relevant
b) Not Relevant

Q49: Something plummeting drops straight down.

a) Relevant
b) Not Relevant

Q50: Something plummeting crashes to the ground.

a) Relevant
b) Not Relevant

3.2.5 Connecting imagery to the writer's purpose

As with word choice, you must connect imagery to purpose, considering how the image helps the writer to convey their ideas and/or opinions. The extracts selected to form Higher RUAE papers are, as you know, most likely to be persuasive in purpose, although they will also at points entertain and inform. As such, imagery will often be used to convey strength of feeling. This is the case in the passage by Isabel Oakeshott from the 2015 Higher RUAE paper.

Examples

1. ... threatened by a wave of intensification from America.

- 'A wave of intensification' —metaphor
- The growing intensive farming movement is being compared to a wave.
- Just as a wave can be vast, overwhelming and engulfing, so too is the intensive farming movement progressing forward with little sense of slowing down.
- Suggests the writer feels we are under attack by the movement, that we too will be swallowed up by it with no trace left of previous ways of life.

....

2. We have become addicted to cheap meat, fish and dairy products ...

- 'addicted' —metaphor
- Our preference for cheap products is being compared to an addiction.
- Just as an addiction is something that controls us, that we cannot escape from, and that can threaten our lives, so too are we unable to stop buying cheap animal products; we are compelled to consume low quality foods because of the price.
- Suggests the writer feels our relationship with food is unhealthy; we no longer make sensible decisions about what we put in our bodies; we are driven by other factors and have lost our free will in the matter.

Writing persuasively using imagery: Both passages in the 2015 Higher paper are written by critics of the intensive farming industry; their purpose is to persuade the reader that farming on an industrial level is damaging to the environment and inhumane.

Try to use imagery to develop the opposite argument —that intensive farming is actually beneficial. So your purpose is to persuade the reader that farming on an industrial level is useful and productive.

You might want to think about the following facts in your writing.

- Food is cheaper.
- Advancements in biotechnology have also created crops that are resistant to diseases.
- Pesticides have improved yields and the quality of the crops grown.
- Food has a longer shelf life.

© HERIOT-WATT UNIVERSITY

- There are fewer geographic or climatic limitations to farming; weather conditions don't matter so much.
- It takes less human labour to produce crops.
- Farmers are able to afford to hire experienced, skilled workers to focus on specialist tasks.

3.3 Sentence structure

Just as writers make decisions about the language they use to create an effect, they also make decisions about how to structure their ideas into sentences.

There are three aspects of sentences structure that a writer can make decisions about.

1. *Punctuation marks* are the devices we all use to organise ideas in a sentence. You will already be familiar with most punctuation marks; you will have been using them since you learned to write. The difference in reading tasks at Higher is that you are being asked to comment on the effect of punctuation marks. In other words, you must explain why the writer chose a particular punctuation mark and how it helps to organise ideas.

2. There are also many different types of sentences. *Sentence types* all perform different functions in communicating more about the writer's ideas. Sentence type describes the function of a whole sentence, from the capital letter at the beginning to the full stop at the end.

3. Sentences often contain language patterns. *Sentence patterns* help writers to make their ideas more vivid, and readers therefore to understand more about an idea. A sentence pattern can occur within a sentence, or across a number of sentences.

To revise the basics of sentence structure —what a sentence is and how that basic structure can be developed —look at the SCHOLAR National 5 pages, 3.3.1 What is a sentence? and 3.3.2 Adding to the basic structure.

3.3.1 Punctuation marks

Punctuation marks are the tools we use to organise sentences into sections, or to join them together. They help us work out how ideas are related to one another.

Before you can answer a question on the effect of a punctuation mark, you have to understand what it does. One of the most effective things you can do to improve the way you tackle sentence structure questions is to learn what each mark does in a sentence.

Practise identifying punctuation marks and their function in articles you use for your reading log from Topic 1. Keep an eye out for any interesting or unusual uses of punctuation.

Punctuation marks activity

Q51: Match the punctuation marks with their definitions.

Adds additional information.	! Exclamation mark
Indicates a question.	, , or ——or ( ) Parenthesis
Indicates dialogue, titles, or quotations. Can also indicate irony.	? Question mark
Indicates strong emotion.	. Fullstop
Indicates words left out.	; Semi-colon
Introduces an expansion.	... Ellipsis
Joins together two related sentences or separates items in a complex list.	, , or ——or ( ) Parenthesis
Marks the end of a sentence.	" " or ' ' Inverted commas
Separates items in a simple list or clauses in a sentence.	: Colon or —Single dash

3.3.2 Sentence types

To comment on a writer's use of sentence structure you should be able to identify the types of sentences used. These might include:

- *statement*: a simple sentence that puts forward information as a fact;

- *exclamation*: a sentence or phrase expressing emotion (often surprise, shock or excitement) - usually marked with an exclamation mark;

- *command*: a sentence that tells or instructs;

- *question*: a sentence worded so as to invite an answer;

- *rhetorical question*: a statement disguised as a question. The answer is implied or obvious;

- *minor sentence*: a sentence without a verb;

- *short sentence*: a simple sentence, often only containing a few words;

- *long sentence*: a sentence noticeably longer than those around it, often containing multiple clauses, parenthesis or a list.

Identify the sentence type

Read the following sentences and identify the correct sentence types.

Q52:
   Intensive farming is brutal and exploitative.

a) Long sentence
b) Statement
c) Exclamation
d) Command
e) Rhetorical question
f) Minor sentence
g) Short sentence
h) Question

....

Q53:
   Buy local; buy organic; buy ethical.

a) Long sentence
b) Statement
c) Exclamation
d) Command
e) Rhetorical question
f) Minor sentence
g) Short sentence
h) Question

....

Q54:
   But what about the benefits of such intensive systems? Well, they too are complex.

a) Long sentence
b) Statement
c) Exclamation
d) Command
e) Rhetorical question
f) Minor sentence
g) Short sentence
h) Question

....

TOPIC 3. ANALYSIS

Q55:
If we knew the conditions the animals lived in, would we be happy eating meat?
a) Long sentence
b) Statement
c) Exclamation
d) Command
e) Rhetorical question
f) Minor sentence
g) Short sentence
h) Question

....

Q56:
It's not just the animals we farm either. Think about the bees. The butterflies. The beetles. Even the hedgerows.
a) Long sentence
b) Statement
c) Exclamation
d) Command
e) Rhetorical question
f) Minor sentence
g) Short sentence
h) Question

....

Q57:
It was more than I could stomach. Quite literally!
a) Long sentence
b) Statement
c) Exclamation
d) Command
e) Rhetorical question
f) Minor sentence
g) Short sentence
h) Question

....

© HERIOT-WATT UNIVERSITY

Q58:

I wondered again what had happened to the farms I remember from my childhood, where cows and sheep were able to graze and wander, where hens were free to lay in pastures, where dairy farmers received a fair fee for their milk, and where fields could be rested, giving the land a chance to regenerate and recoup.

a) Long sentence
b) Statement
c) Exclamation
d) Command
e) Rhetorical question
f) Minor sentence
g) Short sentence
h) Question

....

Q59:

Quite frankly, it's all about money.

a) Long sentence
b) Statement
c) Exclamation
d) Command
e) Rhetorical question
f) Minor sentence
g) Short sentence
h) Question

3.3.3 Sentence patterns

To comment on a writer's use of sentence structure you should also be able to identify common sentence patterns. These might include:

- *repetition*: using a word or phrase more than once for emphasis;

    Example Perhaps the biggest image problem politicians face is the public's perception that they are compulsive liars: when they're not lying about their expenses or lying about tax bills, they're lying about statistics, policies or —worst of all —lying about each other.

- *list*: a series of words or phrases separated by commas or semi-colons;

    Example For those seeking fame these days, there is no shortage of opportunities: croon for Cowell or show Britain your 'talent' on primetime telly; conquer the blogosphere or vlog your every waking moment; bake, cook, sew or paint your way to reality-show stardom. The options are endless.

- *climax*: the highest point of tension, humour, drama, quantity, size, etc. in a sentence;

    Example All toy fads follows a similar trajectory. Each begins in obscurity, waiting to be discovered by an enterprising individual, shared with friends and family, picked up by the wider public, adopted by the media and retailers as the Next Big Thing, at which point popularity explodes and before you can say 'tamagotchi' the world is awash with yo-yos, Rubik's cubes, loom bands, hoverboards...

- *anticlimax*: a sentence that builds in intensity, power of quantity towards a climax, but which is ended with an unexpected disappointment or humorous twist;

    Example Who could look at mankind's long history of technological progress and fail to be impressed? The endless ingenuity of our species has spawned the printing press, the telephone, cars, calculators, space travel, the internet, and, surely the crowning jewel of the digital age, the heated toilet.

- *parallel structure*: phrases or sentences that repeat the same structure, often beginning or ending in the same way, or using punctuation in the same way;

    Example As much as I longed for the big day to arrive, I feared what lay ahead. As much as I prepared and practised, I fretted about the potential for failure.

- *alliteration*: two or more words that begin with the same sound;

    Example There is something so sleek, sophisticated and stylish about a boutique hotel that one can't help but be seduced.

- *antithesis*: two opposing ideas placed together to emphasise a contrast;

    Example As Armstrong said, it's a small step for man, but a giant leap for mankind.'

- *polysyndetic list*: a list where conjunctions (usually 'and') are used repeatedly for effect, even when there is no need for the conjunction;

    Example My problem with fossil fuels is not just about the ozone layer (important though that is); it's about scarring the landscape and polluting the air and exploiting the workers and lining the pockets of large organisations and poisoning the oceans and disturbing the very fine balance required for life on this planet.

- *asyndetic lists*: a list without conjunctions, where they are removed for effect;

    Example Then the miniature beauty queens take the stage: plucked, scrubbed, tanned, preened, sprayed, perfumed, bejeweled, quiffed, glossed within an inch of their very tiny lives.

© HERIOT-WATT UNIVERSITY

- *tricolon:* a series of three parallel words, phrases, or clauses - sometimes called The Rule of Three or The Power of Three;

  Example : The crowd had grown ugly waiting for the official announcement. They hurled insults at one another. They threw empty bottles and cans. They practically pawed the ground.

- *inversion:* the reversal of the normal word order (subject, verb, object —see the SCHOLAR National 5 pages,3.3.1 to revise What is a sentence?) in a sentence, to draw focus to the thing that comes first or last.

  Example A veritable paradise, the whole peninsula stretched out before us.' OR 'There stretching out before us, a veritable paradise, was the whole peninsula.

Identify the sentence pattern   Go online

Read the following sentences and select the correct sentence patterns.

Q60:
   Questions remain however: what about the land? What about the animals? What about the workers? And what about the long term effects of intensive farming that we can only, right now, make a guess at?

a) Alliteration
b) Climax
c) Repetition
d) List
e) Anticlimax
f) Parallel structure

....

Q61:
   As far as the eye could see were fields of rippling corn, grazing cattle, vibrant hedgerows, insects, birds and butterflies.

a) Alliteration
b) Climax
c) Repetition
d) List
e) Anticlimax
f) Parallel structure

....

Q62:

It's easy to clamour and agitate for change as we sit in our comfortable homes in the West, confident that we won't experience widespread cataclysmic crop failure, conflict over water supplies, starvation-triggered mass migration or even stringy roast beef to have with our Yorkshire puddings.

a) Alliteration
b) Climax
c) Repetition
d) List
e) Anticlimax
f) Parallel structure

....

Q63:

There can be no doubt that food is cheaper; just as there can be no doubt that crops are more plentiful and more resilient.

a) Alliteration
b) Climax
c) Repetition
d) List
e) Anticlimax
f) Parallel structure

....

Q64:

Too much will be lost if we adopt a 'wait and see' approach to our farming infrastructure. If we don't act now to halt the industrialisation of our countryside we'll find ourselves tied up like the proverbial pig in a poke.

a) Alliteration
b) Climax
c) Repetition
d) List
e) Anticlimax
f) Parallel structure

....

UNIT 1. READING FOR UNDERSTANDING, ANALYSIS AND EVALUATION

Q65:
If we could only fully harness the public's attention, they would quickly realise that financial gain for the few, means the destruction of the countryside for the many.
a) Alliteration
b) Polysyndetic list
c) Repetition
d) Asyndetic list
e) Antithesis
f) Tricolon structure

....

Q66:
Cheaper food and fewer diseases and greater yields and longer shelf life and less dependence of weather. These are the overwhelming benefits of such a system.
a) Alliteration
b) Polysyndetic list
c) Repetition
d) Asyndetic list
e) Antithesis
f) Tricolon structure

....

Q67:
My concerns, as I researched further, multiplied further: redundancy, food miles, cross-contamination, so-called Frankenstein crops, animal welfare, dietary changes. And no one was able to reassure me that there was nothing to fear.
a) Alliteration
b) Polysyndetic list
c) Repetition
d) Asyndetic list
e) Antithesis
f) Tricolon structure

....

Q68:
A world where everyone has access to nutritious food; a world where drought and famine were things of the past; a world where farmers actually made money instead of losing it hand over fist.
a) Alliteration
b) Polysyndetic list
c) Repetition
d) Asyndetic list
e) Antithesis
f) Tricolon structure

TOPIC 3. ANALYSIS

3.3.4 Connecting sentence structure to the writer's purpose

It is not enough to simply identify features of sentence structure or describe their function. When analysing a text, you must be able to comment on how particular features of sentence structure have been deliberately used by the writer to achieve a purpose. In other words, you have to be able to write about the effect of the sentence structure of the reader.

Common effects of punctuation:

- parenthesis can be used to make an aside, showing the writer's attitude;
- inverted commas can show the writer's attitude by creating an ironic, doubtful or critical tone (see 3.4);
- a semi-colon can emphasise similarity or contrast between the two sentences it joins;
- a colon, dash and ellipsis can create a sense of anticipation or drama.

Common effects of sentence types:

- exclamations can show the strength or a writer's attitude or emotion;
- a question can draw attention to an important idea and encourage the reader to think about it;
- a rhetorical question is a persuasive technique designed to encourage the reader to agree with the writer's point of view, or to emphasise an important idea;
- a short sentence can emphasise or draw attention to an idea;
- long sentences followed by a very short sentence (or vice versa) can emphasise a contrast.

Common effects of sentence patterns:

- repetition and parallel structures can emphasise particular words or ideas;
- alist can emphasise the number, variety or extend of something;
- climaxes can draw attention to the final climactic word or idea in the sentence, or emphasise an change or development;
- anticlimaxes can create humour or show disappointment;
- alliteration can draw attention to particular words and make an idea stand out;
- antithesis can draw attention to particular words and make an idea stand out;
- polysyndetic lists can emphasise the number, variety or extent of something;
- asyndetic lists can emphasise the number, variety or extent of something;
- tricolon can emphasise particular words or ideas;
- inversion can draw attention to particular words and ideas.

© HERIOT-WATT UNIVERSITY

70   UNIT 1. READING FOR UNDERSTANDING, ANALYSIS AND EVALUATION

Remember that only features of sentence structure that have been used deliberately to emphasise or enhance the writer's ideas are worth commenting on. Look at the relationship between the structure of the sentence and the writer's purpose: context is crucial. And remember that good writing —powerful, emotive and passionate writing —will seamlessly blend together a skilful use of word choice, imagery and sentence structure, and there will be more aspects of each of these language features in each passage than you can ever fully comment on.

For example, imagine you were asked to analyse the writer's use of sentence structure in these two paragraphs from the 2015 Higher RUAE paper, passage one.

Examples

1.

> But, as I discovered when I began looking into the way food is produced[1], increasingly powerful forces are pulling us in the opposite direction. We have become addicted to cheap meat, fish and dairy products from supply lines that stretch across the globe. On the plus side, it means that supermarkets can sell whole chickens for as little as £3. Things that were once delicacies, such as smoked salmon, are now as cheap as chips. On the downside, cheap chicken and farmed fish are fatty and flaccid. Industrially reared farm animals —50 billion of them a year worldwide —[2]are kept permanently indoors, treated like machines and pumped with drugs[3].
>
> Notes:
>
> [1] Parenthesis adds in additional information about the process she has undertaken; suggests the process was methodical, logical, to be trusted, rational.
> [2] Parallel structure emphasises the pros and the cons of such a system / Inversion: forces attention to 'industrially reared' making us question the nature of such a system, makes it sound unnatural / Parenthesis offers extra information about the size of the operation; implicitly suggests the writer is shocked by the stat, and that we should be too
> [3] Listing to end the paragraph about the way the animals are cared for in the intensive farming system; outlines the unnatural nature of the system. Could be argued to rise to a climax —to bring the writer's argument about the ills of the system to a high point. Remembering that she began with parenthesis suggesting she had researched the topic, the climax underlines the horrors that have been uncovered as facts.

© HERIOT-WATT UNIVERSITY

TOPIC 3. ANALYSIS

2.

My journey to expose the truth, to investigate the dirty secret about the way cheap food is produced[1], took me from the first mega-dairies and piggeries in Britain to factory farms in France, China, Mexico, and North and South America[2]. I talked to people on the front line of the global food industry: treadmill farmers trying to produce more with less. I also talked to[3] their neighbours —[4] people experiencing the side effects of industrial farms. Many had stories about their homes plummeting in value, the desecration of lovely countryside, the disappearance of wildlife and serious health problems linked to pollution.[5]

Notes:

[1] Parenthesis adds extra information about the idea of 'truth', adds strength to her argument as she presents the truth as unpalatable and 'dirty' / Parallel structure —explicitly links the idea of exposing and investigating; explicitly links together the idea of the truth and the idea of the dreadful way cheap food is created.

[2] Listing suggest the widespread nature of such farming methods (interesting that the list contains European, Asian, Central American and North/South American locations —conveys the idea of it being present all over the world)

[3] Colon introduces an explanation about who is on 'front line of the global food industry', the farmers who are caught up in the system. The colon dramatically introduces the metaphor 'treadmill farmers' and draws focus to the idea of farmers now having to work harder and harder but never experience more success. / Parallel structure —'I talked ... I also talked ...' reinforces her position as a researcher: gathering evidence, taking a rational approach to the matter, dealing with facts and not conjecture.

[4] Dash introduces more information about who the neighbours of the farms are, those with no stake in the industry who are negatively affected by it.

[5] Listing reinforces the problems that come along with intensive farming —economic, environmental and health issues. Could again be seen as a climax —rising to the idea that human life is threatened by the process.

© HERIOT-WATT UNIVERSITY

72   UNIT 1. READING FOR UNDERSTANDING, ANALYSIS AND EVALUATION

Explaining function and effect   Go online

Read the extract from the 2015 Higher RUAE paper, passage one. Choose the comment that analyses both the function and effect of the sentence structure feature.

> As for the cows, they last only two or three years, ten-to-fifteen years less than their natural life span. Crammed into barren pens on tiny patches of land, they stand around listlessly waiting to be fed, milked or injected with antibiotics. Through a combination of selective breeding, artificial diets and growth hormones designed to maximise milk production, they are pushed so grotesquely beyond their natural limit that they are soon worn out. In their short lives they never see grass.

(lines 11-16)

Q69: The writer uses a list —'selective breeding ... growth hormones' —to:

a) demonstrate how many horrible things happened to the cows on this farm in California.
b) emphasise the procedures the cows went through, making this type of farming seem like a cold and uncaring experiment on animals.
c) show how unhappy she is about all the things that happened to the cows.

....

Q70: The writer:

a) uses the final sentence to emphasise the contrast between these cows and the environment with which we would normally associate them.
b) creates drama and tension in the short sentence at the end of the paragraph.
c) brings the argument to a dramatic climax.
d) tells us that the cows' lives are unhappy and unnatural through a short sentence.
e) ends the paragraph using a climax to make us feel sympathy for the animals.

....

Q71: The writer uses inversion:

a) to give us more information about the condition the cows are kept in.
b) in the sentence 'Crammed ... antibiotics.'. This highlights the atrocious conditions in which the cows are kept.
c) to help the reader understand more about intensive farming and cows.

© HERIOT-WATT UNIVERSITY

3.4 Tone

Tone describes how words sound or would sound when spoken out loud. Here are some common words to describe tone.

Tone words	Means...
Apologetic	sorry
Appreciative	thankful; grateful
Acerbic	Harsh, severe, biting
Awe-struck	Overwhelmed; amazed
Candid	Open, frank, revealing
Clinical	Objective, emotionless, forensic
Contemptuous	Showing contempt, disdain, scorn, disregard
Critical	Finding fault
Cynical	Distrustful, sneering, pessimistic
Disappointed	let down; sad because of failure
Doubtful	Uncertain, unconvinced, questioning
Elegiac	Expressing sorrow, or lamentation, usually for something lost
Enthusiastic	passionate; keen
Frustrated	angry or upset at being unable to change or achieve something
Hectoring	Pushy, bullying, nagging
Hopeful	feeling positive about the future
Intimate	Chatty, revelatory, friendly, confiding
Introspective	Looking inwards, examining or contemplating own thoughts or actions
Judgmental	being very critical
Mocking	making fun of something in a cruel way
Menacing	Threatening, dangerous, aggressive
Nostalgic	A bitter-sweet longing for things past, looking back on a 'golden time'
Pedantic	Having a narrow, unyielding focus on small details, rules and accuracy
Reflective	Meditative, thoughtful, contemplative
Sarcastic (also irony)	saying the opposite of what is really meant to show criticism
Scathing	Attacking with severe criticism and vitriol
Self-deprecating	Being modest or critical of one's self, often humourously
Sentimental	feeling soft-hearted and emotional about something
Sympathetic	caring and compassionate
Tongue-in-cheek	Not really meaning what is said, often humorously

74 UNIT 1. READING FOR UNDERSTANDING, ANALYSIS AND EVALUATION

3.4.1 Register

Register describes the level of language. It is a measure of formality. Writers can write in a formal register or an informal register.

A formal register may be created by the use of jargon, sophisticated word choice, an objective third person stance, complex sentence structures and an absence of contractions or colloquial language. To revise jargon, visit Scholar's National 5 pages, 3.1.4 Jargon.

An informal register may be created by contractions, colloquialism or dialect, second person address to the reader through questions or the use of third person plural pronouns (we, our, us).

Sometimes writers will employ a mixed register to create a humorous tone or emphasises a point through that tone.

> Example After undertaking her royal duties —meeting foreign dignitaries, opening hospital wings and delivering addresses to Parliament —there's nothing Her Majesty likes more than chillaxing with Phil, over a new episode of Homes under the Hammer and nice cuppa.
>
> The writer is suggesting, through the mixed register, that there are two sides to her personality.

Part of what makes this example humourous is the use of colloquialisms: words or phrases that are not formal, but are used in ordinary or familiar conversation. 'Chillax' and 'cuppa' are examples of colloquialisms.

3.4.2 Positive and negative tones

Different tones communicate different emotions and attitudes. For this reason, tones are generally positive or negative. When there is no strong emotion or attitude the tone can be described as neutral or matter-of-fact.

Rather than just describing a tone as either positive or negative, try to be as specific as possible. There are many different tones that are positive and many different tones that are negative.

TOPIC 3. ANALYSIS

Positive and negative tones activity

Q72: Identify whether the tones are positive or negative.

Positive	Negative
Accusatory	Acerbic
Celebratory	Happy
Contemptuous	Cynical
Grateful	Enthusiastic
Hectoring	Scathing
Lighthearted	Pedantic
Pessimistic	Optimistic
Sympathetic	Intimate
Menacing	Outraged
Excited	Friendly

3.4.3 Identifying tone

Depending on the question you are asked, you may be given a tone and asked to identify how it has been created. Alternatively, you may have to identify the tone yourself before explaining how it has been created.

Identifying different tones — Go online

Q73: Match the sentences with the words that best describe the tone.

The impact of intensive farming certainly deserves some consideration.	Sympathetic
Intensive farming has brought a new dawn of plenty. Could this be the end of the global food crisis?	Celebratory
One cannot help but be upset by the conditions animals must endure as a result of intensive farming.	Outraged
How dare the big agri-businesses try to justify such suffering and cruelty on economic grounds!	Hectoring
Long gone are the days when free-range was the norm, and farmers were respected members of the community, not just faceless middle managers in a supply chain.	Neutral
Maybe it's time you weighed up the small savings in your shopping basket against the considerable distress factory farmed animals are put through. Maybe it's time you did the right thing, and refused to accept animal cruelty in the a few measly extra pennies in your pocket.	Optimistic
We should loudly applaud the scientific advancements that mean that even in the harshest conditions —flood, drought, pestilence —the boffins have found a way to make secure food sources around the world. In a world of uncertainty, these developments are something to cheer about.	Nostalgic

3.4.4 Explaining how tone is created

A writer's tone is shown through language choices. This means that you use your skills in analysing word choice, imagery and sentence structure to explain how the tone is created.

In the following example from the 2015 Higher RUAE paper, passage one, there is a tone of disgust. Roll over to see some of the language techniques that create this tone.

Example

> 'As for the cows, they only[1] last two or three years, and then 10-15 years less than their natural lifespan. Crammed into barren pens on tiny patches of land[2], they stand around listlessly waiting to be fed, milked or injected with antibiotics[3]. Through a combination of selective breeding, artificial diets and growth hormones designed to maximise milk production, they are pushed so grotesquely beyond their natural limit that they are soon worn out. In their short lives, they never see grass.'[4]
>
> Notes:
>
> [1] Word choice suggests too short, unnaturally short
> [2] Collective word choice expresses idea that conditions are woefully limited and inhumane
> [3] Sentence structure suggests total passivity, dependence on the system. Also suggests that this is all their purpose is. Also, the possible juxtaposition between 'fed, milked' which are natural activities against 'injected with antibiotics' which is unnatural.
> [4] Word choice offers an explicit statement of disgust / Long sentence reinforces how many things are down to the cattle and their lack of agency / Final short sentence reflects the shortness of their lives and the shocking fact they are never outside

Identifying language features that create tone

Q74: Match the sentences with the language features that create the tone.

Sentence	Language features
The impact of intensive farming certainly deserves some consideration.	emotive word choice; inclusive pronoun
Intensive farming has brought a new dawn of plenty. Could this be the end of the global food crisis?	question mark; exclamation mark; emotive language
One cannot help but be upset by the conditions animals must endure as a result of intensive farming.	positive word choice; list; inclusive pronoun
How dare the big agri-businesses try to justify such suffering and cruelty? And on economic grounds!	contrast; direct address; emotive word choice
Long gone are the days when free-range was the norm, and farmers were respected members of the community, not just faceless middle managers in a supply chain.	formal register; statement
Maybe it's time you weighed up the small savings in your shopping basket against the considerable distress factory farmed animals are put through. Maybe it's time you did the right thing, and refused to accept animal cruelty in the a few measly extra pennies in your pocket	contrast; inversion; past tense
We should loudly applaud the scientific advancements that mean that even in the harshest conditions —flood, drought, pestilence —the boffins have found a way to make secure food sources around the world. In a world of uncertainty, these developments are something to cheer about.	question mark; positive word choice; imagery

3.5 Learning points

Summary

- Words have a denotation and connotations.
- Words with powerful connotations are useful in identifying the writer's stance/opinion.
- Words that belong to a particular profession or group are called jargon words.
- Writers choose words with connotations that help them achieve their purpose.
- Similes, metaphors and personification are comparisons used to help the writer achieve their purpose.
- An image transfers qualities from something imagined to the literal thing being described.
- Imagery can make description more vivid, and helps to convey the writer's ideas and/or opinions.
- Sentences come in different types: statement, exclamation, command, question, rhetorical question, minor sentence, short sentence, long sentence.
- Sentences can be structured to create patterns: repetition, list, climax, anticlimax, parallel structure, alliteration, antithesis, polysyndetic list, asyndetic list, tricolon, inversion.
- Punctuation can be used to create an effect.
- Tone describes the way words sound when read aloud.
- Tone shows the writer's emotions and attitudes.
- Tones can be positive or negative.
- Tone can be affected by register.
- Tone is created by other language features such as word choice, imagery, and sentence structure.

3.6 End of topic test

> End of Topic 3 test   Go online

Proms are a terrible, chintzy disappointment —perfect preparation for adulthood

Jean Hannah Edelstein
The Guardian
16 June 2015

It might be 17 years since I attended my high-school prom in upstate New York, but don't think for a moment that the memories aren't still burning bright: the polyester scratch of my don't-stand-near-flames, floor-length frock. The weight of the extravagant corsage that extended from my wrist to my elbow, transforming my arm into a rosy garden border. The inelegant scramble of six formal-wear-clad teenagers as we piled into the back seat of a stretch limousine. Some may say that the increased popularity of American-style high-school proms in the UK is a bad thing for Britain's youth. I disagree. Nothing prepares teenagers better for adulthood than the prom, and that's because it's so terrible.

My mother, an expat Scot with little patience for pointless American rituals, was indulgent in allowing me to attend my high-school prom (and funding it), but was resolute in her insistence on referring to the event as 'the practice wedding'. At the time, I found this insulting; in retrospect, I see its acuity. What is a prom but an early opportunity to celebrate heterosexual gender stereotypes through the ritualistic spending of money on anachronistic things that are completely absent from everyday life? Ballgowns, fancy cars, chicken breasts prepared to be served to 300 people simultaneously: so rare are the occasions when they make sense, we must create and perpetuate rituals around them.

What better way to herald a child's passing from parental dependence to full-time servant of capitalism than an occasion that promises glamour in proportion to expenditure, but which manifests itself as a night with the unglamorous people they see every day? Unglamorous people in uncomfortable outfits, some rented, emitting a chintzy glow under the light of a moon that was made of papier-mache by the kids in third-period art class? The promise of prom is spectacle; the reality is disappointment. Could anything prepare children better for the gruelling realities of human existence? I think not.

Some may say that the Kardashian-inspired scale of today's proms is excessive. But if children are to learn that money can't buy happiness, could there be any better lesson than that given when arriving by helicopter to your school prom only to realise that you still have bad skin and that your math teacher is your chaperone? More is more, I say, when it comes to helping impressionable young people understand that no amount of expense on taffeta frocks and sequined handbags will alleviate the terrible ennui of adult life.

Would we rather that our children wait until they are in their late 20s to get to grips with the fact that a loveless relationship cannot be saved by extravagant expense? No, we wouldn't, for that is the innocence that leads to £75,000 weddings between people who file for divorce before they've reached their one-year anniversary. Much better that a girl should know early on the heartbreak of a boyfriend turning up in a tie that doesn't match her dress. Far more helpful that a young man's fancy should be smashed at the sight of his girlfriend doing a sultry electric slide with her physics lab partner.

TOPIC 3. ANALYSIS

The prom is a microcosm of adulthood: stupid conventions and rules, established by long-gone arbiters of taste. Slut-shaming of women. Relationships modelled according to a socially acceptable script rather than the reality of two individuals and how they feel about each other. Go for it, kids! One might even say it's the night of your lives.

©*The Guardian*
It might be 17 years since I attended my high-school prom in upstate New York, but don't think for a moment that the memories aren't still burning bright: the polyester scratch of my don't-stand-near-flames, floor-length frock. The weight of the extravagant corsage that extended from my wrist to my elbow, transforming my arm into a rosy garden border. The inelegant scramble of six formal-wear-clad teenagers as we piled into the back seat of a stretch limousine. Some may say that the increased popularity of American-style high-school proms in the UK is a bad thing for Britain's youth. I disagree. Nothing prepares teenagers better for adulthood than the prom, and that's because it's so terrible.

Q75: Find the word(s) in paragraph one that suggests the writer can clearly recall her prom.

....

My mother, an expat Scot with little patience for pointless American rituals, was indulgent in allowing me to attend my high-school prom (and funding it), but was resolute in her insistence on referring to the event as 'the practice wedding'. At the time, I found this insulting; in retrospect, I see its acuity. What is a prom but an early opportunity to celebrate heterosexual gender stereotypes through the ritualistic spending of money on anachronistic things that are completely absent from everyday life? Ballgowns, fancy cars, chicken breasts prepared to be served to 300 people simultaneously: so rare are the occasions when they make sense, we must create and perpetuate rituals around them.

Q76: Find the word in paragraph two that suggests the writer now believes her mother was right about prom.

....

What better way to herald a child's passing from parental dependence to full-time servant of capitalism than an occasion that promises glamour in proportion to expenditure, but which manifests itself as a night with the unglamorous people they see every day? Unglamorous people in uncomfortable outfits, some rented, emitting a chintzy glow under the light of a moon that was made of papier-mache by the kids in third-period art class? The promise of prom is spectacle; the reality is disappointment. Could anything prepare children better for the gruelling realities of human existence? I think not.

Q77: Find the word in paragraph three that suggests real life is hard.

....

Some may say that the Kardashian-inspired scale of today's proms is excessive. But if children are to learn that money can't buy happiness, could there be any better lesson than that given when arriving by helicopter to your school prom only to realise that you still have bad skin and that your math teacher is your chaperone? More is more, I say, when it comes to helping impressionable young people understand that no amount of expense on taffeta frocks and sequinned handbags will alleviate the terrible ennui of adult life.

© HERIOT-WATT UNIVERSITY

82 UNIT 1. READING FOR UNDERSTANDING, ANALYSIS AND EVALUATION

Q78: Find the word in paragraph four that suggests that being a grown up is tedious.

....

The prom is a microcosm of adulthood: stupid conventions and rules, established by long-gone arbiters of taste. Slut-shaming of women. Relationships modelled according to a socially acceptable script rather than the reality of two individuals and how they feel about each other. Go for it, kids! One might even say it's the night of your lives.

Q79: Find the word in paragraph six that suggests that proms are a performance.

....

The writer suggests that 'the promise of prom is spectacle; the reality is disappointment.' Throughout the article, she uses word choice to exemplify this contrast.

Q80: Complete the table using the examples listed.

Promise and spectacle	Reality and disappointment

Examples: extravagant corsage, sequined handbags, uncomfortable outfits, arriving by helicopter, math teacher is your chaperone, papier-mâché, glamour, fancy cars, taffeta frocks, inelegant scramble, chintzy glow, bad skin, ballgowns, heartbreak.

For each example of imagery, identify the comment that best describes its effect in the passage.

Q81:
   don't think for a moment that the memories aren't still burning bright
   a) The image suggests the memories are painful.
   b) The image suggests the memories are vivid.
   c) The image suggests the memories are confusing.

....

© HERIOT-WATT UNIVERSITY

TOPIC 3. ANALYSIS 83

Q82:

full-time servant of capitalism

a) The image suggests being enslaved and controlled by money.
b) The image suggests looking after other people.
c) The image suggests running a company.

Q83:

a young man's fancy should be smashed

a) The image suggests being physically attacked.
b) The image suggests breaking a cherished ornament.
c) The image suggests the total destruction of his desires.

Q84:

Relationships modelled according to a socially acceptable script

a) The image suggests behaving in a predetermined manner.
b) The image suggests performing in an entertaining way.
c) The image suggests being cast in a play.

For each example of sentence structure, identify the comment that best describes its effect in the passage.

Q85:

...don't think for a moment that the memories aren't still burning bright: the polyester scratch of my don't-stand-near-flames, floor-length frock. The weight of the extravagant corsage that extended from my wrist to my elbow, transforming my arm into a rosy garden border. The inelegant scramble of six formal-wear-clad teenagers as we piled into the back seat of a stretch limousine.'don't think for a moment that the memories aren't still burning bright: the polyester scratch of my don't-stand-near-flames, floor-length frock. The weight of the extravagant corsage that extended from my wrist to my elbow, transforming my arm into a rosy garden border. The inelegant scramble of six formal-wear-clad teenagers as we piled into the back seat of a stretch limousine.

a) The writer uses a colon to introduce a list of all the specific details she can still remember.
b) The writer uses a colon to introduce a description of her dress.
c) The writer uses a colon to add more information about the memories.

© HERIOT-WATT UNIVERSITY

Q86:
At the time, I found this insulting; in retrospect, I see its acuity.

a) The writer uses a semi-colon to demonstrate how similar the writer is to her mother.
b) The writer uses a semi-colon to create a contrast, illustrating how her feelings towards her mother's attitude have changed over time.
c) The writer uses a semi-colon to suggest the difference between the past and the present.

....

Q87:
The prom is a microcosm of adulthood: stupid conventions and rules, established by long-gone arbiters of taste

a) The writer uses a colon to introduce an explanation of why proms offer a taste of adult life.
b) The writer uses a colon to introduce a personal comment, criticising proms.
c) The writer uses a colon to create a balanced structure to contrast proms with adult life.

....

Q88:
...the polyester scratch of my don't-stand-near-flames, floor-length frock. The weight of the extravagant corsage that extended from my wrist to my elbow, transforming my arm into a rosy garden border.

a) Cynical
b) Self-deprecating
c) Pessimistic
d) Sarcastic
e) Mocking

TOPIC 3. ANALYSIS

For each example, identify the tone that best describes the writer's stance.

Q89:
What is a prom but an early opportunity to celebrate heterosexual gender stereotypes through the ritualistic spending of money on anachronistic things that are completely absent from everyday life?
a) Cynical
b) Self-deprecating
c) Pessimistic
d) Sarcastic
e) Mocking

....

Q90:
But if children are to learn that money can't buy happiness, could there be any better lesson than that given when arriving by helicopter to your school prom only to realise that you still have bad skin and that your math teacher is your chaperone?
a) Cynical
b) Self-deprecating
c) Pessimistic
d) Sarcastic
e) Mocking

....

Q91:
no amount of expense on taffeta frocks and sequinned handbags will alleviate the terrible ennui of adult life.
a) Cynical
b) Self-deprecating
c) Pessimistic
d) Sarcastic
e) Mocking

....

Q92:
The prom is a microcosm of adulthood: stupid conventions and rules, established by long-gone arbiters of taste... Go for it, kids! One might even say it's the night of your lives.
a) Cynical
b) Self-deprecating
c) Pessimistic
d) Sarcastic
e) Mocking

© HERIOT-WATT UNIVERSITY

Unit 1 Topic 4

Evaluation

Contents

4.1 Evaluating effectiveness 88
4.2 Evaluating introductions 89
4.3 Evaluating conclusions 89
4.4 Evaluating supporting details 90
4.5 Practising evaluation skills 91
    4.5.1 Evaluate the introduction 91
    4.5.2 Evaluate supporting detail 91
    4.5.3 Evaluate the conclusion 92
4.6 Learning points 93
4.7 End of topic test 94

Learning objective

By the end of this topic, you should be able to:

- understand what is meant by 'evaluating';
- evaluate the effectiveness of an introduction;
- evaluate the effectiveness of a conclusion;
- evaluate the effectiveness of supporting detail.

88 UNIT 1. READING FOR UNDERSTANDING, ANALYSIS AND EVALUATION

> **Key point**
>
> Many of the activities and examples in these materials are based upon the 2015 SQA Higher RUAE paper, passages 1 and 2.
>
> 1. Adapted from 'Goodbye birds. Goodbye butterflies. Hello… farmageddon,' by Isabell Oakeshott, taken from The Sunday Times, 19 January 2014.
> 2. Adapted from 'Pasture to the Plate' by Audrey Ayton, taken from The Observer supplement, 10 July 1994.
>
> You will find it useful to have a copy of this paper next to you as you work through the resources.

4.1 Evaluating effectiveness

Evaluating involves making a judgement about how well a paragraph or language feature helps the writer achieve their purpose.

You might be asked:

- how effective the first paragraph is as an introduction to the passage as a whole;
- how effective the final paragraph is as a conclusion to the passage as a whole;
- how effective supporting detail is in supporting the writer's main idea.

In order to answer this type of question you will have to show an understanding of both the writer's ideas and their use of language. This means you must draw on your Understanding (Topic 2) and Analysis (Topic 3) skills. While it is possible to make a comment on why an introduction, conclusion or supporting detail is not effective, you should remember that the passages have been selected for their effectiveness. This means it is much easier to comment positively on what is effective.

4.2 Evaluating introductions

To evaluate an introduction, it is useful to remind yourself of the purpose of an introduction. From your own writing you will know that an introduction can:

- grab the reader's attention through something interesting, humorous, surprising, shocking or dramatic;
- establish the writer's point of view or main idea;
- establish conflicting points of view or a question that the writer will go on to explore;
- establish why the subject of the passage is important;
- establish the tone of the passage;
- show how the issue is current, topical, controversial or relevant.

In order to comment on how effective an introduction is, you will have to have read the rest of the passage so you can connect ideas or language features in the introduction to other parts of the text.

4.3 Evaluating conclusions

To evaluate a conclusion, it is useful to remind yourself of the purpose of a conclusion. From your own writing you will know that a conclusion can:

- sum up the main ideas of the passage;
- pinpoint the most important or significant idea in the passage;
- end with a climax;
- end with a 'call to action' or an encouragement to the reader;
- link back to the introduction, creating a 'circular structure';
- return to an idea or image from earlier in the passage;
- link back to the title of the passage;
- answer a question asked earlier in the passage;
- make use of tone by either maintaining a tone used earlier, or offering a positive or negative final message.

4.4 Evaluating supporting details

As well as introductions and conclusions you may be asked to evaluate how well supporting detail develops the writer's argument. Supporting detail might include: statistics, facts, quotes, examples, speculation or comparisons. (You can revise these types of supporting detail in Topic 2.2)

You will comment on how the evidence makes the writer's argument more convincing, persuasive or entertaining.

For instance:

- statistics can lend a sense of scientific objectivity to an argument. Statistics can emphasise the scale or extent of something very small or very large;
- facts can be used to prove (or try to prove) beyond question that the writer's opinions are correct;
- quotes, especially from experts or authority figures, lend an argument more power;
- examples can be used to show a problem or issue is widespread or to take an idea and put it into a real life situation;
- anecdotes can help to show how a wider problem or issue affects the writer, and therefore how it might affect the reader - if the anecdote is amusing it can also help to make a complicated topic more interesting;
- comparisons can emphasise how good or bad something is by setting it side by side with a similar example;
- speculation can present a best or worst case scenario in the event of the writer's hopes or fears coming true, to create optimism or pessimism in the reader.

As with analysis of language features (such as word choice or imagery) it is important not to comment on the supporting detail in isolation, but to connect it back to the writer's wider purpose in that paragraph, or the passage as a whole.

4.5 Practising evaluation skills

This section features questions which will help you to practise the evaluation of an introduction, supporting detail and a conclusion.

4.5.1 Evaluate the introduction

Reread the 2015 Higher RUAE paper, passage one by Isabel Oakeshott.

> **Evaluating the introduction activity** Go online
>
> Look specifically at paragraph one:
>> On a cold, bright November day I stood among a million almond trees and breathed in the sweet air. I was in Central Valley, California, in an orchard stretching over 700,000 acres. Before me was a vision of how the British countryside may look one day. Beyond the almond orchards were fields of pomegranates, pistachios, grapes and apricots. Somewhere in the distance were almost two million dairy cows, producing six billion dollars' worth of milk a year.
>
> The introduction is effective because it...
>
> Q1: ...introduces the personal tone of the article. Identify the way in which it does this.
>
> ....
>
> Q2: ...introduces the idea of the scale involved in industrial farming. Identify the way in which it does this.
>
> ....
>
> Q3: ...introduces speculation about the future of British farming. Identify the way in which it does this.
>
> ....
>
> Q4: ...introduces the idea of the beauty of the countryside, the idea of 'Eden'. Identify the way in which it does this.

4.5.2 Evaluate supporting detail

> **Evaluating supporting detail activity** Go online
>
> Look at paragraph 4 of the passage.
>> Could the British countryside ever look like this? If current trends continue, the answer is yes. Farming in Britain is at a crossroads, threatened by a wave of intensification from America. The first mega-dairies and mega-piggeries are already here. Bees are disappearing, with serious implications for harvests. Hedgerows, vital habitats for wildlife, have halved since the Second World War. The countryside is too sterile to support many native birds. In the past forty years the population of tree sparrows has fallen by 97%.

Q5: Identify the main idea of the paragraph.

....

Q6: Identify the five details mentioned in the paragraph to support the main idea.

....

Q7: What makes these five examples effective?

Look at paragraph 7 of the passage.
I talked to people on the front line of the global food industry: treadmill farmers trying to produce more with less. I also talked to their neighbours —people experiencing the side effects of industrial farms. Many had stories about their homes plummeting in value, the desecration of lovely countryside, the disappearance of wildlife and serious health problems linked to pollution.

The main idea of this paragraph is that the changes in farming affect people just as much as they affect the land and the animals.

Q8: What makes this paragraph effective?

4.5.3 Evaluate the conclusion

Evaluate the conclusion activity   Go online

Look at the final paragraph of the passage:
It may seem hard to imagine such a scene in Britain but it is not-far-fetched. Proposals for an 8,000 cow mega-dairy in Lincolnshire, based on the American model, were thrown out after a public outcry. On local radio the man behind the scheme claimed that 'cows do not belong in fields'. It will be the first of many similar fights, because dairies are expanding and moving indoors. The creep of industrial agriculture in Britain has taken place largely unnoticed, perhaps because so much of it happens behind closed doors. The British government calls it 'sustainable intensification'. Without fuss or fanfare, farm animals have slowly disappeared from fields and moved into hangars and barns.

This is an effective conclusion because it. . .

Q9: ...ends with her most significant concern: that British farming is changing for the worse. Identify the way in which it does this.

....

Q10: ...links back to the rest of the passage being about her visit to California described in the opening paragraph. Identify the way in which it does this.

....

Q11: ...continues the writer's use of emotive language in describing the changes to British farming practice. Identify the way in which it does this.

....

© HERIOT-WATT UNIVERSITY

TOPIC 4. EVALUATION

Q12: ...issues a warning about the future. Identify the way in which it does this.

4.6 Learning points

Summary

- Evaluating involves judging how well a paragraph or language feature helps the writer achieve their purpose.
- Evaluation combines Understanding and Analysis skills.
- You may be asked to evaluate the effectiveness of an introduction, conclusion or supporting detail.
- There are common features of introductions and conclusions you can identify, but it is important to show how these features relate to the passage as a whole.
- To evaluate supporting detail you should comment on how it develops the writer's main idea or argument.

4.7 End of topic test

> **End of Topic 4 test**   Go online
>
> Make sure you have passage two from the 2015 Higher RUAE by Audrey Eyton next to you. Read the passage carefully.
>
> *Paragraph 1*
>
> The founding fathers of intensive farming can claim, 'It seemed a good idea at the time!' Indeed it did, in Britain, half a century ago. The post-war government swung into action with zeal, allocating unprecedented funds to agricultural research. The outcome was that the mixed farm, where animals grazed in the fields, was replaced by the huge factories we see today.
>
> Q13: What makes the first paragraph an effective introduction to the passage?
>
> ....
>
> *Paragraph 4*
>
> The aim of those early advocates of intensive farming was 'fast food' - fast from birth to table. Again, they succeeded. Chicken, once an occasional treat, now the most popular meat in Britain, owes its low price largely to the short life of the bird. Today's broiler chicken has become the fastest growing creature on earth: from egg to take-away in seven weeks. Most farm animals now have less than half of their pre-war lifespan. Either they are worn out from overproduction of eggs or milk, or have been bred and fed to reach edible size in a few short weeks or months.'
>
> Q14: Why is the example of chicken effective in furthering the writer's argument?
>
> ....
>
> *Paragraph 7*
>
> It is also a scientifically proven fact that intensive farming has caused the loss of hedgerows and wildlife sustained by that habitat, has polluted waterways, decimated rural employment and caused the loss of traditional small farms. We need to act in the interests of human health. We need to show humane concern for the animals. We need to preserve what remains of the countryside by condemning the practice of intensive farming. We need to return the animals to the fields, and readopt the environmentally friendly, humane and healthy system we had and lost: the small mixed farm.
>
> Q15: What makes the final paragraph an effective conclusion to the passage?

Unit 1 Topic 5

The comparison question

Contents
5.1 Preparing to answer the comparison question 96
5.2 Identifying areas of agreement and disagreement 97
5.3 Structuring your answer 98
5.4 Practising the comparison question 100

96   UNIT 1. READING FOR UNDERSTANDING, ANALYSIS AND EVALUATION

The comparison question is the final question in the Higher RUAE paper. It is always worth 5 marks and asks you to compare the arguments presented by both writers. Depending on these arguments, you could be asked to find areas of agreement, disagreement, or both.

> **Key point**
>
> Many of the activities and examples in these materials are based upon the 2015 SQA Higher RUAE paper, passages 1 and 2.
>
> 1. Adapted from 'Goodbye birds. Goodbye butterflies. Hello... farmageddon,' by Isabell Oakeshott, taken from The Sunday Times, 19 January 2014.
>
> 2. Adapted from 'Pasture to the Plate' by Audrey Ayton, taken from The Observer supplement, 10 July 1994.
>
> You will find it useful to have a copy of this paper next to you as you work through the resources.

5.1   Preparing to answer the comparison question

Essentially you are asked to summarise the main ideas in each passage, compare them and identify areas of overlap.

To do this you must be able to distinguish main ideas from supporting detail. To revise this skill see Topic 2.2 Main Ideas and Supporting Detail.

You must also be able to present these ideas using your own words. To revise this skill see Topic 2.4 Summarising and Topic 2.5 Explaining in your own words.

Before you read passage one for the first time, make sure you read the final question. This will tell you whether you are looking for areas of agreement, disagreement or both. More importantly, it will specify the particular topic or issue on which the writers agree/disagree.

As you read passage one for the first time, in preparation for answering the questions, it is a good idea to annotate the text. Specifically, make a note in the margin next to each paragraph summarising the main idea in your own words, bearing in mind the particular topic specified in the question. Try to make that summary as concise as possible. It may be as brief as a few words.

Be aware, however that not every paragraph will contain one main idea. Some paragraphs may simply be supporting detail; some paragraphs may contain more than one main idea. A main idea may also span more than one paragraph.

© HERIOT-WATT UNIVERSITY

TOPIC 5. THE COMPARISON QUESTION 97

Preparing to answer the comparison question activity

Q1: Re-read the 2015 Higher RUAE paper, passage one. Make a note next to each paragraph summarising the writer's main ideas about intensive farming. When you are finished, compare your annotations with the suggested answers.

....

When you have completed the questions on passage one, undertake the same annotation process on passage two. This time, focus on the main ideas you identified with annotating passage one. Depending on the question, you may be looking for ideas that are in agreement, or in opposition to those ideas.

Q2: Re-read the 2015 Higher RUAE paper, passage two. Focusing on the writer's points about intensive farming, make a note next to each paragraph summarising the main ideas. When you are finished, compare your annotations with the suggested answers.

5.2 Identifying areas of agreement and disagreement

Identifying areas of agreement and disagreement activity

Once you have annotated both passages, you can see where the passages overlap.

Q3: Identify the aspects of intensive farming upon which the two passages agree. When you have finished, compare your list with the suggested answers.

© HERIOT-WATT UNIVERSITY

5.3 Structuring your answer

The SQA marking instructions for the comparison question indicate how marks are awarded. Structuring your answer appropriately will give you the best chance of gaining all 5 marks available for the question.

You can answer the comparison question in essay-style paragraphs if you choose. However, structuring your answer as developed bullet points, may be beneficial as it will make it easier for you to know when you have identified three distinct areas of (dis-)agreement, and referenced both passages.

SQA Marking Instructions - Comparison Question

- Five marks —identification of three key areas of agreement with detailed/insightful use of supporting evidence
- Four marks —identification of three key areas of agreement with appropriate use of supporting evidence
- Three marks —identification of three key areas of agreement
- Two marks —identification of two key areas of agreement
- One mark —identification of one key area of agreement
- Zero marks —failure to identify any key area of agreement and/or misunderstanding of task

N.B. A candidate who identifies only two key areas of agreement may be awarded a maximum of four marks, as follows:

- two marks for identification of two key areas of agreement
- a further mark for appropriate use of supporting evidence to a total of three marks

or

- a further two marks for detailed/insightful use of supporting evidence to a total of four marks

A candidate who identifies only one key area of agreement may be awarded a maximum of two marks, as follows:

- one mark for identification of one key area of agreement
- a further mark for use of supporting evidence to a total of two marks

What this means in practice is that you can get up to 3 marks simply by identifying 3 areas of agreement or disagreement. So you could begin by selecting three areas from your list, leaving space between each area to then go back and add in supporting detail. It is useful to focus each area of agreement or disagreement on the question. In this case, starting the heading with the words from the question 'Intensive farming...'

Example Intensive farming:

1. is unnatural.
2. is responsible for animal cruelty.
3. influences the consumer.

Then break the list down further.

Examples

1. Intensive farming is unnatural.
   - Passage 1 states that animals are routinely injected with drugs and their lifespan is accelerated.
   - Passage 2 agrees and says that animals are overfed and overbred to make them grow as quickly as possible.

   ....

2. Intensive farming is responsible for animal cruelty.
   - Passage 1 states that animals are kept indoors in tiny pens and never get to go outside.
   - Passage 2 agrees and says that animals are forced to over-produce high qualities of milk and eggs, for example.

   ....

3. Intensive farming influences the consumer.
   - Passage 1 states that consumers changed their diets because produce became so cheap; we can't help but buy cheap meat.
   - Passage 2 agrees and says that we began eating more and more meat and that this caused increases in certain diseases.

Note that each point is structured in the same way, beginning with the position taken by the writer in passage one, and then stating the position taken by the writer in passage two. It can be useful to use 'agrees' or 'disagrees' to keep you focussed on the question, especially if the question asks you for areas of agreement and/or disagreement.

> **Structuring your answer activity**
>
> Using the areas of agreement listed below, return to the 2015 Higher RUAE paper to find supporting detail to develop your answers. When you have added your supporting detail, compare your details with the suggested answers.
>
> Q4: Intensive farming impacts the environment.
>
> ....
>
> Q5: Intensive farming is done on a huge scale.
>
> ....
>
> Q6: Intensive farming should be resisted.

5.4 Practising the comparison question

The Higher Close Reading Past Papers from 2012 to 2015 feature the same style of comparison question as the Higher RUAE and can be used for practise. The 2011 Higher Close Reading Past Paper can also be used for this purpose, by focussing on the attitude displayed by each writer to video games and their effects on young people and identifying the key areas on which they disagree

Unit 1 Topic 6

Exam skills

Contents

6.1 Understanding the exam paper 102
6.2 Skimming, scanning and annotating 105
6.3 Structuring your answer 106
6.4 Using past papers and other articles 107
6.5 Learning points 108
6.6 End of topic test 109

Learning objective

By the end of this topic, you should be able to:

- understand how the RUAE exam paper is structured;
- understand how to skim, scan and annotate;
- understand the different ways to structure answers;
- understand how to use past papers and articles to revise.

> **Key point**
>
> Many of the activities and examples in these materials are based upon the 2015 SQA Higher RUAE paper, passages 1 and 2.
>
> 1. Adapted from 'Goodbye birds. Goodbye butterflies. Hello... farmageddon,' by Isabell Oakeshott, taken from The Sunday Times, 19 January 2014.
>
> 2. Adapted from 'Pasture to the Plate' by Audrey Ayton, taken from The Observer supplement, 10 July 1994.
>
> You will find it useful to have a copy of this paper next to you as you work through the resources.

6.1 Understanding the exam paper

The RUAE exam paper will consist of two passages on a related topic and questions totalling 30 marks. Passage one will contain 25 marks worth of questions, and the final question will ask you to look at both passages and to compare the writers' arguments. This question is worth 5 marks. You have an hour and a half to answer all the questions.

Questions will have line references to guide you to the part of the passage containing the answer.

The majority of the questions will test your understanding of the writer's ideas. These questions should always be answered in your own words as far as possible (see Topic 2).

Questions requiring you to analyse the writer's language are the next most common. Sometimes the question will specify a particular language feature, others will simply ask about the 'use of language' generally, allowing you to choose the language features you analyse (see Topic 3).

Usually there are one or two questions that require you to evaluate (see Topic 4).

Each question will have a number of marks associated with it. Use the number of marks to judge how many separate comments you need to make.

For example, a 3 mark understanding question will require three separate points in the answer.

In analysis questions, no marks are awarded for identifying or quoting a language feature. You can gain up to two marks for your comment on an individual language feature. However, it may be a better approach to provide a separate comment on a language feature for each mark available. For example, if the question is worth 4 marks, analyse 4 features.

Evaluation questions that ask about the introduction or conclusion will typically award up to two marks for each comment. However, like analysis questions, it may be better to provide a comment for each mark available. No marks are awarded for quoting a language feature or idea.

Understanding the exam paper activity   Go online

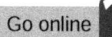

Here are the questions for the 2015 SQA National 5 RUAE exam. Identify what kind of question each is:

- Understanding (U)
- Analysis (A)
- Evaluation (E)
- Comparative (C)

Q1: Identify any two positive aspects of Central Valley, California, which are conveyed in these lines. Use your own words in your answer.

a) U
b) A
c) E
d) C

....

Q2: By referring to at least two examples, analyse how the writer's use of language creates a negative impression of Central Valley.

a) U
b) A
c) E
d) C

....

Q3: By referring to both word choice and sentence structure, analyse how the writer makes clear her disapproval of dairy farming methods used in Central Valley.

a) U
b) A
c) E
d) C

....

Q4: Explain the function of these lines in the development of the writer's argument. You should make close reference to the passage in your answer.

a) U
b) A
c) E
d) C

....

Q5: In your own words, summarise the differences between UK Government food policy and consumer wishes.

a) U
b) A
c) E
d) C

....

Q6: Analyse how both imagery and sentence structure are used in these lines to convey the writer's criticism of industrial farming.

a) U
b) A
c) E
d) C

....

Q7: Explain how the writer continues the idea that the Central Valley dairy farming is 'nightmarish'. Use your own words in your answer. You should make three key points.

a) U
b) A
c) E
d) C

....

Q8: Evaluate the effectiveness of the final paragraph as a conclusion to the writer's criticism of industrial farming.

a) U
b) A
c) E
d) C

....

Q9: Look at both passages.

Both writers express their views about intensive farming. Identify three key areas on which they agree. You should support the points you make by referring to important ideas in both passages.

You may answer this question in continuous prose or in a series of developed bullet points.

a) U
b) A
c) E
d) C

6.2 Skimming, scanning and annotating

Skimming means to read the passage quickly, not taking in specific details, but gaining a general impression of the main ideas and how the ideas are organised. This may be how you first read the passage before looking at it in more detail when answering the questions.

Scanning means to quickly look through the text in order to find a specific detail or word. When the question contains a quotation from the passage, you will scan the lines referenced to find these words. The answer will usually be located nearby or the context will help you answer the question.

Example : Q7 in the 2015 Higher RUAE paper

Read lines 42-55. Explain how the writer continues the idea that the Central Valley dairy farming is 'nightmarish'. Use your own words in your answer. You should make three key points. *(3)*

The first step in answering this question is to scan lines 42-55 to find the word 'nightmarish'. Once you have found this word, reading the context more closely will give you the answer.

Annotating is an important skill that can be an extremely useful way to make sense of the paper. You might find it useful to underline, circle or highlight on the questions:

- the line reference;
- the command verb (explain, summarise, show);
- the number of marks available.

More importantly, you should annotate the passage to help you organise your thinking before writing your answer down. Here are useful steps to follow.

1. Draw a bracket or box around the referenced lines to make sure your answer comes only from the designated section.

2. Read through the entire section from the first line to the last.

3. As you read through the lines, identify every possible answer within the section. For understanding questions, this might involve numbering individual ideas; for analysis questions this might involve finding interesting examples of word choice, imagery and sentence structure and underlining or highlighting it. (Remember to separate ideas when highlighting. See Topic 2.5.1)

4. From the ideas (or language features, if you are answering an analysis question) you have found, make a sensible decision about which you can most successfully put into your own words (or analyse). It is important not to choose the first ideas (or language features) you come across; you may find simpler answers later in the section.

6.3 Structuring your answer

There are many ways you can structure your answers. You may already be working with structures taught to you by your teacher, or you may approach each question differently. The important thing is that all aspects of a question are tackled.

Examples

1. Q1 in the 2015 Higher RUAE paper

Read lines 1-5. Identify any two positive aspects of Central Valley, California, which are conveyed in these lines. Use your own words in your answer. (2)

The question is asking you to do two things.

1. Identify two positive aspects.
2. Write them down using your own words.

You could structure your answer like this:

- The orchard is beautiful.
- The orchard is abundant.

or you could structure your answer like this:

- The writer suggests that the orchard is like a paradise; it is beautiful. She goes on to say that the orchard also supports much life; it is abundant.

....

2. Q5 in the 2015 Higher RUAE paper was a 4-mark summary question

Read lines 23-24. In your own words, summarise the differences between UK Government food policy and consumer wishes. (4)

You could structure your answer like this:

- Government policy is to buy British and not buy food from abroad. They also want to be more environmentally friendly. Consumers want less expensive food and don't really care about where the food comes from.

or you could structure your answer like this:

- the government wants us to buy British;
- the government doesn't want us to buy food from abroad;
- the government wants to be environmentally friendly;
- consumers want less expensive food;
- consumers don't really care where food comes from.

or you could structure your answer like this:

Government

- Buy British
- Don't buy foreign food
- Be environmentally friendly

Consumers

- Want less expensive food
- Don't care where food comes from

All three answers would gain full marks. However, it may be easier for you to keep track of how many separate point you have made if you use bullet points, and it may be easier to check you have covered both parts of the question if you use sub-headings. Note that there was no requirement to provide the same number of points for each part of the question, as long as both the government and consumers are discussed in the answer.

In each answer, there are actually 5 points. The question offered a maximum mark of 4, so you cannot gain any extra credit. However, providing an extra point or two might be a good idea if you are uncertain about the accuracy of some of your points.

No matter how you choose to structure your answer, remember there is no need to repeat the words of the question; this will only waste time. Additionally, you do not need to write in full sentences; RUAE is a test of your reading, not your writing.

6.4 Using past papers and other articles

Resources

- SQA Higher English Past Papers:
  http://www.sqa.org.uk/pastpapers/findpastpaper.htm?subject=English&level=NH
- SQA Discontinued Higher English Past Papers.
  http://www.sqa.org.uk/pastpapers/findpastpaper.htm?subject=English&level=H
- SQA Higher English Exemplar and Specimen Papers.
  http://www.sqa.org.uk/sqa/47904.html

The most obvious way to use past, exemplar, specimen and practice papers is to complete them under timed conditions. However, there are many other things you can do with these papers to develop your skills:

- examine the marking key to understand how marks are awarded, and identify alternative answers to those you found;
- practise reading, annotating and understanding questions;
- select particular question types from several papers to target specific skills.

Passages from past, exemplar, specimen and practice papers can also be used for these activities, once you have completed the questions:

- practise your reading skills to increase your vocabulary;
- practise working out the audience and purpose for each article;
- read and analyse the writer's line of thought;
- practise your analysis skills by selecting your own language features (those not covered by the questions);
- examine introductions and conclusions from several different passages;
- practise summarising the main ideas;
- read the passage out loud to identify the tone;
- practise skimming to improve the pace of your reading;
- practise annotating.

Many of these activities can also be applied to articles taken from the sources listed in Topic 1.2. Remember you could also become an exam setter yourself by making up your own questions and marking scheme and trading them with a friend.

6.5 Learning points

Summary

- The RUAE exam paper is worth 30 marks.
- The paper will contain two passages and a mix of Understanding, Analysis and Evaluation questions. There is also a final comparative question on both passages worth 5 marks.
- Skimming can be used to read the passage quickly.
- Scanning can be used to find specific details when answering questions.
- Annotating can help you understand the passage and organise your answers.
- There are many ways to structure your answers.
- In addition to timed practice, there are many different ways to use past papers and articles to revise.

6.6 End of topic test

End of Topic 6 test — Go online

Q10: How many marks is the RUAE exam worth?

a) 20
b) 30
c) 50

....

Q11: How long do you have to complete the RUAE exam?

a) 45 minutes
b) 1 hour
c) 90 minutes

....

Q12: What skill do you use when making notes on the passage?

a) Skimming
b) Scanning
c) Annotating

....

Q13: What skill do you use when reading the passage through quickly to gain a sense of the writer's argument?

a) Skimming
b) Scanning
c) Annotating

....

Q14: What skill do you use when searching for specific details in the passage?

a) Skimming
b) Scanning
c) Annotating

....

Q15: You must repeat the wording of the question at the start of your answer.

a) True
b) False

Q16: You can structure your answers in any way you choose.

a) True
b) False

Q17: You must always answer in full sentences.

a) True
b) False

Q18: You should never bullet point your answers.

a) True
b) False

Q19: You must never include more points in your answer than the number of marks available.

a) True
b) False

Q20: Using the marking key to mark your own answers can be a useful activity.

a) True
b) False

Unit 1 Topic 7

Practice Papers

Contents
7.1 Practice paper 1: Katie Hopkins 112
7.2 Practice paper 2: Attention and distraction 117
7.3 Practice paper 3: Food and diets 123

Before you start, note that the end of unit tests contain essay questions that are not marked automatically. To get a better understanding of where you are at in your learning you can ask your teacher to look at your answers or use the sample answers, that are provided in this test, and compare your answers to them.

7.1 Practice paper 1: Katie Hopkins

Practice paper 1: Katie Hopkins   Go online

PASSAGE ONE

Katie Hopkins calling migrants vermin recalls the darkest events of history

Zoe Williams, The Guardian, 19 April 2015

The bodies have yet to be counted; from the latest tragedy in the Mediterranean only 28 have so far been saved. There may have been 700 on board. The scale of the loss is extraordinary, but the manner of it entirely ordinary. These deaths are the result of politics; not complicated coups in faraway places, but bland decisions in beige EU meeting rooms resulting in the decision to halt search and rescue operations. In a statement to the House of Lords last October, the Foreign Office minister Lady Anelay justified the move and Britain's support for it thus: "The government believes there is an unintended 'pull factor', encouraging more migrants to attempt the dangerous sea crossing and thereby leading to more tragic and unnecessary deaths".

This move was never going to stop the flight of refugees —people fleeing chemical weapons and public beheadings, political oppression, civil war and starvation do not emigrate to a place because they've heard good things about its coastguard services. Nor do they change their minds when they read that the safety features have had their funding cut.

The rationale as Anelay described it made no sense at all; yet at a deeper level it makes perfect sense. Because we scarcely ever talk about migrants except in terms of what they're worth: how much they grow the economy or take from it, how much wealth they create in student fees or investment, what they do to wages with their pesky hard work and willingness to be exploited.

Political parties talk about migration as something to attract or repel, a tango between economic and political expediency. Human beings have no innate value in this worldview: there is no pride in representing the country that is safe and generous enough to offer a haven. Refugees, arriving with nothing, are worth nothing.

The controversialist Katie Hopkins, writing in the Sun 48 hours before the latest mass drowning, suggested using gun boats on migrants; her idea proved unnecessary, of course. Why waste the money when you can let people die by doing nothing, for free? But Hopkins' phrasing was interesting: "These migrants are like cockroaches. They might look a bit 'Bob Geldof's Ethiopia circa 1984', but they are built to survive a nuclear bomb." The following morning, as an LBC shock jock, she rolled back her position slightly, suggesting the best way to solve the refugee crisis was not to shoot them once they were in the water, but to "burn all the boats in North Africa".

A rather niche debate is underway about whether "Katie Hopkins" is a construct of its owner —like Mrs Merton, an entertainment turn spun out for money - or whether Katie Hopkins is a real person with an antisocial personality disorder. With more urgent questions and so many people dead, this distinction shouldn't detain us. The fault is with those who broadcast her: this is serious stuff.

This characterisation of people as less than human, as vermin, as a "virus" (as she did elsewhere in the article) irresistibly recalls the darkest events in history. It is eerily reminiscent of the Rwandan media of 1994, when the radio went from statements such as "You have to kill the Tutsis, they're cockroaches" to, shortly afterwards, instructions on how to do so, and what knives to use.

It is no joke when people start talking like this. We are not "giving her what she wants" when we make manifest our disgust. It is not a free speech issue. I'm not saying gag her: I'm saying fight her. Articulate the fellowship, the human empathy, that makes these deaths important. Stop talking about how many children were among the dead, as though only children matter. Start talking about everybody's life as cherishable, irrespective of anything they might produce.

As the Hopkins column moved about social media, there gathered that peculiar sense of shame in objecting to it. A representative from Save the Children suggested we should channel that anger in a useful way, and give a donation. Others, scores of others, were of the opinion that if we ignored her she would go away. It's a mixture of social embarrassment and moral nuance.

Are we validating the cockroach-view by engaging with it? Are we feeding off the suffering of others for a luxurious, meaningless ding-dong between people who manufacture conflict because they're so far removed from what real peril feels like? With so much fresh loss, so much more that every one of us could have done, so much collective guilt, isn't silence the only respectful response? I didn't take to the streets in October last year when Anelay made her statement. I didn't even write to my MP. I've never been to Calais to show solidarity with the refugees who are being beaten up there by French police. What right have I to say any of this is wrong?

Compassion is such a rich part of the human experience and yet such a shaming thing to express, because you will always fall short of what your own words demand from you. You will never do enough. It makes you wonder how the concept of human rights was ever born. How did anybody ever overcome the knowledge of their own failings for long enough to establish universal principles that they knew they would probably never do enough to propagate?

Because, fresh from the memory of "barbarous acts which have outraged the conscience of mankind", people knew what the world looked like when nobody stood up to defend "the innate dignity of all the members of the human family". People knew that insufficient was better than nothing. People knew that you don't respect the dead by staying silent about what killed them.

PASSAGE TWO

What Katie Hopkins wrote was monstrous. But save your anger for the politicians who decided to let migrants drown

Sarah Ditum, New Statesman, 20 April 2015

Seven hundred this weekend, and 400 last week, and 300 in February. Last year, more than 3,000. All these souls, swallowed by the Mediterranean as they tried to make the passage from Africa to Italy. They travelled in dinghies and rickety ships, and they likely paid traffickers huge sums of money for the privilege. Not one of us would trust our lives to such a vessel, but then we are safely here, and they were over there. They were escaping war, or poverty, or Isis, or violence. No one would have undertaken this dangerous passage unless they were leaving something much, much worse behind. No one could have overcome their fear at boarding these flimsy craft unless they had hopes of something much, much better beyond —hopes all snuffed in salt water when the boats went down.

Because when the boats go down now, there is little chance of rescue. In November, the Italian fleet suspended its search and rescue mission for migrant boats, called Mare Nostrum ("our sea"). Although the EU contributed euro30m to fund it, the Italian government still had to supply a further euro9m per month, and the remaining EU nations were unwilling to provide more and risk offending popular anti-immigration sentiment. When Katie Hopkins declared in her Sun column that she would send "gunships" to deter the boats carrying migrants she described as "feral", a "plague" and "cockroaches", what she wrote was monstrous —but she did not, after all, actually kill anyone. That honour belongs to the politicians of Europe who terminated Mare Nostrum, every one of them making the repugnant calculation that dead Africans in the sea would be more electorally palatable than live Africans on their soil.

So yes, it's nice to condemn the usefully loathsome Hopkins, but what she has said is merely a frank statement of the politics our government has been enacting at our borders in our name for years now. If we didn't think of migrants as a "plague", why else would we detain those whose applications for asylum have been rejected in facilities such as Yarl's Wood? Here, the guards —employed by private company Serco, but acting on behalf of our state —refer to inmates as "beasties", "animals" and "bitches". A report by the campaign group Women for Refugee Women tells how women at Yarl's Wood are watched over even when they shower; some describe being sexually abused by the staff. Unsurprisingly, more than half of the women interviewed were on suicide watch. There is no public uproar. How much less than human must we think these people are, for us to tolerate such treatment?

If we didn't consider migrants "feral", would we subject them to the kind of brutal controls that we do? Those who seek asylum in the UK are not permitted to work, and then we begrudge them every penny we allow them. While a claim is being processed, asylum seekers are given a place to stay plus £42.62 a week, with an extra fiver if they have a baby —which might just cover the nappies. If their claim is refused, that goes down to £35.39, which they receive on a payment card that can only be spent on certain things in certain shops. What's the worth of that £7.23 to us? Very little, except perhaps that it feels like a punishment. You tried to make a home here, we turned you down, and now we can make your life as miserable as possible. I've watched a man thumbing that card and choosing between soap and apples at the checkout. So many miles travelled to decide whether you can afford hygiene or nutrition in the Co-op queue.

If we thought migrants were more than "cockroaches", wouldn't we give them better treatment than dawn raids? Wouldn't we try to offer them justice and consistency, rather than peremptorily reversed and then suddenly enforced deportation orders? This brutal cycle of faint hope and deep desolation could not have been designed better to crush those it is used upon. The "evidence" that asylum seekers are required to provide in support of their cases is a savage tax on their dignity. Are you really gay? Were you really raped? Show your scars and let us judge you. Tell us your fears and let us weigh their worth.

Yet the parties still tell us we need to do more. You can drink your tea from a Labour mug pledging "Controls on immigration" if you so desire —because however much cruelty we enforce, there will always be a politician ready to say that they would go a little bit further. They'd do it for us. This is the civilisation we think we are defending from incomers. Here, we drive those who wish to make a new home into compulsory poverty. We take the traumatised and pay profit-making companies to turn them into prisoners. And then we have the nerve to damn Hopkins for speaking the violence we consent to have committed in our name. 700 this weekend, and 400 last week, and 300 in February, and last year, more than 3,000: all these souls, and we've barely even begun to count the human cost of our vicious insularity.

Q1: Re-read the first paragraph. The writer opens the article by suggesting that loss on this scale has become 'entirely ordinary'. Analyse how her use of language reinforces this idea. (4)

Marks will depend on the quality of comment on appropriate language feature(s).

2 marks may be awarded for reference plus detailed/insightful comment; 1 mark for reference plus more basic comment; 0 marks for reference alone.

....

Q2: Look at paragraph two. Identify the writer's attitude towards the decision to cut Search and Rescue, and analyse how her language reinforces this attitude. (3)

....

Q3: Look at paragraphs three and four.

a) Using your own words, explain how the public, and/or political parties, view migrants, according to the writer. (2)

b) Analyse how the writer's use of language makes clear her criticism of how the public and/or political parties view migrants. (2)

....

Q4: Look at paragraph six. What is the 'rather niche debate' that is underway'? (2)

....

Q5: By referring to at least two features of language in paragraph eight, analyse how the writer conveys the strength of her belief that it's time to take a stand against 'people talking like this'. (4)

Marks will depend on the quality of comment on appropriate language feature(s).

2 marks may be awarded for reference plus detailed/insightful comment; 1 mark for reference plus more basic comment; 0 marks for reference alone.

....

Q6: Look at paragraph ten. Identify the writer's tone, and go on to show how her use of language creates that tone. (3)

....

Q7: Look at the second to last paragraph of passage one. In your own words, explain the point the writer makes about 'the concept of human rights'. (2)

....

Q8: Evaluate the final paragraph's effectiveness as a conclusion to the passage as a whole. (3)

....

Q9: Look at both passages. Both writers express their views about the response to the migrant crisis. Identify three key areas on which they agree. You should support the points by referring to important ideas in both passages.

You may answer this question in continuous prose or in a series of bullet points. (5)

7.2 Practice paper 2: Attention and distraction

Practice paper 2: Attention and distraction   Go online

PASSAGE ONE

The distraction economy: how technology downgraded attention

Tomas Chamorro-Premuzic The Guardian, Monday 15 December, 2014

After thinking about second screens, behavioural targeting and the success of Buzzfeed, marketers are at last coming to terms with the attention economy: the battle for monetising ephemeral interests. Facebook and Tinder may be leading the race, monopolising users for 15 minutes per day, but what are we doing the rest of the time?

Google reckons that we spend 4.4 hours of our daily leisure time in front of screens. Computers are mostly used for productivity and search, smartphones for connectivity, and tablets for entertainment. Multi-screening is, however, the new norm, with as many as 77% of consumers watching TV while on other devices.

TED talks are threatening to replace books and lectures, turning learning into "edutainment" and celebrating performance and storytelling over factual accuracy. Netflix invites us to spend more time selecting a movie than actually watching it and YouTube provides an infinite cascade of videos to procrastinate in style.

The 341 songs on my main Spotify playlist should take 24 hours to play, but I can usually go through them in one, while answering no fewer than 20 emails per hour. This excludes my social media time, which I leave for when I'm stuck in traffic, or riding my bike. And, unlike most people, I find text messaging and WhatsApp too distracting. Some nations have been far more affected; in South Korea a man died after reportedly playing a 50-hour video game marathon.

Unsurprisingly, there is a crisis of attentiveness. When information is bountiful, attention is limited and precious. Unlike our evolutionary ancestors, who were probably rewarded for absorbing as much of their sensory surroundings as they possibly could, what's adaptive today is the ability to ignore our distracting environments. Indeed, in times of information overload and non-stop media bombardment, distraction is destruction and the only recipe for focus is discipline and self-control.

A one-time theoretical physicist, Michael Goldhaber, defined the attention economy as a "system that revolves primarily around paying, receiving and seeking what is most intrinsically limited and not replaceable by anything else, namely the attention of other human beings". However, it seems more appropriate to describe our era as the distraction economy. Indeed the real war revolves around interrupting consumers' focus and concentration, even for a few seconds. An integral part of this economy is measurement, since digital media allows us to quantify attention via clicks, likes, views and tags, allegedly improving our ability to understand and influence consumers. But if attention is the new currency of the digital economy, what are consumers getting in return?

Not much. In fact, attention is valuable precisely because it is consumed by information overload, producing a vicious circle: we bombard you with content so that your attention becomes more valuable, which in turn justifies yet more content bombardment. "Attention here becomes the scarce quantity which is 'consumed' by that which is abundant, that is, information," says Tiziana Terranova in an insightful essay on this subject. The result is a degradation of attention that causes ADHD-like behaviours, such as impulsivity and boredom. These symptoms are best evidenced during digital withdrawal: those 20 minutes on the tube, or the six hours of downtime while flying over an ocean.

As early as 1971 Herbert Simon observed that "what information consumes is rather obvious: it consumes the attention of its recipients. Hence a wealth of information creates a poverty of attention, and a need to allocate that attention efficiently among the overabundance of information sources that might consume it". Thus instead of reaping the benefits of the digital revolution we are intellectually deprived by our inability to filter out sensory junk in order to translate information into knowledge. As a result, we are collectively wiser, in that we can retrieve all the wisdom of the world in a few minutes, but individually more ignorant, because we lack the time, self-control, or curiosity to do it.

There are also psychological consequences of the distraction economy. Although it is too soon to observe any significant effects from technology on our brains, it is plausible to imagine that long-term effects will occur. As Nicholas Carr noted in The Shallows: What the internet is doing to our brains, repeated exposure to online media demands a cognitive change from deeper intellectual processing, such as focused and critical thinking, to fast autopilot processes, such as skimming and scanning, shifting neural activity from the hippocampus (the area of the brain involved in deep thinking) to the prefrontal cortex (the part of the brain engaged in rapid, subconscious transactions). In other words, we are trading speed for accuracy and prioritise impulsive decision-making over deliberate judgment. In the words of Carr: "The internet is an interruption system. It seizes our attention only to scramble it".

Some scientists take a fatalistic outlook on this, lamenting our inability to assess the long-term damage the attention economy will have on our minds. Professor David Meyer, a leading multitasking scholar, compares the damage to the glory days of the tobacco industry: "People aren't aware what's happening to their mental processes in the same way that people years ago couldn't look into their lungs and see the residual deposits." Although this may be an overstatement, it is clear that our typical patterns of focus have changed dramatically in the past 15 years. To borrow the words of tech writer Linda Stone, we are living in an age of "continuous partial attention".

Thank you for giving me yours.

PASSAGE TWO

Commercial interests exploit a limited resource on an industrial scale: your attention

Oliver Burkeman, The Guardian, Wednesday 1 April, 2015

If, like me, you can't bear those little TV screens in the backs of taxis, just be grateful that you don't live in Seoul (unless you live in Seoul). There, a few years back, bus passengers were exposed to an even more invasive form of advertising: each time the bus approached a branch of Dunkin' Donuts, an "aromatizer" device sprayed the scent of Dunkin' Donuts coffee into the vehicle. The ad executives responsible for this received not lengthy prison sentences, as might have seemed appropriate, but an industry award for "best use of ambient media".

This is one of countless examples in Matthew Crawford's new book, The World Beyond Your Head, of the ways in which every last available scrap of our attention is gobbled up these days with ever-increasing efficiency, usually in an attempt to sell us things. He recounts trips through airports involving the relentless chatter of CNN in the departure lounge, ads on escalator handrails and even in the trays at the security checkpoint —culminating in one instance at a hotel where, sure enough, some bright spark had found space on the plastic key cards to squeeze in another ad.

There's nothing new in the claim that we're living through a crisis of attention, characterized by distraction, shrinking attention spans and an inability to resist checking your iPhone while eating dinner, crossing the road or having sex. (It sometimes feels as if all the articles and books bemoaning the situation do more to contribute to information overload than to alleviate it.) But Crawford makes the crucial point that this is a political problem.

It's not merely that technology enables a myriad of new stimuli, which we need self-discipline to master; rather, it's that the creators of smartphones, social networks designed to hook us, the firms buying ads on escalator handrails and media organizations desperate for your clicks and shares are all helping themselves to something that's ours - the limited resource of our attention - to try to turn a profit.

Crawford's single most important idea may be that of an 'attentional commons': "There are some resources that we hold in common, such as the air we breathe and the water we drink. We take them for granted, but their widespread availability makes everything else we do possible... That is why we have regulations in place to protect these common resources. We recognize their importance and their fragility."

What if we thought of attention as something similar: a collective resource, on which everything else depends? And that, when commercial interests exploit our attention on an industrial scale, what's happening is essentially a transfer of wealth from public to private, no less than if they dumped toxic chemicals in a reservoir?

You can, of course, defend against incursions on your attention by wearing earphones, reading a gripping book, moving to the mountains, staying home, or in some other way avoiding the public spaces where threats to your attention are greatest. But escaping from the attention-colonizers in these ways comes at a cost: the loss of a social existence in which we're not bombarded by efforts to grab attention. "An airport lounge," Crawford writes, "once felt rich with possibilities for spontaneous encounters. Even if we did not converse, our attention was free to alight upon one another and linger, or not. We encountered one another in person, even if in silence."

© Heriot-Watt University

These days, the easiest way to get this kind of silence is to be wealthy: in the airport business lounge, there's no piped CNN, just the clink of glasses as your free drinks are mixed. In a world in which attention has been monetized, you must pay up if you want to be able to hear yourself think. And what are those people in the business lounge thinking about? Why, in some cases, anyway, it's how to monetize other people's attention. "Consider that it is those in the business lounge who make the decisions that determine the character of the peon lounge," Crawford notes, "and we may start to see these things in a political light."

Perhaps the most troubling implication of all this is what it suggests about human freedom. A central assumption of liberalism is that we're free to ignore messages we don't like; that's why freedom of speech involves a right to offend but no right not to be offended. Yet what if, as a matter of empirical psychology, attention doesn't work like that?

Our brains are built to attend to fast-changing aspects of our visual field, more than those that change slowly —so there's a real sense in which the TV screens at the airport command our attention, instead of simply suggesting something we might like to do with it. As Natasha Dow Schull shows in her terrifying study of Las Vegas slot machines, Addiction By Design, the gambling industry likes to defend itself by appealing to the idea that people are free to play its machines or not —all the while designing devices explicitly calibrated to try to rob them of that choice.

This need not necessarily be an argument for draconian regulations on how companies advertise or otherwise seek our attention, and Crawford doesn't propose any. (Much of his book is devoted to exploring other ways in which we might regain attentional sovereignty.) But he does direct a heartfelt plea to architects, interior designers, building managers, politicians and anyone else with influence over the design of public space: "please don't install speakers in every single corner of a shopping mall, even its outdoor spaces. Please don't fill up every moment between innings in a lazy college baseball game with thundering excitement. Please give me a way to turn off the monitor in the back seat of a taxi. Please let there be one corner of the bar where the flickering delivery system for Bud Light commercials is deemed unnecessary, because I am already at the bar."

It's all most depressing. And yet, in the days after finishing Crawford's book, I found myself ironically cheered by noticing all the public spaces not yet claimed in an effort to consume my attention. The paving-stones and asphalt of my street are still a calming expanse of black and gray; the grass in the park doesn't yet have corporate logos dyed into it; give or take the occasional skywriting plane, the skies are free of ads. We may have to fight hard to keep things that way, though.

Q10: Read paragraph one. Explain in your own words what is meant by 'the attention economy'. (2)

....

Q11: Read paragraphs two and three. Analyse how the writer's use of language conveys his criticism of technology. (4)
Marks will depend on the quality of comment on appropriate language feature(s).
2 marks may be awarded for reference plus detailed/insightful comment; 1 mark for reference plus more basic comment; 0 marks for reference alone.

....

Q12: Read paragraphs five and six. In your own words, explain what the writer believes is the difference between 'us' and 'our evolutionary ancestors' (2)
For both marks, a comment should be made on both sides of the contrast.

....

Q13: Analyse how the writer's use of imagery in these lines conveys his criticism of the world in which we live now. (4)
Marks will depend on the quality of comment on appropriate language feature(s).
2 marks may be awarded for reference plus detailed/insightful comment; 1 mark for reference plus more basic comment; 0 marks for reference alone.

....

Q14: 'But if attention is the new currency of the digital economy, what are consumers getting in return?'
Explain the function of this sentence in the development of the writer's argument. (2)

....

Q15: Read paragraphs seven and eight. In your own words, summarise the consequences of 'information overload'. (3)

....

Q16: Analyse how the language in these lines emphasises the negative effect caused by 'information overload'. (4)
Marks will depend on the quality of comment on appropriate language feature(s).
2 marks may be awarded for reference plus detailed/insightful comment; 1 mark for reference plus more basic comment; 0 marks for reference alone.

....

Q17: In your own words, explain what Nicholas Carr believes are the 'psychological consequences of the distraction economy'. (2)

....

Q18: Read the last paragraph of passage one. Evaluate the effectiveness of these lines as a conclusion to the writer's argument. You should make close reference to the passage in your answer.

Marks will depend on the quality of comment on appropriate ideas and/or language feature(s).

2 marks may be awarded for reference plus detailed/insightful comment; 1 mark for reference plus more basic comment; 0 marks for reference alone.

....

Q19: Look at both passages. Both writers express their views about attention and distraction. Identify three key areas on which they agree. You should support the points you make by referring to important ideas in both passages.

You may answer this question in continuous prose or in a series of developed bullet points.
(5)

7.3 Practice paper 3: Food and diets

Practice paper 3: Food and diets Go online

PASSAGE ONE

I'm all for healthy diets but let's not take the joy out of eating

Harder Singh Kohli, The Herald, 15 May 2016

The summer sun had made an early appearance in the little pocket of North London I love. Marcus the Dundonian was behind the bar, my freshly pulled pint was asking no more of me than to be consumed under the canopy of an endlessly blue sky. Life wisnae too bad. A conversation was struck up with a large group sharing the bench with me.

'Are you Scottish?' asked the unbelievably handsome Dane, wearing matching flamingo featured shorts and socks.

'Aye,' I responded, awaiting one of the handful of predictable second gambits.

'Land of the deep-fried Mars Bar...'

We all laughed. There's only one thing worse than being talked about and that's not being talked about. Then followed a forensic cross-examination of all the terrible food in Scotland, an interrogation led, I later learned, by those that had never visited my country.

Irony of all ironies, I had just lunched at a place called The Boisdale, London's Scottish restaurant, serving the very best of Scottish produce in the most elegant, tartan-tinged surroundings.

But my ripostes regarding the amazing food scene across our country were laughed off. It disnae fit the stereotype. The improved health and fitness enjoyed in Scotland over the last decade or so, equally ignored.

We live in an age when food, cooking and the chef are honoured, celebrated and feted. Bookshops sell cookbooks by the thousand; food bloggers wield the greatest power in cyberspace; and TV channels continue their love affair with chefs and their recipes.

The latest trend is for 'clean eating'. Processed foods are prohibited; sugars are shunned; gluten and grains gone. Inspired by Hollywood stars, this mode of cooking and consuming is sent down from Olympus to us mere mortals. The current goddesses promoting eating clean are The Hemsley sisters. With two bestselling cookbooks behind them and an ITV series, Eating Well With Hemsley + Hemsley, starting this week, the sisters are advancing an aesthetic adored by A-list actors, feted by the fashionistas.

And while it's difficult to be critical of any attempt to facilitate a healthier diet, the Hemsleys have been snagged in something of a cross-channel furore. Ruby Tandoh, finalist of the BBC's Bake Off, has posited that 'clean eating' gives 'false hope' to those looking for a sure-fire system to a better life. Warning of 'wellness evangelism', she tweeted: 'Please be cautious taking 'wellness' advice ... your health is too precious to lose to fad, conjecture and bad science.'

The woman that bakes might have a point. One Australian wellness guru, Belle Gibson, told the world that, thanks to her diet and lifestyle changes, she cured herself of terminal brain cancer. A consumer watchdog is currently challenging her assertions.

Food should be fundamentally fulfilling, but it seems to me that the most paramount of pleasures has become a stick that some folk beat themselves with. Research suggests that between 2000 and 2013, eating disorders increased by 15%, and are now known to affect 1.6 million Britons (some researchers believe the true figure might be closer to four million). And while men are a sizeable minority, young women aged 15-19 are most likely to have their lives blighted by a dysfunctional relationship with food.

I've met and known a few women who have developed either anorexia or bulimia. From what I have seen, even for those who have overcome the condition, they can never fully free themselves of its shackles. For many, food and their relationship with it will be a lifelong challenge.

Any parent with a daughter will have some experience of the profound pressure, the eternal expectation, the constant comparison our young women have to contend with when it comes to their body image. I've heard girls as young as six describe themselves as fat. Six. Fat. Where is that coming from?

I'm all for healthy eating. I'm a big fan of managing a change in how we eat, turning us towards a diet that is balanced and nutritious. But food is joy. We raise families over food, we fall in love over food, we enact business over food, we build our lives around food. Food is many things but it is not medicine; it is not a panacea for our every ill and ailment. The more we indulge these scientifically suspect food fads, the less likely we are to restore the detriment and damage already visited upon so many.

PASSAGE TWO

Purity, cleanliness, guilt and modern diets

Eva Wiseman, The Guardian, 21 February 2016

When LA juice bar owner Amanda Bacon's food diary for US Elle went viral there was much hilarity, both at how detached from reality she seemed and at the lack of anything recognisable as food in it. Instead there's 'Brain Dust, cordyceps, reishi, maca, and Shilajit resin', and bee pollen, and activated almonds. Somebody broke down what it would cost Bacon to stock her kitchen with everything she ate in a day —the $48 reishi, the $35 vanilla mushroom protein —and the total came to over $1,200.

Food diaries populate our internet and lifestyle magazines and act as guidebooks for disordered eating —the advice sticks with you, like a burr that hooks to your tights. Off the top of my head, from the magazines of my teens: a handful of almonds at midday, a cup of hot water in the morning, a spoonful of peanut butter on a celery stick as an afternoon treat. All to quiet the sound of your supperless body.

And on one hand, good for Amanda Bacon. Consume, Amanda —ferment your coconut milk, go wild on your pollen, do what you have to do to stay alive and feel sane. But on the other hand, and this is the hand that is wringing itself to the bone, isn't the real reason this food diary struck such a chord with us that, despite it sounding like a foreign language, it feels so oddly... familiar? No, most of us don't splurge on bee pollen, but we understand what it stands for —something precious, an ancient solution to a modern ill. Because this diet —one that screams of paranoia, of a never-ending quest for purity and, of course, of hunger - is one that many people recognise. Whether it's BuzzFeed's 'clean eating challenge' or the Deliciously Ella cookbook selling over a quarter of a million copies, there is clearly a mainstream movement towards the pursuit of dizzying virtue.

People are no longer buying diet foods. Of the 2,000 people market researchers Mintel surveyed, 94% said they no longer saw themselves as dieters. Which doesn't mean they have stopped trying to lose weight - while the concept of dieting may not be popular, thinness shows no sign of going out of fashion.

Enter, then, 'clean food' —it's similar to 'food', but it won't make you fat. It is things like courgette in the shape of spaghetti —half the fun is in pretending. It is 'detoxing'. It is a cookbook called The Naked Diet, with chapter headings 'Pure', 'Raw' and 'Stripped'. It is 'natural', even if it's not entirely sure what that means. It is restrictive. It is dairy free, sugar free, gluten free (the UK market for gluten-free food is forecast to grow 46%, to £561m, by 2017). It is aimed at people who do not have families to feed. It is not about losing weight, officially, but if, after cutting an entire food group out of your diet, you happen to find you take up less space in the world, all the better.

However innocent its intentions (and here I'm being kind - does that come across?), this new market, of which Amanda Bacon's diet is an example of the sharpest edge, is based on fear. For vulnerable people, often mirrored in the young women promoting these recipes, their bright eyes and thriving relationships a testament to the power of buckwheat, 'clean' eating can lead to and support a horribly dysfunctional relationship with food. There is no reason to cut gluten from your diet unless you suffer from coeliac disease - a gluten-free diet is no healthier than any other. There is no reason to do a juice fast —detoxing is a myth, largely because that's what our livers are for, and also because nobody has yet identified which toxins

© HERIOT-WATT UNIVERSITY

need to be de-ed. Of people who class themselves as dairy intolerant, 44% have not been diagnosed as such by a doctor; only 5% of Brits are lactose intolerant - there is no reason for the rest of us to give up dairy.

But the main problem, it seems to me, with the idea of cutting something out of your diet (even sugar —widely seen as a poison, spoken of today as if a Poirot weapon) is how that affects the way you feel about food altogether. To class something as clean is to imply something else is dirty. To talk about health foods is to incriminate other foods as unhealthy. Bread is not evil, sugar is not hell —in moderation, almost everything, be it bee pollen or a Snickers sandwich (copyright) is good for you. There's nothing on our plate we should be scared of.

Q20: Read the first seven paragraphs. Explain, in your own words, the 'irony' of what happened to the writer. (2)

....

Q21: Evaluate the effectiveness of this anecdote as an introduction to the passage. (2)

....

Q22: Read paragraphs eight and nine. Show how the writer's use of language emphasises the popularity of 'food, cooking and the chef'. (4)
Marks will depend on the quality of comment on appropriate language feature(s).
2 marks may be awarded for reference plus detailed/insightful comment; I mark for reference plus more basic comment; 0 marks for reference alone.

....

Q23: Read paragraph ten. Using your own words as far as possible, summarise the criticisms of 'clean eating' made by Ruby Tandoh. (3)

....

Q24: Look at paragraph eleven. Explain the function of this paragraph in the development of the writer's argument. (2)

....

Q25: Look at paragraphs twelve and thirteen. The writer describes people for whom food has become a problem. Analyse how the writer's use of language emphasises the seriousness of this problem.
Marks will depend on the quality of comment on appropriate language feature(s).
2 marks may be awarded for reference plus detailed/insightful comment; I mark for reference plus more basic comment; 0 marks for reference alone.

....

Q26: Read paragraph fourteen. Identify the writer's tone in this paragraph and analyse how it is created. You should refer to at least two language features. (4)
Marks will depend on the quality of comment on appropriate language feature(s).
2 marks may be awarded for reference plus detailed/insightful comment; I mark for reference plus more basic comment; 0 marks for reference alone.

....

© HERIOT-WATT UNIVERSITY

TOPIC 7. PRACTICE PAPERS

Q27: Read the last paragraph of passage one. In your own words, summarise why the writer believes food is important. (2)

....

Q28: Evaluate the effectiveness of the writer's language in the final paragraph as a conclusion to the passage. (2)

Marks will depend on the quality of comment on appropriate language feature(s).

2 marks may be awarded for reference plus detailed/insightful comment; 1 mark for reference plus more basic comment; 0 marks for reference alone.

....

Q29: Look at both passages. Both writers express their views about attention and distraction. Identify three key areas on which they agree. You should support the points you make by referring to important ideas in both passages.

You may answer this question in continuous prose or in a series of developed bullet points. (5)

© HERIOT-WATT UNIVERSITY

Unit 1 Appendix A

Acknowledgements

130 UNIT 1. READING FOR UNDERSTANDING, ANALYSIS AND EVALUATION

- The Guardian (15th December 2014), The distraction economy: how technology downgraded attention

- The Guardian (1st April 2015), Commercial interests exploit a limited resource on an industrial scale: your attention

- The Guardian (19th April 2015), Katie Hopkins calling migrants vermin recalls the darkest events of history

- The Guardian (21st February 2016), Purity, cleanliness, guilt and modern diets

- The Guardian (16th June 2016), Proms are a terrible, chintzy disappointment —perfect preparation for adulthood, https://www.theguardian.com/commentisfree/2015/jun/16/proms-us-uk-schools [accessed 16th August 2016]

- The Herald (15th May 2016), I'm all for healthy diets but let's not take the joy out of eating

- New Statesman (20th April 2015), What Katie Hopkins wrote was monstrous. But save your anger for the politicians who decided to let migrants drown

- The Observer (10th July 1994), Pasture to the Plate

- The Sunday Times (19th January 2014), Goodbye birds. Goodbye butterflies. Hello... farmageddon, http://www.thesundaytimes.co.uk/sto/news/focus/article1364836.ece [accessed 16th August 2016]

Unit 2: Critical reading

1	Scottish Texts: Prose	133
	1.1 Introduction	135
	1.2 Characterisation	136
	1.3 Theme	142
	1.4 Setting	145
	1.5 Style	148
	1.6 Learning points	150
	1.7 End of topic test	151
2	Scottish Texts: Drama	157
	2.1 Introduction	158
	2.2 Characterisation	158
	2.3 Theme	164
	2.4 Setting	166
	2.5 Style	168
	2.6 Learning points	170
	2.7 End of topic test	171
3	Scottish Texts: Poetry	177
	3.1 Introduction	178
	3.2 Form and structure	179
	3.3 Theme	187
	3.4 Sound	192
	3.5 Imagery	197
	3.6 Word choice	203
	3.7 Sentence structure	207
	3.8 Learning points	212
	3.9 End of topic test	213
4	Scottish Texts: Exam techniques	219
	4.1 Introduction	220
	4.2 Key vocabulary	220
	4.3 Exam technique	222
	4.4 End of topic test	238

5 Critical Essay 243
5.1 Introduction 244
5.2 Key vocabulary 244
5.3 Preparation 253
5.4 Criteria 275
5.5 The question 285
5.6 Analysing evidence 292
5.7 Structure 297
5.8 Exam technique 306
5.9 Learning points 307
5.10 End of topic test 308

A Acknowledgements 311

Unit 2 Topic 1

Scottish Texts: Prose

Contents

1.1 Introduction 135
1.2 Characterisation 136
1.3 Theme 142
1.4 Setting 145
1.5 Style 148
1.6 Learning points 150
1.7 End of topic test 151

Prerequisites

Before beginning this topic, you should have read one of the novels or one complete set of the short stories as listed in the Introduction.

You should have a knowledge of what is meant by:

- characterisation;
- theme;
- setting;
- style (particularly use of language).

Additionally, you should be familiar with using word choice and imagery to analyse a text and be able to draw connotations from phrases and a writer's use of word choice.
You should be able to use your skills honed through practice of RUAE papers in another part of your course. You will build on this knowledge through textual analysis of your Scottish Set Text.

134 UNIT 2. CRITICAL READING

Learning objective

By the end of this topic, you should be able to:

- comment on a writer's use of characterisation to create effect;
- identify the theme inherent in your chosen text(s) and explain effect;
- understand the importance of setting in your chosen text(s);
- comment on and analyse distinctive elements of style in your chosen text(s).

TOPIC 1. SCOTTISH TEXTS: PROSE

1.1 Introduction

As part of your Higher course, you will study a Scottish text or texts from one of three genres: drama, prose or poetry. Part of the course assessment will involve answering questions about the text(s) for a total of 20 marks.

This is a relatively straightforward part of the final course examination, one that you can thoroughly prepare for at home, as long as you have the skills to *analyse* a text. You will require a thorough knowledge of your text(s), so should aim to read it through several times over the course of the year.

This section will concentrate on the skills required to textually analyse prose: it will review the different features that an author can employ - in this case, characterisation, theme, setting and style - and support you in being able to consider the effect of this with regards to an author's meaning.

The prose you will study for the Scottish Set Text will either be a novel or a series of six short stories.

Novels:

- 'The Cone Gatherers' by Robin Jenkins (this is a text which can be taught at both N5 and Higher level);
- 'Sunset Song' by Lewis Grassic Gibbon;
- 'The Strange Case of Dr Jekyll and Mr Hyde' by Robert Louis Stevenson.

Short stories:

- 'The Red Door', 'The Telegram', 'Mother and Son', 'Home' by Iain Crichton Smith (these stories can be taught at both N5 and Higher level);
- 'A Time to Keep', 'The Wireless Set', 'The Eye of the Hurricane', 'Andrina' by George Mackay Brown.

You will study one full novel or one full set of stories but only an extract from your text will be printed.

For novels and short stories: 10 out of 20 marks are available for answering questions on the printed text.

For novels: 10 out of 20 marks are available for discussing key areas of the novel as a whole.

For short stories: 10 out of 20 marks are available for comparing the printed text to other short stories by the same writer.

In order to be successful in this part of the course assessment you must be aware of a number of key features and be able to explain their effect with regards to the key ideas and themes of the text(s).

1.2 Characterisation

To recap, characterisation is the way in which authors portray their characters, bringing them to life in unique and vivid ways. This usually helps the authors to convey their overall message. By understanding the different elements used within a character, the readers will be able to enhance their overall understanding of the text.

An author will usually portray characterisation by the way a character acts, speaks, thinks or looks.

For instance, in 'The Cone Gatherers', you will note the abundance of times that Calum laughs, smiles, is kind or cares deeply (think of his reaction after the deer drive). Here we can see how Jenkins uses depictions of Calum's actions to portray him as an innocent, friendly, trusting character.

Similarly, Jenkins allows the reader to see Duror's dark thoughts and imaginings: the diseased tree, the stag struggling in mud, his disgust at Peggy's infirmity and Calum's appearance. Here we see how his thoughts depict him as an evil figure.

Next, we shall look at some examples of famous characters from literature, covering the four key areas of action, speech, thought and appearance. Then there will be examples for you to work through. Italicisation has been added to the following extracts to highlight key words and phrases.

Firstly, look at the way a character acts:

In this extract, taken from Arthur Conan Doyle's Sherlock Holmes tale 'A Study in Scarlet', the famous detective shows his dismay.

> Example Holmes had taken out his watch, and as minute followed minute without result, an expression of the *utmost chagrin and disappointment* appeared upon his features. He *gnawed his lip, drummed his fingers* upon the table...

There are three key phrases here which reveal Holmes' dismay:

- 'utmost chagrin and disappointment' which strongly implies this through the forceful inflection of the word 'utmost' coupled with the idea of deep rooted dismay as suggested with 'chagrin';
- 'gnawed his lip' which emphasises his worry, conveying the idea that he is subconsciously inflicting pain on himself through his stress;
- 'drummed his fingers' which conveys his impatience, thus dismay.

Now, the way a character speaks:

Again, an example from the famous consulting detective as he explains his approach to his work.

> Example You see I have a lot of *special knowledge* which I apply to the problem, and which facilitates matters wonderfully. Those *rules of deduction*... are invaluable to me. Observation with me is second nature.

Like Holmes, we can use the evidence before us to deduct key information about this character: he is both arrogant and methodical. His use of 'special knowledge' implies that he he thinks he is clearly different - and better - than everyone, whilst his reference to 'rules of deduction' suggests his self-confidence comes from adhering to a proven system, or a mental checklist, as he thinks matters through.

Thirdly, the inner thoughts of a character:

From 'Great Expectations' by Charles Dickens we can see a clear example of characterisation revealed through the thoughts of that character. Pip, the main character, is mentally preparing himself to steal food for Magwitch, the escaped convict.

Example The effort of resolution necessary to the achievement of this purpose, I found to be quite *awful*. It was as if I had to make up my mind to leap from *the top of a high house*...

Clearly, we can see that Pip is tortured inside at the thought of doing wrong and stealing. He describes his experience as 'awful' and compares the prospect of stealing to something physically terrifying (jumping from 'the top of a high house').

Finally, the appearance of a character:

Here, we have a description of Magwitch, from 'Great Expectations'. It is easy to see from this initial meeting that he is a frightening character who could easily intimidate young Pip.

Example *A fearful man, all in coarse grey, with a great iron on his leg.*

Clearly, this is a dangerous and frightening character. 'Fearful' has clear connotations of this, whilst the fact he can walk 'with a great iron on his leg' suggests some idea of his physical stature and power. Interestingly (for those who have already read this novel) the connotations of the colour 'grey' (neither positive nor negative) hint at a more complicated character than is revealed in the opening pages.

Understanding and analysing characterisation Go online

Below are some extracts. For each, select the correct analysis for the character based on the connotations of the language used in the extract. You will be told whether you are analysing actions, speech, thoughts or appearance. Remember, when analysing, we want to be as clear and specific as possible.

Actions

There was a violent peal at the bell, and in a few seconds the fair haired detective came up the stairs... and burst into our sitting room.
"My dear fellow," he cried, wringing Holmes's unresponsive hand...

Q1: This character is:

a) arrogant.
b) excited.
c) laconic.

....

Q2: Which word suggests that Holmes is unimpressed with the detective?

With a howl of rage, Stevens thrust his dagger up to the hilt in the defenceless back of Logan. Again and again he thrust it in, until the man's puny squeals for mercy had ended.

Q3: This character is:

a) angry.
b) remorseless.
c) stimulated.

....

Q4: The use of the word 'defenceless' elicits what response in the reader?

a) Ambivalence
b) Disgust
c) Emotional

....

Q5: Why does the writer clarify that Stevens stabbed his victim 'up to the hilt'?

a) To emphasise how short the blade was.
b) To emphasise how violently aggressive he is.
c) To emphasise that he lost the knife.

Speech

"Keep still you little devil, or I'll cut your throat!"

Q6: This character is:

a) violent and threatening
b) cajoling and threatening
c) emotional and threatening

....

"'Hmm," he sighed. "I suppose this was exactly the way you, in your infinite wisdom, intended it to go?" There was a world of biting humour in his voice as he spoke.

Q7: This character is:

a) arrogant.
b) observant.
c) supportive.

....

TOPIC 1. SCOTTISH TEXTS: PROSE

Characterisation within your chosen text

For the text you are studying, copy and complete the following table. You may want to focus on more than one key character, but should have at least four or five aspects covered per character.

The example is based on 'Sunset Song'.

Character	Aspect of character	Quote/evidence	Explanation
Ewan Tavendale	Ewan's ACTIONS show how he can be aggressive and violent.	'He sat up, angrily, the great black cat, sleeked and quick to anger.'	The fact he sits up 'angrily' is a clear indication of this side of his personality; the reference to the 'great black cat' is a sinister reminder of John Guthrie, reinforcing the notion that Ewan is far from perfect.

© HERIOT-WATT UNIVERSITY

1.3 Theme

Just as in poetry or drama, a theme in prose is the bigger idea that the writer is exploring and wanting us, the readers, to think about and relate to, if possible. It is often conveyed through a combination of characterisation, plot and setting. Theme is sometimes referred to as the central concerns.

There are common themes found in all literature:

- death;
- relationships;
- loneliness;
- grief;
- loss;
- change;
- love (positive and negative aspects);
- revenge;
- betrayal;
- greed;
- good vs evil;
- war;
- conflict;
- suffering;
- materialism;
- identity;
- destructive nature of time;
- isolation.

In 'The Cone Gatherers' by Robin Jenkins, there are several key themes running throughout: good versus evil, nature, class structure, religion and war. These themes are largely revealed through analysing the characterisation of the key figures, as well as looking more closely at several key events in the plot (for instance: the deer drive, the storm and the murder of Calum).

In 'Sunset Song' by Lewis Grassic Gibbon, there are several key themes running throughout: change, bravery, the role of women, the ideals of community and the endurance of the land. These themes are largely revealed through an analysis of Chris Guthrie and the destruction which WW1 brings to Kinraddie's rural way of life.

In 'The Strange Case of Dr Jekyll and Mr Hyde' by Robert Louis Stevenson there are several key themes running throughout: duality of human nature, good versus evil, well intentioned plans going wrong. These themes are related from a range of narrative viewpoints.

In the selected short stories by Iain Crichton Smith, there are several key themes running throughout: individuality, humanity and the nature of war. Some of the stories also touch on the nature of individuality whilst constrained in a small village or insular community.

In the selected short stories by George Mackay Brown, there are several key themes running throughout: history, the nature of time, community, religion and the Orkney Islands.

For key events, think of an action, event or occurrence which has major consequences for a main character, moves the plot along or strongly conveys a major theme.

Let's use a sporting analogy: in a game of rugby, one player passes the ball to another. This is a common occurrence, so not a key event. However, after passing the ball, this player punches another, with the result that he is sent off and the other team scores a penalty. In this case the player (character) is affected; the fans have a talking point (plot) and we see the player as overly violent and aggressive (theme).

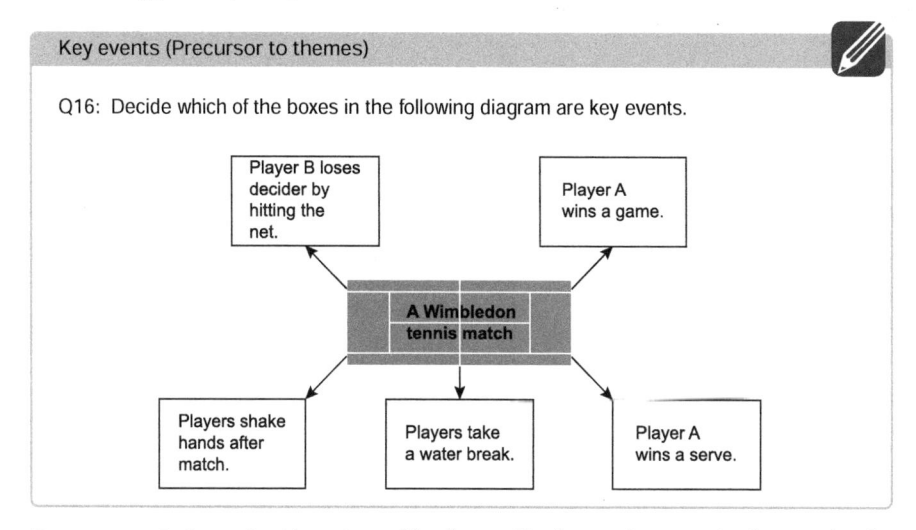

Key events (Precursor to themes)

Q16: Decide which of the boxes in the following diagram are key events.

- Player B loses decider by hitting the net.
- Player A wins a game.
- A Wimbledon tennis match
- Players shake hands after match.
- Players take a water break.
- Player A wins a serve.

For your prose text, you should create a spider diagram like the sporting example above, noting the four or five key events in the text. However, for each event, take a further note on how you believe this has consequences: for the main character; for the plot or for the themes.

For instance, using the sporting example above, Player A is the character who changes through winning the game; Player B hitting the net and losing might suggest the theme of 'chance', highlighting how life sometimes turns on moments of luck regardless of our thoughts and plans.

144 UNIT 2. CRITICAL READING

Understanding theme

For the text you are studying, copy and complete the following table. You may want to focus on one theme and find four or five pieces of evidence for it, or you may want to focus on two or more themes with suitable evidence. Try to cover at least three or four key events from your text. The example is based on 'Sunset Song'.

Key event	Aspect of character	Quote/evidence	Explanation
The fire at Peesie's Knapp	Community; bravery	'Long Rob of the Mill came in about, he'd run over the fields, louping dykes like a hare and his lungs were panting like bellows...'	Here we can see Long Rob's bravery as he runs toward the fire, hoping to save the members of his community. The run is clearly physically painful - made clear through the simile - but his efforts exemplify the importance of community.
Ewan returns from training			
Chae tells Chris how Ewan died			
John Guthrie dies.			

1.4 Setting

To put it simply, the setting in prose is where the event(s) takes place. Location, historical context, weather and time of day can all play a part in setting. As discussed in theme, setting can play a role in conveying the author's message. In this respect, don't think of setting as simply a 'place' of fact, but a way for the writer to manipulate the mood and tone. Setting can act as a symbol.

For example, one setting of 'Sunset Song' by Lewis Grassic Gibbon is rural Scotland (Kinraddie to be precise). The description of this rural aspect is particularly detailed in this novel, giving it an air of gritty realism. This is the location. The weather is typically Scottish: stormy and unpredictable. This reflects the turbulence of the times (WW1 is on the horizon) and the fiery nature of most of the characters, especially Chris who, as a fiercely independent woman, has arguably been shaped and strengthened by her experiences in this location, much like a tree can be bent and be shaped by the wind. The historical context helps to convey several themes: 'change' as wrought by the war and the 'importance of community' as exemplified through the actions of the village (the fire at Peesie's Knapp; Chris' wedding) as a whole.

Understanding setting   Go online

For each extract, choose the correct theme based on the description of a setting; again, think of the connotations of the language being used. These examples are simple, but are designed to get you thinking about how often the theme revealed through setting can be fairly obvious; so don't discount setting when studying your text.

> The sunset painted a soft peach glow over the landscape. The smooth waters of the loch rippled softly as a diving bird kissed it, seeking sustenance. A gentle, warm, summer's breeze whispered through the trees, caressing every branch and every leaf.

Q17: The theme could be:

a) grief.
b) identity.
c) love.
d) materialism.

....

Q18: Pick out at least three words or phrases which gave connotations of this.

> The man wrapped his charcoal scarf tightly around his face and emerged from the shadows. He hissed as the cold air slunk into his lungs, pulled his scarf tighter and strode into the velvety blackness of the city. The buildings towered over him, muffling his footsteps and shrouding him from the gaze of the sun; his reflection wobbled in the windows of the building, giving only a vague impression of who he was.

Q19: The theme could be:

a) grief.
b) identity.
c) love.
d) materialism.

....

© HERIOT-WATT UNIVERSITY

Q20: Pick out the phrase/part of the phrase which best suggests this.

The woman shrieked with joy; the man on his creaking knee inwardly said an incantation of thanks. He had bought the right diamond: the right cut, the right hue, the right setting, the right stone. The right jewel to adorn her perfectly manicured hand, the right jewel to show off here, at their weekly brunch under the gaze of the unforgiving LA sun and in front of the gaze of the greedy LA cameras.

Q21: The theme could be:

a) grief.
b) identity.
c) love.
d) materialism.

....

Q22: Why does the writer use repetition of 'right' in this paragraph?

a) To highlight the character's shallow motives.
b) To highlight that this was for the right hand.
c) To highlight that we should feel proud of the man.

TOPIC 1. SCOTTISH TEXTS: PROSE 147

Setting within your chosen text

You should complete the table for your text, covering at least three key locations and what mood and theme they help to convey. The example is based on 'Sunset Song'.

Location	Historical context	Weather	Time	Mood created
Blawearie farm	Start of the 20th Century pre and post WW1	All seasons	All seasons, key scenes often at dusk or night	The farm is a conflicted place - the changing seasons suggest the changing fortunes of the family and the rural community/way of life as a whole; the advent of WW1 further emphasises this.
Long Rob's mill				
Chris and Ewan's wedding location				

© HERIOT-WATT UNIVERSITY

1.5 Style

A writer's style is often the language that he/she uses to convey effect. In conjunction with your work on creative and discursive writing, and on Reading for Understanding, Analysis and Evaluation, you should be familiar with the following techniques and their effect:

- alliteration;
- metaphor;
- personification;
- sentence structure;
- formal and informal language.

Alliteration

This is where the writer uses the same letters or sounds at the start of two or more words. This is done to draw your attention to this phrase; for you to examine it for connotations or to help create a mood.

Example Big Bad Bob Bullied the Boy.

Clearly this creates a harsh tone.

Q23: What tone is created by using alliteration in the following extract?

The bird soared and swooped in the sky, its wings wide to use the warm air.

a) Triumphant and majestic
b) Depressed and gloomy
c) Giddy and hectic

Metaphor

This is a direct comparison between two things, usually things that you wouldn't expect to be compared.

Example The man had bull strength.

This is used to show how extremely strong the man is.

Often, metaphors in prose at Higher level are more complex. In 'The Cone Gatherers', the diseased tree is a metaphor for Duror's unravelling mind; the 'black cat' imagery in 'Sunset Song' represents repressed sexuality. In your text, you should be aware of these larger metaphors, which, like Duror's crumbling mind being represented by the dark woods, can extend throughout the entire novel.

Personification

This is where human qualities are given to non-human animals or objects. It is often done, in longer prose, to help create atmosphere.

TOPIC 1. SCOTTISH TEXTS: PROSE

> Q24: Imagine reading that a 'forest held its breath as the man crept through it'.
> This tells us that the man, in this situation, is so:
>
> a) terrifying that even the trees (which don't have breath to hold) were frightened into silence.
> b) interesting that even the trees (which don't have breath to hold) were hushed in anticipation.
> c) silent that even the trees (which don't have breath to hold) were so quiet because they wanted to listen to him.

Sentence structure

This is often used to create effect: short sentences to create tension, increase pace; lists to emphasise how long something will take. For a more detailed exploration, look at the pages on RUAE.

Formal and informal language

You also need to be aware of this. For example, if a writer sets a story in a deprived area of Glasgow, but has a character speak formally ('You shall not', rather than 'won't' for instance), it is to show that they don't fit in. In 'Sunset Song', Gibbon uses a dialect true to his setting of the north east of Scotland (but which, technically speaking, is informal in nature) to give his novel authenticity. This makes us relate more strongly to the characters and to care what becomes of them.

Style within your chosen text

You should keep a series of running notes on your text, noting for every chapter or every story key elements of style. As you keep these notes, try to work out how these elements help the writer to convey their theme more clearly. Discuss your ideas with a partner or teacher.

© HERIOT-WATT UNIVERSITY

1.6 Learning points

Summary

- **Characterisation**

  To recap, an author will usually portray characterisation through the way a character acts, speaks, thinks or looks. You should look for the connotations of particular words and phrases to give you clues about the nature of a character.

  Use of characterisation often helps to reveal elements of theme.

- **Theme**

  To summarise, a theme in prose is the bigger idea that the writer is exploring and wanting the reader to consider. It is often conveyed through a combination of characterisation, plot and setting.

- **Setting**

  To recap, the setting in prose is where the event(s) takes place. Location, historical context, weather and time of day can all play a part in setting. Often try to think about the metaphorical implications when analysing setting, rather than just accepting it as simply a place.

- **Style**

  The writer uses language to convey meaning: word choice, sentence structure, metaphor, formal and informal language all play a large role in conveying his/her overall message.

1.7 End of topic test

End of Topic 1 test   Go online

Q25: Authors will usually portray characterisation only by the way characters act and speak.

a) True
b) False

....

Q26: Characterisation is an important way in which the writer conveys theme.

a) True
b) False

....

Q27: The inner thoughts of a main character are the most important method of creating characterisation as they are the only thoughts that a writer will reveal.

a) True
b) False

....

Q28: Theme in prose is slightly different to theme in drama, but the same as theme in poetry.

a) True
b) False

....

Q29: Theme is an important message given by the author, usually commenting on a social issue or the nature of humanity and can be understood through studying characterisation, setting and style.

a) True
b) False

....

Q30: An author uses deliberate choices of style to help convey their theme.

a) True
b) False

....

Q31: An author would use a setting based in real life in their work because they can't think of an original idea.

a) True
b) False

....

© HERIOT-WATT UNIVERSITY

Q32: Setting helps to strengthen a writer's message about theme.

a) True
b) False

....

Q33: Thinking of connotations and metaphorical implications can help to fully understand the message a text gives.

a) True
b) False

....

Q34: The actions of a character are the most important aspect to analyse, especially in prose.

a) True
b) False

Select the words which best describe the characters mentioned in the following extracts.

Q35:
   He was broadly built, earning his frame from countless battles in the pit (battles which he enjoyed; killing others gave him life, gave him joy) wielding his wicked axe with ease.

a) Interesting
b) Powerful
c) Vicious

....

Q36:
   She smiled softly at the waiter, basking in the glow of adoration from the other diners.

a) Sonorous
b) Ambivalent
c) Happy

....

Q37:
   As he entered, the very room was hushed; even the dust motes seemed to pause their eternal dance. The shadows pooled in dark blotches at his feet, following him like a beaten dog. The silvery fingers of moonlight stabbed into the floor, refusing to move, refusing to quiver, refusing to be noticed.

a) Frightening
b) Magical
c) Mysterious

TOPIC 1. SCOTTISH TEXTS: PROSE

....

Q38:

The tree sank its dark roots into the fetid mud, snaking around moss stained boulders, trailing across the shallows as if to pull an unsuspecting traveler to the thick embrace of the swamp floor. He stood beside it, his eyes like pools of the thick mud which sucked greedily at his feet, the faint hint of a canine smile etched in the corner of his mouth.

a) Evil
b) Mad
c) Skilful

....

Q39:

The battle had failed, the plan to take the fortress had floundered in the mud around the walls. The enemy were counterattacking; he summoned his men and organised an orderly retreat. He would return.

a) Cowardly
b) Kingly
c) Weak

....

Q40:

He towered over the man, his shoulders flexing like boulders in a socket. His very breath seemed to crush the man with its weight.

a) Vicious
b) Heroic
c) Intimidating

....

Q41:

Like a mouse, she was silent; like a hawk, she was observant; like a dove, she was gentle; like a shadow, she was there, yet not there.

a) Calculating
b) Invisible
c) Unappealing

....

© HERIOT-WATT UNIVERSITY

Q42:

He beckoned over to the poor peasant lad, glibly tossing him a worn copper. When the lad left, he checked his wallet to make it sure it was still stuffed full.

a) Selfish
b) Selfless
c) Self-made

....

Q43:

He laughed; he twirled; he danced. His manic grin was plastered over his face as thickly and crudely as his homemade clown's makeup. He brandished a knife, his eyes glinting like the blade in the moonlight.

a) Dangerous
b) Entertaining
c) Mysterious

....

Q44:

He glowered. Flexing his grotesquely muscled arms he strode forward, ready to destroy his enemy. Nothing would derail him, nothing would deny him the revenge he had so long sought.

a) Moody
b) Focussed
c) Giant

....

Q45: For novels and short stories, the number of marks that are available for answering questions on the printed text is:

a) 8 out of 20
b) 10 out of 20
c) 12 out of 20

....

Q46: Characterisation:

a) helps the author to draw in readers.
b) helps the author to convey their overall message.
c) usually helps the author to plot a story.

....

TOPIC 1. SCOTTISH TEXTS: PROSE

Q47: Theme is often conveyed through a combination of characterisation, plot and:

a) dialogue.
b) setting.
c) setting; usually one will suffice.

....

Q48: Setting is used by a writer to convey where and when a story takes place so that we can:

a) imagine it.
b) check our historical understanding.
c) work out meaning.

....

Q49: A writer's style is his/her choice of language and is used to:

a) convey effect.
b) create interest.
c) be attractive.

....

Q50: It is important to think of _____ when analysing a writer's use of word choice.

a) connotations
b) personification
c) formal language

....

Q51: You can prepare for the Scottish Set Text by only studying:

a) character, theme, setting and key events.
b) plot, language, theme and setting.
c) character, plot, setting and key events.

....

Q52: One adroitly chosen _____ is all it takes to describe a character, suggest their motives and convey a theme.

a) sentence
b) word
c) paragraph

....

Q53: Use of formal and informal language can help add:

a) realism and help us to relate to a character.
b) realism and help us to ponder the motives of a character.
c) surrealism and help us to relate to a character.

© HERIOT-WATT UNIVERSITY

Q54: A metaphor in Higher:

a) is just like a simile without 'like' or 'as'.
b) can be extended to run through the novel.
c) will indicate a major character.

Unit 2 Topic 2

Scottish Texts: Drama

Contents

2.1 Introduction 158
2.2 Characterisation 158
2.3 Theme 164
2.4 Setting 166
2.5 Style 168
2.6 Learning points 170
2.7 End of topic test 171

Prerequisites

Before beginning this topic, you should have read one of the dramas as listed in the Introduction.

You should have a knowledge of what is meant by:

- characterisation;
- theme;
- setting;
- style (particularly use of theatrical techniques).

Additionally, you should be familiar with using word choice to analyse a text and be able to draw connotations from phrases.

Learning objective

By the end of this topic, you should be able to:

- comment on a writer's use of characterisation to create effect;
- identify the theme inherent in your chosen text(s) and explain effect;
- understand the importance of setting in your chosen text(s);
- comment on and analyse distinctive elements of style in your chosen text(s).

2.1 Introduction

As part of your Higher course, you will study a Scottish text or texts from one of three genres: drama, prose or poetry. Part of the course assessment will involve answering questions about the text(s) for a total of 20 marks.

This is a relatively straightforward part of the final course examination, one that you can thoroughly prepare for at home, as long as you have the skills to *analyse* a text.

This section will concentrate on the skills required to textually analyse drama: it will review the different features that a playwright can employ - in this case, characterisation, theme, setting and style - and support you in being able to consider the effect of these features with regards to a writer's meaning.

The drama you will study for the Scottish Set Text will either be:

- 'The Cheviot, the Stag and the Black, Black Oil' by John McGrath;
- 'Men Should Weep' by Ena Lamont Stewart;
- 'The Slab Boys' by John Byrne.

You will study one full drama text but only an extract from your text will be printed.

10 out of 20 marks are available for answering questions on the printed text.

10 out of 20 marks are available for discussing key areas of the drama as a whole.

In order to be successful in this part of the course assessment you must be aware of a number of key features and be able to explain their effect with regards to the ideas and themes of the drama.

2.2 Characterisation

To recap, characterisation is the way in which writers portray their characters, bringing them to life in unique and vivid ways. This usually helps the writer to convey his/her overall message. Therefore, by understanding the different elements used within a character, the audience will be able to enhance their overall understanding of the text. Remember, it is not just the main character(s) you should focus on: the secondary character(s) reveal aspects of theme to the audience as well.

In drama, a writer will usually portray characterisation through the way a character acts, speaks or looks. Additionally, a writer will employ different dramatic features, such as careful use of props, lighting or sound effects (collectively known as stage directions).

For instance, in 'The Slab Boys', the audience is left in no doubt that Phil is a character who is conflicted: angry, yet hopeful. After he is laid off, he firmly tells his boss, Curry, to '...drop all that gibbon shit.' We see here his bitter and angry nature, symbolising some of the play's commentary on social class and the difficulty for those from the working class in fulfilling ambition. However, the final line of the drama ends on an optimistic note as Phil remembers: 'Giotto was a slab boy!'

Next, we shall look at some examples of famous characters from literature, covering the four key areas of action, speech, appearance and stage directions. Then there will be examples for you to work through.

Firstly, look at the way a character acts:

When studying drama texts, it is important to remember that dramas are written to be performed in front of an audience, so the actor will have a lot of input in terms of a character's actions. When reading in class, the way a character acts can often be inferred through stage directions or dialogue. In this extract, taken from Act 5, Scene 1 of Shakespeare's 'The Tempest', as the character of Prospero boasts of his powers (and the others are enchanted within a magic circle he has made) it is noted:

> Example They all enter the circle which Prospero had made, and there stand charmed; which Prospero observing, speaks...
>
> Some playwrights (like Arthur Miller, who you may have studied in N5, or J.B. Priestley, who you may have studied in S3) are known for writing detailed stage directions to help craft their characters. Shakespeare is more famous for his lyrical lines of dialogue. But here a suggestion of Prospero's power and arrogance is revealed: he 'observes' the others becoming charmed, as though this was expected. Prospero was overthrown and exiled by his brother, yet wields absolute power over the other characters on the island: this conflict between sympathy and loathing makes him such an interesting character.

Now, the way a character speaks:

Now, we see Prospero's speech following the above, which further emphasises his boastful nature.

> Example I have bedimmed the noontide sun, called forth the mutinous winds... Graves at my command have waked their sleepers... By my so potent art.
>
> In performance, an actor would speak these lines in a haughty, arrogant tone. His listing of awesome happenings caused at his command works to emphasise this side of his character; his reference to his skills as 'potent' confirms what the audience believes about Prospero: he is arrogant and boastful.

Thirdly, the appearance of a character(s):

In another of Shakespeare's dramas, 'Macbeth', we can see a clear example of characterisation revealed through the description of Lady Macbeth by King Duncan. In this play, Lady Macbeth plays an influential role in the murder of King Duncan, as she convinces Macbeth to commit the act. Interestingly, as is typical of Shakespeare, the description itself is slight, but says everything it needs to as, in Act 1, Scene 6, he calls her a:

> Example Fair and noble hostess.
>
> Clearly, we can see here two things: an impression of Lady Macbeth's beauty through the word choice of 'fair', but also how Shakespeare is clearly contrasting her appearance with her ruthless nature. This use of juxtaposition is effective in making her later actions and decisions all the more shocking.

Finally, the use of stage directions:

Let us return to an example from 'The Tempest' and, from the opening stage direction of Act 1, Scene 1, we are instantly aware of the dangerous and murky nature of the principal characters, foreshadowing some of the themes of 'men and monsters' and 'justice and injustice':

© HERIOT-WATT UNIVERSITY

Example A tempestuous noise of thunder and lightning heard.

The sound of thunder and lighting used to announce the arrival to the island reinforces the murky nature of the key characters; drawing on the audience's understanding of the danger of storms, Shakespeare hints at violence and danger to come. The fact that the noise is extreme - 'tempestuous' - only reinforces this.

Understanding and analysing characterisation   Go online

Below are some extracts. For each, select the correct analysis for the character, based on the connotations of the language used in the extract. You will be told whether you are analysing actions, speech, appearance or stage directions. Some answers may seem similar, but require a closer analysis of the text to ascertain the correct response.

Actions:
   His singing abruptly stops as he brings the horses and wagon to a halt. He hands the reins to Rachel, before stepping slowly from the wagon.

Q1: This character is:

a) angry.
b) impatient.
c) worried.

....

Q2: Which words give this connotation?
....

Q3: What technique is used here to emphasise his concern?

a) Alliteration
b) Onomatopoeia
c) Metaphor

   Although there is a very joyful atmosphere at the group dinner table, Rachel's eyes continually look up towards the window of Steward's room. Mackenzie notices, but says nothing.

Q4: This character (Rachel) is:

a) distracted.
b) flirtatious.
c) unhappy.

....

Q5: What do the actions of Mackenzie say about his feelings for Rachel?

a) He is secretly in love with her.
b) He is upset with her.
c) He is annoyed with her.

TOPIC 2. SCOTTISH TEXTS: DRAMA

Speech

"A curse, a curse on you all; I will laugh in Hell when fate deals you your just rewards!"

Q6:

This character is furious and:

a) vengeful.
b) upset.
c) powerless.

....

"I don't give a damn what Lord Quint wants. My daughter will not be subject to your questioning. So you go back to that old vulture in his black tower and tell him to go to hell."

Q7: This character is:

a) supportive and acquiescent.
b) threatening and dangerous.
c) brave and strong.

....

Q8: Which words convey this character's hatred for Quint?

....

Q9: What connotation do the words 'black' and 'vulture' have here?

a) Darkness
b) Death
c) Wildness

Appearance

The other man turns slowly to face Lord Swann, his gaunt face masked with a sneering smirk.

Q10: This character is:

a) terrifying and ugly.
b) arrogant and haughty.
c) ambivalent and happy.

....

Q11: What type of alliteration is 'sneering smirk'?

a) Fricative
b) Plosive
c) Sibilant

He is a man of middle years, his long dark hair and neatly trimmed beard now flecked with grey. His handsome face is stern; his grey eyes reflect a lifetime of experience.

Q12: This character is powerful and:

a) wealthy.
b) wise.
c) uncertain.

....

Q13: The words 'stern' and 'handsome' are used to describe the same face. What technique is this?

a) Alliteration
b) Juxtaposition
c) Simile

Stage directions
    Enter Macbeth with two bloody daggers.

Q14:
This character is:

a) Violent and merciless
b) Violent and subtle
c) Violent and careful

....

    ...thunder and lightning. Enter three Witches.

Q15:
.These characters are:

a) Dangerous
b) Overly-dramatic
c) Unfortunate

TOPIC 2. SCOTTISH TEXTS: DRAMA

Characterisation within your chosen text

For the text you are studying, copy and complete the following table. You may want to focus on more than one key character, but should have at least four or five aspects covered per character. The example is based on 'The Slab Boys'.

Character	Aspect of character	Quote/evidence	Explanation
Hector	The APPEARANCE of Hector reveals his vulnerable nature.	'He is shorter and weedier than Spanky. He wears spectacles and carries a portable radio.'	Hector's physical shortcomings are succinctly portrayed with the word 'weedier', with its connotations of straggly, out of place and weak; in the masculine world of the 'The Slab Boys', 'spectacles' are a stereotypical way to reinforce this weakness.

© HERIOT-WATT UNIVERSITY

2.3 Theme

Just as in poetry or prose, a theme in drama is the bigger idea that the writer is exploring and wanting us, the audience, to think about and relate to, if possible. It is often conveyed through a combination of characterisation, plot and setting. Theme is sometimes referred to as the central concern(s).

There are common themes found in all literature:

- death;
- relationships;
- loneliness;
- grief;
- loss;
- change;
- love (positive and negative aspects);
- revenge;
- betrayal;
- greed;
- good vs evil;
- war;
- conflict;
- suffering;
- materialism;
- identity;
- destructive nature of time;
- isolation.

In 'The Cheviot, the Stag and the Black, Black Oil' by John McGrath there are several key themes running throughout: the role of women in Scottish society, power and ownership, inequality of wealth and change. These themes are largely revealed through a study of the key plot points of the play.

In 'Men Should Weep' by Ena Lamont Stewart there are several key themes running throughout: poverty, inequality, unemployment and the role of women. These themes are largely revealed through the setting of the play and through a study of the family dynamics of the Morrison family.

In 'The Slab Boys' by John Byrne there are several key themes running throughout: social classes, ambition, rebellion and mental illness. These themes are largely revealed through the actions, speech and appearance of the titular slab boys.

For key events, think of an action, event or occurrence which has major consequences for a main character, moves the plot along or strongly conveys a major theme.

2.7 End of topic test

End of Topic 2 test Go online

Q22: An playwright will usually portray characterisation only through the way a character acts, and speaks.

a) True
b) False

Q23: Characterisation is an important way in which the writer conveys theme.

a) True
b) False

Q24: The dialogue used by a character can only tell us elements of the plot, not elements of characterisation.

a) True
b) False

Q25: Theme in drama is slightly different from theme in prose, but the same as theme in poetry.

a) True
b) False

Q26: Theme is an important message given by the playwright, usually commenting on a social issue or the nature of humanity and can be understood through studying characterisation, setting and style.

a) True
b) False

Q27: Analysing stage directions can be just as important as analysing dialogue.

a) True
b) False

Q28: A playwright will use props only to make the production look more dazzling when performed.

a) True
b) False

Q29: A drama can explore a theme which is pertinent to real life.

a) True
b) False

Q30: The setting of a play can give the audience clues about the themes being explored.

a) True
b) False

Q31: Stage directions can real aspects of characterisation and theme.

a) True
b) False

Q32: Being aware of the historical context of the drama is important.

a) True
b) False

Q33: The main character is the only one worth studying in detail.

a) True
b) False

Q34: Setting helps to strengthen a playwright's message about theme.

a) True
b) False

Q35: Thinking of connotations and metaphorical implications can help to fully understand the message a text gives.

a) True
b) False

Q36: The actions of a character are the most important aspect to analyse, especially in drama.

a) True
b) False

TOPIC 2. SCOTTISH TEXTS: DRAMA 173

Select the word which best describes the character mentioned in each of the following extracts.

Q37:

He is dressed from head to toe in black: black shirt, black jeans black boots. All is black, except his pearl handled pistol and a silver heart shaped locket around his neck. As the scene plays out, he fingers the locket regularly.

a) Dangerous
b) Villainous
c) Mysterious

....

Q38:

He sits in silence, watching the room like a predator observing the antics of its terrified prey.

a) Dangerous
b) Villainous
c) Mysterious

....

Q39:

He stands silently under the tree, dappled in shadow.

a) Dangerous
b) Villainous
c) Mysterious

....

Q40:

He towers over Jim, a hungry sneer crossing his face. This is a man who is no stranger to suffering.

a) Dangerous
b) Villainous
c) Mysterious

....

Q41:

Before anyone can reply, he cracks out of his chair, his pistol already drawn.

a) Dangerous
b) Villainous
c) Mysterious

© HERIOT-WATT UNIVERSITY

Q42: For drama texts, the number of marks that are available for answering questions on the printed text is:

a) 8 out of 20
b) 10 out of 20
c) 12 out of 20

Q43: Characterisation is the way in which playwrights portray their characters, bringing them to life in:

a) familiar and expected ways.
b) unique and vivid ways.
c) varied and unexpected ways.

Q44: Characterisation usually helps the playwright to convey their overall message and,:

a) by understanding the different elements used within a theme, the audience will find it easier to relate to the characters.
b) by understanding the different elements used within a character, the audience will be able to enhance their overall understanding of the text.
c) by enhancing their overall understanding of the text, the audience will be able to easily pick out their favourite character.

Q45: Theme is often conveyed through a combination of characterisation, plot and:

a) setting.
b) setting: usually one will suffice.
c) style.

Q46: Setting is mostly interested in where:

a) the action takes place so that we can imagine it.
b) and when the action takes place so that we can imagine it.
c) and when the action takes place so that we can work out meaning and theme.

Q47: A playwright's style is his/her choice:

a) a variety of different techniques, from soliloquy, stage directions to dialogue and props.
b) only stage directions and dialogue and is used to create interest.
c) dialogue and tone and is used to be attractive.

TOPIC 2. SCOTTISH TEXTS: DRAMA

Q48: It is important to think of _____ when analysing a writer's use of word choice in describing a character.

a) connotations
b) allusions
c) formal language

....

Q49: You can prepare for the Scottish Set Text by only studying:

a) character, theme, setting and key events.
b) character, plot, setting and key events.
c) plot, language, theme and setting.

....

Q50: A metaphor in Higher:

a) can be extended to run through the text.
b) is just like a smile without 'like' or 'as'.
c) will indicate a major character.

Unit 2 Topic 3

Scottish Texts: Poetry

Contents

- 3.1 Introduction 178
- 3.2 Form and structure 179
- 3.3 Theme 187
- 3.4 Sound 192
- 3.5 Imagery 197
- 3.6 Word choice 203
- 3.7 Sentence structure 207
- 3.8 Learning points 212
- 3.9 End of topic test 213

Learning objective

By the end of this topic, you should be able to:

- identify the theme of a poem and explain how evidence from the text relates to that theme;
- comment on a poet's use of poetic form to create effect;
- identify the rhythm and rhyme scheme of a poem and explain the effect;
- identify different sound techniques in a poem and comment on their effect;
- identify imagery in a text and explain how the root image is being exploited;
- comment on the use of word choice in a text;
- comment on the use of sentence structure in a text and its effect.

3.1 Introduction

As part of your Higher course, you will study a Scottish text(s) from one of three genres: drama, prose or poetry. Part of the course assessment will involve answering questions about the text(s) for a total of 20 marks.

This part of the final course examination is one that you can thoroughly prepare for at home, as long as you have the skills to analyse a text.

This section will concentrate on the skills required to textually analyse poetry: it will review the different techniques that a poet can employ, and support you in being able to consider the effect of this with regards to a poem's meaning and theme.

The poetry available in the Scottish Texts section of the Higher course comes in sets of six poems from the following poets:

Carol Ann Duffy:
- War Photographer
- In Mrs Tilscher's Class
- Valentine
- Originally
- The Way My Mother Speaks
- Mrs Midas

Norman MacCaig:
- Hotel Room, 12th Floor
- Assisi
- Visiting Hour
- Brooklyn Cop
- Aunt Julia
- Basking Shark

Sorley MacLean:
- Hallaig
- Kinloch Ainort
- Girl of the red-gold hair
- Shores
- An Autumn Day
- I Gave You Immortality

Don Paterson:
- Waking With Russell
- Rain
- 11:00 Baldovan
- The Circle
- The Ferryman's Arms
- Nil Nil

Liz Lochhead:
- The Bargain
- My Rival's House
- View of Scotland/Love Poem
- Revelation
- Box Room
- Last Supper

Robert Burns:
- Holy Willie's Prayer
- Tam o' Shanter
- To A Mouse
- A Poet's Welcome to his Love-Begotten Daughter
- To a Louse
- A Red, Red Rose

© Heriot-Watt University

TOPIC 3. SCOTTISH TEXTS: POETRY

This list is correct as of August 2018. For an updated list please refer to the SQA:
https://www.sqa.org.uk/files_ccc/Scottish_Set_Text_List_2018-19.pdf

You will study each poem in the set, but only one, or an extract from one, will be printed.

10 out of 20 marks are available for answering questions on the printed text.

10 out of 20 marks are available for comparing the printed text to other poems (by the same writer).

In order to be successful in this part of the examination you must be aware of a number of poetic techniques and be able to explain their effect with regards to the ideas and themes of the poems.

3.2 Form and structure

Rhythm and rhyme

Rhyme is when words sound similar, usually because the end of the words have the same ending, for example 'bed' and 'red'. Both end with the similar sound created by the letters 'ed'. Many poets use rhyme in their poetry, particularly at the end of the line. The pattern of rhyme in a poem is called a rhyme scheme. We identify the rhyme scheme using letters from the alphabet. If lines have the same letter then they rhyme. For example, a stanza of poetry might have this rhyme scheme: AABB. If so, it means lines one and two rhyme, and lines three and four rhyme.

In 'My Rival's House', Liz Lochhead uses rhyme to emphasise the opulence of the house occupied by her boyfriend's mother. There is no set pattern to the rhyme, but when she does use it, she does so in order to bring our attention to the richness and lavishness of her surroundings, which in turn highlights her feelings of inadequacy and intimidation.

Some poets use internal rhyme. This is when words in a poem rhyme but they do not occur at the end of the line. Duffy uses internal rhyme in 'Mrs Midas' in order to convey the speaker as someone who is quite down-to-earth and resilient.

Additionally, poets can also use half rhyme. This is when the vowel sounds of the half rhyming words do not match, but the end consonant of the words do. This technique is exploited by Don Patterson in 'The Ferryman's Arms' to emphasise the idea of fate: just as the speaker is inexplicably drawn to the pool table, the half rhymes are purposefully used to show how things are destined to be together.

Rhythm is the pattern of syllables in each line of a poem. If the rhythm is consistent throughout a poem it can reflect ideas regarding consistency, solidity. If the rhythm is irregular then it can reflect a lack of clarity in the speaker or ideas surrounding instability.

For example, in 'I Gave you Immortality', Sorley MacLean uses a consistent rhythm with the same number of syllables in every line. The regularity of the rhythm reflects the ideas of immortality, of life constantly going on, which in turn emphasises the theme of time in the poem.

In 'The Bargain' by Liz Lochhead, there is no clear pattern to the number of syllables, giving the poem a conversational poem. It becomes almost narrative in the way the speaker tells the story, perhaps underlining the casualness of the relationship and undermining the integrity of the feelings between the speaker and their partner.

Form

When poets decide to write a poem they must first choose the form that they will write in. This will dictate the number of lines the poem has, how many stanzas it has, how the ideas are mapped out in the text, the number of syllables in a line...

There are a number of common forms used by poets that are exemplified by the Scottish poets on the set text list.

Free verse

Poems written in free verse have no real pattern to them. They have multiple stanzas, of multiple lengths, usually with no clear pattern of rhyme.

An example of such a poem is 'Valentine' by Carol Ann Duffy. The poem is written in free verse and many stanzas are simply one line. She does this in order to emphasise a particular idea in that line to the reader.

Another example would be 'Visiting Hour' by Norman MacCaig. In this poem he uses first person narrative to convey the experience of visiting a close personal friend in hospital. He uses the free verse style to reflect the idea that there is no clear pattern to life or death, and nothing is ever truly predictable or certain. He also uses it to show how these thoughts are uncontrollable and flowing through his mind in no structured way. The lack of uniformity reflects the unsettling emotions experienced by the speaker.

Lochhead also makes frequent use of free verse in her poetry. She does this in 'View of Scotland/Love Poem' where she reflects on her memories of celebrating Hogmanay in Scotland, as well as writing about the love she felt for her husband. These two seemingly separate ideas are skilfully intertwined in the poem and the use of free verse allows her to switch effectively from one idea to the other. It also highlights the fluidity of memory and how one recollection can lead you to another one seamlessly.

Sonnets

Poets often employ the sonnet form as it has a very tight structure with a very specific order to the way in which the ideas are presented. Traditionally, these poems focussed on expressing one's love for another, but they are used very differently in the poems on the set text list.

There are two main sonnet forms: The Petrarchan sonnet and the Shakespearean (or Elizabethan) sonnet. Both sonnet forms are utilised by poets within the set texts.

All sonnets have 14 lines and are written in iambic pentameter. This is how we measure syllables in a line of poetry. A 'foot' in poetry is the pattern of a small group of syllables in a line. For example, an 'iam' is the name given to two syllables with an unstressed/stressed pattern.

Example Take the first line of Shakespeare's Sonnet 12.

When I do count the clock that tells the time

This has ten syllables in it but the pattern is unstressed/stressed to the end of the line. You can annotate this as follows:

U / U / U / U / U /
When I do count the clock that tells the time

U represents an unstressed syllable.

/ represents a stressed syllable.

The patterns of syllables is present in every line of a sonnet.

If we then consider that an iam is two syllables with this pattern, then it is clear that there are 5 iams in this line.

U / U / U / U / U /
(When I) (do count) (the clock) (that tells) (the time)

Petrarchan sonnets

This sonnet form is written in iambic pentameter and has 14 lines. The lines are split into an octave (8 lines) and a sestet (6 lines).

The octave is split into two quatrains (4 lines) and a poet uses the octet to introduce the issue and reflect on its challenges. The first quatrain clearly sets out the problem, which is further developed in the second quatrain.

The rhyme scheme in the octave is as follows: *ABBAABBA*.

The sestet offers an answer or solution to the issue. It is split into two tercets (3 lines).

The rhyme scheme in the sestet is *CDECDE* or *CDCDCD*.

At the beginning of the sestet there is usually a 'volta', a turn which signals a change in tone or perspective with regards to the issue raised and discussed in the octave.

© HERIOT-WATT UNIVERSITY

Example

Here is an annotated sonnet written by John Milton using the Petrarchan form.

> A When I consider how my light is spent,
> B Ere half my days in this dark world and wide,
> B And that one talent which is death to hide
> A Lodged with me useless, though my soul more bent
> A To serve therewith my Maker, and present [1]
> B My true account, lest He returning chide;
> B 'Doth God exact day-labor, light denied?'
> A I fondly ask. But Patience, to prevent
> C That murmur, soon replies, 'God doth not need [2]
> D Either man's work or His own gifts. Who best
> E Bear His mild yoke, they serve Him best. His state
> C Is kingly: thousands at His bidding speed,
> D And post o'er land and ocean without rest;
> E They also serve who only stand and wait. [3]
>
> John Milton
>
> * Volta: The focus of the poem changes from the poet's perspective on religion and how to live your life to imagining the voice of God and what his perspective on this is.
>
> Notes:
>
> [1] In the first quatrain (the first *ABBA*) the poet reflects on how he spends his time on earth, understanding that he will eventually have to die.
>
> [2] He continues to reflect on death and religion by discussing the Day of Judgement and how he will have to justify his lifestyle (the second *ABBA*).
>
> [3] In the sestet (*CDECDE*), the poet discusses the issue from a different perspective and imagines a God that would want mortals to live peacefully and show kindness to each other.

TOPIC 3. SCOTTISH TEXTS: POETRY

Form and structure: Petrarchan sonnet annotation

Q1: Here is another Petrarchan sonnet:

My letters! all dead paper, mute and white!
And yet they seem alive and quivering
Against my tremulous hands which loose the string
And let them drop down on my knee tonight.
This said—he wished to have me in his sight
Once, as a friend: this fixed a day in spring
To come and touch my hand . . . a simple thing,
Yes I wept for it—this . . . the paper's light . . .
Said, Dear, I love thee; and I sank and quailed
As if God's future thundered on my past.
This said, I am thine—and so its ink has paled
With lying at my heart that beat too fast.
And this . . . O Love, thy words have ill availed
If, what this said, I dared repeat at last!

Elizabeth Barrett Browning

See if you can annotate it as per the previous example.

Shakespearean (Elizabethan) sonnets

These sonnets are also written using iambic pentameter and have 14 lines. However the way in which the poem is formed is slightly different. Shakespearean sonnets have three quatrains and a final rhyming couplet. The first quatrain introduces the problem, which is developed through the next two quatrains. The final rhyming couplet offers a solution to the original problem.

The rhyme scheme is *ABABCDCDEFEFGG*.

Example

Here is an example Shakespearean sonnet (Sonnet 30) with some annotations:

A When to the sessions of sweet silent thought
B I summon up remembrance of things past,
A I sigh the lack of many a thing I sought,
B And with old woes new wail my dear time's waste:[1]
C Then can I drown an eye, unus'd to flow,
D For precious friends hid in death's dateless night,
C And weep afresh love's long since cancell'd woe,
D And moan the expense of many a vanish'd sight: [2]
E Then can I grieve at grievances foregone,
F And heavily from woe to woe tell o'er
E The sad account of fore-bemoaned moan,
F Which I new pay as if not paid before. [3]
G But if the while I think on thee, dear friend,
G All losses are restor'd and sorrows end. [4]

Notes:

[1] In the first quatrain (*ABAB*) Shakespeare introduces the problem lamenting about the things you lose as you grow old.
[2] He develops this idea in the second quatrain (*CDCD*) by giving examples of the things that he misses that he has lost, such as friends and experiences that he cannot quite remember.
[3] The problem reaches its climax in the third quatrain (*EFEF*) where Shakespeare when he describes how difficult it is to get over these things.
[4] Shakespeare's solution to feeling forlorn about the things he has lost as he gets older is to think of someone close to him and this will bring joy into his mind again. (*GG*).

TOPIC 3. SCOTTISH TEXTS: POETRY

> **Form and structure: Shakespearean sonnet annotation**
>
> Q2: Here is an example of a Shakespearean sonnet (Sonnet 33):
> Full many a glorious morning have I seen
> Flatter the mountain-tops with sovereign eye,
> Kissing with golden face the meadows green,
> Gilding pale streams with heavenly alchemy;
> Anon permit the basest clouds to ride
> With ugly rack on his celestial face,
> And from the forlorn world his visage hide,
> Stealing unseen to west with this disgrace:
> Even so my sun one early morn did shine
> With all triumphant splendor on my brow;
> But out! alack! he was but one hour mine,
> The region cloud hath mask'd him from me now.
> Yet him for this my love no whit disdaineth;
> Suns of the world may stain when heaven's sun staineth.
> See if you can annotate it as per the previous example.

Both sonnet forms are utilised by the authors on the set text list.

Don Paterson also makes use of the sonnet form in his poetry. He uses it when writing about both his son in 'Waking With Russell'. The poem reflects on the strength of the love he feels for his son. Here, he utilises the Petrarchan sonnet form, although he inverts the structure, beginning with the sestet and ending with the octave. This reversal of the traditional form reflects the disorder that the child has brought to his life. It could also reflect the surprise he feels at the depth of love he has for his son, something that he did not quite expect.

The Standard Habbie

Robert Burns uses a structure to his stanzas which is completely unique amongst the other poets in the set. This is called the Standard Habbie.

A Standard Habbie stanza consists of 6 lines with a particular rhyme scheme.

- Lines 1, 2, 3 and 5 rhyme. These are long lines in the stanza.
- Lines 4 and 6 rhyme. These are shorter lines.

The first 3 rhyming long lines gives Burns the opportunity to build anticipation.

The tension and suspense is brought to fruition in the final three lines of the stanza. This is usually where Burns makes sardonic remarks about the subject matter of the poem, or strengthens the atmosphere of the poem.

Example

Here is the opening stanza from 'To A Mouse'. It is written using the Standard Habbie form.

I'm truly sorry Man's dominion
Has broken Nature's social union,
An' justifies that ill opinion,
Which makes thee startle,
At me, thy poor, earth-born companion,
An' fellow-mortal!

Form and structure: Note-making

Consider the set of poems that you are studying for this part of the course. Make notes about any patterns you see with regards to rhythm, rhyme and the way in which each of the poems is structured.

Consider the following:

- How many stanzas (verses) does the poem have?
- How are lines arranged? Is there a uniformity about them?
- Is rhyme present? What is the effect of this?

Always remember to think about why a writer has decided to employ a particular form and structure when writing a poem. Why have they done this? What is the effect? How does it link to the theme?

3.3 Theme

A theme in a poem is the bigger idea that a poet is exploring and wanting to make a statement about. Sometimes this is referred to as the central concern.

There are common themes found in all literature:

- death;
- relationships;
- loneliness;
- grief;
- loss;
- change;
- love;
- revenge;
- betrayal;
- greed;
- good vs evil;
- war;
- conflict;
- suffering;
- materialism;
- identity;
- destructive nature of time;
- isolation;
- religion;
- nature.

Many of Duffy's poems deal with love and relationships. She explores both the positive and negative impact that this common emotion can have on an individual. She also contemplates other themes, such as change, identity, betrayal, materialism, war, and suffering.

Norman MacCaig's poetry tends to be quite dark and deals a lot with death and grief. Other themes include the inherent evil that exists within man, suffering, hypocrisy in religion, and loss.

Liz Lochhead's poetry focuses on issues related to feminism, particularly the relationship between females, as well as between males and females. She often explores the effects of time on the individual and how it can affect the development of our personality.

Don Paterson's poetry often explores ideas around identity and the individual's relationship to time. His poetry can be quite gloomy in that he focuses on the futility of life and the loss of innocence through maturity. However, this is balanced with some poems that focus on the theme of love and relationships, particularly those between father and son.

Sorley MacLean tackles big themes that affect all of society, such as war, death and time. He is interested in exploring nature, both in terms of the natural world and with regards to humanity. His poems can often be quite bleak in their outlook and message about the destructive nature of mankind.

One of the major themes in Robert Burns' poetry is religious and political prejudice. He ridicules those in society who are prejudiced towards others and promotes themes of fraternity and equality. His poems present life as something precious which we should all appreciate and treasure, regardless of background, social status or religion. Another key theme that permeates Burns' poetry is love, both romantic and familial. He often writes about the joy and happiness that feelings of love bring him and how these feeling should not be something by which you are embarrassed.

Theme: Poetry excerpts Go online

Read the following excerpts from some of the Burns poems on the set text list (correct as of August 2018) and try to choose the most appropriate theme.

Q3: 'To a Mouse'
The best-laid schemes o' Mice an' Men
Gang aft agley,
An' lea'e us nought but grief an' pain,
For promis'd joy!

a) Time
b) Fate
c) Humanity

....

Q4: 'Holy Willie's Prayer'
But yet—O Lord—confess I must—
At times I'm fash'd wi' fleshly lust;

a) Identity
b) Social injustice
c) Religious hypocrisy

....

TOPIC 3. SCOTTISH TEXTS: POETRY

Q5: 'To a Louse'
O wad some Power the giftie gie us
To see oursels as ithers see us!
It wad frae mony a blunder free us,
An' foolish notion:
What airs in dress an' gait wad lea'e us,
An' ev'n devotion!

a) Good vs Evil
b) Realising our own faults
c) Social justice

....

Q6: 'A Red, Red Rose'
Till a' the seas gang dry, my dear,
And the rocks melt wi' the sun;
And I will luve thee still, my dear,
While the sands o' life shall run.

a) Religion
b) Enduring love
c) Conflict

....

Q7: 'A Poet's Welcome to His Love-Begotten Daughter'
Thou's welcome, wean; mishanter fa' me,
If thoughts o' thee, or yet thy mamie,
Shall ever daunton me or awe me,
My bonie lady,
Or if I blush when thou shalt ca' me
Tyta or daddie.

a) Unconditional love
b) Humanity
c) Hate

Explaining Theme

When trying to explain the theme of a poem, it is best to find specific evidence and try to explain what you understand about the theme from it. You could use a table as in the following example.

For example, in 'To A Mouse', Burns uses the incident of destroying the mouse's nest to reflect on the universal themes of nature and fate. Throughout the poem he discusses how the fate of nature and mankind are intertwined, unpredictably affecting one another. When he says that the future plans of both man and beast 'Gang aft agley', he conveys to the reader the erratic and changeable nature of fate. Regardless of precautions put in place by either man or animal, nothing can protect them from suffering and grief.

© HERIOT-WATT UNIVERSITY

Example

Poem	Theme	Evidence	Explanation
'To A Mouse'	Fate	'Gang aft agley'	Both man and animal can both be victims of fate, regardless of the plans they have in place to protect themselves. Plans are transient and are often thwarted by accidental incidents.

Theme: Explanations — Go online

Q8: A table like the one above has been made for the poems mentioned in the previous activity. There is one problem though: it has yet to be completed.
Can you match the explanations with the themes and evidence?

Poem	Theme	Evidence	Explanation
'Holy Willie's Prayer'			
'To a Louse'			
'A Red, Red Rose'			
'A Poet's Welcome to His Love-Begotten Daughter'			

Theme:
- Social equality
- Unconditional Love

- Eternal love
- Religious hypocrisy

Evidence:

- Gae somewhere else and seek your dinner on some poor bodie
- '...mishanter fa' me, If thoughts o' thee, or yet thy mamie, Shall ever daunton me or awe me, '
- Til a' the seas gang dry
- At times I'm fash'd wi' fleshly lust;

Explanations:

- Burns uses irony to suggest that a louse has no place on someone who appears to have class and status.
- By using hyperbolic language, Burns shows that love is eternal. Love ending is impossible.
- Burns calls upon misfortune to enter his life if he is ever embarrassed or ashamed of his daughter, or even the mother of his child. The baby may be born out of wedlock, but Burns is fully committed to being a father and loves this child in spite of the situation surrounding its birth.
- Burns uses the word 'lust' to hint at Holy Willie's feelings of sexual desire and, in doing so, Burns shows that he is capable of sin, just like those he condemns, highlighting the hypocrisy that he sees inherent within the Calvinist faith.

Theme: Note-making

Read the poems in the set you are studying and try to identify two or three themes that the poet is exploring.

Once you have done this, try to find evidence in the text that links to the theme and then try to explain what you think the writer is trying to say about the theme.

You may wish to use a table like you did in the previous exercise to organise your ideas.

© HERIOT-WATT UNIVERSITY

Poem	Theme	Evidence	Explanation

3.4 Sound

Poets often use sound devices in order to create description and convey certain ideas to the reader. The three most common sound devices found in poetry are:

1. alliteration;
2. assonance;
3. onomatopoeia.

Alliteration is the repetition of consonant sounds at the beginning of words close to each other in a sentence. A writer does this in order to focus the reader's attention on a specific idea or to emphasise a point. Duffy uses alliteration in 'War Photographer' ('Spools of suffering') to draw our attention to the connection between the photographic equipment and the emotive content of the war photographs.

> Example *Big brown bear.*

Sibilance is a special type of alliteration where an 's' sound is repeated. This can create a sinister tone and can often slow down the rhythm of a poem. Again, a writer would employ this technique in order to emphasise a particular idea. Liz Lochhead uses sibilance in 'My Rival's House' to create the impressions of perfection and faultlessness in the speaker's rival: the sibilance gives the description of the rival's silverware a sense of flawlessness.

Example Sally sells seashells by the sea shore.

Assonance is the repetition of vowel sounds in words close to each other. This device can slow down the rhythm of a poem and give the line a lilting quality. These tend to be softer sounds that reflect feelings of loss and isolation. Burns uses assonance in 'To a Louse' to create a sense of disgust at the creature.

Example his eyes were the truest of blue

Onomatopoeia is when a words describes a sound. Poets use this in order to give the reader a greater sensory experience when reading the poem. In '11:00: Baldovan', Don Paterson describes the bus journey of two young boys, the first without parental supervision. Paterson uses onomatopoeia to describe the sound of the change the boy has for his bus fare in his pocket. This suggests that the boy found the coins very heavy at the time and of a certain worth, although upon reflection we understand that this money was worth far less than the importance the young man placed on it.

Example Crash, bang or crunch

Sound: Devices

Identify the sound device in each of the following excerpts.

Q9: Tam o' Shanter
'Fast by an ingle, bleezing finely,
Wi' reaming swats, that drank divinely'

a) Alliteration
b) Assonance
c) Onomatopoeia
d) Sibilance

Q10: Tam o' Shanter
'wi' favours secret, sweet and precious'

a) Alliteration
b) Assonance
c) Onomatopoeia
d) Sibilance

Q11: A Poet's Address to his Love-Begotten Daughter
"Tho' I should be the waur bestead,
Thou's be as braw and bienly clad,"

a) Alliteration
b) Assonance
c) Onomatopoeia
d) Sibilance

Q12: Tam o' Shanter
'The wind blew as 'twad blawn its last;'

a) Alliteration
b) Assonance
c) Onomatopoeia
d) Sibilance

TOPIC 3. SCOTTISH TEXTS: POETRY

Q13: Tam o' Shanter

'The *rattling* showers rose on the blast;'

a) Alliteration
b) Assonance
c) Onomatopoeia
d) Sibilance

....

Q14: A Poet's Address to his Love-Begotten Daughter

"Thou's welcome, wean; mishanter fa' me,"

a) Alliteration
b) Assonance
c) Onomatopoeia
d) Sibilance

Explaining the use of sound

When analysing a poem, you must not only identify the use of a sound device, but also comment on its effect.

Good words to use in order to do this are 'emphasises', 'stresses' or 'highlights'.

For example, Burns uses alliteration in 'A Poet's Address to his Love-Begotten Daughter' in order to express his love and adoration for his daughter, regardless of her legitimacy. He explains how he wants her to be 'braw and bienly clad', using alliteration to bring our attention to the idea that he wants her to have the same standards of living as his other children. This emphasises his affection for his daughter and shows him to be dismissive of the prejudice that exists within society towards his baby.

Again, using a table to organise your ideas could be helpful.

Example

A Poet's Address to his Love-Begotten Daughter			
Sound device	Evidence	Explanation	Effect
Alliteration	'braw and bienly clad'	Alliteration is used to bring our attention to the idea that he wants his daughter to have the same standards of living as his other children.	Emphasises his affection for his daughter and shows him to be dismissive of the prejudice that exists within society towards his baby.

© HERIOT-WATT UNIVERSITY

Sound: Explanations Go online

An explanation of the effect of each sound device exemplified previously has been written below.
Can you match the best explanation to the evidence given?

Q15: Tam o' Shanter
'Fast by an ingle, bleezing finely,
Wi' reaming swats, that drank divinely'

a) Burns uses alliteration to bring our attention to the way the alcohol tasted to Tam. He suggests that the beer was being drunk easily by Tam, emphasising the excessive way he is drinking, showing Tam to be a character of little self-restraint.
b) The alliteration brings our attention to the way in which Tam is drinking.
c) Burns uses the alliteration to highlight to the reader the excessive nature of Tam's drinking.

....

Q16: Tam o' Shanter
'wi' favours secret, sweet and precious'

a) The sibilance here imitates the hushed voices of Tam and the pub's landlady.
b) Burns uses sibilance to suggest that Tam and the pub landlady are whispering, suggesting that the nature of their exchange is taboo.
c) Burns uses sibilance to imitate the hushed voices of both Tam and the landlady, showing how they are whispering to each other. This suggests that what they are saying is salacious in some way, highlighting the inappropriate nature of their dialogue, which has been exacerbated by alcohol.

....

Q17: Tam o' Shanter
'The wind blew as 'twad blawn its last;'

a) The assonance is used to slow down the rhythm of the poem.
b) Burns uses assonance to mimic the wind blowing: the repeated vowel sounds slow the rhythm and reflect the continuous force of the wind. This highlights to the reader the severity of the storm and the danger it poses to anyone who has to go out in it.
c) Burns uses assonance to slow the rhythm, of the poem and reflect the long howls of the wind.

....

Q18: Tam o' Shanter
'The *rattling* showers rose on the blast;'

a) Onomatopoeia is used to the constant drumming of the rain falling outside the pub, highlighting the ferocity of the storm and creating a sense of foreboding about what will happen to Tam.
b) The onomatopoeia describes the sound of the rain.
c) Burns uses the onomatopoeia to emphasise how violent the storm is.

TOPIC 3. SCOTTISH TEXTS: POETRY 197

Sound: Note-taking

Read the poems in the set you are studying and try to identify the use of sound techniques by the poet.

Once you have done this, try to explain how it is used and what the effect of it is.

You may wish to use a table to organise your ideas.

Title			
Sound device	Evidence	Explanation	Effect

3.5 Imagery

Imagery (or figurative language) is the name we give to techniques a writer uses that involves comparison. These comparisons help us to build a picture in our head of what the writer is trying to describe or the point he is trying to convey to us.

There are three main techniques that writers employ when using imagery:

1. similes;
2. metaphors;
3. personification.

© HERIOT-WATT UNIVERSITY

Similes compare two things using the 'magic' words 'like' or 'as'.

Example

He was fat like a pig.

He is as fat as a pig.

Here the man is a like a pig because he is fat. This is a very specific comparison.

Metaphors describe one thing as another.

Example

He was/is a fat pig.

Here the man could be like a pig in many ways. He might be: fat, unhygienic, greedy, messy.

Personification is when an object is given human qualities.

Example

The chair was tired.

This does not mean that the chair was literally exhausted but it suggests that it is old, worn and past its best.

Imagery: Identification   Go online

Q19: Read the poem below and identify the poet's use of simile, metaphor and personification.

There are:

- two similes;
- three metaphors;

A Red, Red Rose

By Robert Burns

O my Luve's like a red, red rose,
That's newly sprung in June;
O my Luve's like the melodie,
That's sweetly play'd in tune.

As fair are thou, my bonie lass,
So deep in luve am I;
And I will luve thee still, my Dear,
Till a' the seas gang dry.

> Till a' the seas gang dry, my Dear,
> And the rocks melt wi' the sun:
> I will luve thee still, my dear,
> While the sands o' life shall run.
>
> And fare thee weel, my only Luve!
> And fare thee weel, a while!
> And I will come again, my Luve,
> Tho' it were ten thousand mile!

Specialist terms

Although simile, metaphors and personification are the most popular forms of imagery, there are also a number of specials terms that you should be aware of as they feature in some of the poems on the set text list.

Pathetic fallacy: this is when human emotions are given to the weather in order to convey to the reader the mood of a character or a speaker in the poem to the reader. Robert Browning uses it at the start of 'Porphyria's Lover' when he describes the 'sullen wind'. Here the wind is being described as bad-tempered, but really Browning is using it to create an unsettling and hostile mood at the beginning of the poem.

Transferred epithet: this is when a word that should be used to describe a speaker in a poem or a character is attributed to an object instead. For example, in William Wordsworth's 'Daffodils' he describes the daffodils as 'jocund company', 'jocund' meaning happy. In the poem, however, it is the poet that is in such a cheerful mood, not the daffodils. The emotion that he is feeling has been 'transferred' to the daffodils.

Synecdoche: this is where the part of something is used to refer to the whole. For example, in Samuel Taylor Coleridge's poem 'The Rime of the Ancient Mariner', he writes about the 'western wave'. Here 'wave' refers to the whole sea.

All the poems on the set text lists are full of similes, metaphors and personification. Some also have examples of the specialist terms mentioned above, such as 'Visiting Hour' by Norman MacCaig. In the opening of the poem he refers to nostrils travelling down a corridor. This is an example of synecdoche where the nostrils represent the full physical form of the speaker.

In '11:00: Baldovan', Don Paterson uses a transferred epithet to show how the boys are in a place which seems alien to them, full of streets they do not recognise.

Explaining the effect of imagery

When explaining the effect of imagery you must consider the root of the image, what the writer is drawing upon in order to make a comparison.

For example, in Burns' 'A Poet's Welcome to His Love-Begotten Daughter', he addresses his daughter as the 'sweet fruit'. She is not literally a sweet-tasting piece of fruit, but he uses the image of a sweet tasting fruit, like an orange, to describe the appealing qualities of his daughter and that she is a positive outcome of his exploits.

You must consider the significance of the root of the image first before you can discuss its figurative extension. Again, organising your ideas into a table can be a helpful way of doing this.

Example

	A Poet's Welcome to His Love-Begotten Daughter			
Technique	Evidence	Root		Extension
Metaphor	'sweet fruit'	• Pleasing/delightful tasting • Sugary/moreish • Natural food stuff		Burns is implying that his child's birth is normal and the love he feels for it is pure. He suggests that she is adorable and something that is very attractive to him, emphasising his love and adoration for her.

Imagery: Analysis   Go online

Q20: The following table has been used to analyse some of the imagery in Burns' 'Tam o' Shanter', which is on the set text list. (correct as of May 2016)

However, all the entries have been jumbled up. Can you match the technique and evidence with the correct root and explanation?

		Tam o' Shanter	
Technique	Evidence	Root	Extension
		• Fixed position • Occupying a particular place • Interred in the ground	
	Tam lo'ed him like a vera brither		
Metaphors			
			Just as rainbows are an attractive sight but disappear quickly, so too does the feeling of enjoyment that may be derived from something.

TOPIC 3. SCOTTISH TEXTS: POETRY

Techniques:

- Metaphors
- Simile

Evidence:

- 'Nae man can tether time or tide;'
- 'Or like the rainbow's lovely form/Evanishing amid the storm'
- Tam had got planted unco right

Root:

- Arc of seven different colours in the sky caused by rain and sunshine during a storm.
- Male sibling, Kinsman, Blood relation.
- Tide: unstoppable rise and fall of the ocean, Time: measurements that chart existence, Tether: to control or stop.

Extensions:

- In comparing feeling of satisfaction to our inability to control time and the tides of the sea, Burns is emphasising the fleeting nature of gratification.
- This suggests that Tam is comfortable and relaxed, that he is rooted to the spot and unwilling to move.
- This emphasises the closeness of the two friends and create a convivial mood between them.

© HERIOT-WATT UNIVERSITY

Imagery: Note-taking

Read the poems in the set you are studying and try to identify the use of imagery by the poet. Once you have done this, try to explain how it is used and what the effect of it is. You may wish to use a table to organise your ideas.

Title			
Technique	Evidence	Root	Extension

3.6 Word choice

Poets must be economical with the language they use. Therefore every word they include is significant in some way, some more than others. By choosing certain words, writers can emphasise particular ideas or provoke certain emotions in us. We refer to this as the writer's use of word choice.

For example, in 'A Poet's Welcome to his Love-Begotten Daughter', Robert Burns describes the arrival of his daughter as a 'wee unsought for'. By using the word 'unsought', Burns recognises that this birth was not planned, but by using 'wee' he undermines any scandal linked to the child being born out of wedlock, clearly expressing his affection and love for his daughter.

Word choice: Missing words Go online

The following are lines from Burns' poems on the set text list. (Valid as of May 2016)

Use words from the selection to complete the line.

Q21: O, what a _____ in thy breastie!

a) fear's
b) joy's
c) panic's

....

Q22: An' let poor, _____ bodies bee

a) damned
b) rotten
c) hopeful

....

Q23: Wi' reaming swats, that drank _____ .

a) well
b) disgustingly
c) divinely

....

Q24: Welcome! my _____ , sweet, wee dochter,

a) lovely
b) bonie
c) beautiful

Explaining the effect of word choice

When we discuss word choice we must think about a word's *denotation* and a word's *connotation*.

A word's denotation is its dictionary meaning.

Connotations are meanings we associate with a word.

We can only show how the connotations of words are being exploited by a writer if we understand its denotation too.

Example

A 'cross' is an object or a mark created by intersecting two lines.

However, the word 'cross' has many connotations: we associate it with religion, crucifixion, Jesus, church, jewellery...

When discussing a writer's use of word choice it is important to discuss what a word suggests with regards to the theme of a poem.

A good way to make notes regarding the use of word choice in a poem is to use a table like the one below, which will help you to think about the word's denotation and also how its connotations are exploited by the writer.

Example

Robert Burns			
Word choice	Denotation	Connotation	Link to theme
'wee unsought for'	A little undesired	<ul><li>Not a huge inconvenience</li><li>Not a big regret</li></ul>	Although Burns recognises that this birth was not planned, the use of 'wee' undermines any sense of scandal, highlighting the hypocrisy and disdainful attitude of society towards an innocent child. This emphasises his love and affection for his daughter, regardless of the circumstances of her birth.

TOPIC 3. SCOTTISH TEXTS: POETRY

Word choice: Analysis

Go online

Q25: The table below has been used to analyse some of the word choice in the previous activity.

However, all the entries have been jumbled up. Can you match the word, its denotation and connotation with the corresponding theme?

Title			
Word choice	Denotation	Connotation	Link to theme

Word choice:

- Panic's
- Bonie
- Divinely
- Damned

Denotation:

- Condemned by God to hell
- Uncontrollable fear/anxiety
- Attractive
- Something which is God-like

Connotation:

- Beautiful, charming, engaging
- Evil, cursed, doomed, lost
- Exquisite, attractive, reverential, magnificent
- Out of control, wild behaviour, hysterical

© HERIOT-WATT UNIVERSITY

Link to theme:

- Burns uses the word 'divinely' to describe the ease with which the beer is being drunk by Tam. It gives the beer an almost reverential quality, showing how Tam thinks of the alcohol as being tempting, but also something which is beneficial. This creates a sense of irony as we know the alcohol will lead Tam to trouble.
- Burns uses the word 'damned' to describe those that, according to Calvinism, are not predestined to go to heaven and, therefore, will end up in hell, regardless of their actions when on Earth. This links to the theme of religious hypocrisy as Burns is being ironic in using rhetoric that the Calvinists would use to describe those who they believe to be less worthy than themselves.
- The poet uses the Scots word to describe his baby daughter, clearly expressing his affection for her. This child is clearly very special to him and, unlike the rest of society, he does not view it as something he should be embarrassed by. This links to his criticism of society by highlighting the lack of humanity they express towards something so beautiful and innocent.
- By describing the mouse as feeling panicked, Burns recognises that it feels fear and highlights the disruptive presence of man on the natural world. In some ways he sympathises with the mouse, understanding its plight as running parallel to that of the poor during Burns' era. The humanity Burns shows the mouse is something which he wishes that mankind could show to each other.

Word choice: Note-taking

Read the poems in the set you are studying and try to identify the use of imagery by the poet. Once you have done this, try to explain how it is used and how it links to the theme.

You may wish to use a table like you did in the previous exercise to organise your ideas.

Title			
Word choice	Denotation	Connotation	Link to theme

3.7 Sentence structure

Writers also manipulate sentences and use punctuation in order to create effect in poems.

Here are some of the most popular sentence structure techniques that they employ.

Short sentences

Short sentences are often either one word or just a few words. Poets use it to emphasise the meaning in the words that they use in the short sentence. In 'Valentine', Duffy uses it to convey to us the forcefulness of the speaker and the simplicity of her gift.

Repetition

Poets often does this to emphasise a particular idea to the reader. For example, in 'Visiting Hour', MacCaig uses repetition to convey to the reader the heartache of the speaker and his unwillingness to accept what is happening.

Dashes

Poets use dashes to create a dramatic pause. In 'I Give You Immortality', Sorley MacLean uses a dash in stanza four to create a dramatic pause before going on to explain that the source of his poetic drive is also the source of much of the pain he feels.

© HERIOT-WATT UNIVERSITY

Lists

Poets often use lists to emphasise particular points. In 'Tam O Shanter', Burns uses a list to create a range of ways in which the Cutty Sark witch has wrecked the local community.

Enjambment

This is where the ending of a particular line or phrase in a poem can carry over into the next line or stanza. Poets often do this to give a poem an awkward rhythm or illustrate a particular idea. It can also be employed by writers to make a poem sound more like speech, more natural. In 'Nil Nil', Don Paterson uses enjambment in the first stanza to detail the events which lead to the inevitable destruction of the football team. The uses of enjambment creates a sense of these events being out with anyone's control, completely unstoppable.

Parenthesis

This is when a writer adds extra information to the middle of a sentence or phrase using brackets, commas or dashes. Poets may choose to do this to give us additional information that will help us understand a theme or use it to include more description about a certain image in the poem. Liz Lochhead uses parenthesis in 'My Rival's House' to highlight the fact that the poet's partner is related by blood to his mother, which she recognises as a very strong bond that she will struggle to overcome.

Inversion

This is when the normal word order is subverted to place emphasis on a specific word that the poet wishes to highlight to the reader. In 'Mrs Midas', Duffy uses inversion to show her surprise at her husband's strange powers.

Exclamations

Exclamations are identified by the use of the exclamation mark at the end of the sentence and are used to emphasise the emotion behind what is being said. Burns uses exclamation marks in 'A Poet's Address to His Love-Begotten Daughter' to emphasise the joy and happiness he feels at the birth of his daughter.

Minor sentences

These are sentences which do not contain a main verb. Don Paterson uses two minor sentences to open '11:00 Baldovan'. In doing so he quickly establishes the setting, creating a dramatic impact and drawing the reader in to the poem.

Colon

Used to introduce a list or an explanation/expansion of a particular idea. Sorley MacLean uses this in 'Shores' to give us more information regarding the amount of time he would stay on Talisker Bay to prove the overwhelming love he feels for his partner.

Sentence structure: Identification   Go online

Q26:

Identify the use of sentence structure in the poem below.

There are:

- three examples of repetition;
- two examples of each of:
  - enjambment;
  - exclamations.
- and two examples of each of:
  - listing;
  - parenthesis.

A Poet's Welcome to his Love-Begotten Daughter
By Robert Burns

Thou's welcome, wean; mishanter fa' me,
If thoughts o' thee, or yet thy mamie,
Shall ever daunton me or awe me,
My bonie lady,
Or if I blush when thou shalt ca' me
Tyta or daddie.

Tho' now they ca' me fornicator,
An' tease my name in kintry clatter,
The mair they talk, I'm kent the better,
E'en let them clash;
An auld wife's tongue's a feckless matter
To gie ane fash.

> Welcome! my bonie, sweet, wee dochter,
> Tho' ye come here a wee unsought for,
> And tho' your comin' I hae fought for,
> Baith kirk and queir;
> Yet, by my faith, ye're no unwrought for,
> That I shall swear!

Explaining the use of sentence structure

Most writers use sentence structure to emphasise a particular idea to us.

For example, in 'Hallaig', Sorley MacLean uses enjambment to emphasise symbiotic relationship between mankind and the world of nature, conveying to the reader the importance of the way in which the actions of one affects the other. These never-ending lines reflects this never-ending partnership between man and nature.

In 'Originally', Duffy uses short sentences to focus on a single memory.

Using mind maps is a good way to make notes about the use of sentence structure in a poem.

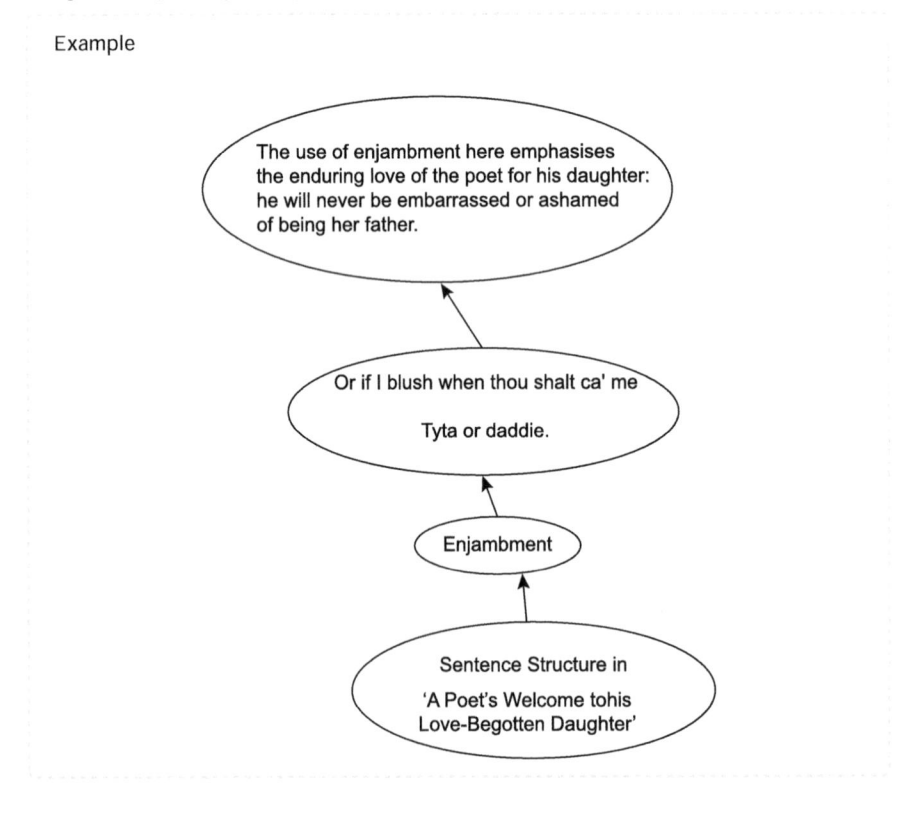

Example

- The use of enjambment here emphasises the enduring love of the poet for his daughter: he will never be embarrassed or ashamed of being her father.
  - Or if I blush when thou shalt ca' me Tyta or daddie.
    - Enjambment
      - Sentence Structure in 'A Poet's Welcome to his Love-Begotten Daughter'

TOPIC 3. SCOTTISH TEXTS: POETRY

Sentence structure: Mind maps   Go online

Q27: The contents of a mind map to discuss the use of sentence structure in the poem from the previous activity have been prepared.

However, none of the links or associated positioning have been made. Can you match up the techniques with the correct examples and explanations?

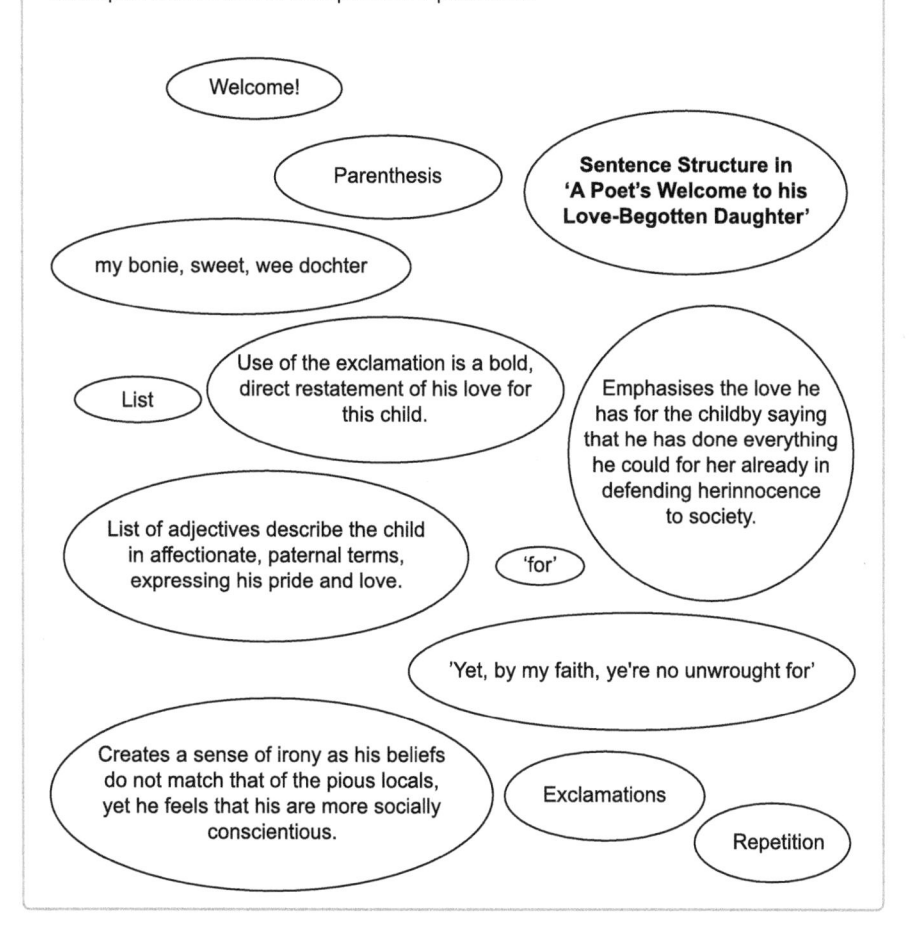

- Welcome!
- Parenthesis
- **Sentence Structure in 'A Poet's Welcome to his Love-Begotten Daughter'**
- my bonie, sweet, wee dochter
- List
- Use of the exclamation is a bold, direct restatement of his love for this child.
- Emphasises the love he has for the childby saying that he has done everything he could for her already in defending herinnocence to society.
- List of adjectives describe the child in affectionate, paternal terms, expressing his pride and love.
- 'for'
- 'Yet, by my faith, ye're no unwrought for'
- Creates a sense of irony as his beliefs do not match that of the pious locals, yet he feels that his are more socially conscientious.
- Exclamations
- Repetition

© HERIOT-WATT UNIVERSITY

3.8 Learning points

Summary

- A theme is the bigger idea that a poet is exploring in their poem through the use of a variety of poetic techniques.

- Poets use different forms and structures in their writing to organise their ideas and create different effects.

- Poets use rhythm and rhyme in their poems to create different effects and help convey the theme to the reader.

- Different sound techniques can be used by poets to create meaning and effect.

- Poets use imagery to create pictures in our minds that help us gain a deeper understanding of the themes being explored.

- The connotations of words are often used by poets in order to create different effects and link to the theme.

- Poets often use different elements of sentence structure to emphasise particular ideas or themes explored in the poem.

3.9 End of topic test

End of Topic 3 test — Go online

Choose the correct poetry technique for the following meanings.

Q28: The pattern of syllables in each line of a poem.

a) Sibilance
b) Rhythm
c) Onomatopoeia

....

Q29: A special type of alliteration where an 's' sound is repeated.

a) Sibilance
b) Transferred epithet
c) Metaphors

....

Q30: When a words describes a sound, for example crash, bang or crunch.

a) Synecdoche
b) Onomatopoeia
c) Inversion

....

Q31: Describe one thing as another.

a) Free verse
b) Onomatopoeia
c) Metaphor

....

Q32: This is when a word that should be used to describe a speaker in a poem or a character is attributed to an object instead.

a) Sibilance
b) Transferred epithet
c) Minor sentences

....

Q33: This is when the normal word order is subverted to place emphasis on a specific word that the poet wishes to highlight to the reader.

a) Inversion
b) Rhythm
c) Parenthesis

....

© HERIOT-WATT UNIVERSITY

Q34: Poems written with no real pattern to them.

a) Metaphors
b) Free verse
c) Inversion

....

Q35: These are sentences which do not contain a main verb.

a) Sibilance
b) Synecdoche
c) Minor

....

Q36: This is when a writer adds extra information to the middle of a sentence or phrase using brackets, commas or dashes.

a) Parenthesis
b) Free verse
c) Onomatopoeia

....

Q37: This is where the part of something is used to refer to the whole.

a) Synecdoche
b) Transferred epithet
c) Minor sentences

The following lines are extracts from the poem 'Tam o' Shanter' by Robert Burns.
But to our tale:—Ae market-night,
Tam had got planted unco right;
Fast by an ingle, bleezing finely,
Wi' reaming swats, that drank divinely;
And at his elbow, Souter Johnny,
His ancient, trusty, drouthy crony;
Tam lo'ed him like a vera brither—
They had been fou for weeks thegither!
The night drave on wi' sangs and clatter;
And ay the ale was growing better:
The landlady and Tam grew gracious,
wi' favours secret, sweet and precious:
The Souter tauld his queerest stories;
The landlord's laugh was ready chorus:
The storm without might rair and rustle,
Tam did na mind the storm a whistle.

Care, mad to see a man sae happy,
E'en drown'd himsel' amang the nappy!
As bees flee hame wi' lades o' treasure,
The minutes wing'd their way wi' pleasure:
Kings may be blest, but Tam was glorious.
O'er a' the ills o' life victorious!

But pleasures are like poppies spread,
You sieze the flower, its bloom is shed;
Or like the snow falls in the river,
A moment white—then melts for ever;
Or like the borealis race,
That flit ere you can point their place;
Or like the rainbow's lovely form
Evanishing amid the storm.—
Nae man can tether time or tide;
The hour approaches Tam maun ride;
That hour, o' night's black arch the key-stane,
That dreary hour he mounts his beast in;
And sic a night he taks the road in
As ne'er poor sinner was abroad in.

The wind blew as 'twad blawn its last;
The rattling showers rose on the blast;
The speedy gleams the darkness swallow'd
Loud, deep, and lang, the thunder bellow'd:
That night, a child might understand,
The Deil had business on his hand.
See if you can identify the techniques used within the poem.

Q38:

'Tam had got *planted unco right;*'

a) Metaphor and word choice
b) Personification and word choice
c) Word choice and onomatopoeia

Q39:

'Wi' *reaming* swats, that *drank divinely*'

a) Onomatopoeia and metaphor
b) Alliteration and word choice
c) Alliteration and repetition

Q40:

'His *ancient, trusty, drouthy* crony;'

a) List
b) Repetition
c) Word choice

Q41:

'Or like the snow falls in the river,
A moment white—then melts for ever;'

a) Enjambment
b) Free verse
c) Simile

Q42:

'Nae man can tether time or tide;'

a) Assonance
b) Word choice
c) Metaphor

TOPIC 3. SCOTTISH TEXTS: POETRY

Q43:

'The rattling showers rose on the blast;'

a) Colon
b) Onomatopoeia
c) Exclamations

....

Q44:

'The speedy gleams the darkness swallow'd'

a) Rhyme
b) Personification
c) Word choice

....

Q45:

'Loud, deep, and lang, the thunder bellow'd:'

a) Word choice
b) List
c) Rhythm

4.1 Introduction

Your knowledge of the Scottish Texts that you have studied in class as part of the Higher course is tested in the Critical Reading paper. This part is worth 20% of your overall grade and it accounts for 20 out of the 40 marks that comprise the Critical Reading paper.

For this section of the Critical Reading paper, an extract from your novel, drama, short story or a poem, or part of one of the poems, you have studied will be printed with accompanying questions. For example, Norman MacCaig's 'Memorial' was published in full in 2016; however only part of Carol Ann Duffy's 'Mrs Midas' was published as it is a relatively long poem.

10 out of the 20 marks are available for questions directly related to the printed extract or poem.

10 out of the 20 marks are available for comparing the printed extract to the rest of the novel or drama. For short stories and poems, the bulk of the marks will come from comparing the printed extract to the other texts.

In this topic we will look at key vocabulary that will feature in some of the questions, how to answer the final comparison questions and how you can use your notes to prepare for the final examination.

4.2 Key vocabulary

In the final exam, understanding the questions and what you are expected to do to answer these questions can be difficult. Students may know their texts well, but using their knowledge to answer the question correctly is what they can find challenging.

Below are some key terms that repeatedly arise in questions.

These key words should help you understand how to use your knowledge to answer the questions.

For example, if the question has the word 'analyse' in it, then you know that you are being asked to identify the uses of technique in the text and discuss the effect. If you begin to explain what you understand from the use of the technique, then you are not answering the demands of the question.

- Analyse
  discuss the effect of the use of techniques such as alliteration, imagery, word choice etc.
- Effective conclusion
  the final lines of the extract summarise the writer's main points or help us understand the theme more clearly
- Example
  give a quotation or reference from the text
- Explain
  make something clear by describing it in detail
- Ideas
  the main concerns, issues or thoughts explored in the text; the main themes and points raised by the writer

TOPIC 4. SCOTTISH TEXTS: EXAM TECHNIQUES

- Main ideas/concerns
  these are the themes and concerns that a writer explores in a text
- Mood/Atmosphere
  something that a writer creates in a text through the use of techniques
- Poetic technique
  this term encompasses all the techniques that a writer uses when creating a poem, such as alliteration, rhyme, simile, single sentences
- Tone
  relates to the way in which a line would sound if it was read aloud, often revealing the attitude of the writer towards the subject matter; it is a way we can gauge a writer's thoughts and opinions
- Writer/poet's use of language
  this refers to any techniques used in a poem by the writer

Key vocabulary: Exam techniques definitions Go online

Q1: Match the definitions with the exam techniques vocabulary.

Definition	Term
Something that a writer creates in a text through the use of techniques.	Effective conclusion
Discuss the effect of the use of poetic techniques such as alliteration, imagery, word choice.	Mood/atmosphere
Refers to any techniques used in a poem by the writer.	Analyse
The final lines of the poem summarise the writer's main points or help us understand the theme more clearly.	Poetic technique
This term encompasses all the techniques that a writer uses when creating a poem, such as alliteration, rhyme, simile, single sentences.	Main ideas/concerns
These are the themes and concerns that a writer explores in a text.	Writer/poet's use of language

© HERIOT-WATT UNIVERSITY

4.3 Exam technique

This section provides information about how to answer questions in the two parts of the Scottish Text section of the Critical Reading paper; the analysis of the printed extract and the final comparison question. General points which apply to prose, drama and poetry are followed by specific points relating to poetry. The section ends with a practice activity.

4.3.1 Analysis of the printed extract

When answering questions in the Scottish Texts section of the exam, it is good to know how the SQA applies the marks available for each question.

In general:

- bullet point your answers - there are no marks given for re-wording the question, which only wastes time, so the more time you can save here, the more you can spend on the final comparison question or writing your critical essay;
- there should be one bullet point for each of the marks available, e.g. if the question is for 2 marks, then you should make two points;
- look for some of the key vocabulary above to help you understand how to use your knowledge of the text to answer the question, e.g. if the question contains the word 'analyse', the question will be asking you to discuss the writer's use of technique to create effect in a particular part of the poem.

Question types

As explained above, there are only a certain number of questions the exam can ask you; it is up to you to work out what is being asked and how to answer it.

1. 'Explain how...'
   This type of question is fairly simple to approach. It is asking you to *quote* and *explain*. Unlike National 5, you will NOT get a mark for the *quotation*, but instead your marks will be rewarded based on the quality of your (correct) *explanation*. In a two mark question you can get two marks for a full and detailed *explanation*, but, in practice, you are better to *quote* and *explain* two separate items.

2. 'Analyse how...'
   This is also fairly simple to approach. It is asking you to identify a *technique, quote* and *analyse* the effects of this technique in relation to the question. Again, unlike National 5, you will NOT get a mark for the *quote*, but instead your marks will be rewarded based on the quality of your (correct) *analysis*. In practice, if it is a two mark question, you are better to *quote* and *analyse* two separate items.

3. 'Identify...'
   This type of question will usually be asked alongside and 'Analyse how' or 'Explain how' - you simply need to name the technique use and/or give an example of the specified technique, then analyse it for effect.

4. 'Explain...'

This is slightly different to 'Explain how...'. Usually you will be asked to 'Explain any [number] of reasons' for/against something; you simply need to bullet point a reason/explanation for each of the number of marks available.

5. 'By referring to...'

Again, this question is asking you to *quote* and *explain*. When you see the words 'by referring to', it is a clear request to refer to the extract and quote from it. Like 'Explain how...' and 'Analyse how...' you need to deal with more than one point.

Read through some examples for the above question types to see how you should answer. These examples are short extracts just so you can see how to lay out your answer; in the actual SQA exam the questions will focus on longer extracts of text, from which you will need to select relevant examples.

Examples

1.

Question

Like a volcano fit to explode, the man stormed into the dark, quiet room.

Analyse how the writer's use of language shows that this character is dangerous. (2)

Answer

- Quote 1: 'Like a volcano'
- Explanation 1: This simile gives us connotations of immense and unpredictable power, suggesting the man's explosive and violent potential. (1)
- Quote 2: 'stormed'
- Explanation 2: This word has connotations of violent and unpleasant weather - usually destructive, like flooding, or hurricanes - therefore reinforces the man's dangerous character. (1)

2.

Question

When he first came to town, all the people gathered round. They bought him drinks and food; they brought him blankets and fuel; they brought their elders and wisemen to see him. He was pleased.

Explain what point the writer is making about the man. (3)

Answer

- Point 1: Everyone came to see to the man and to listen to him. (1)
- Point 2: They brought him things to eat and to drink. (1)
- Point 3: The man was very happy with their response. (1)

© HERIOT-WATT UNIVERSITY

3.

Question
She felt as though she had a dark cloud that hovered over her head, drenching her thoughts with grief, soaking her ambitions with misery, drowning her hopes in the deluge. Identify the tone used here and analyse how he writer conveys the character's emotions. (2)

Tone: depressed and miserable

Answer

- Quote 1: 'drenching'
- Explanation 1: This word choice gives connotations of being utterly covered in water, emphasising that her depression completely envelopes her. (1)
- Quote 2: 'drowning her hopes'
- Explanation 2: This metaphor suggests that her depression is destroying her, causing her great anguish and threatening her life, much like someone drowning would be near death and in pain and hysterics. (1)

....

4.

Question
Cave sat at the piano and pondered. He stared at his reflection in the black polished wood, thinking of how best to tap into his inner muse; he feared, at times, that she had deserted him, that he would never again be able to reveal his soul. He feared he would never be true again. He feared that he would become a fake, a phony, become everything he despised.

By referring to this extract, explain how it is made clear that Cave is worried that he has lost his skills. (2)

Answer

- Quote 1: 'pondered'
- Explanation 1: This word choice suggests he is thinking deeply about his future, almost like he is obsessed. (1)
- Quote 2: 'feared'
- Explanation 2: Repetition of this word emphasises how much it is on his mind - he is fully occupied with his worries. (1)

More questions from the 2015 Higher paper can be found using the link:
http://www.sqa.org.uk/pastpapers/papers/papers/2015/NH_English_all_2015.pdf

TOPIC 4. SCOTTISH TEXTS: EXAM TECHNIQUES

Poetry

Understanding questions

At Higher level, most of the questions will ask you to analyse the poet's use of technique. There will be very little (if any) marks awarded for simply showing understanding. These questions may still crop up from time to time though, so it is best to be prepared for all eventualities.

Understanding questions will ask you to show your knowledge of the writer's main points, ideas, concerns or themes.

These questions usually contain the following phrases.

- Explain how...
- Explain why...
- Explain what...

Analysis questions

The bulk of the marks available for poetry in the Scottish Texts section of the Critical Reading paper will be for analysing the poet's use of techniques. These questions will ask you to identify the use of poetic techniques in the poem and explain their effect.

At Higher level there are no marks awarded for identifying the technique. Marks are awarded for the discussion of the effect of the technique only.

- A more basic comment will receive 1 mark.
- A detailed/insightful comment could receive up to 2 marks.

These questions usually contain the following phrases.

- By referring to at least two examples, analyse how...
- Analyse how...
- Explain the use of...
- By referring closely to lines..., discuss the speaker's attitude to...

Attitude, tone, mood and atmosphere.

Sometimes you may come across a question which asks you to identify the attitude of the poet, or tone, mood or atmosphere of a poem.

You will then be asked to explain how this is conveyed to you by quoting and explaining.

- No marks are allocated for identifying attitude, tone, mood or atmosphere.
- No mark is allocated for quotation.
- One mark is allocated for a more basic comment. (1+1)
- Two marks can be allocated for a more detailed comment. (2)

© HERIOT-WATT UNIVERSITY

Evaluation questions

When we discuss something as being *effective* then we simply mean that it has succeeded in achieving its purpose.

There are two types of evaluation question that appear.

1. Effective openings.
2. Effective conclusions.

Effective openings

The openings lines of a poem can be effective in a number of ways:

- they establish the mood/tone/atmosphere of the poem;
- they introduce the main idea of the poem;
- they introduce the main theme(s) of the poem.

Example

Here are the opening lines from 'A Poet's Welcome to His Love Begotten Daughter'.

Thou's welcome, wean; mishanter fa' me,
If thoughts o' thee, or yet thy mamie,
Shall ever daunton me or awe me,

The opening of lines of this poem are effective in the following ways:

- 'Thou's welcome, wean;'

  Burns opens the poem by whole heartedly welcoming his daughter into the world, expressing gratitude and joy towards her. Using the Scots word 'wean' to refer to her also conveys his affection and love for her. This is effective as it establishes the loving and joyous mood of the poem.

- 'Mishanter fa' me'

  Burns is calling upon misfortune to descend on his life if he at any point shows embarrassment or shame over the birth of his daughter. This is effective as it introduces us to one of the main ideas of the poem, which is that Burns does not believe that the birth of his daughter is something that he should be ashamed of just because she is, in the eyes of the community, illegitimate.

- 'If thoughts o' thee, or yet thy mamie,
  Shall ever daunton me or awe me,'

  Burns claims that he wants misfortune to befall his life if he is ever ashamed of his daughter or her mother. Here he makes it very clear that he will not be pressured by the kirk or the community into feeling guilty for what he has done as he does not agree with their prejudice towards him or his daughter. This is effective as it introduces us to one of the main themes of the poem which is Burns' criticism of the prejudice which exists in society at the time, which is borne from extreme religious observance and a lack of compassion for one's fellow man.

Effective conclusions

The concluding lines of a poem can be effective in a number of ways:

- they can sum up the poet's points or bring about some kind of climax;
- they can make the poet's final comments about the theme;
- they can make reference to the title or the beginning of the poem.

Example

Here are the closing lines from 'A Poet's Welcome to His Love Begotten Daughter'.

I'll never rue my trouble wi' thee,
The cost nor shame o't,
But be a loving father to thee,
And brag the name o't

The closing of lines of this poem are effective in the following ways:

- 'And brag the name o't'

  By using the word 'brag', Burns conveys his pride at the birth of his daughter and says that he will boast about her as a doting father should. This is effective as this is where the poem reaches its climax and the unconditional love that Burns feels for his daughter, which he expresses throughout the poem, cannot be doubted.

- 'I'll never rue my trouble wi' thee,
  The cost nor shame o't,'

  Burns explains that he will never complain about his daughter, regardless of the expense another child will cost him, or the prejudice that he will face because of the circumstances of her birth. This is effective as it sums up Burns' point about the theme of the poem: he will not allow the narrow-mindedness of society to diminish the love he feels towards his daughter.

- 'loving father'

  Here Burns declares his intentions emphatically: he will love his daughter unconditionally and always be someone she can rely on. This is effective as it refers back the title: the title of the poem makes it clear that this is a very personal piece of writing addressed specifically to his daughter. In addition, in the title the daughter is described as 'love-begotten', showing that she was borne out of love, which he repeats in the closing lines of the poem.

4.3.2 Final comparison question

The last question often frightens candidates, but can be answered with little stress if you know your text(s) well and follow a formula.

You know it worth 10 marks, so break your response down into five small paragraphs for 2 marks each, as follows:

1. Identify the area of commonality. (2)

    The commonality is identified in the question asked (i.e. 'Discuss John's role within the family.') Using the words of the question as a driver, you should ensure you do three key things in this first section:

    i. You should then make a comment on this feature/aspect by discussing and referring to the extract.
    ii. Then make a comment on the feature/aspect outwith the extract (from another point in the novel/story or in another story).
    iii. If possible you should then make an over-arching statement binding these two comments together, showing what they have in common: this will help you to show your overall knowledge of the texts, which is essentially what this question type asks you to do.

2. Quote and analyse from extract. (2)

    This is the easiest way to pick up marks in the last question. You need to quote from the example twice and analyse each quote separately. You should make sure this is relevant to the question asked.

3. Make detailed reference to the rest of your text(s) in relation to the question. (4)

    You can either do this by making three detailed comments about a key event/character/theme (depending on question) for two marks each (2) + (2) + (2), or by making six more general comments for one mark each (1) + (1) + (1) + (1) + (1) +(1).

Let's look at an SQA past paper question in order to exemplify the above. The example question and answer relates to 'Sunset Song' by Lewis Grassic Gibbon.

Example

Question

Discuss how Grassic Gibbon presents Chris's growing to maturity in this extract and elsewhere in this novel. (10)

Answer

1. Identify the area of commonality. (2)

    The idea of Chris maturing is explored throughout this novel. In this extract we see Chris reflecting on the death of her mother, realising that her mother killed herself to escape the misery of her life. At this point, Chris begins to realise she loves the land more than anything else. Gibbon explores this idea elsewhere in the novel, notably the way in which Chris handles her deteriorating relationship with Ewan. He uses this idea throughout the novel to convey the themes of the land, endurance and community. (2)

2. Quote and Analyse from extract. (2)

'Oh mother, mother, why did you do it?' - Here we can see, specifically through the repetition of 'mother' how distraught and lost Chris feels; here she realises that she has to take control of her life. (1)

'The rooks cried out across the upland parks of Don far beyond the tunnels of the years' - Here we can see Gibbon using imagery to convey the theme of endurance: rooks often symbolise intelligence, and their colour (black) has connotations of death, suggesting that it is this moment that Chris fully awakens as an independent woman, that her mother's death has acted as a catalyst for her development. (1)

3. Make detailed reference to the rest of your text(s) in relation to the question. (6)

The idea of Chris growing to maturity is covered many more times in the novel. The depiction of her torn affections (one for the land, one for her intellectual desires) suggests the theme of duality: these two Chris' represent the two aspects of her country, Scotland and Britain, and the struggled to find belonging in both. Ultimately she chooses 'the land', chooses to be with 'her people' and is associated with the song 'The Flowers of the Forest' so, when she matures to a decision, chooses 'Scottish Chris'. (2)

You would then write about another key event in which you thought Chris' growth to maturity explored key ideas in the text, just like above. (2)

You would then again write about another key event in which you thought Chris' growth to maturity explored key ideas in the text, just like above. (2)

Layout

There is no single way of laying out this answer. You can write it as a paragraph or you can use bullet points.

Bullet points may help you to formulate your answer in a more coherent way and it may help ensure that you have covered all the areas required to get the 10 marks available.

All the examples above have been written using bullet points.

You may find it helpful to use headings to lay out your answer also. These would be:

- Commonality
- Extract
- Other Poem(s)

Using these headings will help to ensure that you have covered all the areas required to receive the 10 marks available.

The following is an example answer in response to this question using 'Holly Willie's Prayer' as the printed text and 'To A Mouse' as the other text.

Example

Question

Highlight the parts of the answer for which you think the candidate is awarded the mark.

1. Commonality
2. Comments on the printed extract.
3. Comments on another text.

Answer

1. Commonality

   In all of his poetry, Burns tries to engage with his readers by provoking an emotional response in them, usually with regards to themes of love, suffering and injustice that he explores in his poetry. This is true of 'Holy Willie's Prayer' as in this poem he exposes the hypocrisy in the character of Willie, provoking a sense of anger in the reader. Similarly, in 'To a Mouse', Burns' re-telling of discovering that he had destroyed of mouse's nest while ploughing a field provokes a sense of sympathy in the reader, not only for the mouse, but also for mankind as a whole as he uses the mouse's suffering as a representation of human suffering at large.

2. Comments on the printed extract.

   > But, Lord, remember me and mine
   > Wi' mercies temp'ral and divine

   Here, Willie has just confessed to being driven by sexual desire and fornicating with a number of young women, something that, as part of the Elect within Calvinism, he should be immune too. He calls upon God to punish all those who commit the deadly sin of lust, yet he feels that he should be shown compassion. Burns uses the word 'temp'ral' to show how Willie expects God to be benevolent in his case as he is, in his own eyes, a true follower of the faith, yet has succumbed to evil, just like those in society that he condemns. This arrogance provokes anger and resentment in the reader as they side with Burns regarding the moral irresponsibility of believing in divine predestination.

3. Comments on another text.

   > - Wee, sleekit, cowrin, tim'rous beastie,
   >   O, what a panic's in thy breastie!

   In 'To A Mouse', Burns opens the poem by addressing the mouse directly. He uses a list of adjectives to describe the mouse, including 'cowrin' and 'tim'rous' which creates the impression that the mouse is frightened and scared, provoking sympathy from the reader for it. In addition, Burns uses the word 'panic' to describe the state the mouse is in, emphasising the mouse's vulnerable position to the reader, showing it to be weak and defenceless, which again provokes sympathy for it.

- The best-laid schemes o' Mice an' Men
  Gang aft agley,
  An' lea'e us nought but grief an' pain,
  For promis'd joy!

As the poem continues, Burns identifies further with the mouse and its fight for survival. He concedes that both man and animal have to plan in order to live successfully, but that these plans 'gang aft agley', meaning that they are helpless against fate, provoking empathy from the reader as they too understand the frustration of future planning be usurped by destiny and fortune. Furthermore, Burns describes feelings common to both man and beast, such as 'grief' and 'pain'. Here he identifies with the plight of the mouse further as he understands that these feelings are universal and not just felt by humankind. This provokes empathy in the reader as they too identify with the feelings the mouse must go through and can understand the challenges that it must face in order to survive.

- But Och! I backward cast my e'e,
  On prospects drear!
  An' forward, tho' I cannot see,
  I guess an' fear!

Towards the end of the poem Burns reflects on the wider message of the poem. He recognises that the mouse's feelings of anxiety and worry are borne from the instant disruption to its plans: unlike man, the mouse does not worry about the future but only lives in the present. This provokes anxiety in the reader as we too understand the concern and nervousness the speaker feels with regards to being fully prepared for the future. Burns uses the exclamations to emphasise the speaker's feelings of apprehension with regards to preparing for an unknown future and this provokes a similar feeling of disquiet in the reader as they too can identify with that situation.

Poetry

The final question in the Scottish Texts section is for 10 marks and it will ask you to compare the printed poem (or extract) to at least one other poem in the set (or parts of the poem not printed). For full marks, you must deal with at least one other poem in the set which is not printed.

The question will give you a particular idea to focus your answer on: it may ask you to show how the poems are linked thematically, or through ideas, or by a particular technique.

- With regards to Norman MacCaig, the question may ask you to focus on ideas of human suffering in his poetry.

- With regards to Carol Ann Duffy, you may be asked to discuss her use of poetic form to create characters.

- With regards to Robert Burns, you may be asked to look at how he condemns some of the religious prejudice that was present in society during his time.

- With regards to Liz Lochhead, you may be asked to look at the ways in which she explores difficult relationships in her work.

- With regards to Sorely MacLean, you may be asked to discuss the theme of time in his poetry.

- With regards to Don Paterson, you may be asked to explore the fragility of human life in his work.

When marking your answer, the SQA follow the guidance below:

- 2 marks for commonality;
- 2 marks for quotation and comment on the printed text;
- 6 marks for reference to (quotation) and comment on another poem in the set.

Again, there are no marks awarded for simply quoting from the printed text or any other poem in the set.

Commonality

Commonality means to look at the similarities between the printed poem (or extract) and other poems in the set with regards to a particular focus highlighted in the question.

Example

In the 2016 Higher paper, Burns' 'A Poet's Welcome to His Love-Begotten Daughter' was the printed text.

The final 10 mark question read as follows:

Discuss Burns' treatment of the religious and/or moral concerns of his time in this, and at least one other, poem.

In this poem Burns criticises those who judge his innocent baby because she was born out of wedlock. He scorns those who, because of their religious prejudice, think that he should be embarrassed by his daughter and declares his unfaltering love for her.

This links to 'Holy Willie's Prayer' as, in this poem, Burns criticises puritanical religious and moral conventions of the time through the speaker of the poem, Willie. Willie presents himself as a fully committed Calvinist believer, but this is soon undermined by revelations from Willie regarding his feelings of lust, something which, as a true Calvinist and part of the 'elect' he should not succumb to.

An example of how to write about the commonality of these two poems in response to the 2016 Burns question is as follows.

> Example
>
> Commonality
>
> Many of Burns's poems focus on religious hypocrisy and the prejudice that extreme religious belief can breed. This is certainly true in 'A Poet's Welcome to His Love-Begotten Daughter' as he clearly criticises those who judge his innocent new born daughter because she was born illegitimately. He does not understand their disgust at his daughter just because she was born out of wedlock; the love he has for her is unwavering. Similarly, Burns criticises the extreme views of the Calvinist faith in 'Holly Willie's Prayer' where he creates a hypocritical character who firstly extols his devotion to God and his purity of character, before revealing that he often sins by succumbing to his lustful thoughts.

Quotation and comment on printed text

The quotation and comment must be relevant to the focus of the question.

Remember: No marks are awarded for quotation alone.

- You can use one quote with a very detailed comment. (2)
- Or you can use two quotations with a more basic comment. (1+1)

The following is an example of how to quote and comment from the printed text in answer to the 2016 Burns question.

> Example
>
> Extract
>
> > And tho' your comin' I hae fought for,
> > Baith kirk and queir;
> > Yet, by my faith, ye're no unwrought for
> > That I shall swear!
>
> In this part of the poem, Burns uses the word 'fought' to describe the struggle he has had with the church and his community with regards to their acceptance of the birth of his daughter. 'Fought' implies that he has had to deal with a lot of resistance from those around him, showing them to be completely prejudiced as his daughter is an innocent party in this. Furthermore, he uses the exclamation at the end to emphasise his love for his child and shows that he is happy to battle with those around him to ensure that his daughter is accepted into society as he sees love as being more important that religious prejudice.

Reference and comment on other texts

Again, the references or quotations from other poems in the set must be relevant to the focus of the question.

Remember: There are no marks awarded for quotation only.

2 marks can be awarded each quotation and detailed/insightful comment. (2+2+2)

1 mark can be awarded for quotation/reference and more basic comment. (1+1+1+1+1+1)

Either approach is equally valid and depends on your knowledge of the set poems.

The following is an example of how to quote and comment from the printed text in answer to the 2016 Burns question.

Example

- I'm here, a pillar o' Thy temple
  Strong as a rock,
  A guide, a ruler and example
  To a' Thy flock.—

At the beginning of the poem, Willie purports to be part of the Elect, chosen by God to go to heaven no matter how they behave on Earth. Burns uses imagery to show the hypocrisy in Willie's belief in his devotion and faith to God. By describing Willie as a 'pillar', it shows that Willie believes that he fully supports the religion and is a model practitioner. Burns also uses a list to convey Willie's arrogant attitude, something which within itself is a sin. Willie lists himself in a number of leadership roles to show how he is at the forefront of the religion and an example to others of how to resolutely follow the teachings of God.

- But yet—O Lord—confess I must—
  At times I'm fash'd wi' fleshly lust;

Later in the poem, Willie admits to having sinful thoughts himself, even those he is part of the Elect and seemingly innocent. Burns uses the word 'But' to show that there will be a change in the line of thought in the poem: up until this point, Willie has been praising himself for being a firm follower of the faith and condemning all those who succumb to immorality. Yet here Willie admits to having feelings of 'fleshly lust', showing him to be just as immoral as those he judges. Again, Burns brings to light the hypocrisy that he witnessed within Calvinist believers at the time.

- Thy strong right hand, Lord, make it bare
  Upo' their heads!
  Lord, visit them, and dinna spare,
  For their misdeeds!

Willie then goes on to pray to his God to show sinners no mercy. The use of exclamations emphasises the strength of Willie's plea: Willie does not believe in showing compassion to those who are not part of the elect. He firmly believes that they should be punished for their sins. This is humorous and ironic as Willie has just confessed to the same sin that he now condemns, further emphasising the duplicity that exists within religion and the unfounded piousness that believers have.

Preparation for the final question

It is always good to know 3-4 quotations from each of the poems in the list.

These quotations do not have to be long. What is important is their significance to the poem and that there are many points you can make with regards to them in line with the main ideas in the poem, the use of poetic technique and the themes of the poem.

Example

Here is a quotation from 'Tam O'Shanter'.

But pleasures are like poppies spread,
You seize the flower, its bloom is shed;

This is a good quotation to use as there are many points that you can make. You could:

- discuss the use of the word 'But' to indicate a turning point in the poem;
- discuss the word choice of 'pleasures' and 'seize';
- discuss the use of imagery;
- show how these lines relates to the idea of the fleetingness of gratification.

Usually, the opening and closing lines of a poem are good to know as that is where the poet is introducing the main ideas of the text and making his/her concluding thoughts and reflections about the themes.

It is also good to know some key quotations from throughout the poem.

Preparation

When preparing for this exam, it is best to know your poems well.

No doubt you will have annotated copies or notes from class to review, but there are also a number of websites that you can access that have notes on the poems or online exercises that you can complete.

If you missed the teaching of one of the poems in class, or find one of them particularly challenging then there are two things you can do.

1. Read the poem yourself and respond to it as an individual.
   - What do you think it is about?
   - What are the themes?
   - Can you identify and explain the use of any poetic techniques?
2. Research this particular poem on the internet to help secure your knowledge and understanding of the poem.
   - Try searching for the title of the poem with the word 'analysis'. You may find that this takes you to a number of suggested sites that provide notes on the use of poetic techniques in the poem.

It is also helpful to *annotate* you poems. This means highlighting the use of techniques straight on to the page.

The best way to do this is using an A3 copy of the text. Below is an example of an annotated text.

Note-making

Annotate the text, highlighting poetic techniques and making notes about their effect and how they link to the themes of the poem.

It is a good idea to colour-code your annotations so that they are easily identifiable when you review your notes.

For example, you could use a colour key, e.g.

- red for form and structure;
- green for rhythm and rhyme;
- blue for sound;
- purple for imagery;
- yellow for word choice;
- orange for sentence structure.

If you cannot annotate your poems, you can always organise your notes using the above key as a guide and simply bullet point examples of the poetic techniques with an explanation of their effects.

Making links between the poems

If you have colour-coded your annotations and notes on the individual poems, you can start to collate your notes under these headings.

For example, under the heading 'Imagery', you can make a short bullet-pointed list of all the different examples of imagery from across the set.

It is also a good idea to make notes on where there are inter-connecting themes.

For example, death is a prominent theme in Norman MacCaig's poetry. When making notes, use 'Death' as a heading and then list 1 or 2 quotations from each of the poems in the set that links to this theme.

4.3.3 Practice activity

Past/specimen paper question practice	Go online

Using these notes as guidelines, you should practise past paper or specimen paper questions (these are freely available on the SQA website) on your set Scottish texts. You can check the answers yourself or ask your teacher to help you.

4.4 End of topic test

End of Topic 4 test	Go online

Inn 2015, the SQA published 'To A Mouse' as the printed text for Robert Burns.

This paper can be found using the following link:

http://www.sqa.org.uk/pastpapers/papers/papers/2015/NH_English_all_2015.pdf

Below is an answer to each of the printed questions with two sample answers. However, one answer is of better quality than the other.

See if you can choose the one which best answers the question.

To a Mouse, On turning her up in her Nest, with the Plough, November 1785 by Robert Burns

> Wee, sleekit, cowrin, tim'rous beastie,
> O, what a panic's in thy breastie!
> Thou need na start awa sae hasty,
> Wi' bickering brattle!
> I wad be laith to rin an' chase thee,
> Wi' murd'ring pattle!
>
> I'm truly sorry Man's dominion
> Has broken Nature's social union,
> An' justifies that ill opinion,
> Which makes thee startle,
> At me, thy poor, earth-born companion,
> An' fellow-mortal!
>
> I doubt na, whyles, but thou may thieve;
> What then? poor beastie, thou maun live!
> A daimen icker in a thrave
> 'S a sma' request:
> I'll get a blessin wi' the lave,
> And never miss't!
>
> Thy wee bit housie, too, in ruin!
> It's silly wa's the win's are strewin!
> An' naething, now, to big a new ane,
> O' foggage green!
> An' bleak December's winds ensuin,
> Baith snell and keen!
>
> Thou saw the fields laid bare an' waste,
> An' weary Winter comin fast,
> An' cozie here, beneath the blast,
> Thou thought to dwell,
> Till crash! the cruel coulter past
> Out thro' thy cell.

That wee bit heap o' leaves an' stibble,
Has cost thee monie a weary nibble!
Now thou's turn'd out, for a' thy trouble,
But house or hald,
To thole the Winter's sleety dribble,
An' cranreuch cauld!

But Mousie, thou art no thy lane,
In proving foresight may be vain:
The best-laid schemes o' Mice an' Men
Gang aft agley,
An' lea'e us nought but grief an' pain,
For promis'd joy!

Still thou are blest, compar'd wi' me!
The present only toucheth thee:
But, Och! I backward cast my e'e,
On prospects drear!
An' forward, tho' I canna see,
I guess an' fear!

Q2: Look at lines 1—18.

Analyse how Burns establishes at least two aspects of the speaker's personality in these lines. *(4 marks)*

A) Wee, sleekit, cowrin, tim'rous beastie,
O, what a panic's in thy breastie!

The speaker shows that they have an affectionate character. Burns shows this through the use of the exclamation to show that the speaker is concerned for the well-being of the mouse as he seems to worry about the state of shock the mouse is in. In addition, he addresses the mouse as 'beastie', which is diminutive, showing that he is not frightened or appalled by eh mouse but that he recognises its defencelessness.

At me, thy poor, earth-born companion
An' fellow-mortal!

The speaker shows that they are a sympathetic and compassionate person by showing an awareness of the mouse's vulnerability. By using the word 'poor' to describe the mouse, the speaker shows that they understand that the mouse has met with unfortunate circumstances, one which the speaker sympathises with. By calling the mouse a 'companion', he shows an affinity with the mouse, identifying with its plight and fight for survival.

B) Wee, sleekit, cowrin, tim'rous beastie,
O, what a panic's in thy breastie!

The speaker shows that the mouse is scared and frightened as its home has just been disturbed by the poet. He uses lots of adjectives to show how the mouse is terrified of the speaker, yet the speaker does not want to cause it any harm. This shows the speaker is caring.

© HERIOT-WATT UNIVERSITY

At me, thy poor, earth-born companion
An' fellow-mortal!

The speaker recognises that both the mouse and himself are 'mortal', showing that he understands why it is so scared of him. This shows that the speaker is understanding as he shows concern for the mouse and realises the similarities between the two of them.

....

Q3: Look at lines 19-36.

By referring to at least two examples, analyse how Burns creates pity for the mouse and its predicament. *(4 marks)*

A) Thy wee-bit housie, too, in ruin!
Its silly wa's the win's are strewin!

Burns describes the mouse's nest as small and explains that it has been destroyed by him. This creates pity for the mouse as he shows us how the mouse will now have nowhere to shelter from the harsh conditions of winter. In addition, by calling the next a 'housie' he creates sympathy for the mouse as he makes it seem almost human, leading us to identify more strongly with the mouse.

An' weary Winter comin fast,
An' cozie here, beneath the blast,
Thou thought to dwell,
Till crash! the cruel coulter past
Out thro' thy cell.

The poet then goes on to describe some of the challenges the weather will pose for the mouse during the winter. He uses alliteration with 'weary Winter' to show how getting through it will be a struggle for the mouse, creating pity for it. Moreover, he uses onomatopoeia to describe the sounds that the mouse will hear during the winter: 'crash' has connotations of something colliding, creating tensions and anxiety. This makes us feel sorry for the mouse as the winter may bring some significant challenges for the mouse to survive.

B) Thy wee-bit housie, too, in ruin!
Its silly wa's the win's are strewin

Burns uses word choice to underline the smallness of the mouse's nest: he describes it as 'wee' and 'silly', emphasising to us the fragility of its home and conveying the vulnerability of the mouse to the reader, creating pity and sympathy for it. Furthermore, Burns humanises the mouse by calling the mouse's nest a 'housie': this immediately draws parallels between the mouse's life and the reader's life, making use feel sorry for the mouse and sympathising with the loss of its home.

An' weary Winter comin fast,
An' cozie here, beneath the blast,
Thou thought to dwell,
Till crash! the cruel coulter past
Out thro' thy cell.

The poet then goes on to detail the challenges the mouse will face with the ensuing winter. He uses alliteration to bring the reader's attention to some of the hardships that the mouse will face and overcome. For example, he uses 'weary Winter' to underline the difficulty and hopelessness posed by the coming cold, He also uses alliteration on the plosive 'b' to emphasise the harshness of the climate during winter that the mouse will need to shelter itself from. Moreover, he uses onomatopoeia and an exclamation to highlight the danger that the weather poses, implying that the mouse will be scared by the unpredictability of the weather and the storms.

....

Q4: Look at lines 37-48.

Explain how the final two verses highlight the contrast between the speaker and the mouse. (2 marks)

A) 'Still thou are blest, compared wi'me!'

The poet begins the final verse with an exclamation with which he proclaims that the mouse is much more fortunate than he. He describes the mouse as being 'blest' despite the challenges the mouse will face which he has discussed earlier in the poem. This shows how he believes that mankind's struggle to survive is more demanding and difficult than the mouse's. He then goes on to explain how humans are conscious of the past and future, unlike the mouse, which brings with it its own unique anxieties and stresses. Burns' point is that this conscious ability to feel regret about past actions and to worry about what the future might hold sets us apart from animals as they are driven solely by their survival instinct.

B) In the second last verse the poet discusses the shared experiences that humans and animals share: both cannot control fate and both will experience a mixture of grief and joy in their lifetime.

In the last verse the poet shows that he is envious of the mouse as it does not have to think about its past actions or worry about what the future will bring, as mankind has to do.

- Setting
  this is where and when the event(s) takes place
- Structure
  the way in which a text's plot is put together
- Theme
  the bigger idea that is explored in a text; the overall message created

Prose

- Characterisation
  the way in which writers portray their characters
- Climax
  tension or conflict in a text is at its highest point
- Description
  an account of a character's physical appearance, or the setting, or of an incident
- Ideas
  beliefs and concepts conveyed in a text
- Key incident(s)
  important episodes which move the plot on, build to a climax, or are important in developing our understanding of character and/or theme
- Language
  words and rhetoric used by the author to create characters and description
- Narrative technique
  the way in which the story of the text is told (1st/3rd person narrative)
- Plot
  what happens in the text in chronological order
- Setting
  this is where and when the event(s) takes place
- Structure
  the way in which a text's plot is put together
- Turning point
  when a significant change takes place regarding the plot or character development

Prose Non-fiction

- Ideas
  beliefs and concepts conveyed in a text
- Narrative voice
  this includes narrative stance (1st/2nd/3rd person) and the use of the active or passive form of the verbs
- Stance
  a writer's point of view on a particular topic
- Style
  the way in which the text is written, including such aspects as narrative stance, techniques and tense
- Selection of material
  examples, quotations, ideas, anecdotes and information that the writer has included for effect
- Use of evidence
  statistics, facts and anecdotes used to support or exemplify a writer's point

Poetry

- Content
  what is included in a text
- Ideas
  beliefs and concepts conveyed in a text
- Imagery
  literary devices used by a writer to create pictures and images in the reader/audience's mind
- Rhyme
  when two words sound similar
- Rhythm
  the pattern of syllables in each line of a poem
- Sound
  devices used in poetry to create particular oral effects (alliteration/assonance/onomatopoeia)
- Structure
  the way in which a text's plot is put together
- Theme
  the bigger idea that is explored in a text; the overall message created

- Tone

    this relates to the way in which a line would sound if it was read aloud, often revealing the attitude of the writer towards the subject matter; it is a way we can gauge a writer's thoughts and opinions

- Word choice

    words are chosen to emphasise particular ideas or evoke certain emotions in the reader

Media

- Characterisation

    the way in which writers portray their characters

- Dialogue

    words spoken by characters in a text

- Editing

    how scenes and/or camera shots are spliced together to create effect; this can also be referred to as a montage sequence

- Key sequence

    important series of shots or scenes in a film or TV text

- Mise-en-scène

    props and scenery to create shots and background for a film and TV text

- Music/sound

    used to create effects in film and TV texts

- Special effects

    additional effects added to a scene in a film or text

- Plot

    what happens in the text in chronological order

- Special effects

    additional effects added to a scene in a film or TV text

- Setting

    this is where and when the event(s) takes place

- Use of camera

    different camera shots used to create effects in film and TV texts

Key vocabulary: Definitions

Select the correct key term for each definition.

Drama

Q1: This is where and when the event(s) takes place.

a) Climax
b) Setting
c) Characterisation

Q2: What happens in the text in chronological order.

a) Plot
b) Structure
c) Setting

Q3: The bigger idea that is explored in a text; the overall message created.

a) Conflict
b) Key scene
c) Theme

Q4: Disagreement between characters, or within a character.

a) Conflict
b) Climax
c) Characterisation

Q5: Tension or conflict in a text is at its highest point.

a) Structure
b) Climax
c) Setting

Prose

Q6: An account of a character's physical appearance, or the setting, or of an incident.

a) Description
b) Plot
c) Characterisation

....

Q7: The way in which authors portray their characters.

a) Description
b) Setting
c) Characterisation

....

Q8: Episodes which move the plot on, build to a climax, or are important in developing our understanding of character and/or theme.

a) Key incident(s)
b) Structure
c) Climax

....

Q9: The way in which the story of the text is told ($1^{st}/3^{rd}$ person).

a) Setting
b) Narrative technique
c) Plot

....

Q10: Words and rhetoric used by the author to create characters and description.

a) Language
b) Narrative technique
c) Ideas

Prose Non-Fiction

Q11: Statistics, facts and anecdotes used to support or exemplify a writer's point.

a) Use of evidence
b) Selection of materials
c) Ideas

....

Q12: A writer's point of view on a particular topic.

a) Ideas
b) Style
c) Stance

....

Q13: Examples, quotations, ideas, anecdotes and information that the writer has included for effect.

a) Ideas
b) Selection of material
c) Use of evidence

....

Q14: The way in which the text is written, including such aspects as narrative stance, techniques and tense.

a) Style
b) Ideas
c) Narrative voice

....

Q15: Beliefs and concepts conveyed in a text.

a) Use of evidence
b) Selection of material
c) Ideas

TOPIC 5. CRITICAL ESSAY

Poetry

Q16: The form in which the poem is written, for example, sonnet, free verse etc.

a) Content
b) Structure
c) Ideas

....

Q17: The bigger idea that is explored in a text; the overall message created.

a) Theme
b) Content
c) Ideas

....

Q18: The patterns of syllables in each line of a poem.

a) Rhyme
b) Sound
c) Rhythm

....

Q19: Literary devices used by a writer to create pictures and images in the reader/audience's mind.

a) Imagery
b) Word choice
c) Ideas

....

Q20: Devices used in poetry to create particular oral effects (alliteration/assonance/onomatopoeia).

a) Imagery
b) Word choice
c) Sound

Media

Q21: Important series of shots or scenes in a film or TV text.

a) Setting
b) Plot
c) Key sequence

....

Q22: Words spoken by characters in a text.

a) Dialogue
b) Plot
c) Characterisation

....

Q23: Props and scenery to create shots and background for a film and TV text.

a) Key sequence
b) Mise-en-scene
c) Setting

....

Q24: How scenes and/or camera shots are spliced together to create effect.

a) Editing
b) Key sequence
c) Mise-en-scene

....

Q25: Used to create effects in film and TV texts.

a) Special effects
b) Sound
c) Music

5.3 Preparation

> **Learning objective**
>
> By the end of this section, you should be able to:
>
> - identify key evidence in a text you have studied;
> - make notes on key evidence.

Before you can even hope to write a good essay, you need to know your text well.

Although you will have studied your chosen text in class and will have lots of notes from your teacher, you still need to review and organise them so that they are useful and easy to learn for the exam.

For all texts it is good to have a bank of key quotations or evidence that you can manipulate into lots of different essay questions.

Drama/Prose (including Non-Fiction)

For both of these genres, it is important that you pick key quotations that you can link to a variety of overarching topics, like characterisation, theme, key incident and symbolism.

You must also be able to explain the significance of your chosen quotation, what you understand from it and how the writer has used techniques within it to convey particular aspects of the text to the audience/reader.

To do this, it is useful to make up sets of quotations cards. These cards should have the quotation clearly at the top, with an act or chapter reference. Below this quotation should be a series of bullet points where you make notes about the quotation's context, your understanding of it, the use of techniques within it and what overarching topics it links to.

Example

```
                          Quotation

                                       Name of text, act/chapter reference

  • Context
  • Understanding
  • Analysis of techniques
  • Links to over arching topics within the novel/drama
```

Here is an example from 'Othello' by William Shakespeare, a popular play studied at Higher level for this part of the course

Example

> 'Valiant Othello, we must straight employ you
> Against the general enemy Ottoman—'
>
> Act 1, Scene 3
>
> - Context
>   - This is said by the Duke to Othello.
>   - He is greeting Othello to the senate meeting.
>   - This is ironic as Othello is there to be charged with being a traitor by Brabantio, yet the Duke is more interested in making sure that Othello raises the army in time to destroy the attacking Ottoman Empire.
> - Understanding
>   - Othello is clearly a well-respected army general, showing him to be very successful within his position.
>   - Othello is someone the Duke can rely on in order to ensure the safety of Venice.
> - Analysis of techniques
>   - 'Valiant': brave, courageous, strong, a leader, lacking in fear or doubt.
>   - 'straight employ' suggests that there is no hesitation with regards to Othello's ability to deal with the imminent threat.
> - Links to over arching topics within the novel
>   - Delayed character revelation: the high praise from the Duke is in direct contrast with what we hear about Othello from Iago and Brabantio earlier in this act.
>   - Theme of appearance verses reality - Othello does not live up to the expectation set up by the Duke's favourable opinion of Othello.
>   - Theme of racism: Othello occupies a very influential position within Venice, a predominantly white society, and, being a former slave, this admiration that is bestowed on him from others within Venetian society shows how his achievements and successes have helped him overcome any prejudice he may encounter because of his heritage.

Here is an example from 'The Cone Gatherers' by Robin Jenkins, a popular novel studied at Higher level for this part of the course.

© HERIOT-WATT UNIVERSITY

Example

> 'Why then did he hate the cone gatherers and wish to drive them away? Was it because they represented goodness, and himself evil?'
>
> Chapter 10, page ...
>
> - Context
>   - Roderick is on his way to visit the cone gatherers with cake in the beach hut.
>   - He encounters Duror on the way there and cannot bring himself to go any further.
> - Understanding
>   - Roderick is scared of Duror and associates his character with evil: he sees him as sinister and menacing.
>   - Roderick recognises the intense feelings of hatred that Duror has for the cone gatherers.
>   - Roderick understands that Duror's attitude towards the cone gatherers is irrational and unreasonable.
> - Analysis of techniques
>   - The repeated use of questions by Jenkins shows confusion in Roderick's character: he does not understand the motivation behind Duror's contempt for the cone gatherers and this frightens him.
>   - 'Drive' has connotations of force and strength, implying that Duror's hatred will overpower the cone gatherers and bring about their ruin.
> - Links to over arching topics within the novel
>   - Duror is characterised here as an intimidating and daunting character, emphasised by the fear that Roderick feels when he enters the scene.
>   - This is further emphasised by Roderick's reflections on Duror's mental state: he wonders if Duror has been driven mad by his hatred of the two cone gatherers and is actually on his way to the beach hut to kill them both.
>   - Links to theme of good vs. evil: Roderick identifies Duror with evil, symbolising him as a character filled with contempt and lacking in compassion.
>   - Links to the theme of good vs. evil: Roderick identifies the cone gatherers with the forces of good because he does not understand what they have done to deserve the mistreatment they receive from Lady Runcie Campbell and Duror. He admires them for the way in which they deal with the adversity that they contend with.

> *(continued)*
>
> - Links to over arching topics within the novel
>   - Links to the theme of class and social injustice: despite being part of the upper class, he does not agree with the way the cone gatherers are treated just because they are working class. He believes that everyone should be treated fairly and this is shown in the gift of cake that he is bringing to the beach hut.

This novel is also popular for the Scottish Texts section too. Texts written by Scottish authors can be used in both sections of the Critical Reading exam, as long as they are from different genres. For example, you can write an essay on 'The Cone Gatherers' and answer textual analysis questions on Carol Ann Duffy poetry. Many schools in Scotland teach different genres from the set text list in order to give students a choice of texts to do in both sections of the exam.

Here is an example from 'A Modest Proposal' by Jonathan Swift, a non-fiction text that could be studied at Higher level for this part of the course.

Example

> 'It is a melancholy object to those who walk through this great town or travel in the country, when they see the streets, the roads, and cabin doors, crowded with beggars of the female sex, followed by three, four, or six children, all in rags and importuning every passenger for an alms.'
>
> Lines ...
>
> - Context
>   - In the opening of the piece, Swift uses descriptive language to set the scene with regards to poverty present in Ireland in the 1700s.
>   - He describes the gulf between the rich and poor, highlighting the number of children that are growing up in impoverished conditions.
> - Understanding
>   - At this time, many families in Ireland were suffering from living in poverty and relied on begging in the street in order to survive and provide for their family.
>   - As a result, Ireland's streets were often busy with mothers and their children asking for money, which, in the eyes of the gentry, was a frustrating and repelling sight.

> *(continued)*
>
> - Analysis of techniques
>
>   - Word choice of 'melancholy': has connotations of sadness and sorrow, implying that the poverty which overtly existed in the streets of Ireland at that time is depressing and should incite misery in those who witness it.
>   - List of public places where beggars can be found emphasises the depth of the problem that existed in Ireland at the time: by making it seem like it was everywhere, Swift implies that it is an endemic problem.
>   - Word choice of 'crowded': this suggests that Ireland's public places are congested with beggars, highlighting the extent of the problem.
>   - List of the number of children that accompany women beggars on the street emphasises to the reader that it is families that are starving in Ireland and not just individual adults. This creates sympathy for the impoverished of Ireland at the time.
>   - Word choice of 'rags': Swift creates sympathy and pity for the families in Ireland living in poverty as he highlights the poor state of their clothing, showing them to be living in deprived conditions.
>   - Word choice of 'importuning': this has connotations relating to pestering and harassing. Here Swift is being satirical: the upper classes are frustrated with the beggars that exist in Ireland, yet Swift has clearly described them previously as people who are completely dispossessed and in need of help.
>
> - Links to over arching topics within the novel
>
>   - Links to the theme of poverty: Swift describes the scene in Ireland at the time in such a way as to illicit an emotional response from the reader and create sympathy for those living in poverty at the time.
>   - Links to the use of satire: opening of the piece conveys the speaker as a caring individual, genuinely concerned regarding the wellbeing of those more destitute parts of society. This is very quickly undermined in what follows, highlighting the hypocrisy which exists in society and the lack of humanity shown towards the poor by the wealthier classes.

Poetry

Poetry is different from prose and drama because of the concentrated use of techniques. In a poem, a poet has a limited amount of space in which to get his ideas across, unlike a novelist or dramatist. As a result, they have to pack lots of techniques into their work in order to explore a theme, create a character, describe a scene, or explore an idea.

For poetry, there will be a number of key quotations that you can choose that will link to the poet's main ideas and/or theme.

You must also be able to explain the significance of your chosen quotation, what you understand from it and how the writer has used techniques within it to convey meaning to the reader.

To do this, it is useful to make up sets of quotations cards. These cards should have the quotation clearly at the top. Below this quotation should be a series of bullet points where you make notes about the quotation's context, your understanding of it, the use of techniques within it and what overarching topics it links to.

Example

> Quotation
>
> Name of poem, line number

- Context
- Understanding
- Analysis of techniques
- Links to over arching topics within the text

Here is an example from 'To His Coy Mistress' by Andrew Marvell, a popular poem studied at Higher level for this part of the course.

Example

> 'Had we but world enough, and time,
> This coyness, lady, were no crime.'
>
> To His Coy Mistress, lines 1 and 2

- Context
  - Opening of the poem, which sets the scene and describes the predicament of the speaker: his outward show of affection is not reciprocated by his intended lover.
- Understanding
  - The speaker wishes he had more time in which to woo his lady and would happily take his time over courting her properly if time was not a factor.

(continued)

- Analysis of techniques

    - Use of the conditional tense 'Had': by beginning the poem in the conditional tense, the poet makes it clear to us the speaker regrets the current situation and wishes things were much different. He craves for the circumstances to be more in his favour.
    - Use of the collective personal pronoun 'we': assumes that there is a relationship established between the speaker and the addressee and that his feelings are reciprocated by her. Speaker appears possessive in character.
    - Parenthesis: isolates the phrase 'and time', slowing down the rhythm of the line to reflect the desire he has for time to slow down and for there to be much more of it. It also places emphasis on the word 'time' itself, conveying to the reader it's importance to the speaker and to resolving his problem of being intimate with the addressee.
    - Rhyme of 'time' and 'crime': this intrinsically ties these two concepts together in this poem and emphasises the speaker's opinion that to waste time is an offence to humanity.
    - Word choice of 'coyness': the addressee of the poem is being shy and timid, something which the speaker is not too fond of or impressed by.
    - Word choice of 'lady': by referring to the addressee as a 'lady' we can infer that perhaps she is not from the upper classes of society at the time but trying to emulate the way in which aristocratic females behaved at the time in order to improve her self-esteem and image.
    - Word choice of 'crime': Marvell uses this word to show how the speaker seems personally aggrieved by the addressee's behaviour and views it as a social injustice.

- Links to over arching topics within the novel

    - Characterisation of the speaker: he is portrayed as sinister and sneaky, prone to bouts of hyperbole. He seems to flatter the addressee, yet hints towards his frustration at her resistance to his charms.
    - Theme of time: here the speaker sees time as elusive, something that they cannot control, therefore they should waste no time and make the most of the time they have.
    - Theme of gender inequality: there is a clear division between the roles of men and women during the 16th century. This male speaker is empowered to speak freely of his desires for the addressee, yet her defiance and opposition to his flirtations frustrate him.

© HERIOT-WATT UNIVERSITY

Film and TV

Media texts are different from the other three genres discussed above because of the visual element. In a Film or TV text, you will be discussing the use of cinematographic techniques within scenes and sequences to create meaning and impact. Such techniques will include mise-en-scene, sound, lighting, camera angles and editing. Directors use these techniques in media texts to create characters, build tension, create genre markers and create key scenes.

For Film and TV texts, you will mainly be discussing key scenes and sequences, therefore making notes in preparation for the exam will be slightly different from the three more popular genres above.

You must be able to explain the significance of your chosen scene or sequence, what you understand from it and how the director has used techniques within it to convey meaning to the audience.

To do this, it is useful to make up sets of evidence cards. These cards should have the scene or sequence clearly identified at the top. Below this should be a series of bullet points where you make notes about what's happening in the scene or sequence, your understanding of it, the use of techniques within it and what overarching topics it links to.

Example

Scene or Sequence

Name of media text

- Description of action
- Understanding
- Analysis of techniques
- Links to over arching topics within the text

Here is an example from 'Psycho' directed by Alfred Hitchcock, a popular film studied at Higher level.

Example

> Parlour Scene (first 2 minutes)
>
> Psycho
>
> - Description of action
>   - The scene opens with Norman and Marion entering the parlour where Norman has brought a light supper for her to eat after she has arrived late at the Bates Motel. Norman stays with Marion while she eats and indulges in conversation.
> - Understanding
>   - This scene is used to establish the character of Norman, as well as convey the vulnerability and precarious position in which Marion finds herself.

(continued)

- Analysis of techniques

    - Mid-shots and close-ups: these are used in order to establish her reaction to entering the room. The first mid-shot is when she enters and she seems calm. There is then a close-up of a stuffed owl with its wings spread. This shot is angled downwards, so that it looks like the owl, a bird of prey, is threatening Marion, positioning Marion as its prey. There is then another mid-shot of Marion, showing her reaction to seeing the owl and she seems quite disturbed, which is in complete contrast to the mid-shot as she entered. This creates tension and suspense as it suggests that Marion is in an exposed position and is not safe.
    - Mid-shot: this is used to establish the setting. It shows the parlour to be quite cramped with little room to move. It also shows how most of the space is taken up with furniture, albeit very little. This suggests that Marion may be trapped in some way and that there is little room for escape from her current situation. It could also reflect the mental state of Norman: a mind cluttered with irrational and insane thoughts that stop him from functioning normally as part of society.
    - Lighting: There is a single lamp in the parlour and it acts as the only light for the whole scene. This casts half of Norman's face in shadow, symbolising his split personality and the tension between his well-mannered self and his uncontrollable jealousy. The lighting also creates powerful shadows behind Norman of both himself and objects in the room. These seem to loom over Marion, creating tension and suspense. In contrast, Marion is sitting much closer to the lamp meaning that she is bathed in light, making her appear angelic, suggesting that she is an innocent victim. This is ironic as we know that she is in fact a thief, but there is still the possibility that Marion could correct her mistake and it is clear that she feels guilty about it, showing her to be compassionate and caring.

- Links to over arching topics within the text

    - This scene builds tension and suspense as it presents Norman as a character that behaves in a strange way and is not entirely confident in himself. It suggests that he is not to be trusted.
    - This scene is foreboding as it suggests that, in some way, Norman is a potential threat to Marion and that she is not safe.
    - This scene also establishes the differences in character between Marion and Norman: she is presented as someone who is logical and rational, whereas Norman is portrayed to us as a dark character, one who cannot be trusted and is a bit strange.

TOPIC 5. CRITICAL ESSAY

Preparation: Activity

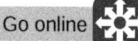

Go online

Here are further examples of quotation/evidence cards that students have created for the texts they have studied, however the notes are all in the wrong order.

Drama

> 'Keep up your bright swords, for the dew will rust them'
>
> Act 1, Scene 2

Q26: The use of the command shows that Othello is authoritative and dominating. He takes the lead in the situation, undermining Brabantio's power and position.

a) Context
b) Understanding
c) Analysis
d) Link to overarching topics

....

Q27: Theme of betrayal: as the words spoken by Othello echo those of Christ in the Bible, we expect the story arch of Othello's character to parallel that of Christ. Like Christ, Othello has been betrayed by someone he trusts (Iago) and this will eventually lead to a fatal ending.

a) Context
b) Understanding
c) Analysis
d) Link to overarching topics

....

Q28: Brabantio intends to force Othello to go before the Senate as he has married Desdemona without his permission.

a) Context
b) Understanding
c) Analysis
d) Link to overarching topics

....

Q29: Othello shows that he has no intention of being forced to do anything and immediately takes control of the situation.

a) Context
b) Understanding
c) Analysis
d) Link to overarching topics

....

© HERIOT-WATT UNIVERSITY

Q30: This is said by Othello in response to the arrival or Brabantio and his men who have come to confront him about his marriage to Desdemona.

a) Context
b) Understanding
c) Analysis
d) Link to overarching topics

....

Q31: Dialogue: these words parallel those said by Christ when he is arrested by the Roman soldiers. This is symbolic in showing us how Othello is inherently good. This is foreshadowing as it suggest to the audience that he too will have to make sacrifices in order for good to prevail over evil.

a) Context
b) Understanding
c) Analysis
d) Link to overarching topics

....

Q32: Theme of appearance verses reality: Othello appears to be very different from the character described by Iago in the opening of the play. He seems to be well-respected and more powerful than we expected. He seems measured and disciplined, which in complete contrast to the unruly and disobedient character presented to the audience through Iago's dialogue.

a) Context
b) Understanding
c) Analysis
d) Link to overarching topics

....

Q33: Theme of good versus evil: in echoing the words spoken by Christ, Shakespeare aligns Othello as a force for good in the play. He is naturally a good person, acting in the best interests of those around him, making his eventual downfall even more tragic.

a) Context
b) Understanding
c) Analysis
d) Link to overarching topics

....

Q34: He tells Brabantio's men to stand down and to stop threatening him.

a) Context
b) Understanding
c) Analysis
d) Link to overarching topics

Prose

> 'Screaming in sympathy, heedless of the danger of being shot, Calum flung himself upon the deer, clasped it round the neck, and tried to comfort it.'
>
> Chapter 6, page ...

Q35: This scene is ominous as it indicates that there is little Calum can do to escape his fate: he will be a victim of Duror's hate, just like the deer. In addition, the violence with which the deer is murdered will also be experienced by Calum.

a) Context
b) Understanding
c) Analysis
d) Link to overarching topics

....

Q36: 'Screaming': has connotations of pain and fear. This suggests that Calum is shocked by the brutal murder of the deer and completely identifies with it. He suffers its pain, just as much as the deer does.

a) Context
b) Understanding
c) Analysis
d) Link to overarching topics

....

Q37: This is a key incident in the novel which exposes the depth of Duror's corruption and his hatred of Calum.

a) Context
b) Understanding
c) Analysis
d) Link to overarching topics

....

Q38: He is completely horrified by what he has just witnessed, showing him to be vulnerable and in danger of becoming a victim of Duror's revulsion of him.

a) Context
b) Understanding
c) Analysis
d) Link to overarching topics

....

Q39: Links to theme of good vs. evil: Calum is clearly symbolic of good as he is innocent and devoid of sin, much like the deer. He will be sacrificed, just like Christ, in order to purge Duror of his evil ways.

a) Context
b) Understanding
c) Analysis
d) Link to overarching topics

Q40: Symbolism of the deer: the deer is symbolic of Calum as, like Calum, it is vulnerable and hunted by Duror. It's tragic ending foreshadows what will happen to Calum because of his innocence and Duror's disgust of Calum's disabilities.

a) Context
b) Understanding
c) Analysis
d) Link to overarching topics

Q41: Parenthesis: this gives us more information about the way in which Calum reacts to the deer's death. It tells us that he acted without any consideration for his own safety and was not aware of the potential danger he was in. This portrays Calum as being as weak and defenceless as the deer. He too is a target for Duror, just as the deer was.

a) Context
b) Understanding
c) Analysis
d) Link to overarching topics

Q42: This describes Calum's reaction to witnessing the deer being slaughtered by Duror during the Deer Drive where the cone gatherers were acting as beaters for the hunters.

a) Context
b) Understanding
c) Analysis
d) Link to overarching topics

Q43: Calum is characterised as helpless and susceptible to the danger that Duror poses.

a) Context
b) Understanding
c) Analysis
d) Link to overarching topics

Q44: Calum is intrinsically linked with nature and animals, showing him to be compassionate and kind.
a) Context
b) Understanding
c) Analysis
d) Link to overarching topics

Non Fiction

'That the remaining hundred thousand may, at a year old, be offered in the sale to the persons of quality and fortune through the kingdom; always advising the mother to let them suck plentifully in the last month, so as to render them plump and fat for a good table.'

Lines ...

Q45: Black humour: Swift makes reference to the idea that mothers must increase the breastfeeding of their children in the last month before they are sold to ensure that they are 'plump' and 'fat' for prospective buyers. This is humorous as it suggests that the adults will be preoccupied with the successful sale of children as meat, undermining the horror of the cannibalism that underpins the whole proposal.

a) Context
b) Understanding
c) Analysis
d) Link to overarching topics

....

Q46: Links to the theme of poverty: Swift, through the suggestion of this absurd proposal, exposes the prejudice that exists towards those living in poverty, especially children who are portrayed as defenceless and at the mercy of the adults who are in charge. In doing so he emphasises the vulnerability of these children, forcing the upper classes to face the inconsiderate way that they treat these young people.

a) Context
b) Understanding
c) Analysis
d) Link to overarching topics

....

© HERIOT-WATT UNIVERSITY

UNIT 2. CRITICAL READING

Q47: Parenthesis: tells us that children could be used as a source of food from one year of age. This highlights how young some of the children living in poverty are. Children at this age are completely dependent on adults for their well-being, something that the upper classes ignore in their condemnation of the poor. This emphasises the lack of sympathy the upper classes have towards these children.

a) Context
b) Understanding
c) Analysis
d) Link to overarching topics

....

Q48: This is the speaker's proposal: sell children to rich households as meat. This comes after many statistics about the number of poor children in Ireland at the time, as well as rejecting all other possible ways in which children could possibly contribute effectively to society.

a) Context
b) Understanding
c) Analysis
d) Link to overarching topics

....

Q49: 'quality' and 'fortune': Swift uses these words to describe the more affluent members of society. In using the word 'quality', we can infer that some of the wealthier classes do not value the poor and see them as a scourge upon society, not a part of it. Using the word 'fortune' reminds us that those born in to money are lucky and should appreciate their position. Swift is hinting at the fact that they could very easily be living in poverty should they not have been born in to a privileged family.

a) Context
b) Understanding
c) Analysis
d) Link to overarching topics

....

Q50: The speaker's idea to solve the poverty crisis amongst children in Ireland during the 1700s. He is being satirical as he does not actually perceive this as a solution: what he does is expose the prejudice and lack of compassion of the upper classes who are offended more by the children being visible on the street, rather than the fact that they are living in poverty.

a) Context
b) Understanding
c) Analysis
d) Link to overarching topics

....

TOPIC 5. CRITICAL ESSAY

Q68: Close-up zoom: the camera is in front of Marion and zooms in past her shoulder to the black figure that appears behind the shower curtain. This creates dramatic irony as the audience is aware of the imminent attack and fear for Marion's life.

a) Description
b) Understanding
c) Analysis
d) Link to overarching topics

....

Q69: This scene creates lots of tension and suspense as Marion's death signals her disappearance and will undoubtedly have consequences for Norman and his mother.

a) Description
b) Understanding
c) Analysis
d) Link to overarching topics

....

Q70: Jump cuts: during the attack there are a series of jump cuts of close-ups of Marion's face as she is stabbed. This use of editing reflects how frantic and violent this attack is. Marion is clearly in shock and this creates sympathy for her.

a) Description
b) Understanding
c) Analysis
d) Link to overarching topics

....

Q71: This scene builds tension and suspense as it is full or dramatic irony: Marion is unaware of the danger she is in while the audience can see it taking place. Marion is oblivious to the imminent attack, making the attack even more dramatic and horrific.

a) Description
b) Understanding
c) Analysis
d) Link to overarching topics

....

Q72: Non-diegetic sound: there are short, high pitched notes played on string and brass instruments, creating a screeching and unpleasant sound. It creates a mood of hysteria, reflecting how frenzied the attack is, showing Mrs Bates to be completely out of control.

a) Description
b) Understanding
c) Analysis
d) Link to overarching topics

© HERIOT-WATT UNIVERSITY

Preparation: Note-making

Consider the text you have studied for the critical essay section of the Critical Reading paper.

Depending on the genre, use the templates as a guide to help you organise your notes and prepare for final examination.

TOPIC 5. CRITICAL ESSAY

5.4 Criteria

> **Learning objective**
>
> By the end of this section, you should be able to:
>
> - understand the criteria used by the SQA to grade your essays;
> - use this to evaluate your own critical writing.

When teachers and SQA markers assess your critical essay, they use a set of criteria which they apply to your essay in order to award it a grade.

Understanding the criteria by which your essay will be assessed is vital in helping you understand what should be included in the content of your essay and how it should be written.

The link below will take you to a copy of the marking grid used to assess critical essays at Higher level (correct as of April 2016). These grids are regularly updated so check the SQA website for an updated version:
http://www.sqa.org.uk/pastpapers/papers/instructions/2015/mi_N5_English_all_2015.pdf

There are four broad general areas against which you essay is assessed:

1. Understanding.
2. Analysis.
3. Evaluation.
4. Technical accuracy.

Knowing what each of these broad general areas includes will help you to write a more focused essay.

Understanding

In your essay you must show understanding of the following:

1. The text.

    You must show that you understand what happens in the text, the characters, the plot and the central concerns.

    For example, if you have studied Othello and begin to discuss the lack of love he had for his wife, then you show a lack of understanding of the play, particularly the theme of love and the relationship between Othello and Desdemona. While it could be argued that he does in fact hate Desdemona at certain points in the play, most of his jealous feelings are derived from a position of love and it is clear at the end of the play that he kills her in order to ensure justice is upheld, not because he despises her.

2. The themes and main ideas.

    You should be discussing themes throughout your entire essay, even if you are discussing other aspects of the text, such as character or poetic technique. You should be linking the points you make about these other aspects to theme throughout your essay.

© HERIOT-WATT UNIVERSITY

3. The question.

You must also show that you have understood the question. This will show the examiner that you understand how your chosen texts relates to the demands of the question and what it asks you to focus on.

For example, if the question asks you to choose a poem in which the use of poetic form helps to clarify and develop the central concerns, and you respond to this by writing on To His Coy Mistress, then you show a lack of understanding of the question and your chosen text. The poem may be a dramatic monologue with a particular form and structure which aids our understanding of the central concerns, but it is not the most prevalent technique employed by the writer and it would be very difficult to write a whole essay solely on the poetic form of this poem. The dense imagery and use of word choice in To His Coy Mistress are more effective in developing the theme.

Analysis

When analysing a text in your essay, you must discuss how a writer or director uses techniques and stylistic devices to create meaning and effect.

For example, when writing about a prose text, you could discuss how a writer uses description to create a vivid image of a character. This description may include an effective simile. You should be able to discuss this simile and how it helps us to understand aspects of the character's personality.

Example

In Othello, Iago warns Othello about jealousy, calling it 'the green-ey'd monster'. When discussing this piece of evidence in an essay, you could comment on Shakespeare's use of personification in order to convey jealousy as a wild, uncontrollable emotion which has devastating effects on the individual. You could also discuss the symbolism in using the colour 'green', a colour we associate with envy and jealousy.

In addition, you could use this to discuss Iago's manipulation of Othello and how, in saying this, he wishes to present himself as a true friend of Othello, despite the audience knowing that he wants to bring about Othello's downfall, thus creating dramatic irony.

Evaluation

When you evaluate a text in a critical essay you must show how the evidence/quotation you have discussed links to the question you are answering.

For example, you may be able to discuss the use of religious imagery in To His Coy Mistress, but of what relevance is it? Is the question about how poetry can help us think differently about something? If so, then you must link the analytical comments that you have made about the use of this imagery to the idea that it makes us think about time in biblical terms and consider the continuum of history, from B.C.E. to C.E.

Similarly, if writing about Psycho, you may be able to discuss the use of sound in the shower scene, but of what relevance is it? Is the question about how the director creates tension and suspense in a film? If so, then you must link the analytical comments that you have made about how sound is used to the way in which it creates tension and suspense in the audience.

Technical accuracy

This area covers the following:

1. Spelling
2. Grammar
3. Sentence construction
4. Punctuation
5. Structure
6. Paragraphing

At the very least, your teacher or the SQA marker should be able to understand your essay and follow your line of thought at first reading. It is assumed that any Higher candidate has a certain level of technical accuracy that is in line with the level of study they are undertaking.

Essays which achieve below a 10

Some essays may achieve less than 50% of the marks available.

These essays do so for the following reasons:

- what you write does not answer the question. For example, the question may ask you to focus on the writer/director's use of setting, but you have focussed solely on the main character;
- analysis and evaluation are weak: you tell the story, rather than make critical points about theme, character, setting, key scene etc.;
- the answer is thin in ideas and is too short as a result.

5.4.1 Descriptors

For each band there are a set of *descriptors* linked to each of the general areas to help teachers differentiate between the different bands.

It is useful to be familiar with these descriptors and what they look like in a practical sense.

Some of the most important areas in the criteria and their descriptors are discussed below.

Understanding

	...knowledge and understanding of text	
Band	Descriptor	What it means
19-20	Thorough	A full and exhaustive knowledge of the text and its central concerns.
16-18	Secure	A firm comprehensive understanding of the text and its central concerns.
13-15	Clear	An accurate knowledge of the text and its central concerns, but lacks some depth.
10-12	Adequate	A satisfactory understanding of the text and its central concerns, but lacks depth and accuracy.

	...textual evidence to support line of thought...	
Band	Descriptor	What it means
19-20	Perceptive selection	Wide ranging and insightful evidence chosen from lots of different parts of the text.
16-18	Detailed	Thorough and comprehensive evidence chosen from many different parts of the text.
13-15	Clear	Accurate and suitable evidence chosen, although some of it may not be as relevant as others.
10-12	Adequate	Satisfactory evidence chosen, although better evidence could have been selected in its place.

	Line of thought that is...	
Band	Descriptor	What it means
19-20	Fluently structured and expressed	Sophisticated with lots of salient points.
16-18	Coherently structured and expressed	Comprehensible with many salient points.
13-15	Clearly structured and expressed	Easy to follow, although lacks some sophistication.
10-12	Adequately structured and expressed	Easy to follow, although it may be a bit simplistic with some superfluous points.

© HERIOT-WATT UNIVERSITY

Analysis

...analysis of the effect of features if language/filmic techniques		
Band	Descriptor	What it means
19-20	Perceptive	Insightful and in depth discussion of techniques' effect and impact.
16-18	Detailed	Thorough and comprehensive discussion of techniques' effects and impact.
13-15	Clear	Accurate understanding shown of the impact and effect of techniques employed, but lacks some depth.
10-12	Adequate	Narrow understanding shown of the impact and effect of techniques employed.

Evaluation

...evaluative stance with respect to the text and task		
Band	Descriptor	What it means
19-20	Committed	Points and comments focus solely on the question and show a depth of understanding of the central concerns of the text.
16-18	Engaged	Clear and detailed involvement with the text that relates to the question.
13-15	Clear	Good engagement with the text in relation to the question, although this is not sustained throughout the essay.
10-12	Adequate	Satisfactory engagement with the text, but lacks depth and is unconvincing in parts.

Technical accuracy has not been included as essays usually pass this if they can be easily understood at first reading.

Criteria: Explanations

Go online

Q73: The explanations of the four broad general areas of criteria are shown in the following table.
Can you link the areas of criteria to the explanations?

	Appertains to what you know about the text in terms of plot, character, setting and theme. You must show understanding of the following: 1. The text. 2. The themes and main ideas. 3. The question.
	When analysing a text in your essay, you must discuss how a writer or director uses techniques and stylistic devices to create meaning and effect.
	When you evaluate a text in a critical essay you must show how the evidence/quotation you have discussed links to the question you are answering.
	This area covers the following: 1. Spelling 2. Grammar 3. Sentence construction 4. Punctuation 5. Structure 6. Paragraphing

Areas of criteria: Analysis, Evaluation, Technical accuracy, Understanding.

TOPIC 5. CRITICAL ESSAY

Criteria: True and false   Go online

Q74: Your essay must answer the demands of the question.

a) True
b) False

....

Q75: The evidence you choose to analyse and support your line of thought needs to be relevant to the question.

a) True
b) False

....

Q76: There is no need to discuss themes in your essay unless the question specifically asks you to.

a) True
b) False

....

Q77: The structure of your essay and the way you organise your ideas is not important.

a) True
b) False

....

Q78: When you evaluate evidence, you should make links to the plot of the text.

a) True
b) False

....

Q79: In the marking criteria, it states specifically that you have to have a clear line of thought.

a) True
b) False

....

Q80: Essays can fail for weak technical accuracy.

a) True
b) False

....

Q81: When you analyse evidence you should explain what you understand about the text from it only.

a) True
b) False

Criteria: Descriptors	Go online

Below are examples of candidates' critical writing.

Choose the descriptor which you think best characterises the writing.

Q82: 'Othello is greeted with high level of respect when he arrives at the senate:

> Valiant Othello, we must straight employ you
> Against the general enemy Ottoman—

By using the word 'valiant' to address Othello, it is evident that the Duke holds him in high regard and that Othello is thought of very highly, not only by the Duke, but also within the society of Venice. However, this may seem strange to the audience initially: Othello has been brought before the senate by Brabantio to answer the charges he has brought against him and the Duke, before knowing it to be Othello, promised Barbantio that he would punish the perpetrator for his crime. As soon as the Dukes realises it is Othello, he renages on this, showing how important Othello is to the safety and security of Venice.'

Knowledge and understanding of the text is:

a) thorough.
b) secure.
c) clear.
d) adequate.

....

Q83: 'Othello is greeted with high level of respect when he arrives at the senate:

> Valiant Othello, we must straight employ you
> Against the general enemy Ottoman—

By using the word 'valiant' to address Othello, it is evident that the Duke holds him in high regard and that Othello is thought of very highly, not only by the Duke, but also within the society of Venice.'

Textual evidence to support the line of thought is:

a) perceptive.
b) detailed.
c) clear.
d) adequate.

....

Q84: '... it is clear to the audience that Othello is a very admirable and heroic character'

When it comes to line of thought, this answer is:

a) fluently structured and expressed.
b) coherently structured and expressed.
c) clearly structured and expressed.
d) adequately structured and expressed.

....

TOPIC 5. CRITICAL ESSAY

Q85: 'This is further emphasised when the Duke claims that he must 'straight employ' Othello with regards to the threat of the Ottoman Empire, showing that the Duke has no doubt about Othello's skills and leadership as an army general. He is clearly someone that the Duke can rely on, which contrasts with Brabantio's view of Othello.'

Analysis of the effect of features of language is:

a) perceptive.
b) detailed.
c) clear.
d) adequate.

....

Q86: 'This high praise from the Duke establishes Othello as a character who is well thought of within Venetian society; add to this the challenges that his race would have posed for him at the time, and it is clear to the audience that Othello is a very admirable and heroic character.'

The evaluative stance with respect to the text and task is:

a) committed.
b) engaged.
c) clear.
d) adequate.

Criteria: Note-taking

Read over any essays which you have completed already.

Try to identify the areas which you need to improve on in your own critical writing.

Ask yourself the following evaluation questions:

1. Have I shown understanding of how the themes are developed?
2. Have I shown understanding of how your text relates to the question?
3. How relevant is my evidence? Does it support my line of thought?
4. Have I discussed the effect of techniques used by the author/director?
5. Have I linked your evidence back to the question?

You can use these questions to identify strengths and areas for improvement in your own critical essays.

Here is an example of part of a paragraph from a critical essay on 'A Modest Proposal'. The question focuses on how the text makes the reader consider their views on a political, social or ethical issue.

© HERIOT-WATT UNIVERSITY

Example

> Swift opens the piece by setting the scene in Ireland with regards to the social division that exists[1]. He described the poor on the streets of Ireland and the reaction of the more affluent classes to them:
>
>> It is a melancholy object to those who walk through this great town or travel in the country, when they see the streets, the roads, and cabin doors, crowded with beggars of the female sex, followed by three, four, or six children, all in rags and importuning every passenger for an alms.[2]
>
> He describes the gulf between the rich and poor, highlighting the number of children that are growing up in impoverished conditions[3]. At this time, many families in Ireland were suffering from living in poverty and relied on begging in the street in order to survive and provide for their family. As a result, Ireland's streets were often busy with mothers and their children asking for money, which, in the eyes of the gentry, was a frustrating and repelling sight. He uses the word 'melancholy', which has connotations of sadness and sorrow, to imply that the poverty which overtly existed on the streets of Ireland was depressing and should incite misery in those who witnessed it. He then goes on to list the public places where beggars can be found, emphasising the depth of the problem that existed in Ireland at the time: by making it seem like it was everywhere, Swift implies that it is an endemic problem that existed within society at the time[4]. Swift describes the scene in Ireland at the time in such a way as to illicit an emotional response from the reader and create sympathy for those living in poverty at the time.[5]
>
> Notes:
> [1] Understanding of questions
> [2] Selection of relevant evidence
> [3] Understanding of the themes
> [4] Discussion of effect of the technique
> [5] Link back to the question

As you can see, the candidate has used the evaluation questions above to reflect on the strengths of their essay. In doing so they have also identified areas for improvement:

- selection evidence: could have made reference to other parts of the opening of this piece to show how Swift establishes the prejudice attitudes of the upper classes;
- more analysis: could have discussed more, and perhaps more relevant, techniques used within the evidence;
- more evaluation: could have discussed how the sympathy created makes the reader consider how similar attitudes to the poor still exist in contemporary society.

> You could do a similar exercise with any essays you have written thus far using the evaluation questions.

5.5 The question

> **Learning objective**
>
> By the end of this section, you should be able to:
>
> - use the question to structure an essay;
> - identify the key words in the question;
> - identify some of the main question types for each of the genres.

A critical essay is an extended response to a question. The question will often focus on a particular feature of the text, such as the theme, a character, a key scene/incident or the ending.

When writing a critical essay, you should imagine that you are a 'lawyer' building a case in defence of the text that you have studied. You need to gather all your evidence and organise it in a clear and coherent manner.

The question is the key to doing this.

Here is an example of an SQA question for a drama text.

> **Example**
>
> Choose a play in which there is a scene involving a moment of conflict or of resolution to conflict.
>
> By referring to details of the scene, explain how the dramatist presents this moment and discuss how this contributes to your appreciation of the play as a whole.
>
> (SQA Higher paper 2015)

As you can see, the question is set out in two parts. These two parts introduce the demands of the question and direct you to what you have to discuss in your essay.

The first part of the question tells you which text to choose and why. It will provide you with a focus for your essay.

> **Example**
>
> Choose a play in which there is a scene involving a moment of conflict or of resolution to conflict.
>
> (SQA Higher paper 2015)

Above is the first part of the second drama question from the Higher 2015 paper. The key words have been highlighted in bold. These key words should guide you towards formulating your ideas and organising your line of thought.

With regards to the question above, your answer should focus on a scene where there is conflict or conflict resolution within a dramatic text.

The first thing you should do is choose whether or not you will focus on a scene which involves conflict or a scene which involves conflict resolution. For example, you could discuss both these aspects in relation to Othello. You could discuss the conflict between Othello and Desdemona, or when the conflict between these two characters is resolved at the end.

The next thing you need to decide on is the scene you will focus on and why. The 'why' is important as the more specific you can be about this from the beginning, the more focused your essay will be with regards to answering the question. If you chose to write about conflict in a scene, then you could choose Act 3 Scene 4 where Desdemona and Othello are in conflict over the handkerchief. If discussing conflict resolution in the play, you could discuss Act 5 Scene 2, where the conflict is resolved through the deaths of the couple.

The second part helps you to structure the initial ideas from first part and how these should be organised. The second part of the question usually contains two or three instructions.

> Example
>
> By referring to [details of the scene, explain how the dramatist presents this moment] and [discuss how this contributes to your appreciation of the play as a whole.]
>
> (SQA Higher paper 2015)

Above is the second part of the second drama question from the Higher 2015 paper. The instructions given in this question have been identified using square brackets and highlighted in bold. These instructions should guide you towards structuring your ideas.

For example, if you had chosen to write about the conflict between Othello and Desdemona in Act 3 Scene 4 of the play, then the first thing to tackle in this essay would be a detailed analysis of the scene itself, discussing the way in which Shakespeare employed dramatic and poetic techniques to convey the conflict to the audience.

Then the instruction is to show how this conflict is pivotal to the text as a whole. You may choose to go back and analyse the relationship between Desdemona and Othello at the beginning of the play in order to show the extent of the breakdown in their relationship. After doing that you could choose to look at how their relationship develops in the rest of the play, perhaps discussing Othello's physical attack on Desdemona before killing her (and himself) in the denouement.

TOPIC 5. CRITICAL ESSAY

Just to recap:

- The question comes in two parts:
    - The first part tells you which text to choose and why
    - The second part helps to structure your essay.

To help plan your essay using the question, you could do the following:

- underline the key words in the first part of the essay and makes notes about what the focus of your essay will be;
- identify the instructions using square brackets in the second part of the question and use them to help structure your ideas into paragraphs.

NB: some of the questions may feature a phrase similar to this: 'by referring to appropriate techniques'. This acts as a reminder to comment on techniques used within the text and the evidence you use to support your argument. The techniques for each specific genre are listed in the question paper in a box above the questions.

Even if your chosen question does not include this phrase, you will still be expected to discuss a range of techniques exploited in your chosen text.

> Example
>
> Answers to questions on Prose Fiction should refer to the text and to such relevant features as characterisation, setting, language, key incident(s), climax, turning point, plot, structure, narrative technique, theme, ideas, description ...
>
> (SQA Higher paper 2015)

You should not structure your essay around these techniques but discuss how they have been used by the writer throughout the text.

In the Critical Reading paper, you have a choice of three questions per genre, including non-fiction.

These questions can be described as generic: they must cover broad general aspects of the particular genre in order to allow all students to be able to answer at least one of the questions, regardless of the text they have studied.

As a result, there are certain 'types' of question for each genre that appear year after year, although presented differently.

Some of these types have been bullet pointed below. These are a good starting point for organising your evidence. If you do this, you will soon see that some of the evidence can be used in multiple question types.

Drama:

- Theme
- Breakdown in relationships/conflict between characters
- Character (development/evokes our sympathy)
- Theme/central concern/important human issue
- Key scene
- Turning point
- Effective opening and closing scenes

Prose:

- Breakdown in relationships/conflict between characters
- Character (development/evokes our sympathy)
- Theme/central concern/important human issue
- Key incident
- Setting
- Style: symbolism/narrative technique

Prose Non-Fiction:

- Recreates a moment/experience/event
- Structure
- Explores a social/ethical/political issue
- Texts written in a particular form (journalism/essay/biography)
- Writer's use of language to explore central concerns/provoke thought
- Texts written in a particular style (persuasive/satirical)

Poetry:

- Theme/central concern/important human issue
- Atmosphere/mood
- Describes person/place/incident
- Form

TOPIC 5. CRITICAL ESSAY

Film and TV:

- Example of a specific genre
- Conflict
- Theme/central concern/important human issue
- Key scene/sequence (dramatic/build tension/climax/turning point)
- Effective opening and closing scenes

The question: Past paper questions Go online

Below are the past paper questions from the Higher 2014 paper.

See if you can identify the key words in the first part of each question (shown in bold italics in the answers) and the instructions in the second part of the question (shown in square brackets in the answers).

Q87: Choose a play in which a major character's actions influence the emotions of others.

Briefly explain how the dramatist presents these emotions and actions and discuss how this contributes to your understanding of the play as a whole.

....

Q88: Choose a play which explores an important issue or issues within society.

Briefly describe what happens in this scene then, by referring to dramatic techniques, go on to explain why the scene is important to the play as a whole.

....

Q89: Choose a novel or short story in which the method of narration is important.

Outline briefly the writer's method of narration and explain why you feel this method makes such a major contribution to your understanding of the text as a whole.

....

Q90: Choose a novel or short story in which there is a moment of significance for one of the characters.

Explain briefly what the significant moment is and discuss, with reference to appropriate techniques, its significance to the text as a whole.

....

Q91: Choose a non-fiction text which recreates a moment in time.

Discuss how the description effectively recreates this moment and show how important this is to your appreciation of the text as a whole.

....

Q92: Choose a non-fiction text which is structured in a particularly effective way.

Explain how the structure enhances the impact of the writer's message.

....

© HERIOT-WATT UNIVERSITY

Q93: Choose a poem which takes as its starting point a memorable experience.

Discuss how the poet's presentation of the experience helps you to appreciate its significance.

....

Q94: Choose a poem which encourages you to think differently or to understand something in a new way.

Discuss how the poet's ideas and techniques led you to change your thinking or understanding.

....

Q95: Choose a film or television drama in which the setting in time or place is important.

Explain how the film or programme makers use media techniques effectively to create this setting.

....

Q96: Choose a film or television drama where the hero is not completely good and/or the villain is not completely bad.

Explain how the film or programme makers use media techniques to develop the hero and/or villain.

Extension: choose one of the questions above that suits the text you have studied. Use it to make notes about what you would include in your essay and how you would structure it.

TOPIC 5. CRITICAL ESSAY

The question: Note-making

Read over the list of the different 'types' of questions for the genre of text you have studied for the critical essay section.

Use each type as a heading and make notes underneath about specific events or pieces of evidence that you would use in an essay to answer that type of question if it was printed.

A good way of doing this would be to make up mind maps, an example of which for 'Othello' follows.

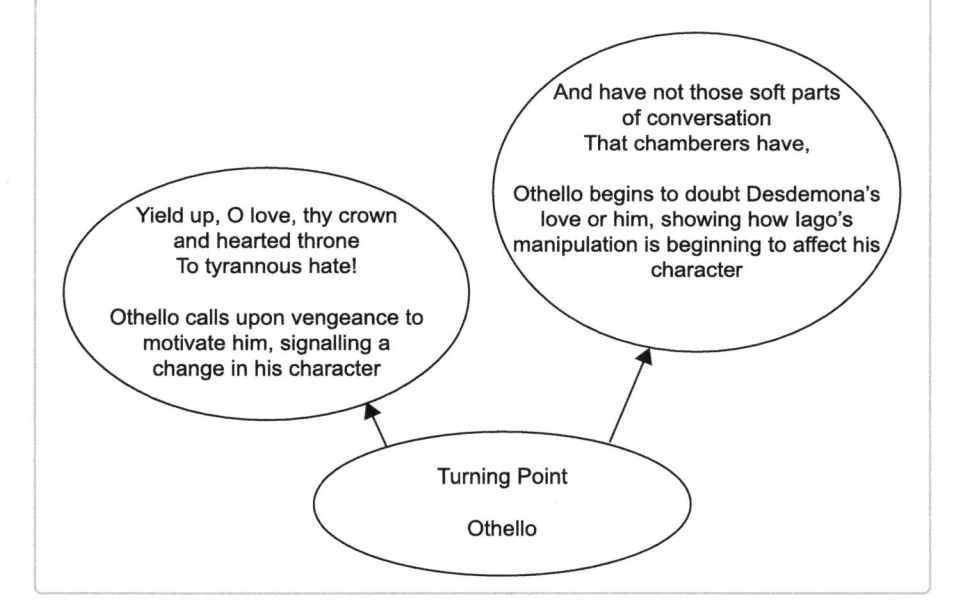

> Yield up, O love, thy crown
> and hearted throne
> To tyrannous hate!
>
> Othello calls upon vengeance to motivate him, signalling a change in his character

> And have not those soft parts
> of conversation
> That chamberers have,
>
> Othello begins to doubt Desdemona's love or him, showing how Iago's manipulation is beginning to affect his character

Turning Point

Othello

5.6 Analysing evidence

Learning objective

By the end of this section, you should be able to:

- understand the term 'analysis' within the context of critical writing;
- identify good quality analysis of evidence.

Candidates often display an in depth understanding of the text they have studied for the critical essay section of the Critical Reading paper. You can confidently tell the story of the text and discuss the themes, but essays often lack in analysis. Candidates fail to discuss the use of techniques and literary devices by the writer in enough depth. If so, the essay becomes narrative: you end up telling the story, rather than making critical points about the way in which the text has been created.

When analysing evidence in a critical essay, you should be using critical terminology to discuss the text and the impact it has on the reader or audience. This terminology differs from genre to genre and is outlined by the SQA in a box above each genre in the question paper.

The way in which we analyse evidence also differs from genre to genre.

Prose/Drama

With extended pieces of writing, like novels, short stories, plays and non-fiction pieces, your analysis of evidence does not need to focus entirely on the quotation and/or reference that you have used to exemplify your point.

You can use your evidence* as a 'jumping off' point to make links to other parts of the text and discuss literary devices used by the writer, such as characterisation, theme, turning point, symbolism ...

Only concentrating on the techniques used in the quotation and/or reference is called 'micro-analysis'. Doing this does not allow you to show the marker that you understand the way in which this particular evidence adds to your understanding of the text as a whole.

*At Higher level, it is entirely possible that you could write an essay without any quotations. Rather than quote directly from the text, you can make detailed reference to it. Essays of this nature can achieve full marks if the references are thoroughly detailed and there is still analysis of the techniques used by the writer, however this is not recommended. It is always good to be able to quote directly from the text.

The following is an example of weak analysis in a prose essay. This essay is focussing on the conflict between Duror and Calum in 'The Cone Gatherers'.

Example

> For Calum the tree-top was interest enough; in it he was as indigenous as squirrel or bird.

Calum is shown to be an expert in climbing trees and is very nimble, despite his disabilities. This proves that he has something positive to contribute to the world and is capable of working to support himself. Jenkins also makes reference to animals, emphasising how natural it is for Calum to be in that environment. Using the animals, Jenkins conveys to us Calum's innocence, linking him to good, but also making him vulnerable to the evil present in the character of Duror.

In the previous example, there are some points made about Calum's character, but these are superficial and lack depth. There is very little mention of Duror and how the conflict between the two is conveyed to the reader.

The following example shows how this same quotation could be used to provide more analysis.

Example

> For Calum the tree-top was interest enough; in it he was as indigenous as squirrel or bird.

Jenkins uses the word 'indigenous' to convey to the reader the ease with which Calum is able to climb the tree, something that Duror fails to do later in the novel. Reaching the 'top' is symbolic of Calum's agility, despite his disabilities, and this only incenses Duror further: it is a direct challenge of Duror's superiority in the wood. This is unsettling for Duror: he views the wood as his 'sanctuary', something which belongs to him, yet Calum shows himself to be more connected to nature than Duror. Jenkins compares Calum to animals throughout the novel to emphasise his innocence and align him with the positive forces of good. This is further highlighted by Calum's attempts to save the rabbits and the sympathy he feels for them; this is in direct contrast to Duror as he is preoccupied with killing and hunting animals, as witnessed in the Deer Drive.

In the previous example, the candidate discusses the use of word choice in the analysis, but also discusses Jenkins' use of symbolism and contrast. In addition, the candidate makes reference to other parts of the novel, making links with the evidence they use. Although the quotation focuses on the characterisation of Calum, the candidate is able to use it to discuss Duror and the way in which both are presented in the opening chapters of the novel.

Poetry

'Micro-analysis' of poetry is very difficult to avoid because of the nature of the genre itself. When analysing evidence from a poem, you must discuss the use of poetic technique and how the poet uses this to create meaning and impact.

Again, if you fail to do this, you will end up explaining what you understand about the line(s) that you have quoted, rather than discuss the effect of the use of poetic techniques.

The following is an example of a poem in an essay. The essay is focussing on the creation of a sinister character.

> Example
>
> Thy beauty shall no more be found,
> Nor, in thy marble vault, shall sound
> My echoing song;
>
> The speaker begins to focus on what will be lost through time, not what the couple could do if they had endless amounts of it. The speaker almost threatens the addressee: he explains to her that her 'beauty' will fade and she will no longer be attractive. This is supposed to persuade her to take advantage of the time they have together and give in to his desires. This is very different from the use of flattery in the first stanza. Marvell uses references to death to take the poem in a much darker and more sinister direction, exposing the speaker as someone who is becoming frustrated by the addressee's self-restraint.

In the previous example, the candidate only explains how the speaker may feel and makes some reference to the poet's use of death imagery, but there is no discussion of the poetic techniques employed by Marvell to create the sinister character of the speaker.

The following shows how this same quotation could be used to provide more analysis.

> Example
>
> Thy beauty shall no more be found,
> Nor, in thy marble vault, shall sound
> My echoing song;
>
> The speaker, rather than flatter the addressee, tries to scare and frighten her into succumbing to her sexual desires. He focuses on the addressee's 'beauty': he explains to her that time will ravish her attractive looks and the implication is that she will no longer be able to attract men, hence the reason why she should have her fun now. Marvell also makes reference to the 'marble vault' that the addressee will be laid in when she dies, creating a dark and gloomy atmosphere. There is also a distinct change in the use of pronouns by the speaker: the collective pronouns used in the first stanza are replaced by singular ones like 'thy' and 'my', showing there to be some distance between the speaker and the addressee. The two are now in conflict, making the speaker's threats more sinister.

In the previous example, the candidate discusses the use of word choice, symbolism and the use of pronouns by the poet. In addition, the candidate also makes references to the first stanza in order to how the poet exploits the techniques in the evidence to create a contrast in the mood of the second stanza to the mood of the first stanza.

Film and TV

Film and TV texts can encompass a mix of the two approaches to analysis exemplified above. The approach depends upon the question.

If the question centres on creating atmosphere, tension or genre, then micro-analysis of scenes is required. This will include specific comment on a number of techniques used in particular scenes, shots and sequences.

If the question focuses on character or theme, then broader analysis, as exemplified in the prose

TOPIC 5. CRITICAL ESSAY

example, is more appropriate.

The following is an example of weak analysis of a film text. Without focussing on techniques and literary devices, this becomes a summary of what happens in the scene.

> Example
>
> In the parlour scene, Hitchcock creates tension and suspense through the character of Norman. He is clearly unhappy with Marion's suggestions regarding placing his mother in a home and comes across as quite threatening. This makes the audience fear for Marion's safety and his aggressiveness towards Marion makes the audience uncomfortable, just like Marion herself.

In the previous example, the analysis only focuses on what is happening in the scene, not on how the scene has been created using techniques and devices.

The following example shows how the same scene can be used to answer a question on the creation of tension and suspense:

> Example
>
> Norman is clearly unhappy about the suggestion that his mother could be put in a home. The camera does not move from the mid-shot position, but Norman moves closer into the camera, making him appear larger and much more menacing. He speaks directly into the camera, placing the audience in the position of Marion. This is an intimidating stance by Norman, which makes both Marion and he audience feel uncomfortable. In order to emphasise the threat that Norman poses to Marion, Hitchcock uses mise-en-scene in order to create foreshadowing. There are two pictures in the background of women: one who is naked and the other one is of a women being attacked. This foreshadows what will happen to Marion: Norman will take the advantage of her vulnerability in the shower later in the film in order to successfully kill her. This creates even more tension as we know that Marion will fall victim to Norman and end up dead.

The following is an example of the broader type of analysis, similar to that exemplified in the prose example. This uses the same scene as the other two examples, but the question focuses on character development.

> Example
>
> In this scene, we see a different side to Norman. When we first meet him he seems mild-mannered and shy, but in this scene he is portrayed as threatening and dominant. He challenges Marion's assertion that his mother could be put in a home. He scoffs a few times at Marion's suggestion, showing that he is mocking Marion and does not believe her to have any understanding of what 'institutions' are like. Additionally, he asks a few rhetorical questions to show that he does not agree with Marion and is agitated by her idea. This use of dialogue by Hitchcock shows us a different side to Norman: he seems unpredictable and threatening, which is in complete contrast to the polite and humble character that we are first introduced to. This is ominous as it becomes clear that Norman is a much more complex character than the audience are initially led to believe.

© HERIOT-WATT UNIVERSITY

Analysis: Quotations and references

For each of the quotations and/or references given below, choose the best analysis that corresponds to the question and the genre.

Q97:
'The Moor is of a free and open nature
That thinks men honest that but seem to be so'

a) Iago explains that Othello is a very trusting individual, which is something that plays to Iago's advantage. He will exploit this flaw in order to manipulate Othello and bring about his downfall.
b) Shakespeare uses the words 'free' and 'open' to show how Othello is a very trusting character. He is not naturally suspicious of others, something that Iago intends to fully exploit. In addition, Iago uses the word 'honest', which is something he is described as by Othello, highlighting Othello's gullibility.

....

Q98:
'To look after his brother, he had never got married, though once he had come very near it: that memory often revived to turn his heart melancholy.'

a) Jenkins uses the word 'melancholy' to describe the way in which Neil feels when he remembers his past love. This shows a softer, more vulnerable side to Neil which contrasts with the tetchy and grumpy character the reader has become accustomed to.
b) Jenkins explains to the reader that Neil has made many sacrifices in his life in order to care for his brother. This makes us sympathise with Neil and characterises him as someone who is responsible.

....

Q99:
'And your quaint honour turn to dust,
And into ashes all my lust.'

a) The speaker threatens the addressee with the destructive power of time: he explains to her that if she does not give in to her sexual desires then she may die a virgin, which, in turn, means that he will not be able to satisfy his 'lust'.
b) By using the word 'quaint', Marvell implies that the speaker views the addressee's attitude as old-fashioned and conservative. He then uses a metaphor to warn against the destructive nature of time: by using 'dust', Marvell makes reference to the idea that soon she will die and will regret her decision.

....

Q100:

> 'For first, as I have already observed, it would greatly lessen the number of papists, with whom we are yearly overrun, being the principal breeders of the nation as well as our most dangerous enemies;'

a) Swift uses the word 'papists' to refer to the Catholic population of Ireland at the time. This derogatory term reflects the anti-Catholic feelings that existed in Ireland at the time and, by using it, Swift highlights the bigotry present within society and the prejudice with which the poor were met with. This is further emphasised by describing them as 'enemies', showing the hostility that existed towards the poor at the time.
b) Swift, by imitating some of his peers and fellow countrymen, places the blame of the number of poor children with the Catholic population of Ireland. He characterises them as 'enemies', feeding into the religious division that existed within the country at the time.

....

Q101: There is a slow close-up zoom to Norman's face as his grimace turns to a maniacal smile.

a) This shot focuses our attention on Norman's face and it would seem that he is almost pleased with himself for the murders he has committed.
b) Using this shot focuses the audience's attention on Norman's face. He is staring directly in to the camera as if he is directly addressing them as an individual. The menacing stare is almost defiant: he does not care if the audience judge him for his evil deeds.

5.7 Structure

Learning objective

By the end of this section, you should be able to:

- write an introduction;
- write a summary of a text;
- use some strategies with which to organise your ideas in response to a Critical Essay question.

The ideas and line of thought in your essay will be determined by the question, as discussed in the previous section.

However, you will still need to structure these ideas into a coherent essay. This must not be a retelling of the story or guided tour of the poem: you must make critical points about the text in order to provide an extended answer to a question.

It is important that your answer includes detailed textual evidence, usually in the form of a quotation.

There is no 'correct' way to structure a critical essay, but there are some general rules that you can use to organise your ideas and create a clear line of thought.

In general, there are two ways in which to approach structuring a critical essay.

1. One quotation per main paragraph.

    These essays should use the following structure:

    - Paragraph 1: Introduction
    - Paragraph 2: Summary *
    - Paragraph 3-6/7: Main paragraphs (one quotation in each)
    - Paragraph 8: Conclusion

2. Two quotations per main paragraph.

    These essays should use the following structure:

    - Paragraph 1: Introduction
    - Paragraph 2: Summary *
    - Paragraph 3-5: Main paragraphs (two quotations in each)
    - Paragraph 6: Conclusion

* Not everyone will recommend the inclusion of a summary and it is not always necessary. Please see the note on how to write summaries for clarification.

Introduction

All introductions should follow roughly the same format, including the following:

- Author - Title - Reference to the question	Try to fit these three elements into the opening sentence. When you refer to the question, try to be as specific as you can.
- Outline of what you will discuss in your essay	This should outline the points you will make in your essay. Try to use the phrase 'variety of techniques' rather than mentioning specific techniques. This will give you freedom to discuss any techniques/literary devices and help you avoid writing an essay structured round techniques.

It is also a good idea to refer to the central concern of the text in the introduction also.

The following is an example of an introduction to an essay in answer to a character question on Othello. The relevant parts have been identified for you.

TOPIC 5. CRITICAL ESSAY

Example

In one of Shakesepare[1]'s most catastrophic tragedies, 'Othello[2]', he creates a protagonist bound to succumb to his fatal flaw, gullibility[3]. It is this flaw which allows him to be easily manipulated by Iago into thinking that he has been betrayed by his wife and provoke within him a 'tyrannous' jealousy[4]. Shakespeare uses a variety of techniques[5] to initially portray Othello as an inspired army general, before showing the devastating effects this manipulation has on his character. By the end of the play he has is completely consumed by his jealousy and fully believes that the murder of his wife by his own hands is the only way in which Desdemona can fully atone for her sins[6].

Notes:

[1] Author
[2] Title
[3] Reference to the question
[4] Reference to central concerns (themes)
[5] Phrase encompassing all possible techniques/literary devices
[6] Outline of what will be discussed: in this essay, you would discuss Othello's initial characterisation in the opening act, before going on to discuss the changes in his character in the turning point and beyond. You would finish by discussing his actions and how it impacts on your understanding of his character in the final scene of the play.

Structure: Introduction

The following is an introduction to an essay in answer to a theme question.

Answer In Robin Jenkins' eponymous novel, 'The Cone Gatherers', he skillfully constructs the conflict between Calum and Duror in order to parody the story of Christ and the perennial fight between good and evil. In the novel, Jenkins uses a variety of techniques to show how the conflict that exists between the two characters develops and can only be resolved through the sacrificial killing of Calum by Duror.

Q102: Looking at the introduction from the sample answer, identify:

- Author
- Title
- Reference to the question
- Reference to the theme
- Outline of what will be discussed in the essay

Main paragraphs

One quotation per paragraph

You can use the following structure as a guide to organise the ideas for your paragraphs:

- Topic sentence:
    - Introduces the topic for the paragraph (what you are discussing?)
    - Refers back to the question (why you are discussing it?)
- Point:
    - Introduces the quotation/reference to the text
    - May involve giving some context regarding the plot and what is happening in the text at this point
- Evidence:
    - Quotation/detailed reference to the text
- Analysis:
    - Discuss the techniques and literary devices used by the writer in the evidence provided in order to create meaning and impact
- Evaluation:
    - Refer back to the question
    - Explain the reason for discussing this evidence with regards to the demands of the question

Two quotations per paragraph

You can use the following structure as a guide to organise the ideas for your paragraphs:

- Topic sentence:
    - Introduces the topic for the paragraph (what you are discussing?)
    - Refers back to the question (why you are discussing it?)
- Point:
    - Introduces the quotation/reference to the text
    - May involve giving some context regarding the plot and what is happening in the text at this point
- Evidence:
    - Quotation/detailed reference to the text
- Analysis:
    - Discuss the techniques and literary devices used by the writer in the evidence provided in order to create meaning and impact

- Evaluation:
    - Refer back to the question
    - Explain the reason for discussing this evidence with regards to the demands of the question
- Linking Point:
    - Use as linking word or phrase to link your ideas together
    - Introduces the quotation/reference to the text
    - May involve giving some context regarding the plot and what is happening in the text at this point
- Evidence:
    - Quotation/detailed reference to the text
- Analysis:
    - Discuss the techniques and literary devices used by the writer in the evidence provided in order to create meaning and impact
- Evaluation:
    - Refer back to the question
    - Explain the reason for discussing this evidence with regards to the demands of the question

An example of an annotated main paragraph using just one quotation follows.

Example

The extent of the psychological damage that Othello suffers at the hands of Iago is fully shown in Act 4.[1]Othello loses all sense of himself and the mental instability he feels because of jealousy manifests itself physically:[2]

> Is't possible? Confess! - Handkerchief! - Oh devil!
> Falls in a trance[3]

This act opens with Iago agitating Othello further by discussing Desdemona and Cassio kissing. This outrages Othello and he loses control of his emotions. This is evident in the use of prose employed by Shakespeare to convey to us that Othello has fell from the lofty position that he held before: he has become more base, like Iago, and is no longer in an honourable position where he can use blank verse. In addition, the questions, short sentences and dashes mean that his speech is stilted and erratic, reflecting his inability to think logically at this time. Add to this Shakespeare's clever use if exclamations, and it is clear to the audience that Othello is in a heightened emotional state. This directly contrasts with the calm, controlled character that is presented to us in the opening scenes of the play. This contrast is further emphasised by Shakespeare's use of stage directions: Othello has some sort of fit as a result of being overcome with his emotions. The lack of control he feels emotionally is demonstrated to the audience through the lack of control he has over his body.[4]This is very shocking for the audience as it presents us with a very different character from the one we were introduced to in the opening acts, emphasising the change in his character due to Iago's exploitation of his fatal flaw.[5]

Notes:
[1] Topic sentence
[2] Linking point
[3] Evidence
[4] Analysis
[5] Evaluation

TOPIC 5. CRITICAL ESSAY

Structure: Main paragraphs   Go online

The following are a series of main paragraphs on the different genres. They have been written using the structuring ideas from above. What is the correct order for each series?

Q103:

- Through using the word 'wisely', Shakespeare shows that Othello has come to understand his mistake: he recognises that his jealousy was driven by his love for Desdemona, which clouded his judgement and ability to look objectively at the situation. He acknowledges the lack of jealousy within his character, but knows that he was manipulated to feel that way, placing some of the blame with Iago. In describing himself as 'perplexed', Shakespeare conveys to the audience Othello's acceptance of the tyrannical way in which he behaved, expressing regret with regards to his actions.
- Othello regains some of his honourable and heroic character in the closing lines of the play.
- Othello wants his story to be a warning to others and urges those around him to tell it as cautionary tale as he recognises how easily he was manipulated and how devastating the consequences were. In killing himself, he dies with honour, not allowing himself to be disgraced upon his return to Venice. His suicide is his own decision, taking the control and power away from Iago and restoring some of the audience's respect for him.
   - Of one that loved not wisely, but too well.
- Of one not easily jealous, but being wrought,
   Perplexed in the extreme.
- He is completely devastated after Iago's evil plot has been revealed and realises he has mistakenly murdered his wife:

  ....

Q104:

- Jenkins uses words like 'rushing' and 'frantic' to convey the chaos of the scene. Duror leaps on the opportunity to violently and unrestrainedly kill the deer, in order to agitate and frighten Calum. The short sentence 'Blood spouted' adds to the horrific description of the scene, emphasising the brutality and cruelty that Duror is capable of. It foreshadows Calum's death: the deer is sacrificed by Duror to satiate his hatred of Calum, much like Calum will be killed in order to cleanse the wood of the evil represented by Duror.
- 'rushing upon the stricken deer and the frantic hunchback, he threw the latter off with furious force, and then, seizing the former's head with one hand cut its throat savagely with the other. Blood spouted.'
- He mercilessly slaughters the deer in front of Calum with no regard for his feelings:
- The killing of the deer exposes Duror's lack of compassion towards Calum: he subjects Calum to this level of violence in the full knowledge that it will have a devastating effect on Calum.
- The depth of Duror's hatred for Calum is fully exposed in the Deer Drive.

  ....

© HERIOT-WATT UNIVERSITY

Q105:
- Marvell uses a simile to describe the speaker and the object of his desire: he compares them to 'birds of prey', placing them in the role of hunters. Birds of prey are violent creatures that prey on smaller animals, and this suggests that the couple must be more powerful and commanding in their attitude to time. He continues this imagery by using the word 'devour', linking to the carpe diem theme: 'devour' has connotations of being overwhelmed and the couple must make the most of the time they have together before it inevitably runs out.
- The speaker calls upon the addressee to join him in thwarting time by taking advantage of the time they do have:
- Marvell uses increasingly violent imagery in order to convey the devastating effects of the passing of time.
- The poet is able to convey to us, through imagery, the importance of using our time wisely: he cleverly conveys the destructive power of time as something we can overcome by being proactive and enjoying the time we have to its fullest.
- And now, like am'rous birds of prey,
  Rather at once our time devour,

....

Q106:
- The speaker refers to 'an hundred thousand' poor children being on the streets in Ireland, but there is little evidence to compound this statement. It is clear that Swift is using hyperbole in order to exaggerate the extent of the problem, mimicking the overly dramatic response of the upper classes to the poor. The speaker then claims that Ireland's GDP will increase by 'fifty thousand pounds a year', a sum based on the hypothesised numbers with no substantial evidence to back them up. Although this number would have seen impressive at the time, Swift employs hyperbole once more in order to entice the upper classes as he knows that their weakness is money and profit, not the care and well-being of other human beings.
- Thirdly, whereas the maintenance of an hundred thousand children, from two years old and upward, cannot be computed at less than ten shillings a-piece per annum, the nation's stock will be thereby increased fifty thousand pounds per annum, beside the profit of a new dish introduced to the tables of all gentlemen of fortune in the kingdom.
- Swift continues to expose the prejudice against the poor at the time by giving reasons as to why his proposal is valid.
- Through the use of hyperbole to create humour, Swift skilfully exposes the discrimination that the poor in Ireland are met with and shows those more affluent members of society to be lacking in compassion for others less fortunate than themselves.
- In his third point, the speaker uses statistics and facts to outline the benefits that his proposal will bring to the community:

....

Q107:

- Hitchcock immediately unsettles the audience and makes them feel tense.
- From the opening credits alone, it is clear the Hitchcock intends to subvert all the audience's expectations.
- In the opening credits there is loud string music played staccato and the screen is split into bars that move frantically across the screen.
- The sound and the graphics on screen point towards instability, which is something that Hitchcock builds throughout the entire film, keeping the audience in suspense.
- The music is repetitive and short in length, foreshadowing the way in which Marion will be slashed later in the film. The sound is unpleasant and chaotic, adding to the sense that this will not be a relaxing film to watch and that the audience will spend most of their time on edge. This is further emphasised by the bars that whizz across the scene with no apparent pattern. This reflects the mental breakdown of Norman: his ability to think logically has been completely disturbed. This echoes the feeling of the audience in response to the opening credits: the unstable and disordered movement of the bars points toward the dual personality of Norman.

5.8 Exam technique

> **Learning objective**
>
> By the end of this section, you should be able to:
>
> - use strategies regarding planning and timing to help you write under examination conditions.

Planning

Planning your essay is essential to success in this part of the examination. A plan is like a route map for your essay: doing so will ensure that your essay has a clear line of thought and answers the question in the paper. This is your 'thinking' time, allowing you to formulate your ideas and organise them into a coherent structure.

When planning, you only have to think about your main paragraphs. It is helpful to identify the topic of the paragraph and the evidence you will use to exemplify your points. You do not need to write the evidence out in full: you can simply bullet point one or two words to remind you of what it is you want to discuss in each paragraph.

The following is an example of a plan for 'Othello'. The question asks you to focus on the development of a character.

Example

Revelation of character in the exposition

- 'Keep up...'
- 'She loved...'

Turning point

- 'Haply...'
- 'Yield up...'

Othello's loss of control

- 'Is't possible?...'
- 'Devil!...'

Denouement

- 'O balmy...'
- 'I kissed...'

NB: other quotations could be used from the text, other than those above, to make comments about Othello's character development.

Timing

It is also essential that you keep track of time in this part of the examination as, in order to do well, your essay must show knowledge of the full text and have a conclusion.

Approximately, you should spend around 45 minutes on your essay.

You should spend at least 5-10 minutes reading the question thoroughly and planning your essay.

This will leave you 35-40 minutes to write your essay. If you know your text well and have thoroughly planned your essay then this is plenty of time to get all your ideas on the page.

Proof reading

If you have time, it is always a good idea to read over your essay to correct any errors with technical accuracy (spelling/punctuation/grammar). A marker would rather see technical corrections than technical errors.

5.9 Learning points

Summary

- There is key vocabulary linked to each genre which should be used when analysing evidence from a text.
- Evidence from a text can take the form of a quotation or detailed reference.
- You can organise your notes and evidence under broad themes such as conflict, characterisation, setting.
- The SQA have four broad general areas against which they assess your essay.
- The question can help you to formulate your essay and structure your ideas.
- Analysis of evidence should be thorough and discuss techniques or literary devices exploited by an author/ director.
- There are certain details that must be included in an introduction and a conclusion.
- Main paragraphs can be structured using the terms: topic sentence; point; evidence; analysis; and evaluation.
- Planning your essay, managing your time and proof reading your work are all essential to being successful in this part of the examination.

5.10 End of topic test

End of Topic 5 test Go online

Q108: When showing _____ of evidence, you must explain what you know about the text from that particular piece of evidence.

a) context
b) evaluation
c) understanding

....

Q109: When _____ a text in your essay, you must discuss how a writer or director uses techniques and stylistic devices to create meaning and effect.

a) analysing
b) evaluating
c) understanding

....

Q110: When you _____ a text in a critical essay, you must show how the evidence/quotation you have discussed links to the question you are answering.

a) analyse
b) evaluate
c) understand

....

Q111: The essay questions come in _____ parts.

a) one
b) two
c) three

....

Q112: The first part will provide you with _____ for your essay.

a) a focus
b) an idea
c) a theme

....

Q113: The second part helps you to _____ the initial ideas from first part and how these should be organised.

a) sequence
b) structure
c) write

....

© Heriot-Watt University

Q114: When analysing poetry, you use _____ analysis.

a) macro
b) mega
c) micro

Q115: All introductions must include: author, title, reference to the question and reference to the _____ .

a) main characters
b) setting
c) central concerns

Q116: Topic sentences should introduce the _____ and refer back to the question.

a) technique
b) topic
c) setting

Q117: When planning your essay, you need to plan the _____ .

a) conclusion
b) main paragraphs
c) introduction

Unit 2 Appendix A

Acknowledgements

- *Elizabeth Barrett Browning*, My Letters! all dead paper...
- *Robert Burns*, To A Mouse
- *Robert Burns*, Holy Willie's Prayer
- *Robert Burns*, Address to the Deil
- *Robert Burns*, A Man's a Man For a' That
- *Robert Burns*, A Poet's Welcome to His Love-Begotten Daughter
- *Robert Burns*, A Red, Red Rose
- *Robert Burns*, Tam o' Shanter
- *John Byrne*, The Slab Boys
- *Charles Dickens*, Great Expectations
- *Arthur Conan Doyle*, A Study in Scarlet
- *Lewis Grassic Gibbon*, Sunset Song
- *Robin Jenkins*, The Cone Gatherers
- *Andrew Marvell*, To His Coy Mistress
- *John Milton*, When I consider how my light is spent
- *William Shakespeare*, Hamlet
- *William Shakespeare*, The Tempest, Act 5, Scene 1 & Act 1, Scene 1
- *William Shakespeare*, Macbeth, Act 1, Scene 6
- *William Shakespeare*, Othello
- *William Shakespeare*, Sonnet 12
- *William Shakespeare*, Sonnet 30
- *William Shakespeare*, Sonnet 33
- *Bram Stoker*, Dracula
- *Jonathan Swift*, A Modest Proposal

Unit 3: Portfolio

1 Creative writing 315
   1.1 Introduction 317
   1.2 Common skills 318
   1.3 Prose fiction 335
   1.4 Personal writing 365
   1.5 Exemplar work 382
   1.6 Learning points 407
   1.7 End of topic test 408

2 Discursive writing 411
   2.1 Introduction 412
   2.2 Common skills 412
   2.3 Argumentative writing 435
   2.4 Persuasive writing 442
   2.5 Planning 446
   2.6 Exemplar work 449
   2.7 Learning points 463
   2.8 End of topic test 464

3 Talking: Tips and techniques 469
   3.1 Introduction 470
   3.2 Ideas and content 472
   3.3 Language choice 473
   3.4 Communicating meaning 474
   3.5 Non-verbal communication 475
   3.6 Visual aids 476
   3.7 Talking from notes 477
   3.8 Introductions 478
   3.9 Conclusions 478
   3.10 Planning 479
   3.11 Learning points 480
   3.12 End of topic test 481

Unit 3 Topic 1

Creative writing

Contents

- 1.1 Introduction 317
- 1.2 Common skills 318
    - 1.2.1 Creating a setting 318
    - 1.2.2 Using commas 326
    - 1.2.3 Show, don't tell 328
    - 1.2.4 Symbolism 333
    - 1.2.5 Paragraphs 334
- 1.3 Prose fiction 335
    - 1.3.1 Characters 335
    - 1.3.2 Using dialogue 342
    - 1.3.3 Themes 346
    - 1.3.4 Narrative voice 352
    - 1.3.5 Plot structure 354
- 1.4 Personal writing 365
    - 1.4.1 Getting ideas 365
    - 1.4.2 Structure 366
    - 1.4.3 Reflection 377
- 1.5 Exemplar work 382
- 1.6 Learning points 407
- 1.7 End of topic test 408

> **Prerequisites**
>
> Before beginning this topic, you should have worked on Creative Writing skills over a number of years in school. You will have produced Creative Writing for your Portfolio in National 5 English. Reading professional writer's Creative Writing will also help you learn to be an effective writer.
>
> You should have a knowledge of what is meant by the terms used on the contents page. These resources will help you develop your skill at integrating these features effectively and skilfully into your own writing.

UNIT 3. PORTFOLIO

Learning objective

By the end of this topic, you should be able to:

- produce a complex piece of writing that will fit into the Creative section of your Portfolio.

TOPIC 1. CREATIVE WRITING

1.1 Introduction

For your final Portfolio submission you have to produce two pieces of writing. Your school will have procedures about handing in plans and essay drafts and you should follow these. You will also have studied many of the skills needed to be a good writer in other parts of the course and can build on the work done when studying National 5 English. When you studied literature, you will have analysed the skills of effective creative writing. Similarly, in Reading for Understanding, Analysis and Evaluation (RUAE) you will have analysed the style of non-fiction and this will help you write an effective discursive essay if you use elements of that style in your own writing.

The Scholar materials will help you think of some ideas and revise the skills needed to write a successful Portfolio. These materials use examples of genuine Portfolio work submitted in the past and students have kindly given their permission for it to be used.

Portfolio requirements

One piece of writing which is broadly creative:

- a personal essay / reflective essay;
- a piece of prose fiction (e.g. short story, episode from a novel);
- a poem or thematically linked poems;
- a dramatic script.

This is covered in this section of the course.

One piece of writing which is broadly discursive:

- a persuasive essay;
- an argumentative essay;
- a report for a specific purpose;
- a piece of transactional writing.

This is covered in the Discursive section of the course (Please see the next topic).

1.2 Common skills

There are a number of similarities in the skills needed to produce the different types of creative writing to a complex level. For example, personal essays could use direct speech to create a sense of character. Even if you decide to do a Personal essay, you should look through the Prose Fiction section as well for ideas and to revise your creative writing skills. If you choose to write a drama script, you could use the sections on creating characters and structure to help you.

1.2.1 Creating a setting

In your short story or personal essay for your portfolio there is a word limit which means that you don't have the opportunity to have a detailed developments of multiple settings. A detailed exploration of one complex setting can work well. Additionally, creating a stark contrast between two very distinctive settings could allow you to show mood development or character development.

Sometimes the setting is just the background to the story but in more complex stories it is really important: it is like a character in a story or in travel writing it is central to the whole reflective element of the essay.

It is far better to have a really well established setting rather than a piece of writing that moves from one place to the next with very little description.

- Your setting could be based on somewhere that you know or have been and then you can develop in detail.
- You could use pictures or photographs to generate ideas for your setting.
- Appeal to more than one of the five senses when you describe the setting - sight, sound, smell, touch, taste.
- Build atmosphere by writing about a hidden secret within the setting.
- Describe the weather and show how this helps set the mood.
- Show how your character interacts with the setting.
- Make the setting have a direct link to the theme of your story.

There are some picture-based activities in the next section which you can use to evaluate settings.

For your own story, you could find an image which you think will suit the setting (s) and use headings to make notes.

1.2.1.1 Generating story ideas

Story idea 1

Look at the pictures and think of how they create a mood of hope or optimism. Apart from visual aspects, what other senses would be engaged in a setting like this?

Perhaps the picture could be used as a setting for a journey, an adventure or an escape. Use the following words to make notes:

- Atmosphere
- Feelings
- Colours
- Senses

Think about how the colours add to the mood of this setting. Remember that journeys can be literal and metaphorical so you could use a real journey to explore a figurative journey for a character. Think of how a crossroads could be used to represent a choice.

Story idea 2

Look at the picture and think of how you could use it as a setting for a short story. Perhaps this picture could be used as a setting for a story where a character is trapped or limited by his or her circumstances. Think of the struggles that could exist in such an environment and how they can be used to generate a story.

Use the following words to make notes:

- Atmosphere
- Feelings
- Dreams and lost dreams
- Senses

TOPIC 1. CREATIVE WRITING

Story idea 3

Look at the picture and think of how you could use it as an idea for a short story. Giving your story a very distinctive setting (Venice in this case) means that you can work with a lot of the ideas associated with that place. These could include iconic buildings associated with the place or famous events in its history.

Use the following words to make notes:

- Atmosphere
- Feelings
- Thoughts
- Senses
- Colours

Story idea 4

Look at the picture and think of how you could use it as a setting for a short story. Perhaps this picture could be used as a setting for a journey, an adventure or someone coming to a city for the first time - perhaps to start a new life. What might the character be thinking as they look at this scene?

Use the following words to make notes:

- Atmosphere
- Feelings
- Dreams
- Senses

TOPIC 1. CREATIVE WRITING 323

Story idea 5

Look at the picture and think of how you could use it as a setting for a short story. Looking at the fine detail of a building might help you find some imagery and motifs that you can work into the plot of your story or use to reflect on the personality of characters.

Use the following words to make notes:

- Atmosphere
- Feelings
- Dreams
- Senses

1.2.1.2 Setting in Portfolio examples

Setting in Portfolio activity: Shipwrecked

Look at the paragraph from the short story 'Shipwrecked'.

> This fine 'establishment' that our club used as a base was filled with drunks and luckless 'men'. This 'bar' was a 'treasure trove' of 'authentic' marine materials. Even the owners of this 'sea themed' 'pub' disgusted me. The walls were splattered a sea sick yellow. The tables, mere barrels. Pungent smells filled the atmosphere - the aroma was intoxicating - everyone but me was as drunk as a sailor. The drunken type of course. The sickly bile that these 'associates' of mine spewed was nauseating in itself, but the corny pick-up lines they tried to deliver made me gag.

You can read the whole story in the section of Exemplar work.

Discussion questions

1. What colours are used in the scene?
2. What mood do these colours suggest?
3. Read the whole story and explain how this idea very subtly creates the right mood for the story as a whole where a character experiences false feelings.

© HERIOT-WATT UNIVERSITY

TOPIC 1. CREATIVE WRITING

Setting in Portfolio activity: Olivia's Choice

Look at the paragraph from the introduction to the short story 'Olivia's Choice'.

> As I tried to lift my eyelids after another rough night's sleep, my eyes focused onto a vast sky of grey fog. A tiny droplet of water glistened in the corner of my eye until blinking and feeling it slowly slide down my left cheek. My back ached after another night sleeping on cardboard. Even the thought of sitting up began to tire me out. The time was unknown to me, and so was my location. I just lay there and tried not to accept the situation that I knew I was in, but the thought was still there and there was no way of escaping it. The city's laughter echoed down hollow alleyways. As the sound faded, I remembered what it was like to have friends, people around me, to go home to a warm bed, to close the door behind me and shut out the world knowing I was safe. But now I was at the mercy of the elements, my fate decided by the drop of a coin into an empty paper cup.

Write down three ideas that you think about when you think of fog. Use what you have learned about connotations in other parts of the English course. In your notebook, make notes about how the writer has made a connection between the atmosphere made by the fog and the character who is unsure of her situation.

Look at some of the weather images below. How could they be used to reflect the mood of a character?

You can read the whole story in the section of Exemplar work.

© HERIOT-WATT UNIVERSITY

1.2.2 Using commas

> **Top tip**
>
> Examiners' tips:
>
> Work on technical accuracy to improve your marks.

It is really essential that writing has controlled expression. As well as choosing the right words you also need to construct sentences accurately. Using the comma properly is an important part of sentence building.

Here are some of the ways in which a comma should be used:

1. To separate the items in a list.

   Example Into his bag he placed his keys, his wallet and his passport.

   When making lists for personal writing or short stories, you could use them in the following ways:

   - Long lists to show many details and perhaps this could suggest the character being overwhelmed in a difficult situation.
   - Lists of three - make the final point the climax. In the above example, leading up to the passport helps build the plot about the character leaving the country.

2. To separate clauses in a sentence.

   Use a comma to separate introductory clauses from the main part of that sentence. Usually, these can be clauses that contain adverbial phrases.

   Examples

   1. Treading carefully, Michael ghosted past the slightly open door.

   2. As the darkness came, he fearfully entered the forest.

3. Using commas to create parenthesis.

   Parenthesis is a part of the sentence that can be removed without changing the meaning of the sentence.

   Example Mr Brown, his teacher, was always nagging about working harder.

   If you are using a comma to do this, it is important that the phrase begins and ends with a comma.

TOPIC 1. CREATIVE WRITING

4. To punctuate direct speech.

   Example "Be careful not to wake it," he whispered.

   With this kind of speech, the comma can be replaced by a question mark or an exclamation mark as well.

1.2.2.1 The comma splice

This is one of the most frequently made mistakes when using the comma. It means that a sentence has been 'spliced' or joined by a comma when either a full stop or a conjunction was needed. If the clauses make sense on their own then using the comma is wrong.

   Example David crept into the room, he knew that he should not be heard. *(Incorrect)*

   Q1: Which of the following sentences is correct?
   a) He crashed into the room, he tripped over the table as he did so.
   b) As he crashed into the room, he tripped over the table.
   c) I sometimes wish I had never gone there, it was the worst day of my life.

There are some ways to fix comma spliced sentences.

You can use a full stop.

   Example David crept into the room. He knew that he should not be heard.

You can use a *conjunction* to connect the sentences. If you do this then you show cause and effect.

   Example David crept into the room as he knew that he should not be heard.

The comma splice questions   Go online

Use commas to punctuate the following sentences.

Q2: "We need to go soon" Jane pleaded.
   ....

Q3: The river Nile the longest in Africa brought more dangers to his adventure.
   ....

Q4: As he left for school he snatched his bag his coat and a soggy piece of toast.
   ....

> Q5: Following the path carefully he entered the shelter of the silent forest.

1.2.3 Show, don't tell

This section will be helpful for creating effective characters for short stories or describing your own feelings subtly in personal writing.

It is common advice in creative writing that you should 'show' how a character (or the writer in personal writing) is feeling rather than just 'tell' the reader. This is important for several reasons:

- you have to engage the reader and one way to do this is to help them visualise the scene;
- you will engage the reader by making them work on inference;
- it can help you move the story on by describing actions that fit into the plot.

Sometimes you have to tell the reader what a character is thinking but do this by choice rather than doing it all the time. Here is an example.

> Example
>
> *Telling*
>
> The boy did not want to go to school.
>
> *Showing*
>
> He scuffed his feet on the ground and his pace shortened as if by routine as he approached the ominous gate.
>
> *Advantage*
>
> As well as giving a clearer description, 'showing' helps set the idea that this was a frequent occurrence any by adding the detail of the gate and transferring an adjective describing his mood onto the object, we can hint that there is a real reason for him not going. It is not just he doesn't like school but there is something going to happen that day.

1.2.3.1 Show, don't tell in Portfolio examples

Show, don't tell in Portfolio activity: All Creatures Great and Small

Look at the paragraph from the reflective essay 'All Creatures Great and Small'.
Note how the writer shows us the character's feelings rather than telling us.

> It was a depressing drive to the house as the vet and I sat in silence[1]. After fifteen minutes of this dead, endless reticence we approached the house and turned into the drive. As we walked through the door we were greeted by a woman and a grandmother. The grandmother seemed composed but the lady was distraught with tear stains streaked down her cheeks. As she led us upstairs we approached the room where the silenced dog lay. As I entered the room I shuffled past[2] the dog lying in front of me. The vet deduced it had died in the night from a sudden stroke or fit. At least they gained some comfort from the fact it had been quick and painless. The German shepherd looked peaceful as he lay in his eternal slumber. I could feel the emotion rising up in me, choking me. I swallowed[3].
>
> Notes:
> [1] Apprehensive
> [2] Uneasy feeling- unsure of own role in events
> [3] Physical gesture indicating nervousness / lack of confidence

You can read the whole reflective essay in the section of Exemplar work.

Show, don't tell in Portfolio activity: Journeying

Look at the paragraph from the reflective essay 'Journeying'.

> The hot, grainy sand melted effortlessly into the glistening Mediterranean Sea. My eyes squinted, adjusting to the bright midday July sunlight as I woke from snoozing on an uncomfortable plastic sun lounger which had slowly sunk into the sand. The bright green material of the lounger was covered in sand so I had to get up. The parasol above provided little shelter, and the smell of the sea was pungent. Surrounded by rows of the same cheap style of lounger, it looked like a typical tourist resort brimming with holidaymakers. Spending the day on the beach seemed like the perfect oasis, acting as an escape from mundane everyday life.

Discussion question:

1. The essay seems to present a typically idyllic holiday setting with a day on the beach. Which details from this extract help establish a more negative mood and suggest that a less pleasant experience is being set-up?

You can read the whole reflective essay in the section of Exemplar work.

TOPIC 1. CREATIVE WRITING 331

Show, don't tell activity

Look at the following pictures and discuss the emotions and feelings that could be suggested by the action. Remember, when you write describe what the character is doing rather than tell the reader directly what they are thinking. Describing gesture, posture and facial expression are great ways to 'show' a character's thoughts. The situations might even give you an idea for a story. Some gestures are just natural poses but some are symbolic and could be used to introduce the idea of symbolism to your writing.

Image	'Show'	Emotions and feelings
	His fist clenched as he waited and watched the clock.	Anger, nervousness. A clenched fist is also a SYMBOL of defiance especially when held in the air.

© HERIOT-WATT UNIVERSITY

332 UNIT 3. PORTFOLIO

Image	'Show'	Emotions and feelings

TOPIC 1. CREATIVE WRITING 333

1.2.4 Symbolism

Symbolism is when you use an object to represent an abstract idea or a set of values. Some organisations also use symbols to represent themselves. They achieve their impact by being strong visual images but also by appealing to the connotations associated with the object.

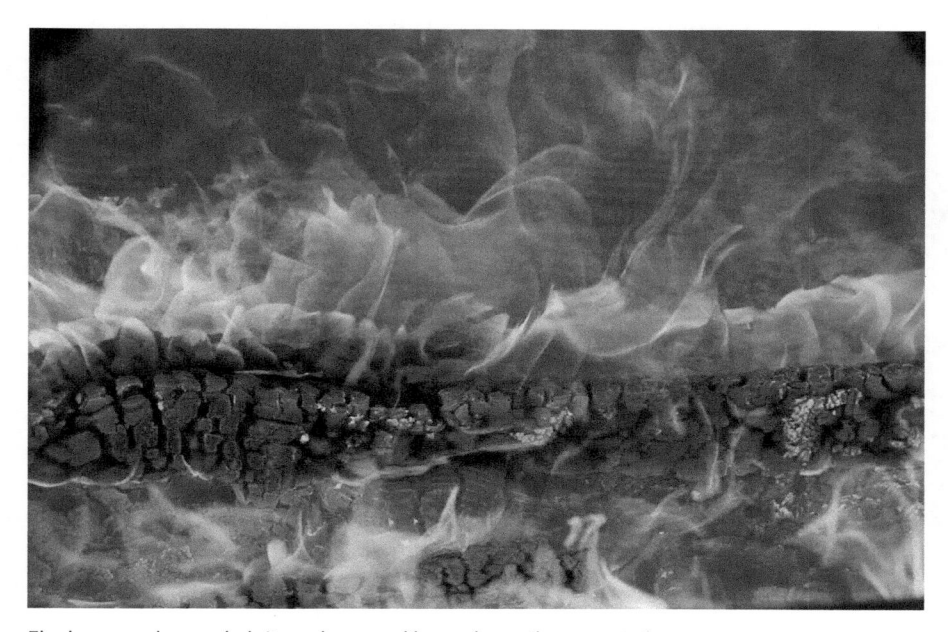

Fire is a complex symbol. It can have positive and negative connotations.

Q6: Complete the table using the attributes listed.

Positive	Negative

Attributes

- Protection
- Destruction
- Hope of rescue
- Pain

© HERIOT-WATT UNIVERSITY

Using an object or an idea that can be applied symbolically could help your story achieve some complexity.

1.2.5 Paragraphs

Writing in paragraphs is important. Paragraphs that are too long overwhelm the reader- apart from being grammatically incorrect. If there are too many short paragraphs, it is likely that the story is moving around quickly with no extended descriptions.

Take a new paragraph in creative writing when:

- you change time - 'Later that day...', 'A few moments later...' You can use changes in time to structure a story or a personal essay;
- you change place - think of it like changing the scene that you would like the reader to visualise;
- a new person begins to speak;
- you want to create a dramatic moment - perhaps with a single sentence paragraph;
- you introduce a new character and describe them in some detail.

1.3 Prose fiction

Imaginative writing covers writing in poetry, drama or prose. Most often, pupils choose prose and write short stories. Some ideas that you need to think about when you create stories are:

- creating characters;
- using dialogue;
- having a theme;
- structuring a plot;
- creating a narrative voice.

By planning and thinking about these features you will create a more developed and complex short story.

1.3.1 Characters

Really well made characters are perhaps the most important part of story writing. The reader engages with the people in the story far more readily than they do with the setting or the themes. Getting characters right is worth taking time to plan properly.

There are ways in which we can get the idea for a inventing a character.

Creating characters activity   Go online

Q7: Complete the table using the advantages and disadvantages listed.

Technique	Advantages	Disadvantages
Using someone that you know		
Using a famous person- perhaps from history		
Creating a character from looking at pictures		
Basing them on characters that you have read or seen in film/television		

Advantages and disadvantages

a) You can visualise the person
b) You might forget that the reader does not know this person
c) The characters are not yours and only copies of another writer's ideas
d) You will realise that the reader will know this person
e) In your story, you might not create enough of a personality for them
f) You might not know enough about them to make them realistic
g) You understand this person and know all their habits/ mannerisms
h) You have a lot of ideas about the character

Discussion points

1. Which of the above strategies do you think would allow you to create the most original characters?
2. Should we just create characters who are similar to ourselves in terms of age and background?

Regardless of how you get your ideas, you can use the following points to make notes about one or two characters who will be central to your story.

- Physical description: Age, height etc. - you will not use this much in the story but it will help you see the character.

- Back-story: Tell us what has brought them to the place where they are now. What has their life been like? If your character has a different background to yourself, you may need to research some details.

- Personality: What kind of person are they?

- Relationships: What relationships do they have in life? What is their family background?

You can prepare by collecting lots of information about your character. You won't use all of this in a story but by preparing thoroughly, you will make the character more realistic.

TOPIC 1. CREATIVE WRITING 337

1.3.1.1 Creating characters from pictures

Story idea 6

Look at the following picture and use the following points to make notes about the character.

- Physical description
- Back-story
- Personality
- Relationships

Story idea 7

Look at the following picture and use the following points to make notes about the character.

- Physical description
- Back-story
- Personality
- Relationships

TOPIC 1. CREATIVE WRITING

Story idea 8

Look at the following picture and use the following points to make notes about the character.

- Physical description
- Back-story
- Personality
- Relationships

1.3.1.2 Characters in Portfolio examples

> **Characters in Portfolio activity: Olivia's choice**   Go online
>
> Read this extract from the short story 'Olivia's Choice'.
>
> > I thought back to the first day I ran away. A decision quickly made in haste, out of frustration at someone my father loved, but someone I didn't.[1] I couldn't understand how he could move on when I couldn't, and why he would want to. All my anger about my mother's death I took out on her, and now only realising now how unfair that was.[2] I remember the moment when I left the front door knowing I wasn't coming back[3] - yet I so deeply wanted to. The air smelt cleaner than it did before and the outdoors more welcoming. I walked over to somewhere I called my second home, somewhere frightening to others yet for myself a place of tranquillity. I sat beside her grave and talked with her - "I'm sorry I let you down". I didn't need to tell her how upset I was - she could see it.
> >
> > Notes:
> >
> > [1] Reveals the motive for running away.
> > [2] Summarises a story of how problematic living at home became.
> > [3] Defines the moment that she left.
>
> This is a story about a character who has run away from home. Notice how her back story is used.
>
> You can read the whole story in the section of Exemplar work.

TOPIC 1. CREATIVE WRITING

Characters in Portfolio activity: Magnum Opiate   Go online

Read this extract from the short story 'Magnum Opiate'.

Although his thoughts were that of a content disposition, even against the discomfort of the cardboard backseat he crumpled over, they were quickly shot down as the taxi came to an alarming brake stop in the middle of the dirt road. He rose quickly from his slouch to observe the surroundings outside the window caked in the midday heat. There was no house here. It wasn't even an 'artistic' illusion. It was gravel followed by gravel and a little bit of sand. Emptiness. Why had we stopped? He had heard the 'artists' (he was quite happy at how well he had continued this odious analogy of 'artists'; it was one of the few humorous things he had left) hid their... ehm... art well but this level of isolation was laughable, in a horribly self-loathing kind of way. He rubbed his eyes and leaned forward to confront the driver but was set aback upon witnessing the small hairy man hunched over the wheel and bleeding. He himself, hated the sight of blood and started to feel sickness in the dusty sauna of the harboured Honda. Panting melodramatically, he let himself out of his door - it's not like the dead taxi driver was going to do it - and fell back into the barren, sandy waste in a state of shock.

Which phrases in the extract suggest that this character is unpleasant? List five.

You can read the whole story in the section of Exemplar work.

1.3.2 Using dialogue

Direct speech

Direct speech is important in creative writing. It can be a way of making a character more realistic and a way of developing his or her personality. There are two features of the use of speech that you should consider.

1. How to punctuate it properly.
2. How to use it effectively in creative writing.

Punctuation of speech

When using direct speech in creative writing, there are some straightforward rules.

- The speech marks go round the words spoken.
- The speech begins with a capital letter.
- There is always a punctuation mark before the second set of speech marks - always.
- Take a new paragraph when you change speaker in sections of dialogue.

Examples

1. "You will never see anything like this, " he announced.

   ....

2. He announced, "You will never see anything like this."

TOPIC 1. CREATIVE WRITING

Punctuation of speech — Go online

Q8: Choose the appropriate elements from the following list:
- ?
- Hand
- hand
- "
- "
- ,
- .

to complete the following sentence:

me that screwdriver he demanded
....

Q9: Choose the appropriate elements from the following list:
- ?
- It
- it
- "
- "
- ,
- .

to complete the following sentence:

I heard a distant voice scream was you
....

Q10: Choose the appropriate elements from the following list:
- ?
- It
- it
- "
- "
- ,
- .

to complete the following sentence:

How did you discover the body he asked

1.3.2.1 Effective speech in creative writing

- Don't use speech to tell the story or have the character explain what she or he is doing.
- Use it to give your character personality by copying the individuality of real people speaking:
    - use dialect;
    - give them an idiosyncrasy - some phrases that only they use;
    - have the character say things which are different from what they are thinking.

A hundred ways to not say 'said'!

There is nothing wrong with the word 'said' but if it gets overused in dialogue it can really spoil the effect of the speech. Using alternatives which are less neutral also help you build in the character's feelings. Here are one hundred alternatives:

accused	declared	started	chattered	commanded
corrected	nagged	blurted	hinted	interrupted
screamed	argued	promised	thought	replied
added	demanded	stated	cheered	commented
cried	snarled	boasted	hissed	requested
moaned	asked	proposed	ranted	whimpered
shouted	denied	stormed	reasoned	jeered
admitted	sneered	boomed	reassured	responded
croaked	objected	giggled	urged	whined
mumbled	babbled	protested	choked	concluded
shrieked	prayed	bragged	recalled	whispered
advised	ordered	greeted	implied	confessed
sighed	exclaimed	suggested	informed	joked
announced	sobbed	groaned	remarked	roared
dared	explained	growled	inquired	wondered
muttered	begged	grumbled	remembered	worried
answered	pleaded	queried	wailed	laughed
decided	sputtered	teased	insisted	sang
smirked	bellowed	tested	warned	continued
approved	stammered	quoted	repeated	yawned

1.3.2.2 Dialogue in Portfolio example

Dialogue in Portfolio activity: Shipwrecked

Read the extract from the short story 'Shipwrecked'. It uses dialogue to create a scene where the main character is taunted by an illusion of a past lover.

"Now don't you think that's a bit unfair? I came all this way to greet you, and you still hold a grudge against me," she said with in her facetious way. "Isn't it a bit babyish? I mean it's not even my fault now is it?" she spewed lies in my face. "I get it you are angry, but still isn't it manipulative of you to still play victim after so long? Shouldn't you move on? It is almost like you crave the attention? You even forgot my name," her face turned into a bitter smile. "You are alone. You only have yourself to blame. It is pathetic really, you create strawmen, make me into a siren. When someone wrongs you, you demonise them. Make them into stereotypes, generic husks of what they originally were." The verbal assault did not stop. "Why? Because other opinions scare you? Other ways of life frighten you? You don't like the idea of being wrong? You can't handle being wrong. You can't handle responsibility of your actions. You just can't."

Marker's commentary

We know that the character until now has been upset by his past. The writer uses dialogue to externalise his own doubts and to create a nagging voice for the ex-partner. This helps to suggest what the relationship might have been like but it also uses to dialogue explore the insecurity of the main character. The repeated use of questioning helps aid this.

You can read the whole story in the section of Exemplar work.

1.3.3 Themes

There are many themes that you could use in imaginative writing of prose fiction. If you can tie in the theme with the development of your character, then you create a purpose for the character in the story.

You can also make the theme at its most tense in the conflict of your story and in this way it drives the plot. By looking at the section of the notes on plot structure, you could take your idea for a theme and develop it appropriately.

Some ideas for themes:

- a character at a key moment in life - perhaps the first step into the adult world;
- ambition - a character driven by an (impossible) ambition;
- a character discovering something new (about him/herself);
- being let down or betrayed;
- getting revenge;
- facing fears;
- breaking free;
- good versus evil;
- isolation - physical and/or emotional;
- a character envious or jealous of someone else;
- the search for truth;
- overcoming prejudice;
- survival.

> **Top tip**
>
> **Examiner's Tip**
>
> Think of how you could use the theme of the story in a subtle reference dropped into the title. Then the title acts as an enigma for the reader and it will draw them to the central idea of the story.

TOPIC 1. CREATIVE WRITING 347

1.3.3.1 Using theme to generate a story

Story idea 9

You could use the character section to build a character and then take this idea to create a situation for her or him.

Alternatively, you could start with the theme and build an appropriate character from the situation.

Looking at the section on story structure will remind you of the need to start with the theme in the set-up and developing it as the story builds.

1. Think of a situation where a character has massive ambition to achieve something.
2. What is in the way of the character achieving this? If you explore some complex obstacles, perhaps focussing on relationships with other characters, you will create the conflict for your story.

© HERIOT-WATT UNIVERSITY

Story idea 10

You could use the character section to build a character and then take this idea to create a situation for her or him.

Alternatively, you could start with the theme and build an appropriate character from the situation.

Looking at the section on story structure will remind you of the need to start with the theme in the set-up and developing it as the story builds.

1. 'A journey of a thousand miles begins with a single step' Lao Tzu.

2. Create a character and take them on a journey of discovery. Make them learn about their own potential or limitations. You could interpret the journey metaphorically as well as literally as you explore them learning about themselves.

TOPIC 1. CREATIVE WRITING

Story idea 11

You could use the character section to build a character and then take this idea to create a situation for her or him.

Alternatively, you could start with the theme and build an appropriate character from the situation.

Looking at the section on story structure will remind you of the need to start with the theme in the set-up and developing it as the story builds.

1. Think of a situation where a character is trapped metaphorically rather than literally.
2. What is keeping them in? Is it:
    1. physical?
    2. emotional?
    3. circumstances (poverty for example)?
3. What do they need to do to break out?
4. In the picture above, the image of a web is used to suggest the idea of being trapped. What other images could you use? Refer to the image several times during the story (in different ways) and you have created a motif which will bring elements of improved style to your writing.

Story idea 12

You could use the character section to build a character and then take this idea to create a situation for her or him.

Alternatively, you could start with the theme and build an appropriate character from the situation.

Looking at the section on story structure will remind you of the need to start with the theme in the set-up and developing it as the story builds.

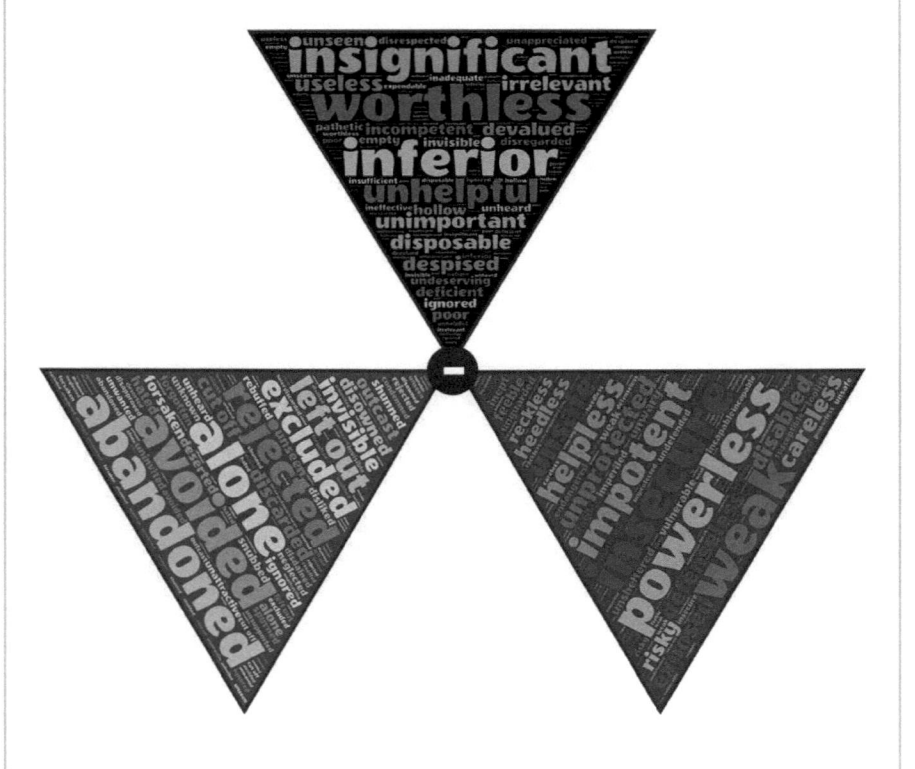

1. Place a character in a situation where they have to face their worst fear.
2. Create a tense climax where they find the means to overcome this fear.

TOPIC 1. CREATIVE WRITING

1.3.3.2 Themes in Portfolio examples

Themes in Portfolio — Go online

Q11: Complete the table using the themes listed to match the story titles.

Story	Theme
'Olivia's Choice'	
'The Apple Incarnate'	
'Shipwrecked'	
'Magnum Opiate'	

Themes

- Dealing with rejection and self-doubt.
- Obsession and self-destruction.
- We get inside the mind of a conspiracy theorist.
- Family strife and coping with death.

You can read all the stories in the exemplar section.

By reading a story and looking for its theme as your main focus, you will see how a writer integrates a theme into character development.

1.3.4 Narrative voice

This is the 'voice' of the story - the person telling the events to the reader. You will have covered this idea when you studied prose in the Literature section of the course. There are two realistic possibilities that you should consider in the writing of prose fiction. Think about this before you write and stick to the same voice.

First person narrative voice

This is when the person telling the story is actually in the story. They are telling the reader the events.

Advantages

- You get to know one character really well.
- You get to really know what the character is thinking.
- As a writer, you get to develop the character.
- You can let the reader see the flaws in the character.

There are some more sophisticated ideas that you should consider when using first person narrator.

- Is the first person narrator the protagonist?
- Does the action of the story happen as if in 'real time' so as the narrator does not know what is going to happen?
- Has time elapsed between the events of the story? How long? Has the narrator developed or matured since the events?
- Is the writer talking to herself or himself or aware that he/she is narrating to a reader?
- Is the style of writing 'stream of consciousness'? This means it is written as if it is thoughts rather than extended, fully grammatical prose. You could even use this as part of the story.
- The narrative voice might be a secondary character giving his or her opinion of the main character.
- You could deliberately create an unreliable narrator. Someone who is manipulating the reader by not telling the whole truth. Gradually the reader will see through the narrative voice and understand the flawed nature of the character.
- You could use a dual narrator. Two different characters, each using first person, to give different and opposing views of the same situation.

Third person narrative

This is where the voice of the story is external. You would refer to characters by name or use pronouns like he, she, his, her etc.

Advantages

- You can enter the mind of more than one character.
- You can offer different views of the same scene or events by use of narrative.

TOPIC 1. CREATIVE WRITING

- You can add more physical description of the character.
- The story can go to places without the main character being present.

There are some more sophisticated ideas that you should consider when using third person narrator:

- *Third person objective:* The narrator can only relate to the reader what is seen or heard. The narrator does not tell us what the character is thinking. To make this work well, you will need strong skills at showing and not telling.
  (Please see previous section 1.2.3 - Show don't tell)
- *Third person omniscient:* The narrator knows everything and can choose to tell us how characters are thinking. When using this you need to be careful that you don't just tell the reader what the character is thinking and planning all the time.
- *Third person limited:* The narrative voice is third person but focusses on a single character and tells the story from their point of view. With this narrative voice, you can still get the reader to really understand a single character in the same way as first person narrative voice. However, this narrative voice can stop and describe setting and atmosphere in a way that would seem really artificial in a first person narrator story.

1.3.4.1 Narrative voice in Portfolio example

Narrative voice in Portfolio activity: Olivia's Choice

Look at the following paragraph from the short story 'Olivia's Choice'. It is the part of the story where the character thinks about her choice in relationships.

> I thought back to the first day I ran away. A decision quickly made in haste, out of frustration at someone my father loved, but someone I didn't. I couldn't understand how he could move on when I couldn't, and why he would want to. All my anger about my mother's death I took out on her, and now only realising now how unfair that was. I remember the moment when I left the front door knowing I wasn't coming back - yet I so deeply wanted to. The air smelt cleaner than it did before and the outdoors more welcoming. I walked over to somewhere I called my second home, somewhere frightening to others yet for myself a place of tranquillity. I sat beside her grave and talked with her - "I'm sorry I let you down". I didn't need to tell her how upset I was - she could see it.

Discussion questions

1. Which narrative voice is being used?
2. Which parts of this story really let us see the character's inner thoughts?
3. Which parts let us see her inner dreams that only she would know?

You can read the whole story in the section of Exemplar work.

> **Narrative voice in Portfolio activity: The Apple Incarnate**
>
> Look at the paragraph from the short story 'The Apple Incarnate'.
>
> > The stairs felt cold against his exposed foot. The hairs on his chin finally found their purpose, clotting the trails of drying blood running down his face. The wiping of it acted as a subtle prompt for him to hurry on. He hoped they were no longer out there. He feared them - like vultures they encircled him, stabbing away at his weaknesses and tormenting him with attraction. And considering all that he gave them. *But he wasn't to be caught.* Maimed as he was, he was determined to reach the rather hollow safety of the room.
>
> Discussion questions
>
> 1. Select a part where the narrative voice enters the mind of the character.
> 2. Look at the parts of the extract where the character's physical sensations are described. Explain how the writer is using them to show how the character is feeling rather than telling us more directly.
>
> You can read the whole story in the section of Exemplar work.

1.3.5 Plot structure

When thinking up an idea for a plot, it is too easy to get carried away with the story and try to make too much happen. You have a word limit and can only develop a single situation effectively within that limit.

It is better to have a more realistic story with developed characters than an over elaborate, dramatic plot that really isn't all that believable. Complications in s story for Higher should focus on character and theme development rather than being plot based.

You can think of a straightforward story as having four sections. They won't all be of equal length and every story will balance the length differently. For a more complex story, you can change this structure but it is a good idea to understand the basic structure. Then, any adaptation of the structure will be done for a sound reason.

1. Set-up - the start of the journey.
2. Conflict - complications arise.
3. Climax - the problem reaches its highest point.
4. Resolution - the final thoughts on the journey down.

TOPIC 1. CREATIVE WRITING

Set-up — Conflict — Climax — Resolution (mountain diagram)

Story structure

Go online

Q12: Complete the table by matching the descriptions listed with the structural terms.

Story structure	Description
Set-up	
Conflict	
Climax	
Resolution	

Descriptions

- The problem develops and it reaches a worst moment.
- You set up the story by introducing the main character.
- The problem is concluded. The character has learned what they need to.
- You introduce a problem or a challenge for the character.

More complex structures

The straightforward structure for a short story can produce an effective story at any level of writing. There are some ways that you can show writing skill by adapting the structure.

- A character can have flashbacks. This can let you write tense scenes with more drama that a narrative voice telling the back-story.
- Flashforwards can let you do time jumps and keep the story moving at pace.
- Dual narrative structures (perhaps with dual narrative voices) lets you converge two plots and make the climax the point where they meet.
- You can miss out the typically slow set-up and take the reader right to the point of conflict.
- You can shorten the resolution. Don't leave hanging endings but make the reader work out the ending from clues dropped during the story.

1.3.5.1 Set-up

A set-up of a short story has to do more than just be an introduction. You need to:

- establish the main character;
- set up the situation in terms of plot;
- hint at where the conflict might be;
- set some narrative 'hooks' - leave some details out that keep the reader wanting to read on.

A good set up tells the reader lots but not everything. It is subtle and intriguing.

TOPIC 1. CREATIVE WRITING

Set-up in Portfolio examples: Magnum Opiate

Look at the set-up from the short story 'Magnum Opiate'.

> It was both the dry stench of the cab and the complete carelessness of its less than friendly driver that made it a very uncomfortable journey to the 'artists' house. He really couldn't be doing with this hassle - the travelling alone had already lasted twelve hours. However, he was in ways fixed to this task more than others. Well to put it into a rather brutal but realistic fashion, his job and frankly his livelihood were on the line.

Discussion questions

1. What do we learn about the character?
2. What things are hinted at but make us want to learn more?
3. Describe the mood of the opening scene.

You can read the whole story in the section of Exemplar work.

© HERIOT-WATT UNIVERSITY

Set-up in Portfolio examples: The Apple Incarnate

Look at the set-up from the short story 'The Apple Incarnate'.

> Exhaustion. It followed him, dragging him back as he struggled through the motel doors. The intoxicating magenta sign spoke out in uncaring and invasive patterns - the welcome of it felt as hollow as the holes encasing his being. The manager was out so he raced towards the first corridor, toward his room, leaving a trail of spattered vermillion over the cheap lobby carpets.
>
> *There was no time for explanations.*

Discussion questions

1. What can we infer about this character?
2. What can we infer about the hotel?
3. What plot details are given and which are left out to keep us reading on?

You can read the whole story in the section of Exemplar work.

1.3.5.2 Conflict

The conflict phase moves the story on. In this phase you can:

- develop the main character;
- develop the plot;
- develop the sense of tension;
- perhaps hint at different outcomes.

A good conflict moves the story on and keeps the reader interested. It begins to establish the nature of the problem facing the central character and will build to the next phase of the story.

Conflict in Portfolio examples: Olivia's Choice

Look at the opening from the short story 'Olivia's Choice'.

Identify the parts where you think conflict is introduced.

> I had been living like this for seven days now. It may not seem long, but after counting every hour, every minute, and every second; it felt like an eternity. I was my own prisoner, but ironically I held the key to my escape. However my freedom would mean going back and I didn't know if I was ready to leave my self-inflicted cell just yet. I knew he would be worried and I knew he wanted me back but I didn't know if I could let go of the past and what the future would bring. Sitting alone staring into the darkness my stomach growling, twisted in pain from hunger was my choice. How could this be right?
>
> I don't think I had come to terms with losing her. I don't think I ever would but I had to find a way of living, I had to find a way of living without her and for myself, something she had always insisted on. My mother had only been gone a year and it all just seemed too soon, too sudden, too new. I couldn't accept the change, I didn't want to - all I wanted to be wrapped in the blanket of her arms, to hear her voice and to feel her warmth yet that was nothing but a distant memory.

You can read the whole story in the section of Exemplar work.

> **Conflict in Portfolio examples: Magnum Opiate**
>
> Look at the opening from the short story 'Magnum Opiate'.
>
> Identify the parts where you think conflict is introduced.
>
>> The dust smeared the car windows and the thin tyres seemed to accentuate every bloody bump they hit on the bare dirt road. He began to realise where he really was headed for - forget the 'artists' - metaphorically. This was the one story that really mattered, the magnum opus, his very own evidence to prove that behind all the dormant years scripting ads for lousy catering companies he was actually a competent and rather gifted collector of information. He thought of the irony that would ensue. All the papers that previously rejected his stories, laughed at his inaudible evidence tapes of countless 'artists' and even went as far to declare him deluded and bearing the same mindset as the 'artists' themselves. But alas, here he was basking in the glory of an overheated Honda hatchback heading into God knows where to catch the mad fools in their artistic act. It was priceless, reminding him of his watch - beautifully handmade but utterly worthless and to be honest, when he really thought about it, lacking in any aesthetic appeal.
>>
>> Although his thoughts were that of a content disposition, even against the discomfort of the cardboard backseat he crumpled over, they were quickly shot down as the taxi came to an alarming brake stop in the middle of the dirt road. He rose quickly from his slouch to observe the surroundings outside the window caked in the midday heat. There was no house here. It wasn't even an 'artistic' illusion. It was gravel followed by gravel and a little bit of sand. Emptiness. Why had we stopped? He had heard the 'artists' hid their....ehm... art well but this level of isolation was laughable, in a horribly self-loathing kind of way. He rubbed his eyes and leaned forward to confront the driver but was set aback upon witnessing the small hairy man hunched over the wheel and bleeding. He himself, hated the sight of blood and started to feel sickness in the dusty sauna of the harboured Honda. Panting melodramatically, he let himself out of his door - it's not like the dead taxi driver was going to do it - and fell back into the barren, sandy waste in a state of shock.
>
> You can read the whole story in the section of Exemplar work.

1.3.5.3 Climax

The climax of a short story is:

- where the high point of the action is;
- it will usually be tense;
- will tend to involve lots of action rather than description;
- could use speech to reveal the dramatic moment.

TOPIC 1. CREATIVE WRITING

Climax in Portfolio examples: Olivia's Choice

Look at this section from the short story 'Olivia's Choice'.

> All of a sudden, I faintly made out a familiar voice through the crowd. "Olivia... Olivia..." A warm hand lightly pressed down on my shoulder which gave me a false sense of security, and a false sense of hope. Before I knew it she was next to me. I couldn't bear to look at her. The wind was blowing my hair in her direction as if to urge me to look round, but I couldn't bring myself to do it. "Olivia?" I paused. "We miss you". How dare she come here to find me; I was only trying to escape her.
>
> "You will never replace my mother!" I yelled at her. "How could you even want to try?" She just didn't understand and she never would. I turned further away from her. Harsh and bitter tears were streaming down my cheeks, lashing onto the pavement in front of me. There was no point trying to stop and conceal them. She knew not to touch me then. She had done enough. My weeping turned to a soft whimpering. I was too weak and too limp to cry anymore, there were no more tears left. She started to wrap her arms around me like a blanket, a feeling I haven't experienced for a long time. "Replacing your mother was something I had never wanted to do, all I wanted was to help you and your father be close again and be someone to look after you". There was an unbearable silence. I couldn't hear the loud buzz of people any more. I thought the world had stood still. The sun began to appear and once again the city was brought to life. Shadows grew fainter on the faces of buildings and the bustle of people began to fill the streets.

This extract is almost at the end. When you read the whole story you will see how the main character has to face the conflict that has been set up- she has to meet the step mother figure from whom she ran away. It is a balance of positive actions from the step mother and the rejection felt by the central character. Using the table below, make notes of three examples of each.

Positive actions	Negative Thoughts

You can read the whole story in the section of Exemplar work.

> ### Climax in Portfolio examples: Shipwrecked
>
> Look at this section from the short story 'Shipwrecked'.
>
> > The storm raged on. Surprisingly I didn't notice, growing more in sheer power. Thunder booms crept slowly. Lightning danced wildly on the surface of the sea, edging closer with every step. "Flashy enough for you? I mean you could have been more creative. A god complex? Seriously? And why am I Zeus? That guy is a detestable degenerate. Oh I see. Clever huh. You made me your worst aspects." His suave attitude irked me. The messy hair, the unkempt beard, the pointy nose, the condescending eyes -all of it irked me. "You could have made things interesting and made me your good side - just like that one movie - but 'someone' was lazy and so I am just a generic egotist." He rolled his eyes just to copy what I did. "So how does it feel to be honest? Because right now you really aren't being truthful." his smug attitude had no bounds. "Well, let us talk about love, eh? Or the lack of it in your life. Either way you can't force her to love you," he paused uncouthly. "Anyway, now why are you here? ... Don't hate people, how they think differently from you, how they lie to you, how they 'use and abuse' you, just like what you are doing now. They have abandoned you. You can't accept that. You just don't want to be lonely. Give me a PhD because I have successfully psychoanalysed you. Don't be a baby. Be a man. Great last words huh?" with that he left.
>
> This extract is almost at the end and the conflict is created as a drunken apparition taunts the character.
>
> Discussion questions
>
> 1. How does the use of the storm imagery add to the impact of the scene?
> 2. How does the physical appearance of the apparition add to the character's sense of self-loathing?
> 3. How is dialogue used to torment the central character?
>
> You can read the whole story in the section of Exemplar work.

1.3.5.4 Resolution

The resolution finishes the story. The climax may be dramatic and full of action so there is little time for the character to reflect. Some hints regarding resolutions are:

- 'show' how your character has changed. (Don't tell);
- tie off any loose ends;
- don't create 'hanging endings'. They can often look like you could not be bothered to think of a decent ending;
- first person narrators can really reflect in this part of the story;
- don't make time jumps or use it to condense what could easily be the plot of another story.

Resolution in Portfolio examples: Shipwrecked

Look at this section from the short story 'Shipwrecked'.

> I slumped on the wheel as the last of these waves crashed over me.

You can read the whole story in the section of Exemplar work.

Marker's comment

All good short stories end at a key moment and know when to stop. The character has been tormented by an apparition whilst drunk. The setting is in a ship based theme pub. This single sentence resolution reinforces the wave imagery that has been used in several places throughout. The point of the story has been reached the character has been crushed by his past. No doubt, he will wake up the next day with more regrets or a sense that he needs to start again. Those details would have been the plot for another story and not the continuation of this one.

Resolution in Portfolio example: The Apple Incarnate

Look at this section from the short story 'The Apple Incarnate.

You will see how the writer concludes by using the same colour imagery to link to the hotel scene at the start. It is an effective conclusion because it does not simply suggest the character is over his obsession and shows that he is trapped. The contrast of pleasure and pain ideas highlights this.

> A foggy night. He rose, wounded but awake from them. This familiar serenity. Ephemeral. He walked doggedly around the twisted metropolis. The sky looked kaleidoscopically pained and he too felt the air awakening. They'd be back out soon. But he was so cosily nestled in this small pocket of thoughtlessness, he decided he'd walk on. For the bright magenta light of the motel was bound to welcome him back to his place of sanctuary - the home of resting off his latest mess and avoiding them until the urge for repetition took over.

1. Highlight the words / ideas that suggest he is now content.
2. Highlight the words / phrases which contain unpleasant ideas of images of pain.

You can read the whole story in the section of Exemplar work.

1.4 Personal writing

Personal writing is when you write about an incident or a memory from your own experience. It might be about something that you have taken part in or maybe your memories of a place or a person.

Good personal writing does more than just describe what happened. You should describe your feelings and reactions in detail. You are also trying to show a sense of self-awareness and show that you have really thought about, and maybe learned from the experience. Some very effective personal writing reflects and shows how the writer has changed as a result of the experience. Another way to reflect is to look back and contrast your views now with how you felt at the time.

The section on prose fiction has lots of ways that you can generate ideas. You could use some of those for personal writing and many of the skills of writing good prose fiction apply to non-fiction too. In personal writing you still need to build characters- just because you know the people in your essay doesn't mean that the reader does so you need to create them just as you would in prose fiction. Good dialogue will also bring personal writing to life. Look over the prose fiction sections to revise your skills.

In addition, we will look over some areas specific to personal writing. These are:

- getting ideas;
- structure;
- reflection.

By planning and thinking about these features you will create a more effective piece of personal writing.

1.4.1 Getting ideas

There are many possible ideas for personal writing but here are some to get you started. What is important is that the idea is original to you and written about in depth.

- Parents are a necessary evil - examining family relationships.
- Write about a time when you gave in to peer pressure or temptation. Explain the complex and contrasting feelings.
- Oh to be an only child!
- The best things in life are free.
- I wish I knew then what I know now.
- Write about a time that changed your life.
- Write about a time that you felt let down.
- Have you ever felt left out?

- Thoughts and impressions on:
    - looking at old photos;
    - listening to old records;
    - seeing old films;
    - going back to an old school or home.
- What your possessions say about you.
- A place with memories.

1.4.2 Structure

When thinking up an idea for a personal essay, it is too easy to think that you must have an elaborate story to tell or that you must cover a long time period. You have a word limit and can only develop a single situation effectively within that limit.

It is better to have a well described single incident than try to cover the events of a week or even a whole day.

You can think of a personal essay as being like a short story with four sections. They won't all be of equal length and every story will balance the length differently. This is the basic structure which can be adapted to make more complex structures.

1. Set-up - the start of the journey.
2. Conflict - complications arise.
3. Climax - the problem reaches its highest point.
4. Resolution - the final thoughts on the journey down.

TOPIC 1. CREATIVE WRITING

Set-up — Conflict — Climax — Resolution

Story structure

Q13: Complete the table by matching the descriptions from the list with the appropriate structural terms.

Story structure	Description
Set-up	
Conflict	
Climax	
Resolution	

Descriptions

- The problem develops and it reaches a worst moment.
- You set up the story by introducing the main character.
- The problem is concluded. The character has learned what they need to.
- You introduce a problem or a challenge for the character.

1.4.2.1 More complex structures

The straightforward structure for a personal essay can produce an effective piece at any level of writing. There are some ways that you can show writing skill by adapting the structure.

- You can use flashbacks. This can let you write tense scenes with more drama that a narrative voice telling the back-story. Perhaps beginning with adult perspective lets you bring reflection into the beginning of your essay.
- Flashforwards can let you do time jumps and keep the story moving at pace You can miss out the typically slow set-up and take the reader right to the point of conflict.
- You can shorten the resolution. Don't leave hanging endings but make the reader work out the ending from clues dropped during the story.
- You could use a motif - an idea or image that runs throughout the story and provides a framework for the story. Having the motif in the title helps your writing use symbolism.
- Make the title a problem or an enigma. Make the reader wonder what the title means and at a key point in the structure (perhaps in climax or resolution) make the symbolic meaning of the title clear.

1.4.2.2 Set-up

The set-up of a personal essay has to do more than just be an introduction.

You need to:

- Establish you and your personality.
- Set up the situation in terms of plot.
- Hint at where the conflict might be.
- Set some narrative 'hooks' - leave some details out that keep the reader wanting to read on. It is easy to ruin an essay by making the start too factual and just directly telling the reader where you are and when it took place.
- You can reflect at this stage by suggesting that looking back your feelings have changed.

A good set up tells the reader lots but not everything.

TOPIC 1. CREATIVE WRITING

Set-up in Portfolio activity: Trossachs Trauma

Look at the set-up from the personal essay 'Trossachs Trauma'.

> Embarking on my Silver Duke of Edinburgh hike, just two days after my National Five exams were over, was nowhere near the celebration I'd been hoping for. All my exam stress had been turned to both physical and mental preparation for this three day hike. Over the period we were scheduled to walk a grand total of fifty-nine kilometres. Twenty kilometres roughly a day doesn't sound too bad does it?

Discussion questions

1. What do we learn about the character?
2. What things are hinted at but make us want to learn more?
3. How does the writer create a tone of doubt?

You can read the whole personal essay in the section of Exemplar work.

Set-up in Portfolio activity: Bursting the Bubble

Look at the set-up from the personal essay 'Bursting the Bubble'.

> For a sheltered boy who spent his early years in the affluent areas of Pimlico and Wimbledon in Southern London, it would be logical to think that a similarly affluent area in the heart of the Renfrewshire countryside would feel like home. Big houses, wealthy people, fancy cars, sounds like a good place for a cerebral, naive, inexperienced child like myself, does it not? Having lived here for seven years now I am almost adjusted to this new lifestyle but - trust me - it wasn't straightforward. The experience of Kilmacolm has pleased some but traumatised the majority, which is why I will keep a special place in my heart for my utter loathing for that despicable village.

This is successful because of the conflict between what the writer was expecting and what he experiences. Which details are about his expectations and which are the real experience?

Expected	Experienced

You can read the whole personal essay in the section of Exemplar work.

1.4.2.3 Conflict

The conflict phase moves the story on. In this phase you can:

- develop our understanding of you;
- develop the plot;
- develop the sense of tension - this can be internal as well as external;
- perhaps hint at different outcomes.

A good conflict moves the story on and keeps the reader interested.

Conflict in Portfolio Example: All Children are Artists

Look at the opening from the personal essay 'All Children are Artists'.

> Thinking back to when I was five, I learned how to add numbers together and one afternoon we got to colour in and I made a tower with the Jenga blocks. I really loved school. Ignorance is bliss, right? I have tried to remember at which point I was educated beyond ignorance, at which point the blissful bubble of colouring in, Golden Time and playing games pretending we were anything and everything, popped and left a hollow filled with Past Papers and late nights fuelled by caffeine desperately trying to finish the thousand or so words that are "...Due first period tomorrow, mum!" It doesn't really matter when I finish whatever homework I'm trying to complete though. I'll stay up late pretending that I won't be woken up at 6.15 by an alarm so loud it causes me pain, and struggle through another exhausting day, tired as always. Primary school seems like a distant bliss, waking up half an hour before going to school for a fun-filled day and finishing homework by four o'clock.

Highlight the different kinds of conflict:

1. conflict with self over behaviour;
2. conflict with self over different feelings as she gets older;
3. conflict with mother.

You can read the whole personal essay in the section of Exemplar work.

Conflict in Portfolio Example: Crossing the divide

Look at the conflict from the personal essay 'Crossing the Divide'.

> As we stepped off the short plane journey from Glasgow, we were greeted by the same weather as home. The short bus journey into the city was just like home. As we reached the city, it seemed like any other British city I had ever been to. But as we left the bus station and strolled past the Europa hotel (Europe's most bombed hotel), and down the pedestrian lane adjacent to the court house, closed to traffic because of a persistent stream of bombs, everything seemed normal. The people were fresh faced and friendly, never shying away from a polite nod as you passed them in the street. Everyone seemed to be living in perfect harmony. However as my trip progressed, I learned that harmony is a word that should never be used when describing Belfast.
>
> We spent the next few days seeing the very tourist-orientated side of Belfast, the side of the city that they wanted you to see. We marvelled at how wonderful the Titanic was and were ushered round 'Belfast's very own leaning tower of Pisa'. All very nice and, well, touristy. It wasn't until our third and final day that I started to get a true indication of what Belfast was really like, not what it was supposed to be like, when I visited the Crumlin Road Jail (Or 'the Crum' as it had been nicknamed by the tourist board) there was the odd inscription on the wall, or mark on the floor that hinted at the deep divisions in the city.
>
> As we walked into the prisoner's registration area, there were cubicles where they were stripped and put into their prison clothes. As I look into each of the cubicles, I noticed that each one was marked at least 20 times with either 'IRA' or 'UVF'. It seemed like every prisoner had a political preference, and I found it unthinkable that the divisions in the city weren't just limited to the streets, but even the prisons had to be completely divided. How they could keep people imprisoned alongside the very people they were imprisoned for trying to kill was beyond me.

Highlight how this conflict is built by presenting one side then the other:

- Comfortable and familiar
- unsettling

You can read the whole personal essay in the section of Exemplar work.

1.4.2.4 Climax

The climax of a personal essay is:

- where the high point of the action if this is appropriate;
- it will usually be tense;
- could use speech to reveal the key moment of learning;
- the writer may highlight their own flaws or flawed attitudes at this moment;
- the title of the story could become apparent at this moment.

TOPIC 1. CREATIVE WRITING

Climax in Portfolio activity: Journeying — Go online

Look at the climax from the personal essay 'Journeying'.

In this section, the writer creates a climax by observing how the character is hiding from the police.

> As I read, the sound of police sirens was in the distance. I remember not taking any notice of it, yet when it became louder and more recognizable. I glanced behind me to see where it was coming from. On returning to my page from not seeing anything, I noticed the masseuse's behaviour. I suddenly realised that she must be here illegally. The woman looked like a terrified child, her eyes broadening and her body springing to life from a peaceful manner. The sight filled me with pity and selfishness- my week long break was a luxury that she would never have, yet I could not help her. How could a life of constant fear be better than what she has left behind, or what she has escaped from? Maybe her country could be war torn, or in great poverty. The sirens were so close that they demanded to be heard. I turned around again, and two police officers rode motorbikes smoothly yet rapidly along the clean, stone promenade that was basking in the shade of palm trees. The *policía* lettering boldly stuck out of the silver and blue vehicle and drew my attention. What would they do to her if they saw her? The thought terrified me, because she had nobody to speak up for her, nobody to help her- the immigration policy had already failed her.

Q14: Put these details that add tension into the correct order. This will show you how to build to a tense climax.

Writer thinks of her own comforts
Distant sirens
The police arrive
Observes the woman hiding
Writer speculates on the woman's life

You can read the whole personal essay in the section of Exemplar work.

> **Climax in Portfolio activity: Trossachs Trauma**
>
> Look at the climax from the personal essay 'Trossachs Trauma'.
>
> > We started to wander further round the loch where we spotted a fence at the top of a hill that looked mountainous from where we stood.
> >
> > "Guys, I think that's the fence they were talking about..." Jen anxiously pointed out.
> >
> > "What? The one all the way up at the top of that hill? That can't be it" Hannah expressed hopefully.
> >
> > But it was. We knew that was the fence the supervisors had been talking about. If only we'd just taken a minute to spot and use the handrails on the map rather than just heading off the minute we were 50% sure it was the right way.
> >
> > That did tend to be the problem with our group. We just never thought things through long enough, we tended to play it by a democracy vote rather than tactically working things out. We learned the hard way that that was never going to bring success. Three men do make a tiger. In the ancient story, once three people had told the King that there was a tiger in the market, he believed it despite that he had not seen it for himself. In our case, the more people that said that we were going the right way, the more we all started to believe it yet none of us had given it thorough thought.
>
> We can examine this extract for more subtle techniques. Explain how:
>
> - dialogue is used to bring in the feelings of others in the group;
> - the legend used helps the writer to reflect on her flawed attitudes.
>
> You can read the whole personal essay in the section of Exemplar work.

1.4.2.5 Resolution

The resolution finishes the essay. The climax may be dramatic and full of action so there is little time for you to reflect. Some hints regarding resolutions are:

- 'show' how your feelings has changed. (Don't tell);
- tie off any loose ends;
- you could reflect strongly in this part of the story;
- you can look to future if this fits your essay;
- if appropriate, make the meaning of the title evident at this point.

Resolution in Portfolio example: Crossing the divide

Look at the resolution from the reflective essay 'Crossing the divide'.

The writer has been on a tour of Belfast and in particular is questioning why people want to see this type of place as somewhere to visit with any sense of nostalgia.

> Besides, I find it hard to understand why the government of Northern Ireland would want to promote this as any kind of tourist attraction- a vile war, fuelled by religious bitterness and hatred that killed thousands of civilians only to come to the 'conclusion' after nearly thirty years of fighting that they simply could never live together and resolved this by planting a huge wall between the two communities. But still people come in their droves to see the 'Divide'.
>
> It seems that people love the romantic side of war and conflict and are 'touched' by the brave Republicans and Loyalists who fought to stand up for their beliefs and religion. Their delusion has become part of the mythology that becomes history and converts to fact. Understanding this is a barrier I cannot cross.

Discussion questions:

1. Explain how the resolution summarises the writer's feelings.

2. Explain how the writer uses the title of the story effectively at the ending. Look for the literal reference and the metaphorical interpretation of the idea of a divide.

You can read the whole reflective essay in the section of Exemplar work.

Resolution in Portfolio activity: Trossachs Trauma

Look at the resolution from the personal essay 'Trossachs Trauma'.

Having finished the hike for the day, the writer presents:

- the memory at the time,
- considers where she went wrong
- and evaluates how she will be different in the future.

> Being eaten alive by midges, we pitched up our tents faster than we'd done anything else that day, consumed a plateful of hard raw pasta which we were too tired to cook properly, and threw ourselves into our tents... only to wake up the next morning and hike all over again.[1]
>
> Overall, looking back it was clear from day one it was never going to go to plan. We saw our training days as just a necessary aspect of the award rather than an effective preparation tool for our hike, and didn't take them as seriously as, evidently, we should have.[2] Our group were a walking disaster (literally) but nevertheless we made it... barely.[3] Despite the near failure of Silver, and the drastic detour, the experience has only made me feel more prepared for my Gold hike which I will be participating in in 2016 and I will not be as 'navigationally challenged'.[4]
>
> Notes:
> [1] the memory at the time
> [2] considers where she went wrong
> [3] the memory at the time
> [4] evaluates how she will be different in the future

You can read the whole personal essay in the section of Exemplar work.

TOPIC 1. CREATIVE WRITING

1.4.3 Reflection

Personal essays can be a very well written and detailed account of your experience. They can show your feelings in great depth and capture the reader's attention.

When you reflect, you show the ability to think more deeply about an experience. Some ways to be reflective are:

- to reflect on how the experience has changed the way that you think;
- to reflect on how the experience has changed your life;
- to reflect on how you would behave differently now;
- to think about how others might react to the situation;
- to consider how your behaviour exemplifies a type of generic human behaviour;
- to examine the source and nature of your behaviour (where did the value system originate?);
- to examine the psychology of your behaviour.

Some aims of a reflective essay are that it will:

- be genuinely contemplative;
- communicate to the reader a clear sense of the writer's personality;
- to have a strong sense of self awareness;
- start with your experience but widen out by reflecting on the theme of your essay.

Your essay should include a range of sections:

- descriptive;
- narrative;
- sections of well written dialogue;
- reflective *(but the process of reflection should exist throughout)*.

1.4.3.1 Reflection in Portfolio examples

Reflection in Portfolio activity: In the Grand Scheme of Things

Effective reflective writing has a reflective narrative voice throughout and not just in the last paragraph. Look at the example sections from the reflective essay 'In the Grand Scheme of Things'.

> We all have these funny aspirations and desires for things in our lives, something as simple as a good job or a nice car; personally I like clothes and appreciate a good quality leather. However these things are only material, one thing you cannot be taught in a classroom is that the only way you can be happy is to stop trying to be. Life has a habit of throwing events at us we cannot prepare for in a classroom or with a university degree. We must to an extent try to grasp the true feeling of living and being alive and cherish it while we can. We find it in that awkward moment when you laugh at your own fake laugh and end up crying, that moment when you lose your concentration and rub conditioner all over your face. You can't recreate these moments; somehow getting conditioner in your eye wouldn't be as funny if you deliberately put it there. Constantly striving for new goals and aspirations will mean if we don't already appreciate what we have in that moment, as said by Omar Khayyam "Be happy for this moment. This moment is your life."

Highlight the phrases which set-up a reflective tone.

When you read the rest of this essay, you will see that reflection is built in at every stage. This helps the writer create a dramatic and forceful ending rather than looking like it was written to a formula.

You can read the whole reflective essay in the section of Exemplar work.

TOPIC 1. CREATIVE WRITING

Reflection in Portfolio activity: All Creatures Great and Small

In this section, we will examine a whole essay with commentary after each section explaining why it is a very effective piece of writing.

Exhibit 1: All Creatures Great and Small

Higher Reflective Essay by Rhona MacPhail, St Columba's School, Kilmacolm

What's the biggest animal you've ever killed? A spider, mouse, hare, either way you probably didn't have any emotional connection to it whatsoever. However what if it was a cat, a dog or a horse? You would care then. This is what a vet has to go through every day, despite the common misconception that being a vet includes saving all creatures cute and fluffy. This is the reality.

The writer establishes a tone which surprises the reader and challenges their misconceptions regarding the nature of a vet's working life.

It was a depressing drive to the house as the vet and I sat in silence. After fifteen minutes of this dead, endless reticence we approached the house and turned into the drive.

A short scene establishes the mood as they approach the house. It is efficient and keeps the limited words allowed for the section that will matter most.

As we walked through the door, we were greeted by a mother and a grandmother. The grandmother seemed composed but the lady was distraught with tear stains streaked down her cheeks. As she led us upstairs, we approached the room where the silenced dog lay. I entered the room and shuffled past the dog lying in front of me. The vet deduced it had died in the night from a sudden stroke or fit. At least they gained some comfort from the fact it had been quick and painless. The German shepherd looked peaceful as he lay in his eternal slumber. I could feel the emotion rising up in me, choking me. I swallowed. I had to let my emotions subside. We then continued to wrap him in soft blankets to hide the sight. I was thankful; the lifeless eyes had been glaring at me making me uncomfortable. Karen talked to the family and asked them if they would like to say their final goodbyes. Two small children who could have only had been about six years old trundled into the room. They crawled down next to their pet and hugged him tears streaming down their faces. Throughout this I had to remain emotionless. After five torturous minutes of watching the family make their tearful farewells, we carried the heavy dog out to the car and delicately placed him in the back seat. We then gave them our condolences and left to head back to the surgery. This was my first experience of death.

The paragraph captures a range of responses and uses a variety of sentence construction patterns. It leads efficiently to a conclusion as to why the incident was important.

This had been my worst recollection from working at a veterinary surgery during my four years of volunteering as a Saturday worker. It still amazes me at how death has had an impact on me and how it's changed my perception of the job as a vet. Of course there are times where

© HERIOT-WATT UNIVERSITY

UNIT 3. PORTFOLIO

I look at the jump ahead of me, thinking of all the possible outcomes. I could avoid it, fail or just maybe, actually clear it.

> The writer subtly introduces the metaphor of a horse jump as a barrier to our progress in life. This will be picked up again in the conclusion.

I don't know what actually enticed me to become a vet in the first place. I know my love of animals originated from a young age but I can't seem to place why I chose animals. I could have hoped to be a doctor, lawyer even an accountant but I guess animals were the only choice. Many people say it's a hard career choice what with the extensive training at university as well as the never-ending amount of work experience. However, what would normally have put someone off the job - actually convinced me to give veterinary medicine a go.

I recall at Christmas one year eagerly unwrapping a box set of James Herriot 'All Creatures Great and Small' and being mesmerised as soon as I gazed down at the page. Since then I've read all the books in the box set given to me and watched his programme. One particular memory I remember distinctly was when he was helping a cow to calf. The birthing process was encountering difficulties and I could see the physical exertion etched onto the vet's face as he tried to contort the calf to the right position. I recollect looking behind my shoulder and glaring at the pale shocked faces of my family members as they watched the brutal scene unfold. While I merely sat watching with admiration. It wasn't glamourous, it involved long strenuous hours with often many dangers but when I watched him work I knew then that this was the career for me.

> The writer reflects on what attracts her to the job in the first place. She subtly indicates why the essay has the title.

All of my memories weren't all sombre; there have also been some life-changing experiences that I've witnessed. Watching an exceedingly ill patient recuperate to treatment and be able to return home with a smiling owner is probably the best reward of the job. I was in awe observing a mother see her 'children' for the first time and it taught me that death is balanced with life and I've been one of the fortunate few who has had the privilege to behold the wonder that is new life. Life, death and the uncertainty that surrounds existence is something that a vet confronts on a daily basis.

It had been an ordinary consultation. Until one of the junior vets came round panting, stumbling over her words informing Rebecca (one of the most valued members of the surgery) about a whelping bitch that was having birthing difficulties. Rebecca hustled the owner and his dog into the consulting room. It had been sudden and the apparent outcome wasn't promising. Rebecca had checked her over and after a tense couple of minutes she broke the news that she suspected that all four puppies were dead since she could only hear a singular heartbeat. I couldn't help but feel sympathy towards both the owner and dog since they didn't have any control over the situation. It made me rethink on the fragility of life. One instant and that could be the end. I realised this didn't apply just to animals either; it applies to us all. In our prime and youth we can all believe we are invincible but the harsh reality is that we are all vulnerable. This was the false façade I had cocooned myself in for years, and in that moment I truly felt the joy of being alive and healthy.

© Heriot-Watt University

TOPIC 1. CREATIVE WRITING

I was brought back to reality when I heard the vet say how the bitch was still in a life or death situation since the puppies still needed to be removed so that she didn't contract septicaemia. They quickly whisked her out of the consulting room into the operating theatre where they gave her a suitable dose of anaesthetic. They lifted her and placed her gently on the operating table and prepared her for a Caesarean. When everything was ready, a couple of nurses were monitoring the bitch with her breathing and blood flow while others were on standby in case any problems arose. Rebecca quickly but steadily opened up the dog and found the puppies, gently cutting away the amniotic bag and tying off the placenta. She then passed them one by one to the nurses to dry. It wasn't a pretty sight. They started rubbing them frantically with towels, encouraging them to breathe. I watched holding my breath; questions running through my mind until my thoughts are interrupted by a nurse shouting, "He's breathing!" Everyone in the room gave a relieved sigh. The nurse then placed the puppy delicately into a breathing compartment pumping life into his lungs. After a while, two other puppies started breathing. The situation was turning itself around. One nurse was still frantically trying to resuscitate the runt of the litter to no avail. The situation was growing dire as minutes crawled away. Finally she stopped and shook her head to the rest of the room but as she did so the tiniest cough could be heard. He was alive. Relieved and exhausted the nurse gave him to me to be towelled off. I could feel the rise and fall of his chest through the towel.

The writer focusses on the positives of being a vet and exemplifies with a tense anecdote highlighting the fragile line between life and death. She reflects on the impact that this has had on her and her own attitude to life.

My mind spurred as a horse jolts onwards to a jump. I felt the force through its legs as I soared over the barrier.

The writer concludes by returning to her animal metaphor. The experience of witnessing an expert at work and saving life has released her emotions and her mind is resolved to become a vet. Any barriers (emotional or physical) have been overcome and the positive tone creates a strong resolution.

1.5 Exemplar work

The following pieces of work have been published with the kind permission from students of St Columba's School, Kilmacolm

Olivia's Choice

Exhibit 2: Olivia's Choice

Higher Short Story by Katya Guyler, St Columba's School, Kilmacolm

As I tried to lift my eyelids after another rough night's sleep, my eyes focused onto a vast sky of grey fog. A tiny droplet of water glistened in the corner of my eye until blinking and feeling it slowly slide down my left cheek. My back ached after another night sleeping on cardboard. Even the thought of sitting up began to tire me out. The time was unknown to me, and so was my location. I just lay there and tried not to accept the situation that I knew I was in, but the thought was still there and there was no way of escaping it. The city's laughter echoed down hollow alleyways. As the sound faded, I remembered what it was like to have friends, people around me, to go home to a warm bed, to close the door behind me and shut out the world knowing I was safe. But now I was at the mercy of the elements, my fate decided by the drop of a coin into an empty paper cup.

I had been living like this for seven days now. It may not seem long, but after counting every hour, every minute, and every second; it felt like an eternity. I was my own prisoner, but ironically I held the key to my escape. However my freedom would mean going back and I didn't know if I was ready to leave my self-inflicted cell just yet. I knew he would be worried and I knew he wanted me back but I didn't know if I could let go of the past and what the future would bring. Sitting alone staring into the darkness my stomach growling, twisted in pain from hunger was my choice. How could this be right?

I don't think I had come to terms with losing her. I don't think I ever would but I had to find a way of living, I had to find a way of living without her and for myself, something she had always insisted on. My mother had only been gone a year and it all just seemed too soon, too sudden, too new. I couldn't accept the change, I didn't want to - all I wanted to be wrapped in the blanket of her arms, to hear her voice and to feel her warmth yet that was nothing but a distant memory.

As the sun crept back into its sanctuary, it felt as if I should be doing the same. The numbing cold was made it even harder to fall asleep and all I could wait for was the rising of the sun and the unveiling of a new day.

Not knowing what the future held frightened me and I had no one and nowhere to run to. I was only running from myself and my fears. Suffering in unbearable pain was my only coping mechanism.

I thought back to the first day I ran away. A decision quickly made in haste, out of frustration at someone my father loved, but someone I didn't. I couldn't understand how he could move on when I couldn't, and why he would want to. All my anger about my mother's death I took out on her, and now only realising now how unfair that was. I remember the moment when I left the front door knowing I wasn't coming back - yet I so deeply wanted to. The air smelt cleaner than it did before and the outdoors more welcoming. I walked over to somewhere I called my second home, somewhere frightening to others yet for myself a place of tranquillity.

I sat beside her grave and talked with her - "I'm sorry I let you down". I didn't need to tell her how upset I was - she could see it.

From the day the doctor told me about the terminal cancer I made it my mission to make sure she was never replaced, I couldn't hide my heartache and it was tough not to show her that I was so miserable. That moment he introduced me to her I hated her and knew I always would. I never knew how he would ask her to marry him; it was the last thing I wanted. But only now I was beginning to see why he did it - he was only trying to help me move forward.

When looking up my eyes levelled with a sea of people's feet flowing right past me as if I wasn't even there. It was all a blur of colours which made me dizzy. A loud murmuring hum of voices echoed about my ears. Seeing the world from this perspective allowed me to realise what I had become; a mindless object obstructing other people's lives.

All of a sudden, I faintly made out a familiar voice through the crowd. "Olivia... Olivia..." A warm hand lightly pressed down on my shoulder which gave me a false sense of security, and a false sense of hope. Before I knew it she was next to me. I couldn't bear to look at her. The wind was blowing my hair in her direction as if to urge me to look round, but I couldn't bring myself to do it. "Olivia?" I paused. "We miss you". How dare she come here to find me; I was only trying to escape her.

"You will never replace my mother!" I yelled at her. "How could you even want to try?" She just didn't understand and she never would. I turned further away from her. Harsh and bitter tears were streaming down my cheeks, lashing onto the pavement in front of me. There was no point trying to stop and conceal them. She knew not to touch me then. She had done enough. My weeping turned to a soft whimpering. I was too weak and too limp to cry anymore, there were no more tears left. She started to wrap her arms around me like a blanket, a feeling I haven't experienced for a long time. "Replacing your mother was something I had never wanted to do, all I wanted was to help you and your father be close again and be someone to look after you". There was an unbearable silence. I couldn't hear the loud buzz of people any more. I thought the world had stood still. The sun began to appear and once again the city was brought to life. Shadows grew fainter on the faces of buildings and the bustle of people began to fill the streets.

Then faced with the biggest problem of all: A choice. I could either go back home or I could stay in my self-inflicted cell. The thought toiled with me. Being too proud was a constant struggle for me yet also was being weak. I was at war with myself and I didn't know which side to take. You can make choices that can change your future but you can never change the choices you made in the past. I knew what I had to do. I had to do it for her, but more importantly I had to do it for myself.

The Apple Incarnate

Exhibit 3: The Apple Incarnate

Higher Short Story by Dominic Bogle, St Columba's School, Kilmacolm

Exhaustion. It followed him, dragging him back as he struggled through the motel doors. The intoxicating magenta sign spoke out in uncaring and invasive patterns - the welcome of it felt as hollow as the holes encasing his being. The manager was out so he raced towards the first corridor, toward his room, leaving a trail of spattered vermillion over the cheap lobby carpets.

There was no time for explanations.

Passing the same magnolia-plagued walls at every new turn didn't appease his crazed state of mind. He felt like a dense, cut-up mess of mass pin-balling off the walls, leaving behind subtle reminders of the consequences of his urges. Relapse, its enriching fruit cast a rainbow of complex pain over him. He felt no regrets. Even now panting against the second staircase, he still felt invincible. It all still raced through his blood. It was letting him know it was enjoying his company for now.

Though he already felt it fading.

The stairs felt cold against his exposed foot. The hairs on his chin finally found their purpose, clotting the trails of drying blood running down his face. The wiping of it acted as a subtle prompt for him to hurry on. He hoped *they* were no longer out there. He feared them - like vultures they encircled him, stabbing away at his weaknesses and tormenting him with attraction. And considering all that he gave them. *But he wasn't to be caught.* Maimed as he was, he was determined to reach the rather hollow safety of the room.

The murky Urban. Standing over, taunting, pushing. The Noise was piercing, the needles all too loud. eyes closing and swollen phalanges reaching out, begging, vainly showing innocence against the upper arms - no longer hiding their blackened waste within. Wet. The ground, a feeling, a texture, he could still feel - he wanted to remain feeling. Black. They cast their shadows.

The room's door was locked. His eyes groaned with pain as he started to bang his head against the flimsy sheet of wood and the rusted lock just managing to cling on to what it needed to. His mauled torso cast its own opus of monochromatic proclamation as he slid down the door, crying if he could have remembered what ducts to open for it. He felt more than desperate and less than helpless crawling over the empty hall, warding away the invisible ghosts before the real ones were bound to appear.

He was no sooner starting to see them when the corroded door pin gave way. A hope. His vacant brain was needing his red spheres for eyes to be truly seeing this. He rose wearily patting down the shivers that ran through his spine, and careered towards the entrance, hearing only faint white noise from the Television he left on. He stared at the unrecognisable image of himself within the room's mirror. It worried him. *Was it him?* Two bulging pupils in a skeletal gathering of fear and torment. It wasn't him. It couldn't be. These red streaks covered his body. The sickness was reaching its surface. They were finding their ways to get to him after all. Ways he had never thought of. He had to fix these wounds. He rushed to close the door. Footsteps outside mimicked his heartbeat till they became it - asking questions of their exterior existence within his own discomposed skull. He wouldn't let them in either way.

The shadows spoke harshly. Enquiring information already received, manipulating their needs upon this corpse lying on asphalt in the heat of the storm. He choked under the rain and blood but had his prize. He thanked them, for at last it seemed worthwhile. Retreating to a corner in the road, he sat hunched, avoiding further contact that wasn't needed. He tore apart the bag, crying, weeping tears of frustration, as he advanced once again in the action he and they needed.

He was lying sprawled across the small bed staring up at the aged ceiling, finding small comfort in the static blaring from the equally antique television set. He had treated the wounds as best he could: One of his socks sparingly offered service as a tourniquet. It would take hours until his waist would fester. He had hours. The clock wasn't cooperating but he had hours. All he could do was wait. They *would* find him. Distant shouting echoed through the single pane of the balcony window and into the bedroom. He smiled with fear. *Not quite here yet.* He laughed as he slithered off of the bed and started opening the balcony door that led out to the night. A wall of rain was met as he stepped into the chaotic dark. His mind played games with how many lights he was seeing, though he persevered in focusing down to street level. *Just where will they... Ah I've found you.* The wind and rain danced in a fire of city fog as he alighted the parapet, carefully balancing to allow his voice to be heard, wiping his bloodied mouth so as to better his appearance against these makers, fixated as he now was.

'Here! Look, fools, see how I have grown. You will not reach me. I am unreachable.'

Hysteria, it broke out like the rashes over his face. A thousand coated tears running down a false smile. He was scared. Why wasn't it working? He felt nothing again, amidst the rain and storm. A sagging pain. They were moving. He hunched as far as he was willing scanning the street with no luck. They had left. Clouds formed in the dense sky as he continued calling out. This night felt like his last. They were everywhere. His waving arms felt like nothing more than blades of grass in a prairie - present but with no presence. This must have been it. The comedown. The thing they so needed to happen so as to justify their approach. He felt it. The insipid loop, over and over again, how many times he'd given in to their calls after that first time. That first fatal taking of the fruit - The Apple Incarnate. How he'd love to go back, beyond himself, beyond the bloody mess he'd become. His hands. Look at his hands, they ached and ached and yet still gave remorse to the other sickening sights of his body.

Not this time, not this time! Leaping back into the room, pulling the stained curtains down in a fit of anxiety he stumbled away toward the television, undressing the polyester sheets in a worried, though now nihilistic, fashion. The white noise was replaced by voices, alienating him to believe it was them, like everything else he was seeing now as he reached the sour end of his latest plunge into lubricity. The door's voice - shut but singing - resonated in the air. He shook his head, panicking, crying - his emotions all jumping into the same blender and pressing play. He tried to reassure himself as he continued frantically pacing back and forth from the door, each lap getting closer to opening up and confronting them. No. He would hide. The bathroom, behind the shower, sleep it off, they would leave that way - leave him sleeping.

A foggy night. He rose, wounded but awake from them. This familiar serenity. Ephemeral. He walked doggedly around the twisted metropolis. The sky looked kaleidoscopically pained and he too felt the air awakening. They'd be back out soon. But he was so cosily nestled in this small pocket of thoughtlessness, he decided he'd walk on. For the bright magenta light of the motel was bound to welcome him back to his place of sanctuary - the home of resting off his latest mess and avoiding them until the urge for repetition took over.

Shipwrecked

Exhibit 4: Shipwrecked

Higher Short Story by Michael Zwizwai, St Columba's School, Kilmacolm

"The 48th conference of Could Be Cute Couples Candidates in College Clique will now commence!"

The illogical name we decided to call our club, only a drunk would be satisfied with it.

This fine 'establishment' that our club used as a base was filled with drunks and luckless 'men'. This 'bar' was a 'treasure trove' of 'authentic' marine materials. Even the owners of this 'sea themed' 'pub' disgusted me. The walls were splattered a sea sick yellow. The tables, mere barrels. Pungent smells filled the atmosphere - the aroma was intoxicating - everyone but me was as drunk as a sailor. The drunken type of course. The sickly bile that these 'associates' of mine spewed was nauseating in itself, but the corny pick-up lines they tried to deliver made me gag.

These 'colleagues' tried to communicate with me. I was too distracted by their blatant failures as human beings. All I heard was the static that buzzed through. This 'meeting' was nothing more than a farce. These drunkards just wanted to badger women. I would be better off on a windy day at sea than here. "-Why was I here?" Silence. The drunks were too intoxicated to care about my question. They were lost in a sea of vodka, too drunk to navigate and I sat on a stool beside a fake ship's wheel.

"So," said our leader, the drunkard captain. "Who is going to follow my lead and help me plan the ultimate line?" Many hands were up, by that I mean that five out of seven of us raised our right hand but also sailed their left into the sky.

My eyes wandered. Her. I saw her, a glimmer of a pearl hiding in the deep sea. A sadistic smirk slid through her face. Only for me. A tear rolled like a wave down my face. I can't. A man mustn't. She laughed. Submerged amongst her friends, she was still taunting me. The atmosphere made me drunk on emotions. The waves in my mind calmed to the loud eccentric 'motivational' chants.

"So who's ready to make this a night to remember!" yelled our captain, full of false confidence. Drunken ayes were heard. One, was silent.

"Ok, lets us try this line out," the captain stated. "Who's with me?"

Again many hands were up. The 'loyal' crew followed him, staggering on to the barrels left and right until they boarded the table adjacent to us. The captain approached a young woman. She was a 'beauty' at sea.

She spoke. An alluring melody floated out. A dream-like mist enveloped me. She engulfed me, taunting all the way. Again. The bar seats turned into a rocky bay at sea. The sickly walls became thunderous clouds above. The 'lovely', 'endearing', stained floor became wild waves above an abyss. The intoxicating yet warm atmosphere turned into a cold isolation. Reality became murky water. I was alone. Again. The familiar lullaby warped its way towards me, disturbing the cold solace. The tempting vocals wrapped themselves around me. A face emerged from the grey waves, edging close to my position. The sonata ceased, a wicked smile emerged. I 'tried' to sound a violent threat, 'tried' being the key word. Every word I forced out was sucked into the whirlpool of silence. It was her. She was the cause of all my problems.

"Now don't you think that's a bit unfair? I came all this way to greet you, and you still hold a grudge against me," she said with in her facetious way. "Isn't it a bit babyish? I mean it's not even my fault now is it?" she spewed lies in my face. "I get it you are angry, but still isn't it manipulative of you to still play victim after so long? Shouldn't you move on? It is almost like you crave the attention? You even forgot my name," her face turned into a bitter smile. "You are alone. You only have yourself to blame. It is pathetic really, you create strawmen, make me into a siren. When someone wrongs you, you demonise them. Make them into stereotypes, generic husks of what they originally were." The verbal assault did not stop. "Why? Because other opinions scare you? Other ways of life frighten you? You don't like the idea of being wrong? You can't handle being wrong. You can't handle responsibility of your actions. You just can't."

Stop. I begged, but to no avail. These daggers that she threw at me, this insipid vile bile that she spat in my face hurt, but I was used to it. Her face softened while it slowly melted into the dark sea.

"It's ok. I mean you survived this long with that mind-set."

Another more aged face appeared, it too sporting a cruel smile. I regrettably got used to the fact that I couldn't speak so I held no opposition.

"Hey. How are you doing? Fine? Ready to comfortably listen to what I have to say for once, ready to soak up my knowledge?" smiling the face muttered, "Ready, to not be a brat!? Failure! Or coward!?" I was used to these vague attempts at mockery. "No, well I guess you have nothing going for you. I mean your family has ostracized you. Your girlfriend has broken up with you. Your dream has been crushed and yet you don't blame yourself." Vile words came out with even more venom. "You are so immature, the girlfriend who loves you still, who just wants to wait because she isn't ready. You turn her into a monster in your eyes." She knew nothing. "You are just like your father. Now you want to cry? What a selfish child." Her eyes slowly dimmed and a blue hue appeared around the edges. Her faced aged even further. "I was young once, I understand you. I do. Though my words are harsh I love you, truly. That is not an excuse for my words. However that doesn't give you an excuse to act so impish. Wouldn't you agree?" The face slowly dissolves into the dark sea.

The storm raged on. Surprisingly I didn't notice, growing more in sheer power. Thunder booms crept slowly. Lightning danced wildly on the surface of the sea, edging closer with every step. "Flashy enough for you? I mean you could have been more creative. A god complex? Seriously? And why am I Zeus? That guy is a detestable degenerate. Oh I see. Clever huh. You made me your worst aspects." His suave attitude irked me. The messy hair, the unkempt beard, the pointy nose, the condescending eyes -all of it irked me. "You could have made things interesting and made me your good side - just like that one movie - but 'someone' was lazy and so I am just a generic egotist." He rolled his eyes just to copy what I did. "So how does it feel to be honest? Because right now you really aren't being truthful." his smug attitude had no bounds. "Well, let us talk about love, eh? Or the lack of it in your life. Either way you can't force her to love you," he paused uncouthly. "Anyway, now why are you here? ... Don't hate people, how they think differently from you, how they lie to you, how they 'use and abuse' you, just like what you are doing now. They have abandoned you. You can't accept that. You just don't want to be lonely. Give me a PhD because I have successfully psychoanalysed you. Don't be a baby. Be a man. Great last words huh?" with that he left. I slumped on the wheel as the last of these waves crashed over me.

Magnum Opiate

Exhibit 5: Magnum Opiate

Higher Short Story by Dominic Bogle, St Columba's School, Kilmacolm

It was both the dry stench of the cab and the complete carelessness of its less than friendly driver that made it a very uncomfortable journey to the 'artists' house. He really couldn't be doing with this hassle - the travelling alone had already lasted twelve hours. However, he was in ways fixed to this task more than others. Well to put it into a rather brutal but realistic fashion, his job and frankly his livelihood were on the line.

The dust smeared the car windows and the thin tyres seemed to accentuate every bloody bump they hit on the bare dirt road. He began to realise where he really was headed for - forget the 'artists' - metaphorically. This was the one story that really mattered, the magnum opus, his very own evidence to prove that behind all the dormant years scripting ads for lousy catering companies he was actually a competent and rather gifted collector of information. He thought of the irony that would ensue. All the papers that previously rejected his stories, laughed at his inaudible evidence tapes of countless 'artists' and even went as far to declare him deluded and bearing the same mindset as the 'artists' themselves. But alas, here he was basking in the glory of an overheated Honda hatchback heading into God knows where to catch the mad fools in their artistic act. It was priceless, reminding him of his watch - beautifully handmade but utterly worthless and to be honest, when he really thought about it, lacking in any aesthetic appeal.

Although his thoughts were that of a content disposition, even against the discomfort of the cardboard backseat he crumpled over, they were quickly shot down as the taxi came to an alarming brake stop in the middle of the dirt road. He rose quickly from his slouch to observe the surroundings outside the window caked in the midday heat. There was no house here. It wasn't even an 'artistic' illusion. It was gravel followed by gravel and a little bit of sand. Emptiness. Why had we stopped? He had heard the 'artists' (he was quite happy at how well he had continued this odious analogy of 'artists'; it was one of the few humorous things he had left) hid their....ehm... art well but this level of isolation was laughable, in a horribly self-loathing kind of way. He rubbed his eyes and leaned forward to confront the driver but was set aback upon witnessing the small hairy man hunched over the wheel and bleeding. He himself, hated the sight of blood and started to feel sickness in the dusty sauna of the harboured Honda. Panting melodramatically, he let himself out of his door - it's not like the dead taxi driver was going to do it - and fell back into the barren, sandy waste in a state of shock.

God he was prepared for things a bit crazy but he never really expected to witness a spontaneous death slap-bang in front of his face. How did it happen anyway? His mind was a collection of fragmented pieces of anxious trails untraceable to what he was truly feeling. He couldn't help but look into the front window of the car now being painted in different biological shades of red as the drivers slumping head slid down the dry, thirsty glass.

A mistake had definitely been made somewhere. How did they know or find out? They were so cooperative, between his exchanges, it seemed they revelled in the chance of an interview, and he was adamant he played his part, of which he was crazy enough to go for, to a T. Yes, he was wearing a wire but under the 'double-life' lying and beyond the policies of agencies, he was someone genuinely interested in these people. Where others sought to stay away, he felt the need to continue advancing and advocating, to find out their motives beyond their lucrative 'art'. These very 'artists' were the men who dominated his TV screen as a young boy - legends, rumours shrouded behind a lack of outreach and an almost over abundant fear of knowing interaction would be deadly.

However, he couldn't help but believe this death, this unexpected turn of events was a sign that they knew exactly what was happening.

His eyes were wide and weary and he invaded his breast pocket, ferociously searching for his medication. The sun bled a hole in the sky dominating the blue vastness like an arsenal of light. Why did he move it about in every pocket different days? - it was difficult enough that he had to take about twelve of them. The jeans. There they were... In that, slightly soggy, plastic bag. He fired half of them in, and swallowed. His heart was racing but hopefully a copious dosage of pills would calm the nerves - it always worked for job interviews... Or maybe not considering this was the first real job he'd managed to get in twelve years and there was hardly any competition for it.

He wanted to get up, escape this floor of sand but he wasn't sure what the next course of action would exactly be. The driver. part of him wanted to find out, to go over and try and fathom how they got to him. Poison? Most probably but who knew? He certainly didn't. They never once mentioned he'd have to make to the house on foot. He wasn't sure his shoes could handle it. Probably more important was the fact he wasn't sure his mind could handle it. He was a desperate individual, diving into this kind of suicide mission like some blind brainwashed civil servant. Who was he to serve truly? The ones who appeared to have left him to rot with the devils they so wanted to apprehend. Maybe these 'artists' were truly artists and the Government just a jealous Big Brother-like entity devoid of creativity. That was it, they were too scared to shame themselves into compromising such a lucrative and popular movement that they'd blame it on him.

In a crazed jolt of energy, he hopped up, wrapping the wire from under his waistcoat laughing - He realised they would have heard his conversations that, although directed towards a rock, were just spoken to himself. No he'd get away, this was it, forget the job and the opportunity. The livelihood? Well he was happy enough it didn't end, sprawled across a cardboard labyrinth in an automobile of decades past. He would get his stuff and leave. 'Abort' was a harsh word, he preferred 'redirect'. Yes, that was it. The 'artists' would stay in mystery and he would leave in one piece and although he wanted to embed himself in their operations, experience their beautifully tangled mess of networking and muling, he was now satisfied that these were powers unconceivable, the only brave enough men to puncture a hole in the shrouding cape of the Government. And that he thought....

-'Down now.'

It had appeared in the chaos of arranging his affairs he hadn't managed to notice the figure walking towards him, armed so heavily, one could say he was 'legged'. He turned slowly to face the strong, if slightly boeotian looking figure.

The tattoos were enough to indicate this was indeed an 'artist.'

- God they were resourceful. He motioned to start speaking but just at that a black bag was thrust over his head and right at that instant, the first thing he felt was happiness (albeit in a slightly nihilistic manner. In all fairness of the truth (which is clearly important at this point in the story) the first thing he felt was the surprisingly soft texture of the bag... Then the potent scent of chemicals. The happiness really came as a close third.) He didn't know what was happening - if he was even dead - but the realisation that the knowledge that was fed into his brain, piped into the cranium by the oppressive forces of his 'society' could be overturned, proving wrong, shone in from a different perspective? Well that was enough to make this adequately painful absolution believable.

All Children are Artists

Exhibit 6: All Children are Artists

Higher Reflective Essay by Rachel Mosley, St Columba's School, Kilmacolm

> "All children are artists. The problem is how to remain an artist once he grows up."
>
> - Pablo Picasso

One of my favourite ways to spend time is wasting it, which of course is problematic when it comes to getting anything done. I could spend weeks doodling and daydreaming, and often choose cloud watching over concentrating, so my work ethic frequently disappears, pops off for a holiday at a moment's notice without so much as a "Cheerio!" I find clouds to be much more relaxing than many of my classes, so I choose seats that face windows as often as I can. The fact I prefer to spot Vikings battling dragons in masses of floating water vapour than factorise polynomials says a lot about my attention span and imagination. Imagination, in fact, is something I believe does not receive nearly enough representation beyond primary school. Picasso believed it too, apparently.

Thinking back to when I was five, I learned how to add numbers together and one afternoon we got to colour in and I made a tower with the Jenga blocks. I really loved school. Ignorance is bliss, right? I have tried to remember at which point I was educated beyond ignorance, at which point the blissful bubble of colouring in, Golden Time and playing games pretending we were anything and everything, popped and left a hollow filled with Past Papers and late nights fuelled by caffeine desperately trying to finish the thousand or so words that are "...Due first period tomorrow, mum!" It doesn't really matter when I finish whatever homework I'm trying to complete though. I'll stay up late pretending that I won't be woken up at 6.15 by an alarm so loud it causes me pain, and struggle through another exhausting day, tired as always. Primary school seems like a distant bliss, waking up half an hour before going to school for a fun-filled day and finishing homework by four o'clock.

There is one distinct memory I have, of a dull day in a bland concrete playground, of a group of six year olds, making their own game. It was one of those games where other people ask "Can I play?" every few minutes and the 'cast' grows until it makes no sense whatsoever. There were no props other than stones or discarded items of uniform, no cues, no sound effects other than those we could make and certainly no rules, but it was wonderful. The best part was, when the next playtime came, an approximation of where the game was left off was made and the madness continued as before. It seems unlikely that sixteen year olds would be capable of such organisation and loss of inhibitions, pretending to be animals and fusing ideas together to have fun as a group. Pretending to be an animal would in reality most likely be considered very embarrassing outside of a drama class.

Perhaps imagination takes a different form when you're grown up, perhaps my excitement in seeing a fox wandering across a frosty field from the school bus is not as out of place among my peers as it seems. I can think of one person in particular who finds my fascination with native wading birds to be extremely perplexing. For example, out on an evening walk, I spot a large grey heron standing silent on the shore, gazing west towards the sunset. It is now that my excitable alter ego appears, jumping up and down on the spot, tugging on the poor boy's elbow with a finger on my lips, gesturing vigorously towards the majestic creature. He sighs, exasperated, and continues walking as if it were no more than a crumpled leaf on

© HERIOT-WATT UNIVERSITY

the pavement. He cannot understand what I find to be so extremely exciting about a bird, a species we will no doubt see a number of on our walk, but he has imagination too. It is extraordinary to see the change in his face, the sparkle in his eye as he tells me a well-imagined story, how he wants to find the girl of his dreams, how he wants to take her to some extraordinary place owned by an anonymous squillionaire and propose to her among hedges sculpted to peacocks, rooms filled with mirrors, polished into nonexistence. Perhaps this is a cliché, perhaps it is the dream of many, the only thing they wish for. Perhaps it is the remainder of his imagination, developed during days climbing trees and skipping stones, wishing he was on an adventure, or perhaps it is the same imagination, that has matured as he has, changed to become something new and brilliant, never dying out.

However, this imagination cannot be used to its full potential, the potential to create worlds and imagine the ridiculous. It is limited to imagining what the weather is like outside during an exam in a cold hall behind closed doors. It is limited to calculating what percentage of a chemical is a pure element, and answering mind-numbing questions disguised as 'interesting' scenarios. It is in this way that imagination is crushed, all but lost in a sea of guidelines. Some people may lose their spark of imagination and creativity by forgetting it, pushing it aside and losing the ability to think of the impossible. Does this mean that there's no hope of completing Higher exams with this childlike spark intact? Who knows at what ungodly hour this very essay will be concluded, word counted and printed... so should I give up now and begin cutting snowflakes from folded paper? Perhaps not. Gel pens are prohibited to answer exam questions with, so it's extremely doubtful that decorating the margins is allowed, preventing a creative outlet during the process of determining your future, perhaps in some cases narrowing the margin of possible thought.

Of course I would love to be organised, finish all my schoolwork two weeks in advance and have endless hours of relaxation time, but I don't think that will ever happen. This dedication is difficult to achieve and with an attention span like mine it is even further from reality. I frequently begin homework but never finish in one sitting, not getting far before finding something else infinitely more fascinating to do... like watching a spider meander across the floor or playing with an unfinished Rubik's Cube. I could get work done... or not.

Instead, I'll procrastinate until the hour demands I begin, and while I write I'll imagine that I'm a unicorn in a helicopter, that I'm best friends with a fox darting across a field on a cold November morning, who wonders why the strange, tall creatures travelling by have no fur. I'll wish it was midnight, and I'll wish I was out in the cold night air, lying on an empty pavement watching satellites, or perhaps I'm watching alien craft that will soon touch down to live on Earth with us as unfortunately their home land exploded and they're very sorry to impose but they simply couldn't find anywhere else at such short notice. I'll imagine that some handsome prince will get down on one knee in some far-off land filled with strangers who don't speak any English, and those strangers won't understand what's going on between us, but will follow tradition and clap and cheer with everyone else, imagining a future life for us that is nothing like the truth.

Even if it is seldom used, seldom considered of value, imagination is everywhere, best observed among the young. It may not be used however, as, to quote Picasso once more:

"It takes a long time to become young".

Trossachs Trauma

Exhibit 7: Trossachs Trauma

Higher Personal Essay by Lucy Grant, St Columba's School, Kilmacolm

Embarking on my Silver Duke of Edinburgh hike, just two days after my National Five exams were over, was nowhere near the celebration I'd been hoping for. All my exam stress had been turned to both physical and mental preparation for this three day hike. Over the period we were scheduled to walk a grand total of fifty-nine kilometres. Twenty kilometres roughly a day doesn't sound too bad does it?

...

"Where's the dam, though?" I questioned nervously.

"It says on our route cards and on the map we're supposed to have passed a dam," Lauren hastily agreed.

"No honestly, Iona, we've to follow this fence until we reach the dam- we're on the right track," Emily said confidently.

After great debate amongst the group, we made the bold decision just to keep on going down the hill and continue to follow the fence, hoping to dear God we come across this dam we were supposed to have passed. We travelled on and on and on, and the further down the hill we went, the surer we were that we were lost. Never were we supposed to be by the water's edge of Loch Katrine, yet here we stood. An overwhelming atmosphere of sadness took charge of the group as we stood by the water's edge in the baking heat. Tiredly and grumpily, we thought back to earlier on in the day and tried to pinpoint at what stage we had got lost. How long we had been lost for? How we would get back on the right route?

I guess we had it coming to us. Our group had never been the most organised, most attentive group of all- we just thought we could sail through it on the hike and everything would turn out just fine. We could have done a lot more during our training days which would have prevented us from getting as lost as we did. Had we taken more time writing our route cards and drawing up our routes on our maps rather than wanting to just 'get it done' we probably would've never followed the wrong fence and got so drastically lost. We thought it was all just about getting there rather than the journey we took to get there... we could not have been more wrong.

As we stood at the bottom of the hill contemplating what the best thing was to do next, the group morale started to fall. We were hungry, we were thirsty and had been lost for about two hours now still not knowing where we were supposed to be. We started to wander further round the loch where we spotted a fence at the top of a hill that looked mountainous from where we stood.

"Guys, I think that's the fence they were talking about..." Jen anxiously pointed out. "What? The one all the way up at the top of that hill? That can't be it" Hannah expressed hopefully.

But it was. We knew that was the fence the supervisors had been talking about. If only we'd just taken a minute to spot and use the handrails on the map rather than just heading off the minute we were 50% sure it was the right way.

That did tend to be the problem with our group. We just never thought things through long enough, we tended to play it by a democracy vote rather than tactically working things out. We learned the hard way that that was never going to bring success. Three men do make a tiger. In the ancient story, once three people had told the King that there was a tiger in the market, he believed it despite that he had not seen it for himself. In our case, the more people that said that we were going the right way, the more we all started to believe it yet none of us had given it thorough thought.

As we began to climb up the hill, the group morale surprisingly started to lift as we became more confident we were on the right tracks, lifting our heads a little. Our saturated feet felt numb and heavy with pain, mentally and physically we were drained from exhaustion... and this was only day one.

Finally after a long steep climb, we reached the top. Immediately we decided to phone the supervisors and considering it was four o'clock and we still had a good seven kilometres to walk we thought it'd be best to let them know how late and lost we were. After several attempts, we got a hold of them and they told us to figure our grid reference and then set foot for them to meet us half way.

It took us some time to figure out exactly where we were on the map but that was not surprising for us. When we were confident about our whereabouts, we reluctantly dragged ourselves up and trekked onwards. The positive thing about our team was our good spirits. Although we were lost for four hours, hungry and thirsty we still managed to crack a few jokes here and there but needless to say when we met the supervisors, they were far from jovial.

That was understandable though. If I were to put myself in their position I would not have been in the best of spirits either. They were sent out on a rescue mission at eight o'clock, causing them to miss their dinner and set out again in the cold all because we took the wrong track and weren't checking our maps on a regular basis. The two things we were told were key to success on our hike were the only two reasons that we came just an arm's length away from failing the hike.

All in all, it was no surprise our group got lost. We just weren't thoughtful enough. We were so focused on making it all a good experience and having laughs and joking about that when it came down to serious navigation skills, we fell at the first hurdle.

Considering our group was, to say the least, a complete liability, we were followed home by the supervisors making sure we were going to right way and checking our maps and route cards. And finally, after the end of what seemed like the longest day of my life, we arrived at the campsite.

Being eaten alive by midges, we pitched up our tents faster than we'd done anything else that day, consumed a plateful of hard raw pasta which we were too tired to cook properly, and threw ourselves into our tents... only to wake up the next morning and hike all over again.

Overall, looking back it was clear from day one it was never going to go to plan. We saw our training days as just a necessary aspect of the award rather than an effective preparation tool for our hike, and didn't take them as seriously as, evidently, we should have. Our group were a walking disaster (literally) but nevertheless we made it... barely. Despite the near failure of Silver, and the drastic detour, the experience has only made me feel more prepared for my Gold hike which I will be participating in in 2016 and I will not be as 'navigationally challenged'.

In The Grand Scheme of Things

Exhibit 8: In The Grand Scheme of Things

Higher Reflective Essay by Olivia McNee, St Columba's School, Kilmacolm

This year I am sitting my Curriculum for Excellence Higher exams, obviously, and I, like most other people my age often find myself sitting slumped at a desk, blankly staring at an inanimate object- if I'm lucky and it's not another human- questioning the meaning of life. Many people may shake this off as a waste of time and say that I should ultimately be listening and they are probably right as the amount of information I am taking in has by this point most likely shrunk to the size of a literal pea. However, I would argue quite the opposite. I truly believe that it is in these moments of what can only be described as teenage zombification I have had some rather significant thoughts and made some debatably inconsequential decisions. I am not claiming to have daydreamed myself into the discovering the structure of an atom or to writing the next 'Dr Jekyll and Mr. Hyde', nevertheless I have taken the time to question certain things in my life, and possibly change my perspective.

I love learning, and I want to give myself the best opportunities in life and whatnot, but sometimes I cannot help but ask, why? What is the point of relentless studying to get qualifications, to get into university, to get qualifications, to get a job, to get a better job, to be financially stable, to have a family, and so the cycle begins. It is difficult for the best of us to look ahead of the literal mounds of homework and hormones to see the light at the end of the tunnel. This has led me to believe that the mundane life of a teenager may not be so mundane after all.

Every day I get up at six thirty to the sound of The Smiths, a ringtone that after hearing it for what I can only say is far too many mornings, still makes me smile. I then follow through the necessary procedures, showering and the like, and hopefully say good morning to the bus driver-If I don't miss the bus- and then sit in the same seat every single day. Initially this may seem insignificant and trivial but I have learned to appreciate the things I would have previously ignored and found it really is a matter of perspective. If you view a mundane and repetitive cycle as mundane and repetitive that is exactly what it will be. Everyday I get on the school bus I try to imagine somebody else's morning, what side of the bed they got out of, what they had for breakfast, who the first person they spoke to was, what was the first thing they smiled at today? Suddenly my complaining about having to put my makeup brushes back in the jar begins to seem rather pathetic.

We all have these funny aspirations and desires for things in our lives, something as simple as a good job or a nice car; personally I like clothes and appreciate a good quality leather. However these things are only material, one thing you cannot be taught in a classroom is that the only way you can be happy is to stop trying to be. Life has a habit of throwing events at us we cannot prepare for in a classroom or with a university degree. We must to an extent try to grasp the true feeling of living and being alive and cherish it while we can. We find it in that awkward moment when you laugh at your own fake laugh and end up crying, that moment when you lose your concentration and rub conditioner all over your face. You can't recreate these moments; somehow getting conditioner in your eye wouldn't be as funny if you deliberately put it there. Constantly striving for new goals and aspirations will mean if we don't already appreciate what we have in that moment, as said by Omar Khayyam "Be happy for this moment. This moment is your life."

© Heriot-Watt University

I have started to think that asking questions like: What is the meaning of life? Why do I have to do this? What is the point? Is about as productive as Douglas Adam's answer to the first. We simply cannot ask non-questions like these and expect anything other than a non-answer. Much like the not so mundane daily routine, I sometimes question whether life's *big questions* are really so big. If one day you asked someone, "What is the meaning of life?" and they turned around and told you the answer. What would you do next? Is there really anything we could do with that information we cannot do without it, personally I think not. It would be impossible to go through life knowing what the purpose of it all was, there would be nothing to look forward to.

At the end of the day, the purpose is to take life as it comes and enjoy it while we can. Do we really want the philosophical answers we are asking for? *"Question everything. Learn something. Answer nothing."* As far as Euripides' philosophy goes, I think this is why we still don't have answers to life's big questions, we don't need them. What gives us the right to answer these questions, I suppose again it boils down to perspective. These questions are there to make us think, by all means ask someone what their perspective is on these non-questions, why not? However we need to stop expecting that one day we'll understand life's big questions in some sort of eureka moment we may have experienced previously in the classroom. I believe that the meaning of life is to live, we cannot ask for anything more. The little we know about the world we live in confirms this; we need to explore the bottom of our oceans before we go looking for the end of the universe. The only thing I would add to Euripides' philosophy is to think and to think for yourself, although it may be implied it is a thing we often forget to do, we can't possibly expect to understand the complex workings of society or others before we can understand ourselves.

With regards to my future, I intend on working for the results I need to apply for university regardless of the fact I don't necessarily know the end goal, I challenge you to find anyone who knew exactly what they would be doing in even five years from now let alone for the rest of their lives. So far, I can't say anything particularly capricious has occurred in my life that has made me question my attitude and I cannot say I'm anxiously waiting for the day that it does. I am rather enjoying making questionable decisions and even enjoying making none, and I look forward to the many more negligible mistakes. In the grand scheme of things, I cannot promise I won't scream the next time I see a daddy long legs or a perfectly formed leather boot, all I can hope for is the ability to put it into perspective.

Bursting the Bubble

Exhibit 9: Bursting the Bubble

Higher Reflective Essay by Alex Schellekens, St Columba's School, Kilmacolm

For a sheltered boy who spent his early years in the affluent areas of Pimlico and Wimbledon in Southern London, it would be logical to think that a similarly affluent area in the heart of the Renfrewshire countryside would feel like home. Big houses, wealthy people, fancy cars, sounds like a good place for a cerebral, naive, inexperienced child like myself, does it not? Having lived here for seven years now I am almost adjusted to this new lifestyle but - trust me - it wasn't straightforward. The experience of Kilmacolm has pleased some but traumatised the majority, which is why I will keep a special place in my heart for my utter loathing for that despicable village.

I spent most of my childhood up until the age of 8 in the beautifully upper middle class area of Wimbledon, which is primarily best known for being the site of the annual tennis championships. The memories I have of my time living there are overwhelmingly positive Just a ten minute walk from my old house there was a cluster of elegant boutiques and florists, charming coffee shops, as well as a Waitrose (of course). Not only that but nearby there was a local park with tennis courts, extensive grassy areas and a gigantic kids' play area which appealed to me greatly at that age. It really was an idyllic area to live in and I greatly enjoyed my time at school, my social groups and the fact I was surrounded by others who were blissfully ignorant of the hardships of life.

However, the time came for my family to transport itself north of the border and without much warning I found myself living in the small village of Bridge of Weir and going to a private school in the neighbouring village of Kilmacolm. Now, let's describe the issues I was faced with when encountering Kilmacolm. Where should I begin? I'll start with school. It did take me while to find my footing in a year group that had known each other for four years previously and were Scottish born and bred. Thankfully, I had a teacher who was from England originally called Mrs Andrews, and she was a great help in trying to make me feel more familiar in my new surroundings. She helped me find friends, get involved in school, and answered such ridiculous questions like, "what's a jotter?" Furthermore, there was the uniform. I was used to sticking to informal polo shirts and shorts when dressing for school. At St Columbas? Oh no. Those ghastly polo shirts are shunned to be worn only during PE and the norm is to wear shirts, ties, and horrifically oversized, and stiff blazers. The social world of Kilmacolm was the most interesting issue of all. Cliques are everywhere. There are year group cliques. There are school cliques. And there are village cliques. It didn't take me long to realise that us outsiders from Bridge of Weir were seen as an inconvenience and were not welcome in the layered social web of Kilmacolm. Whether you interpret that as being inward-looking or just plainly being rude, it was certainly a shock to the system upon arriving in this bubble.

What effect has Kilmacolm had on me? Well... there are plenty of negatives. There is a pretty noticeable trend that in Kilmacolm very little population movement occurs and it took me a long time to realise that people tend to come to this area, stay in this area, and some will attend St Columba's school for the entirety of their education. This was a stark contrast from the nature of being in a school near London when students frequently came and went and I got to know children that were from countries around the globe. Some came to London for a year and then went back to their home country, and there were regular changes of school for those who lived in London as well. This is far more representative of what happens in most regions, and to stumble across an area as stagnant as Kilmacolm is highly unusual. Being small, there is also the very prevalent sense that everyone knows everyone and if you tell one thing to one person it is almost guaranteed to make it to someone else. Rumours spread disturbingly easily. In real life, there are people whom you cannot trust and sometimes it's better to be suspicious and to think before you talk to others. If you live in Kilmacolm for a bit, you'd need to learn that lesson pretty swiftly if I were you.

I like to view almost all my experiences as important life lessons and I'm glad I learned so much through interacting with others and about what certain individuals in the adult world are like. Not to play on the stereotypes, but there truly is no shortage of snobbery in Kilmacolm. Sometimes perceptions are the truth. I knew a few people who could be successfully described by the analogy, 'big fish in a small pond.' It's easy to see how in Kilmacolm it is common for a successful family to become full of their own self-importance and a bit smug. The small size of the village means that people can feel confident that they are top of the neighbourhood hierarchy, and, by God, do they let everyone know about it.

In a city such as London, the chances are that there will always be a person earning a higher salary than you, with a bigger house, more expensive car, and it becomes less of a competition and more of a personal goal. In Kilmacolm it's easy to be the leader of the pack and this motivates people, which to me seems absurd. I remember the parents of one of my classmates buying a Ferrari and the next day their neighbours bought one too. As a person who is interested in business and might contemplate pursuing a career in it one day, I have found it useful to realise that arrogance does exist and to find ways of putting up with people who are like that. Through this I have also realised that I'd rather be a happy, less wealthy person than a wealthy individual who is constantly stressed at the prospect of earning more money and I feel that this is of great importance. On reflection, I now realise that it is important to widen your horizons and the harms of living in the same, small place for too long. The world is a far more exciting place than the inward looking Kilmacolm.

There will always be an element of resentment between the rich and poor in our society. Having been brought up in a privileged household has made me feel very fortunate but not everyone is in that position and there is still very much a divide between those on lower incomes and those on higher incomes. What makes someone belong to a social class? I believe it can depend very much on economic status but also impacts a person's lifestyle, their attitudes and their priorities in life. Kilmacolm is the type of place that appears to breed people who are intolerant of others, and who do not realise what life is like in the real world for people struggling to earn a living. Resentment comes when people become arrogant and lose the feeling that happiness should take priority over wealth. Kilmacolm is simply an isolated case that symbolises a widespread issue across wealthy rural areas in the UK. The poverty in Greenock just down the road, simply doesn't exist in Kilmacolm. Despite being only twenty minutes drive away, the standard of living is a world apart, and this ignorance is selfish as well as unnecessary. As a result, people on a higher income are despised by many and this is very obvious throughout the country, and exacerbates this split. I feel that it was innocent of me to believe in my early years that the entire world was like Kilmacolm, when in the reality it couldn't be farther from the truth.

So, in summary, for me, Kilmacolm symbolises everything that is wrong in British society. It stands for arrogance and despite it teaching me valuable life lessons, I feel very fortunate that I simply encountered it rather than living in it (for that would have been a nightmare.) Kilmacolm is just one of plenty of areas filled with patronising individuals throughout the nation that are full of some self-centred, egotistical people that simply have the wrong priorities in life. I only hope that as time goes on I don't become one of them.

Journeying

Exhibit 10: Journeying

Higher Reflective Essay by Alix Reid, St Columba's School, Kilmacolm

The hot, grainy sand melted effortlessly into the glistening Mediterranean Sea. My eyes squinted, adjusting to the bright midday July sunlight as I woke from snoozing on an uncomfortable plastic sun lounger which had slowly sunk into the sand. The bright green material of the lounger was covered in sand so I had to get up. The parasol above provided little shelter, and the smell of the sea was pungent. Surrounded by rows of the same cheap style of lounger, it looked like a typical tourist resort brimming with holidaymakers. Spending the day on the beach seemed like the perfect oasis, acting as an escape from mundane everyday life.

The beach echoed with English in a variety of accents, the language seemingly exchanged more than Spanish dialect. The morning passed ordinarily, rolling into early afternoon and the peak of the heat. Glancing up from the pages of my book I noticed a small-framed woman sitting on the beach, dressed differently than the tourists. She was wearing long trousers and flimsy, old sandals. Her only sun protection was a greyed and saggy sun hat. The woman's physical shape was that of a malnourished, small child, her arms protruding clumsily from a blue polo shirt. She wasn't a tourist as she was alone with no bags or typical holiday clothes, seemingly uninterested in the loungers behind her or the sun that most other tourists crave. Her eyes were fixed on the horizon, beyond the waves that lapped the sand directly in front of her. The water was fascinating, tossing and turning in the sun like an agitated animal, but her gaze was beyond the water.

Maybe she had travelled to Europe by boat, the sea holding memories beneath the surface, or maybe the sea had allowed her to escape her previous life in the developing world. I sympathised with her from a distance when she stumbled to her feet, and walked over to the loungers a few rows forward from my own. At first, I thought she might be returning to her sun lounger, but she started weaving amongst people and talking to them. After moving to the row in front of me, I realised that she was a masseuse, perhaps working illegally, although I thought nothing more of it, returning to my book and tuning out of my environment.

As I read, the sound of police sirens was in the distance. I remember not taking any notice of it, yet when it became louder and more recognizable. I glanced behind me to see where it was coming from. On returning to my page from not seeing anything, I noticed the masseuse's behaviour. I suddenly realised that she must be here illegally. The woman looked like a terrified child, her eyes broadening and her body springing to life from a peaceful manner. The sight filled me with pity and selfishness- my week long break was a luxury that she would never have, yet I could not help her. How could a life of constant fear be better than what she has left behind, or what she has escaped from? Maybe her country could be war torn, or in great poverty. The sirens were so close that they demanded to be heard. I turned around again, and two police officers rode motorbikes smoothly yet rapidly along the clean, stone promenade that was basking in the shade of palm trees. The *policía* lettering boldly stuck out of the silver and blue vehicle and drew my attention. What would they do to her if they saw her? The thought terrified me, because she had nobody to speak up for her, nobody to help her- the immigration policy had already failed her.

The woman rushed to beside the stout British lady who she was massaging, immediately stopping her work and concealing herself. The British tourist seemed content enough to shield the woman yet I had no doubt that if the police became involved the tourist would do nothing more to protect the masseuse. She was willing to lend the woman a large straw sunhat which she then covered her face with. The woman knelt down in the sand, replicating a prayer position, and covered her face with the borrowed hat. The woman's blue polo shirt and trousers burrowed into the sand as quickly as the police officers drove past like an animal desperate for safety.

As soon as the police had passed, the woman immediately relaxed, her body scuttling out of the sand. She smiled gratefully at the British woman; thanking her without saying any words- I presume she could not speak English. She then returned to her job as a masseuse and didn't seem to think anything of the police, continuing for a short time before gratefully accepting her money from the tourist and wandering away in search of more work. This could be an everyday occurrence for her, hiding whilst trying to earn enough money to survive. The money earned must be minimal without having the concern of presumably either not having a work permit for European countries or being an illegal immigrant.

I could see in her eyes and her posture how afraid she was after she realised the police were close, and this added to my already huge sense of pity and despair for the woman. Why is it fair that she has to live in constant fear whilst our mediocre holiday ailments are often no more than unfamiliar food or language barriers? The luxury of travel which most people don't even think about when handing over passports to foreign police at customs whilst globetrotting is a dream to that woman. Her travelling in search of hope and a future has left her in fear yet travelling to most is a privilege that is taken for granted. My holiday is an opportunity to relax and not worry about daily life, school or homework, yet my ideal holiday location is her home, a home which she is not legally allowed to be in.

What must the woman have run away from in her own country for a life of hiding from the police to be better? A life of running and despair does not seem like a life yet it is hers and she evidently chose to leave worse circumstances for this. Concealing herself regularly is probably the easier part of her new life; her journey to Spain could have been long and dangerous, yet costing her not only money but the guarantee of a new life and restored hope is never certain.

An event which may be a common occurrence for that woman has left me with questions about society and the unfairness. Being able to freely travel from country to country over the long summer months was always something which I didn't put any thought in to before freely leaving the UK by handing over a passport- a booklet with a few sheets of paper, seemingly not too important- but this simple action is a privilege which should not be taken for granted.

Like a child in a sweetie shop

Exhibit 11: Like a child in a sweetie shop

Higher Reflective Essay by Lucy Grant, St Columba's School, Kilmacolm

The phrase 'like a child in a sweetie shop' is one that could not have been more literal to me. Like many other children I was only allowed sweets at the weekend or on special occasions. I'm sure most people can remember that feeling when your Mum gave you 50p to go and buy a sweetie on a Friday after school, sending you off into your local co-op to select that week's treasure. The inexplicable excitement of Halloween is also a fabulous time as a child. Receiving more than your bodyweight in brightly coloured gummies, lollypops and decoratively wrapped chocolates, enough sweets to last at least a week. Maybe even two with careful planning. All these memories I suspect are common ones amongst most people, though for me looking back I see them as the foundation of an obsession.

I always had a sweet tooth as a child, alongside being a fussy eater. A sickeningly unhealthy combination. When I was very little, obviously I did not have enough control to be that unhealthy. I had no money, no freedom to walk to the shops or even the height to reach the sweetie cupboard. At this time my sugar intake could be massively restricted. However by Primary 3, I started to walk home from school. It was only a short route, though it was one that went directly past 'The Video shop'. An excellent source of delectable goodies. I still didn't have money but I did have more intelligence.

At 3:45 each day I knew that there would be a herd of boys from senior school all rampaging into this tiny shop. They were never very careful with their coins, dropping 5p here and 10p there. Every day I would venture into the sea of sugar crazy animals, sliding between their legs checking to see if anyone had dropped any coins. Now looking back, yes I am aware that this could technically constitute as theft, however as a child these minor details did not bother me. I was only focused on the end result. Once the herd had left I usually had around 30p to spend. And ten years ago, back when Freddo's were only 7p that was enough to buy a world of sweets. I became such a regular customer that by the age of 9 the grey haired delicate old man who owned the shop would make all the older boys let me through to the front and he would let me pick a sweetie for free. He'd call me "a little trooper fighting off all those big boys" and this apparently meant I needed calories to replenish me. I'd scoff down these sweets before I went home or I would hide them in the folds of my tie. This happened every day until the shop closed and my genius plan- that for the record I had never been caught for- was foiled.

Now, personally I believe that a child of that age should not have been able to conjure up plans this complex for something as little as a sweet. So- much into the future I have come to the conclusion that considering more effort went into this daily ritual than any other aspect of my life- I was obsessed.

As time went on I did become slightly less obsessive in that I no longer hunted for sweets every day, though come the time that I started to receive pocket money, the amount that I bought, when I did have the chance grew. Anytime I had a sleepover I would go down to the co-op and buy at least £5 worth of cheap sweets. Despite this being for a sleepover. I did not share these sweets. If they wanted sweets then they should have bought their own. I could easily consume all that I had bought in one night. This then resulting in me not eating any dinner. This was not a massive problem until around second year at school when I was having sleepovers every single weekend. My diet mainly consisted of Maltesers, Jelly Tots,

Irn Bru, Diet Coke, and Yum Yum's. My parents didn't even know the extent to my unhealthy eating and still every day at dinner I was told many such things like "all your teeth are going to fall out" and the famous "You're going to grow up and be 20st". I did not listen.

On top of eating this magnitude of rubbish I wasn't eating my meals. At 12 I was becoming more womanly, shall we say. My hips grew wider and the food I ate started to correspond with my weight. I have a twin sister, who was not developing as early as me, and so she was a lot skinnier. Although she still ate a lot it wasn't as bad as me and she was quite a bit smaller than I was. I became increasingly self-conscious as she was beginning to be referred to as "the skinny one". This would probably have steered most people away from sweets but for me it simply meant cut down calories. But why would I give up the tasty calories? I thought. And so I started skipping meals. Not in any anorexic way or anything, I just figured I'd rather have the calories from tasty food. It didn't really bother me that this meant consuming virtually no nutrients in my diet whatsoever. I didn't think it mattered so long as I wasn't going over the 2000kcals a day. If I stayed under that then I was fine.

However, after a few months of eating like this most days, I started to get sick. At first it wasn't that bad. Then I started to get headaches every day- sometimes to the point that I couldn't open my eyes. I was randomly waking up in the night being sick, only to be fine the next morning. I even started to randomly collapse. Me being me, I decided I was dying. Obviously. And so I decided I needed to tell my Mum. She was very concerned. At this point she didn't know quite the extent to my sugar filled, nutrient lacking diet so she took me to the doctors. I was desperate for an answer as my National 5 prelims were coming up and I knew that constantly having headaches would be a bit of an inconvenience. The first thing my doctor asked me was what my diet was like. It had never occurred to me that that might have been the cause. With that one question I became so embarrassed. I was a perfectly mature teenage girl, who lived off sugar. My mum was appalled disgusted. The doctor probably was too. I know I was.

The doctor wrote me up a diet plan which I tried my best to stick to. I began to eat my breakfast and had lunch every day. I cut down on the sweet stuff though it was a very slow and gradual process. The headaches and the collapsing and the sickness all began to stop in time for my prelims. I still had the odd bad day, but it was nothing like it was before. And a year on I can safely tell you that my diet is reasonable. I eat my meals and I eat plenty of fruit to substitute my cravings though unfortunately to curb my desire for sugar I drink a rather obscene amount of diet coke. I'm aware this isn't healthy either but it is progress. I don't think my extreme desire for sugar will ever go away but I know now that I can restrain myself, and not let it consume my diet- even though I had to become severely unhealthy before I decided change was necessary.

Crossing the divide

Exhibit 12: Crossing the divide

Higher Reflective Essay by Cameron McIntyre, St Columba's School, Kilmacolm

As we stepped off the short plane journey from Glasgow, we were greeted by the same weather as home. The short bus journey into the city was just like home. As we reached the city, it seemed like any other British city I had ever been to. But as we left the bus station and strolled past the Europa hotel (Europe's most bombed hotel), and down the pedestrian lane adjacent to the court house, closed to traffic because of a persistent stream of bombs, everything seemed normal. The people were fresh faced and friendly, never shying away from a polite nod as you passed them in the street. Everyone seemed to be living in perfect harmony. However as my trip progressed, I learned that harmony is a word that should never be used when describing Belfast.

We spent the next few days seeing the very tourist-orientated side of Belfast, the side of the city that they wanted you to see. We marvelled at how wonderful the Titanic was and were ushered round 'Belfast's very own leaning tower of Pisa'. All very nice and, well, touristy. It wasn't until our third and final day that I started to get a true indication of what Belfast was really like, not what it was supposed to be like, when I visited the Crumlin Road Jail (Or 'the Crum' as it had been nicknamed by the tourist board) there was the odd inscription on the wall, or mark on the floor that hinted at the deep divisions in the city.

As we walked into the prisoner's registration area, there were cubicles where they were stripped and put into their prison clothes. As I look into each of the cubicles, I noticed that each one was marked at least 20 times with either 'IRA' or 'UVF'. It seemed like every prisoner had a political preference, and I found it unthinkable that the divisions in the city weren't just limited to the streets, but even the prisons had to be completely divided. How they could keep people imprisoned alongside the very people they were imprisoned for trying to kill was beyond me.

We left the jail and ventured up Shankill road and down Falls road. The two most affected areas of the city. It was like two different worlds, never mind two neighbouring roads. The Shankill area was a sea of red white and blue, huge wall murals celebrated the glory of the Queen and her empire. One particularly immaculate one, right in the centre of the area, was of a loyalist fighter - 'Top gun' Mackeag. He seemed no different to any other fighters who had lost their lives, but actually he was one of the most prolific murderers during the troubles. He was responsible for the deaths of 12 Catholics, many of whom had only committed one crime in McKeag's mind, and that was their religion. Why he seems like an appropriate person to rebuild a community around remains a mystery. This wasn't there to celebrate this man, it was there to fuel the next generation's hatred towards their neighbours.

As we turned at the top of the road, and ventured down the Falls area, it couldn't have been any more different. It was ablaze with green white and orange, murals celebrated the pope and the republican fighters who died for their 'noble' cause. Similarly to the Shankill area, they had a particularly bitter one at its centre. It showed perhaps the most famous republican from the troubles, Bobby Sands. Bobby Sands was an IRA terrorist who died under self-imposed hunger strike, protesting about the loss of his political status. He is seen by some as a great role model, who fought and died for his cause. This however, does not take away from the fact that he was a violent criminal fuelled by hatred.

Granted, the contrasting neighbourhoods were shocking, but what hit me was not the neighbourhoods themselves, but what was separating them. A huge metal fence, laced with barbed wire. It was difficult for me to appreciate the sheer size of it, scaling high into the presently peaceful sky, and running deep into the heart of the city.

It was put up in the late 1990s by the northern Irish government and was named the 'peace wall'. At the top and bottom were the 'Peace gates', which even now are only open during business hours. On the wall adjacent to the gate, a mural read, 'united we stand, divided we fall', a chilling reminder that even now, almost 20 years after the end of the sectarian conflict in northern Ireland, these tensions still threaten the city.

This huge barrier was put into place to promote peace and on the surface it worked. People from the falls could no longer launch bombs and grenades into the Shankill and likewise, but that was only on the surface.

The wall was meant to be a temporary barricade during the latter years of the troubles, but has evolved into a permanent symbol of division and hatred. Each side of it is stained with vile murals celebrating the deaths of opposing soldiers, even civilians.

This isn't a traditional war-torn country, I was never threatened with any real danger, but even though the war ended 20 years ago people are still unable to live side by side. It's more that it has been torn apart by war, and hasn't been able to heal the deep divisions.

The situation isn't exactly helped by the tourists who flock to the city, with no knowledge or understanding of the atrocities that took place there.

Every day thousands of people flock to Enniskillen church, just outside Belfast, where one of the most universally condemned terrorist attacks took place. An IRA bomb planted in the church hall, detonated mid-way through an act of remembrance celebrating those, on both sides of the racial divide, who died fighting for their country. But to many of the tourists, it doesn't seem real. They comment on how 'awful' and 'barbaric' it was, then hop back onto their bus and move along to the next destination of their 'troubles experience'.

Don't get me wrong, I'm not suggesting that these events should be closed from the public, and there are sadly many more, but is there no limit to how far it will go? This is not a war lodged deep in the veins of history, but a war that only ended less than two decades ago. There are still thousands of people living having been injured as a result of it. Thousands living without family members who were killed, it seemed almost everyone that we spoke to had lost somebody. Yet still people disrespect this, albeit unintentionally, by seeking to stand over the bodies of those who died by visiting these sights and taking sides on a finished war in which both sides were disastrously out of line.

Besides, I find it hard to understand why the government of Northern Ireland would want to promote this as any kind of tourist attraction- a vile war, fuelled by religious bitterness and hatred that killed thousands of civilians only to come to the 'conclusion' after nearly thirty years of fighting that they simply could never live together and resolved this by planting a huge wall between the two communities. But still people come in their droves to see the 'Divide'.

It seems that people love the romantic side of war and conflict and are 'touched' by the brave Republicans and Loyalists who fought to stand up for their beliefs and religion. Their delusion has become part of the mythology that becomes history and converts to fact. Understanding this is a barrier I cannot cross.

© Heriot-Watt University

1.6 Learning points

Summary

In my creative writing, I can:

- create complex settings;
- show the feelings of characters and explore relationships between characters;
- punctuate and paragraph accurately;
- utilise complex narrative structures.

In Prose Fiction, I can:

- create detailed and realistic characters;
- structure a story effectively;
- have a complex theme for my story;
- use dialogue accurately and effectively.

In personal writing, I can:

- express my feelings in detail;
- engage the reader with my choice of language;
- express how events in my life have changed me and made me reflect.

1.7 End of topic test

End of Topic 1 test — Go online

Q15:
Which two of the following concerns the setting in a short story or personal essay?

a) The time / era that the story takes place
b) The people in the story
c) The place where the action happens
d) The events of the story

....

Q16: What does a character's back-story mean in a short story?

....

Q17: Why should you only have one or two main characters in a story?

....

Q18: Which of the following is correctly punctuated?

a) "This is the last time we will meet" she asserted.
b) "This is the last time we will meet," she asserted.
c) This is the last time we will meet", she asserted.

....

Q19: Show three reasons why this sentence of speech is incorrectly punctuated. Write the correct answer and then check it.
She pondered "when will this ever end"?

....

Q20:
Which two of the following are good uses of dialogue?

a) To help create a character's personality
b) To move the story on
c) To use dialect
d) To show that you can punctuate dialogue

....

Q21: Which of the following speech markers might be best used to describe sarcastic speech?

a) Shrieked
b) Offered
c) Sneered
d) Warned

TOPIC 1. CREATIVE WRITING

....

Q22: What does 'show, don't tell' mean in creative writing?

a) Use graphics and pictures.
b) Use lots of verbs to describe action and have the characters moving around.
c) Use gestures and actions to make the reader work out how a character is feeling.

....

Q23: When should you take a new paragraph in creative writing? (Select all that apply)

a) You change time - 'Later that day...' 'A few moments later...' You can use changes in time to structure a story or a personal essay.
b) When a paragraph looks too long.
c) When you tell us your opinion in personal writing.
d) You want to create a dramatic moment- perhaps with a single sentence paragraph.
e) You introduce a new character and describe them in some detail.
f) You want to say what a character is thinking.
g) A new person begins to speak.
h) You change place - think of it like changing the scene that you would like the reader to visualise.

....

Q24: What do you call it when the first person narrative voice is written in the thought pattern of the narrator?

a) Reflective writing
b) Stream of consciousness
c) Autobiographical writing

....

Q25: Complete the table by matching the terms listed with the definitions.

	The narrator can only relate to the reader what is seen or heard. The narrator does not tell us what the character is thinking.
	The narrator knows everything and can choose to tell us how characters are thinking.
	The narrative voice is third person but focusses on a single character and tells the story from their point of view.

Terms

- Third Person Omniscient
- Third Person Limited
- Third Person Objective

....

Q26: Which of the following is only possible with third person narrator?

a) You can learn what a character is thinking
b) The story can go to places without the main character being present
c) You can use dialogue

....

Q27: Put the following four terms in the correct order for a conventional plot of a short story:

- Conflict.
- Resolution.
- Climax.
- Set-up.

....

Q28: Which of the following would make a piece of writing reflective rather than just personal?

a) Strong plot with lots of well described events.
b) Developed characters.
c) Comparing how the writer feels now compared to the time when the action took place.

....

Q29: You can write poetry for your Portfolio.

a) True
b) False

....

Q30: You can write a play script for your Portfolio.

a) True
b) False

Unit 3 Topic 2

Discursive writing

Contents

- 2.1 Introduction 412
- 2.2 Common skills 412
  - 2.2.1 Topic choice 413
  - 2.2.2 Research skills 416
  - 2.2.3 Use of logic 420
  - 2.2.4 Drafting and redrafting 422
  - 2.2.5 Use of statistics 423
  - 2.2.6 Paragraph plans 427
  - 2.2.7 Linking ideas and creating a line of thought 431
  - 2.2.8 Vocabulary 434
- 2.3 Argumentative writing 435
  - 2.3.1 Structure of argumentative writing 438
  - 2.3.2 Techniques of argumentative writing 440
  - 2.3.3 Argument handling in Portfolio example 441
- 2.4 Persuasive writing 442
  - 2.4.1 Features of effective persuasive writing 445
- 2.5 Planning 446
- 2.6 Exemplar work 449
- 2.7 Learning points 463
- 2.8 End of topic test 464

Prerequisites

If you are approaching Higher after sitting National 5, then you already have many of the skills that you need to produce a Portfolio.

Learning objective

By the end of this topic, you should be able to:

- produce a piece of writing that will fit into the Discursive section of your Portfolio.

2.1 Introduction

For your final Portfolio submission you have to produce two pieces of writing. Your school will have procedures about handing in plans and essay drafts and you should follow these. You will also have studied many of the skills needed to be a good writer in other parts of the course and can build on the work done when studying National 5 English. When you studied literature, you will have analysed the skills of effective creative writing. Similarly, in Reading for Understanding, Analysis and Evaluation (RUAE) you will have analysed the style of non-fiction and this will help you write an effective discursive essay if you use elements of that style in your own writing.

The Scholar materials will help you think of some ideas and revise the skills needed to write a successful Portfolio. These materials use examples of genuine Portfolio work submitted in the past and students have kindly given their permission for it to be used.

Portfolio requirements

One piece of writing which is broadly creative:

- a personal essay / reflective essay;
- a piece of prose fiction (e.g. short story, episode from a novel);
- a poem or thematically linked poems;
- a dramatic script.

This is covered in the Creative section of the course (Please see the previous topic).

One piece of writing which is broadly discursive:

- a persuasive essay;
- an argumentative essay;
- a report for a specific purpose;
- a piece of transactional writing.

This is covered in this section of the course.

2.2 Common skills

There are a number of similarities in the skills needed to produce the different types of discursive writing. The different types are:

- a report for a specific purpose;
- an argumentative essay;
- a persuasive essay.

These materials will focus on the two types which are most often created: argumentative and persuasive. Persuasive writing is where you take a strong line on one side of a topic and argue

TOPIC 2. DISCURSIVE WRITING 413

vigorously for your point of view. Argumentative writing is where you take a more balanced approach and look at a range of points of view on a subject. You can still support a point of view of your own in this kind of writing.

All discursive essays need carefully selected topics and need to be researched. They all need to be planned and structured thoroughly. They also needed to be redrafted and checked for technical accuracy. The final submissions need to be set out properly and all sources acknowledged in a bibliography. If you break the task up and work effectively at each stage, you will increase your chance of success.

2.2.1 Topic choice

Choose your topic carefully. It needs to be something which will allow you to construct a clear and logical argument about a complex topic. The more you are genuinely interested in the topic the better your writing will be.

There are a range of issues to consider.

1. Be original and make your essay stand out. With this in mind, it is worth rejecting common topics such as euthanasia, legalisation of drugs, drugs in sport, death penalty, immigration...

    Apart from their lack of freshness, these topics are very wide and are not likely to be covered in any depth in the word limit. They will not offer you the opportunity to write a complex essay.

2. Select a topic which is of personal interest to you. What issues really matter to you? Are there particular things going on in your local area or community that you could focus on? Perhaps issues like the Edinburgh Trams or localised building proposals might be productive.

3. Broad topics cannot be covered in 1300 words. For example, the topic of 'Energy' has many aspects. Narrowing the topic down to one topic will allow that topic to be covered in more depth. From the bigger topic of 'Energy' you could break it down to: issues relating to power generation; nuclear power (which could be broken even further into examining the validity of the new power station at Hinkley Point); down wind farming (and again this could be localised to a particular site). Similarly, fracking is a current issue and of particular relevance to Scotland. Tightly focussed topics will let you explore the complexities of an issue in detail.

4. Selection of topics from other school subjects.

    You can use ideas from other subjects. You need to consider the extent to which a piece of work from another subject will meet the success criteria for a discursive essay in the English Portfolio. It may well present facts / opinions but it has to do it in a different way to achieve success in English. At best, you should see prior study of a topic as useful background knowledge.

    Some ideas from other subjects could be:

    - *Science*
      Look at scientific developments. This would lead you to areas like cell research, cloning, new treatments, alternatives to animal research...
      Exploring how society deals with these moral or ethical issues makes for a complex discursive essay rather than just presenting the facts.

© HERIOT-WATT UNIVERSITY

- *Modern Studies*
  Any political topic either from Scotland, the UK or worldwide might well be complex enough for a discursive essay. These topics are also likely to be very current so the essay is focussing on an issue that matters now. This can give a sense of importance to your topic. You are also likely to have a specific law to study rather than vague general knowledge.
- *Technology*
  There are always lots of ways in which technological change is having an impact on us. Looking at the ones which are very new gives you a current topic with lots of details and opinions about it. Maybe even the law is a few steps behind the technology and this gives you another social dimension to study. Get to the moral or legal complexity behind the topic.

  Technology doesn't just have to be about inventions. There are always changes in the way that people interact with technology, perhaps using something like social media, and these can be productive for essay topics.

5. When looking for topics, examining current news stories can be useful. There will be many current opinions about the subject and it is also likely to be an issue which is of social relevance.

Topic choice   Go online

Q1: Complete the table using the listed topics.

Topic	Comment
	A vague topic and it covers too many areas.
	It is topical and because it is in the area where you live you will see campaigns on both sides often.
	There is no topic to study. No-one is seriously considering reintroducing this.
	You can use a range of health statistics and public funding statistics to explore the topic. By describing facilities in your own area you could localise the topic.

Topics

- Evaluating proposals to close a local hospital.
- The death penalty.
- Does the government spend enough on public sports facilities?
- Drugs in sport.

Some places to find topics

The following organisations all have websites with interesting articles. Reading them may help you find a topic.

http://www.bbc.co.uk/news Apart from the main news stories, the BBC news section has lots of interesting articles on a vast range of topics. You can search by subject and the news is localised so you can find out what is going on in your area.

http://www.bbc.co.uk/news/magazine The BBC site also has a 'magazine' section where there are articles exploring topics.

http://www.theguardian.com/ or http://www.heraldscotland.com/ Online newspapers, e.g. The Guardian or Herald Scotland, will help you research.

http://www.theguardian.com/uk/commentisfree 'Opinion' sections of newspaper may provide some good ideas for topics.

https://www.amnesty.org/ Amnesty International

https://www.un.org/ The United Nations

https://www.newscientist.com/ The New Scientist

http://www.nationalgeographic.com/ National Geographic

Final word on topic choice

Take a little time and choose the topic carefully. It is actually better if you have two or three ideas to discuss with your teacher at the early stage.

You should also think about why your topic is suitable for a Higher English essay. Is it detailed? Does it have a range of ideas around it? If you can justify this to yourself then you are well on the way to choosing a topic that will work.

2.2.2 Research skills

1. *Breaking the topic up*

Researching and planning is a cyclical process. If you know your topic well, construct a plan based on sub-topics. Vague research leads to a vague plan and a weak essay. If you are unsure about your topic, do one phase of research and then plan in detail. If you don't have enough materials for one sub-topic, then research again.

Some of these sub-topic ideas may work for your essay. Remember, they are sections in the essay - not necessarily single paragraphs. By thinking about them, you can bring detail and structure into your writing.

It is important to do research but remember the overall word limit of your essay is 1300 so don't let the research phase take over and stop you getting on with writing.

TOPIC 2. DISCURSIVE WRITING

Sub-topic	Issues
Facts / main ideas	• Look for statistics about your topic. • How many people does it affect? In what way? • How big a problem is it?
Main groups for or against	• Who supports or disagrees with your topic? • Can you name individuals? • Can you name groups or organisations?
Finance	• What facts about money / finance can you find in relation to your topic? • How much does the government spend on it? • What kind of costs might be involved in fixing your problem? • How much do people / tax payers spend on the problem?
Legal details	• Does the law at the moment cover the issue? • Which laws? • Will the law need changed because of the issues? In what way?
Government attitudes	• Does the government have a policy on your topic? • What do political opponents say about it?
Solutions	• What are the solutions to the problem that you have identified? • Are the solutions reasonable? • Could the solutions lead to a different problem?
Public attitudes	• Do people write about your problem? Letters to newspapers? Blogs? • Do people protest about it?

© HERIOT-WATT UNIVERSITY

2. Extending your research

Often, reading articles in the media can generate the idea for a topic. Newspaper articles are not (and should not be) the only source used. You should try to include a range of sources covering a variety of opinions. Four news articles on the same topic may not provide a balanced or complete picture of a topic. It is advisable that your sources have credibility and some depth.

- written journalism extracts, newspaper special investigations and features;
- essays in biography/autobiography;
- pressure-group handouts;
- advertising;
- speeches;
- blogs;
- TV programmes, such as documentaries;
- encyclopaedias / information books and websites.

3. Quality of sources

a) You also need to consider the authenticity of the source. Information about government policy sourced from the government's own website has authority. Information gleaned from blogs / publicly generated sources (like Wikipedia) may be less authentic and in some cases incorrect. It does not mean that they can't be used but you have to recognise that any opinion or 'fact' taken from them needs to be treated with care. These types of sources should certainly not be your main supply of information. As you explore a range of sources, you should be aware of issues of bias. A biased source can be used. You just need the ability to recognise it as such.

The BBC and articles in the quality press such as The Guardian, The Telegraph, The Scotsman or The Herald are at about the right level of detail. Because they have to follow the rules about publishing carefully, they have to be authentic and are less likely to be blatantly biased.

b) Remember that informal sources are also relevant:
- TV programmes that you watched;
- anecdotes from your own experience;
- school course notes.

What is important to remember is that it is the quality of your use of information and the presentation that matters. Quality sources on their own will not make your essay better.

4. Searching

When using search engines, such as Google, frame your search with a specific question. Searching with key words such as 'homework' or 'studying' will produce masses of results which are unfocussed. Searching with a question like 'do Scottish pupils spend too much time on homework?' is more likely to be productive. Frame your questions carefully and you will get faster and better results.

5. Plagiarism

Passing off other writers' ideas as your own is cheating. There are several issues to consider.

- As you research, take notes by putting ideas into your own words. Copying from sources or highlighting is inappropriate as it may lead you to use selected phrases without any attempt at changing them.
- Copying statistics is not plagiarism. You will acknowledge sources at the end of your essay.
- Quoting is not plagiarism as long as you identify the source.
- Plagiarism will not lead to a well written essay. Bolting together a range of writing styles (some of which may be very informal) will not lead to the measured, formal tone needed for a Higher English Discursive Essay.
- Use short quotations and integrate them into your ideas. Long quotations from sources do not help.

6. The bibliography

At the end of your Discursive Essay you should provide a full bibliography of all sources used. Vague comments like 'newspapers' or 'the internet' or 'various web-sites' is not the correct way to do this.

All bibliographies should be in alphabetical order and referenced as follows:

- Books
  Authors name(s) in italics, Title of Book, Publisher, Date of publication
- Websites
  Name of website with date of production (if known) in brackets, Name of article (if known), Full URL with [date accessed in square brackets]

  > Example BBC (23rd Sept 2011), IOC chief demands 2012 boxing bribe evidence from BBC, http://news.bbc.co.uk/sport1/hi/olympics/15033864.stm [accessed 14th October 2011]

- Course notes
  You can refer to course notes from other school subjects in your bibliography.

> **Top tip**
>
> Create your bibliography at the research stage. This will mean that you can easily find the sources again rather than doing it at the end and going through all the problems of trying to find a website that you looked at several weeks before.

2.2.3 Use of logic

A Higher English essay has to handle sophisticated arguments and an awareness of some of the more common flaws in use of logic and reasoning will help you build arguments more effectively. Sometimes in Persuasive writing you are try to manipulate logic but you need to be careful that you don't go too far.

Generalisation

Sweeping statements based on an anecdote or one piece of evidence.

> Example People say that young people are no good. I saw a young person save a kitten from drowning so this proves that teenagers are misunderstood.

Be cautious about using vague statements.

> Example
>
> Some people don't agree with smoking in public.
>
> Question: Which people?
>
> Answer: People who don't agree with smoking in public.
>
> Rewritten:
>
> People who don't agree with smoking in public don't agree with smoking in public.

If you can define a group, then do so. It will help you gauge how large a group who oppose / favour something is and also, perhaps, you might be able to show the depth of their feelings.

Vague language can make it look like you didn't want to research.

Misuse of statistics

> Example British exports to Germany rose by 2% last year. Our exports to Vanuatu rose by 6%. Vanuatu is clearly three times more important to British economic growth than Germany.

You can't compare percentages like this. You need to know the underlying value of the exports in this example.

Straw man arguments

Setting up an invalid argument just to knock it down like a straw man.

> Example
>
> Some people believe that nuclear waste is harmless. This is clearly nonsense.
> (If it is 'clearly nonsense' why are you offering it as a reasonable counter-argument?)

Associative statistics versus causal statistics

This one is complex. You have to prove that the statistic being claimed is the cause rather than something merely associated or connected to the fact.

> Examples
>
> 1. Many people believe otters to be harmless. This is not so. In 2011, two people drowned whilst hunting otters.
>
> ....
>
> 2. Boys are less intelligent that girls. Exam results show that 60% of girls achieved and A whereas only 56% of boys achieved the same grade.

Two statistics can seem to belong together but that does not mean that they prove each other or that the cause is hidden in the statistic.

Ad hominem arguments (irrelevant)

> Example
>
> Young people can fight for their country at 16 yet we can't buy alcohol and drink in pubs.
>
> There are some assumptions behind this statement.
>
> - That joining the army at 16 is correct. (Also the fact is wrong. People may join the army at 16 but can't see active service until they are 19).
> - Because someone else wants to join the army, others should be allowed to drink.

Beware of making irrelevant comparisons that simply don't follow logical scrutiny.

Tu quoque arguments

Beware of suggesting inconsistency in an opponent's argument and citing it as a reason for invalidating it.

> Example Some people want the death penalty brought back for murder. The death penalty is the same as killing and just makes us as bad as the criminals.
>
> Assumption - that execution is the same as murder. Is it?

Appealing (without reason)

Making an appeal is, in itself, not wrong (especially in Persuasive Writing). Just make sure that there is a connection between the appeal and the argument.

> Example
>
> > Most people don't want nuclear weapons so we ought to abolish them. (appeal to popularity)
>
> Not everything can be decided by majority vote. In fact, most complex things can't. The arguments pertaining to the existence of nuclear weapons do not correspond to the number of people who want them.

Other types of appeal could be to:

- authority - someone important agrees with me therefore I must be right!
- pity - emotive appeals;
- history - we have always done this therefore it must continue.

2.2.4 Drafting and redrafting

You are allowed 'reasonable assistance' with your Portfolio and can be given comments on a first draft. The SQA has clear guidelines about what 'reasonable assistance' means. This means that it is your responsibility to choose a topic; find the research materials; plan your own work; and be responsible for your own choice and use of language.

It is strongly recommended that you see your first draft as important and make it as good as you possibly can. Any feedback that you get will help you improve but if there are many things wrong with a draft of an essay, then the feedback can only cover some of them. The Portfolio is worth a significant number of marks so it is worth the effort.

After the first draft, you should use the argumentative and persuasive checklists to see how effective you have been. These can be found in the 'Planning' section of this topic.

2.2.5 Use of statistics

Use statistics to show that you have done some research and have some hard facts to back up your argument. Remember statistics are only part of your argument so don't just drop them in and expect the reader to analyse them for you.

Some places to find statistics:

Apart from within news articles, you can find statistics at:

https://www.ons.gov.uk/ - The Office of National Statistics who state that 'Our main responsibilities are collecting, analysing and disseminating statistics about the UK's economy, society and population.'

https://yougov.co.uk/ - A worldwide community who share their views on topics.

Examples of use of statistics:

> Example The statistic is: 43% of Scottish teenagers are opposed to nuclear weapons.
>
> Now if you wish to portray this in a negative light, for example if you are doing an essay on the dangers of nuclear weapons, you could say:
>
> > Nearly half of Scottish teenagers are opposed to nuclear weapons.
>
> (This sounds like a greater amount than the reality).
>
> If, however, you wished to use this statistic in a more positive way then you need to manipulate it:
>
> > i. only 43% of Scottish teenagers are opposed to nuclear weapons;
> >
> > ii. 57% of Scottish teenagers are not opposed to nuclear weapons;
> >
> > iii. the majority of Scottish teenagers are not opposed to nuclear weapons.

Numbers

Numbers in an essay can be overused. You need to choose when, and how often, to use mathematical data and when to convert it into words that can be more forceful.

> Example
>
> > Last Saturday 3105 students took part in a protest against nuclear weapons.
>
> (This is not really such a large number that it makes an argument stronger.)
>
> However, if you write:
>
> > Last Saturday thousands of students took part in a protest against nuclear weapons.
>
> (This instantly sounds like more people and makes the argument stronger).

Saying the same thing in different ways

Different words can be used to convey the same meaning.

> Example
>
> - 40% of people in a national survey believed that...
> - Nearly half of people in a national survey agreed that...
> - Only four out of ten people...

Numbers or words?

Use numbers for:

- Money (£3.5 million)
- Dates
- Percentages (42%)
- Large numbers (the population of the USA is 321 million)

Use words for:

- anything else!

Don't write sentences like - 'There are 4 reasons not to support the government over this policy.'

2.2.5.1 Top tips for language

Fewer or less?

This is a common mistake made in discursive writing when using statistics.

Use fewer where the noun is countable - that is to say you could come up with a precise number in the situation.

> Examples
>
> 1. Wales has fewer MPs at Westminster than Scotland.
>
> 2. The new laws mean that we will pay a fewer number of taxes.

TOPIC 2. DISCURSIVE WRITING

Use less where the noun is not countable.

> **Examples**
>
> 1. Unemployment will be less under the new policy.
>   ....
> 2. The new law will mean less taxation.

Fewer or less?   Go online

Q2: There will be _____ pupils in each class under the new guidelines.

a) fewer
b) less

....

Q3: Better food packaging will mean _____ damage to the environment.

a) fewer
b) less

....

Q4: The banks have been told to take _____ risks in the future.

a) fewer
b) less

....

Q5: We need to spend _____ on administration and more on patient care.

a) fewer
b) less

© HERIOT-WATT UNIVERSITY

2.2.5.2 Statistics in Portfolio example

Statistics in Portfolio activity: The Jury's Out Go online

Read this extract from the essay 'The Jury's Out'. This essay is about abolishing the jury system.

> I believe that juries are too expensive for this country to sustain. Juries are unpaid, although expenses can be claimed, ranging from loss of earnings expenses and child minding to travel expenses and even lunch costs. Loss of earnings claims alone can be over £64 per juror per day for the first 5 court days, so in one court loss of earnings claimed in total could reach £960 per day as 15 jurors are used in courts. The total 255 day court use in 1 year (excluding weekends and public holidays) could cost up to £244,800 in jury loss of earning expenses. This is for one court. If juries were scrapped, the costs of wages/work expenses in a year could decrease by over 240% in High Courts and decrease by over 280% in Sheriff Courts based on the figures that in 2013, the salary for high court judges was £174,481 and for sheriff court judges was £129,579. Abolishing juries would save the Government a monumental sum of money per year.

Q6: Complete the following table by matching the impacts from the list with the appropriate statistics.

Statistic	Impact
£244,800	
£129,579	
15 jurors	
Decrease by 280%	

Impacts

- Implies the size of jury in relation to one accused.
- Provides the salary for a judge- implies that more judges could be paid rather than juries.
- Proves how much is wasted on expenses.
- Shows the extent of reduced costs.

You can read the whole essay in the section of Exemplar work.

TOPIC 2. DISCURSIVE WRITING 427

> **Statistics in Portfolio activity: Give Without Being Asked**
>
> Read this extract from the persuasive essay 'Give Without Being Asked'. This essay is about an opt-in organ donation system.
>
>> Those in favour believe that one of the main reasons such a small percentage of the population are donors is due to the fact that people simply don't get around to registering or because people do not wish to discuss their death. According to the NHSBT (NHS Blood and transplant) around 90% of the population would agree to donate their organs however only 37% of the population are registered. It can be assumed that that these two figures differ so drastically because many don't find the time to register themselves. The theory then being that if everyone was automatically registered then the full 90% of those willing to donate could be donors. Therefore there would be far more organs available for donation and this would ultimately result in fewer people dying waiting for a transplant which is the most important thing.
>
> **Commentary**
>
> Can you see how the writer has cleverly balances statistics. She presents the statistic showing that 90% of the population are willing to donate organs. This is balanced against the much smaller statistic about the number of people actually registered to donate. This allows her to draw a logical conclusion that an opt-in system would actually be bringing about a practice which most people would, in principle, agree with.
>
> You can read the whole essay in the section of Exemplar work.

2.2.6 Paragraph plans

Getting the structure of your essay correct is important and having structured paragraphs helps you make your argument clearly.

The sections on argumentative writing and persuasive writing have some tips on the overall shape of an essay. If you are doing the Report then you could look at the persuasive writing section. Remember, if you are doing this type of writing don't make it just about presenting facts, names, dates etc. You have to discuss the ideas about your subject.

Avoid using paragraph formulae with topic sentence; quotation; explanation or any other repeated pattern. This makes for a very mechanical essay and it doesn't help you explore topics properly.

The whole essay should show progression through a topic. Generally, the progression should be as follows.

From	To
Present	Future
Simple	Complicated
Factual	Opinion
Problem	Solution

© HERIOT-WATT UNIVERSITY

For example, an essay could start with a brief description of the situation at present, work through the problems and attitudes and then conclude by looking to the future if we don't change our views.

Paragraphs can be varied in length and sometimes a single sentence paragraph can be used for dramatic effect. More developed paragraphs should have:

- a topic sentence which is clear and not overloaded with details;
- a sense of an argument being explored and proved;
- a clear conclusion of your own point of view.

Paragraphing in Portfolio example

Here is an extract from an essay about UK membership of NATO. The annotations reveal the underlying structure of the paragraph into sub-sections.

NATO - Not Another Terrible Organisation

The UK spends a lot of money each year on NATO. £5.3 billion to be exact.[1] So what could this extra money be spent on if the UK made the justifiable decision to say 'Bon voyage' to NATO and stopped contributing to the NATO budget?[2] There are many areas of society that would benefit from having extra funds pumped into them, like the state education system, schemes to help unemployment, state welfare, and of course, the saviour that is the NHS. The list is endless. Last year, the NHS budget was cut by 3.4%, which has led to a decrease in staff wages and a limit in the amount of money at can be spent on updating crucial hospital equipment and purchasing medicines for patients.[3] Furthermore, to add insult to injury, NATO isn't renowned for being frugal with its finances either. How NATO spends its large budget is mainly classified and unknown to the UK. For example, questions concerning 378 NATO investment funds worth £4.5 billion have remained unanswered for decades, and these have never been reviewed or accounted for.[4] This lack of transparency makes it impossible to tell if NATO is using the UK's money wisely, or whether it is being spent on operations and weapon development as is claimed.[5]

Notes:

[1] The topic sentence indicating the paragraph is about finance
[2] Rhetorical question creates a tone of doubt
[3] Provides alternatives
[4] Raises concerns over how the money is spent
[5] Conclusion

You can read the whole essay in the section of Exemplar work.

TOPIC 2. DISCURSIVE WRITING

2.2.6.1 Using the comma

It is really important in your writing to control your expression. As well as choosing the right words you also need to construct sentences accurately. Using the comma properly is an important part of sentence building in discursive writing.

Here are some of the ways in which a comma should be used.

- To separate the items in a list:

  Example We need to stop animal testing, find alternatives and petition the government to change the existing legislation.

  When making lists for discursive, you could use them in the following ways:
  - long lists to show many details and perhaps this could suggest the number of solutions or even the scale of the problem;
  - lists of three - make the final point the climax.

- Using commas to create parenthesis:

  Parenthesis is a part of the sentence that can be removed without changing the meaning of the sentence.

  Example Michael Gove, a member of the Cabinet, has proposed that Britain should leave the EU.

  If you are using a comma to do this, it is important that the phrase begins and ends with a comma.

The comma splice

This is one of the most frequently made mistakes when using the comma. It means that a sentence has been 'spliced' or joined by a comma when either a full stop or a conjunction was needed. If the clauses make sense on their own then using the comma is wrong.

  Example We need to stop dumping nuclear waste, it is harmful to the environment. *(Incorrect)*

Q7: Which of these sentences is correct?

a) This situation cannot continue, the government has to act now.
b) Unless the First Minister changes her mind, the policy will continue as planned.

There are some ways to fix comma spliced sentences:

- you can use a full stop;

  Example We need to stop dumping nuclear waste. It is harmful to the environment.

- you can use a conjunction to connect the sentences. If you do this then you show cause and effect.

    > Example   We need to stop dumping nuclear waste because it is harmful to the environment.

2.2.6.2   The colon and semi-colon

It is desirable to use these punctuation structure when argument handling at this level. Like any sentence type, don't overuse them: have them as a range of sentence types that you use to show a high level of literacy.

Colon

Colons have two uses.

1. Introduce a list, an explanation, or a magnification.
2. Separate two parts of a sentence when one part is explaining or expanding upon the other.

    > Examples
    >
    > 1. The government has changes its policy: they observed opinion polls and saw how unpopular they were.
    >
    > ....
    >
    > 2. There are three concerns over the use of drones over urban areas: the potential for a crash; civil aviation authorities needing to monitor flights; and citizens' rights.

Semi-colon

Semi-colons have two uses.

1. Separate items in a list. Note this use in the last example of the colon. It is especially useful when the items are more than single words.
2. Used where two clauses are independent but balance each other in some way. It suggests a sense of contrast.

    > Example   A majority of the population in Edinburgh voted against Scottish Independence; In Dundee, over 57% of those who voted were in favour of a political break from the UK.

TOPIC 2. DISCURSIVE WRITING 431

2.2.7 Linking ideas and creating a line of thought

Strong linkage will lead to a well-structured essay with a clear line of thought. There are different ways of linking ideas.

Linking ideas — Go online

Q8: Complete the table using the words/phrases listed.

Adding	Changing direction	Being more specific	Moving on	Reasoning	Summarising
	Alternatively	In terms of	Although	Subsequently	Finally
In addition to...	On the other hand	In relation to	Even though	Consequently	
Similarly		In terms of	Despite		In conclusion
Likewise	However			Therefore	In summary

- Ultimately
- Specifically
- Conversely
- As a result
- Notwithstanding
- Furthermore

© Heriot-Watt University

> **Linking in Portfolio example: Remembrance** — Go online
>
> Here is an extract from an essay about the treatment of ex-servicemen.
>
> Highlight the words and phrases that are used to link arguments.
>
> Remembrance
>
>> Service in the Armed Forces may, in some cases, also lead to an increased risk of alcohol misuse and mental health difficulties. These include anxiety, depression and post-traumatic stress disorder (PTSD). Therefore, it is likely that those ex-Service personnel who do come into contact with the criminal justice system may be affected by one or more of these vulnerabilities. On returning from prison, ex-offenders often suffer from mental health issues as well. Most commonly, these are anxiety disorders such as panic disorder and agoraphobia (being afraid of places where it might be hard to escape or worrying that there would be no access to help if something went wrong). Finally, research has suggested that ex-Service personnel suffer from more problems surrounding finance, benefit and debt, a lack of employment opportunities and higher rates of homelessness due to a lack of help for their mental illnesses. This makes it harder to make a smooth transition back into normal life.
>
> You can read the whole essay in the section of Exemplar work.

Linking paragraphs

When studying Reading for Understanding, Analysis and Evaluation (RUAE), you might have come across linking questions. These ask you to show how a sentence (often a topic sentence) acts as a link. In other words, the topic sentence should help join the paragraphs. In order to do this, it needs to:

- refer directly to a phrase or an idea from the previous paragraph;
- set up the idea to be discussed in the paragraph to follow.

TOPIC 2. DISCURSIVE WRITING

Here is an extract from the essay on embryonic stem cell research.

> Adult stem cells are cells are found in different tissues and can only specialise into cells from the same tissue. For example, an adult cell extracted from bone marrow can only specialise into a bone marrow cell- it does not have the ability to specialise into any cell in the body unlike embryonic cells. Therefore, people believe that the use of embryonic stem cells are a more convenient and more efficient method of treatment. However, for the treatment of leukaemia, adult stem cells could be extracted from the bone marrow and specialised into bone marrow cells. This could be an effective treatment for leukaemia and would not involve the destruction of an embryo. However as adult stem cells are in short supply and as they are not as easy to manipulate as embryonic stem cells are, scientists believe that embryonic stem cell treatment is more efficient.
>
> Despite the effectiveness of this treatment[1], there are further arguments[2] as to why embryonic stem cell treatment is morally complex. The development from a fertilized egg into a baby is a continuous process and there is no distinct point in the development when the embryo is classed as a 'human'. A human embryo is a human being in the embryonic stage, just as an infant is a human being in the infant stage. Although an embryo does not currently have the characteristics as a living person would, it will become a person and should be given the respect, dignity and rights as a living person would.
>
> Notes:
>
> [1] referring to the stem cell treatment at the end of the previous paragraph
> [2] these are explained in detail in the following paragraph

You can read the whole essay in the section of Exemplar work.

2.2.8 Vocabulary

Most discursive writing requires a formal tone so this means choosing your words carefully. You need to think of the effect on the reader of the words chosen by you. In Reading for Understanding, Analysis and Evaluation (RUAE) and the Critical Reading Paper, you do a lot of work on word choice so this will help you when you write.

Vocabulary activity — Go online

Think about the impact of using each of the following words to complete the sentence:

- *reconsidered*
- *surrendered*
- *changed*

Successive government has _____ its position over intervention in the Middle East.

Complete the table by deciding which connotations and impacts the words have.

Word	Connotations	Impact
	Suggests defeat	A word which suggests that they have been beaten- forced to change
	More neutral	Neutral- more even handed
	Suggests control and foresight	Suggests that the policy was an active decision

Word choice in Portfolio example — Go online

Rewrite and improve each of the following draft sentences and then check them against the final versions used in the essay.

Q9: There are big differences between the member countries that make up NATO.

....

Q10: A jury is more likely to not just see the fact, feel sorry for someone and be influenced by what they read in the papers or see on television to reach an answer.

....

Q11: However, the issue with the opt-out system of organ donation is that it could result in bad choices being made and people's choice being taken away.

TOPIC 2. DISCURSIVE WRITING

> **Top tip**
>
> Examiner's tip: Use a thesaurus to look for better alternatives at the first draft stage. Some word processing packages have a built in thesaurus.

2.3 Argumentative writing

Structure

The main feature of argumentative writing are that it will:

- present two or more sides of an argument;
- express ideas in an argumentative tone which is reasonable and yet carries a strong sense of your own opinion;
- communicate to the reader a clear sense that you have considered different aspects of the argument before reaching conclusions;
- make effective use of a number of argumentative techniques such as comparison, contrast, confirmation, refutation, counter-argument, proof, disproof;
- communicate a clear line of thought.

The first point on the list above tends to make people think that an argumentative essays is about 'fors' and 'againsts'. Often the structure of the essay reflects this and essays take the shape like the paragraph plan below.

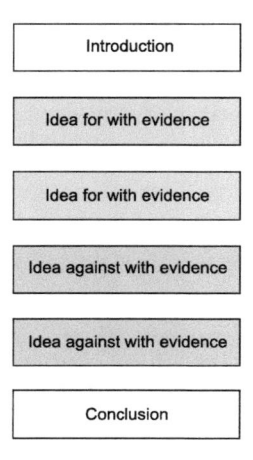

```
Introduction

Idea for with evidence

Idea for with evidence

Idea against with evidence

Idea against with evidence

Conclusion
```

© HERIOT-WATT UNIVERSITY

Some points about this approach (good and bad):

- it is logical and structured;
- it can look too much like the essay was written to a formula;
- the ideas don't necessarily flow easily;
- it will cover both sides of an argument;
- the plan dominates and the writer doesn't always cover the aspects of the topic needed;
- it might be better to put the side of the argument with which you don't agree first. This way, your essay builds in force and gives your opinions more prominence;
- you can show your argument is more important by covering more points from the side with which you agree.

Another way of planning is to use sub-topics like the ones you thought about at the research stage. Within each sub topic, there may well be arguments in favour and against and they can be dealt with in the same paragraph rather than split them up and having two disjointed paragraphs.

Argumentative writing activity: Give Without Being Asked Go online

Q12:

Here is an example from the essay 'Give Without Being Asked'. Highlight the parts of the paragraph which consider the negative aspects and then highlight the positives.

> Furthermore, there is still a lot of debate as to whether an opt-out system is morally correct. Given a utilitarian view the donation of organs would be more beneficial to society and therefore it would seem that organ donation is nothing other than good. However as human beings we are given the right to make decisions for ourselves. The concern is that although people may feel good about going and signing up for organ donation, there may be a certain amount of peer-pressure not to opt-out if presumed consent were introduced. People may feel ashamed of not wanting to donate their organs despite the fact that it is a purely personal decision and it could result in similar abuse to that regarding abortion clinics. This could once again lead to unwilling donations if someone is too afraid to opt-out and therefore introduces many issues with it becoming unethical as well as it potentially causing unnecessary conflict within our society.

You can read the whole essay in the section of Exemplar work.

TOPIC 2. DISCURSIVE WRITING

The visual structure of the paragraph plan for an essay like this may look like:

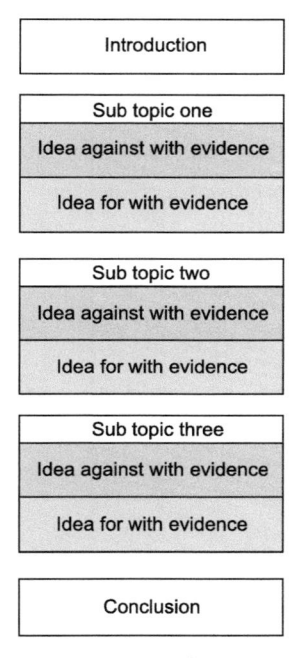

```
┌─────────────────────────────┐
│        Introduction         │
└─────────────────────────────┘

┌─────────────────────────────┐
│        Sub topic one        │
├─────────────────────────────┤
│  Idea against with evidence │
├─────────────────────────────┤
│   Idea for with evidence    │
└─────────────────────────────┘

┌─────────────────────────────┐
│        Sub topic two        │
├─────────────────────────────┤
│  Idea against with evidence │
├─────────────────────────────┤
│   Idea for with evidence    │
└─────────────────────────────┘

┌─────────────────────────────┐
│       Sub topic three       │
├─────────────────────────────┤
│  Idea against with evidence │
├─────────────────────────────┤
│   Idea for with evidence    │
└─────────────────────────────┘

┌─────────────────────────────┐
│         Conclusion          │
└─────────────────────────────┘
```

You may need to mix these two broad essay paragraph structures.

For example, in an essay about the issue of smoking, there is no point in trying to write a balanced paragraph about health issues. On the other hand, a paragraph about rights can be balanced. You can balance the individuals right to smoke against the rights of others not to breathe in something that is harmful.

The following lists will help you to plan your essays.

For and Against planning

- Introduction (key facts, overview, line of thought)
- First idea against (point, evidence, conclusion)
- Second idea against (point, evidence, conclusion)
- Third idea against (point, evidence, conclusion)
- First idea for (point, evidence, conclusion)
- Second idea for (point, evidence, conclusion)
- Final and main idea for (point, evidence, conclusion)
- Conclusion (go over main points and make overall statement)

© HERIOT-WATT UNIVERSITY

Topic based planning

- Introduction (key facts, overview, line of thought)
- First topic (point, evidence from both sides, conclusion)
- Second topic (point, evidence from both sides, conclusion)
- Third topic (point, evidence from both sides, conclusion)
- Fourth topic (point, evidence from both sides, conclusion)
- Conclusion (go over main points and make overall statement)

2.3.1 Structure of argumentative writing

Introduction in Portfolio example - Argumentative

Your introduction should clearly set out the problem. It can also use some overarching facts which let the reader see the scale of the problem. It should also give an outline of the main arguments for and against but don't overload it with facts. Here is an example from the essay 'Give Without Being Asked'.

> **Give Without Being Asked**
>
> For years there has been a dramatic shortage of organ donors in the UK. As of December 2014 there are 6926 people waiting for a transplant.[1] The average waiting time for a kidney is 1,114 days for adults and 354 days for children and about 1,000 people die each year in the UK alone waiting for a transplant.[2] These statistics have left some people in our society questioning the current system for organ donation in the UK including the chief Medical officer who in 2006 expressed his enthusiasm for a well organised and thoroughly explained opt-out system. If an opt-out system were introduced it could be beneficial for those needing transplants, the families of those who have lost their lives and even the government.[3] However, the issue with the opt-out system is that it could result in unethical donations and accidental destruction of people's right to freedom.[4] What's more there is no way to be certain that it will have positive effects.[5]
>
> Notes:
>
> [1] This section sets out the topic.
> [2] The average waiting time for a kidney is 1,114 days for adults and 354 days for children and about 1,000 people die each year in the UK alone waiting for a transplant.
> [3] This section highlights the solution to be discussed in this essay.
> [4] This section hints at there being potential problems with the solution.
> [5] The introduction concludes by explaining that there is no simple anwer.

You can read the whole essay in the section of Exemplar work.

Conclusions in Portfolio example - Argumentative

Your conclusion should clearly set out your final views. Go over the main points but don't restate the facts and evidence. Try to make a final new point and perhaps you can do this by looking to the future. Here is an example from the essay about embryonic stem cell research.

From the following conclusion, highlight:

1. the acknowledgement of other's arguments;
2. this sentence develops and explains the scale of the problem;
3. the writer's own views.

The ethicality of the use of embryonic stem cells for the treatment of leukaemia

> To conclude, although all my sympathy goes to those who have had to live with cancer or watch someone suffer from the horrors of it, I do not believe that it is morally correct to destroy the life of developing embryo in order to save the life of another. When there are other potential treatments for example the use of adult stem cells that could be used instead, I don't see why embryos need to be destroyed. Although the embryo is destroyed at an early stage in its development, it has the potential to become a human from the moment it is created and therefore I do not believe it is morally correct to destroy the life of a developing human in order to save the life of a living one.

You can read the whole essay in the section of Exemplar work.

2.3.2 Techniques of argumentative writing

There are some techniques which are specific to argumentative writing. These techniques will help you control your argument and also will help you cover opposing ideas.

Argumentative writing: Techniques — Go online

Q13: Complete the table by matching techniques from the list with the definitions.

Technique	Definition
	Showing how one situation is like another
	Showing how one situation is like another but with some differences
	Stating how valid your argument is or showing complexity of your argument
	Denying the validity of opponents' arguments
	An alternative argument
	Using hard evidence to back up your point
	Using hard evidence to prove the opposing argument wrong

Techniques

- proof
- disproof
- contrast
- refutation
- comparison
- confirmation
- counter-argument

2.3.3 Argument handling in Portfolio example

Argument handling in Portfolio activity

Look at the example below from the essay on embryonic stem cell research.

The ethicality of the use of embryonic stem cells for the treatment of leukaemia

> Firstly, I will be discussing the arguments in favour of the use of embryonic stem cells. The arguments include, the use of IVF and the fact that many believe anything that can be done to cure cancer, should be done.
>
> During IVF, an egg is surgically removed from the woman's ovaries and fertilised with sperm in the laboratory- the fertilised egg is then returned to the womb for foetal development. However, during this process many eggs are fertilised and only the strongest embryos are returned to the womb- the rest are then discarded. This causes many to question why IVF is not viewed as unethical as in both processes embryos are destroyed. However, I disagree with this argument as the treatment of IVF has the aim to create and grow a new baby and to bring a new human with all sorts of potential into our world. Whereas the use of embryonic stem cells for the treatment of leukaemia aim to destroy a human embryo and therefore prevent a new baby to be born into our world in order to save the life of a living human. This also raises the question of who exactly will be receiving the treatment. In our society it is illegal to refuse treatment to anyone with leukaemia or indeed any type of cancer, so does this mean that a human embryo with all sorts of potential is being destroyed to save the life of a criminal? Or does it mean that this embryo will be saving the life of an innocent child?

Show where the writer has used:

1. Comparison
2. Confirmation
3. Contrast
4. Disproof

You can read the whole essay in the section of Exemplar work.

2.4 Persuasive writing

Structure

The main feature or argumentative writing are that it will:

- have a clear sense of your own views;
- try to persuade the reader with the tone. This could be trying to pressure the reader or appeal to their better nature;
- make effective use of a number of persuasive techniques, such as manipulating information, claiming necessity, employing technical rhetoric.

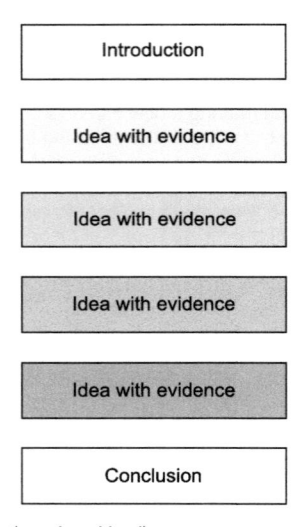

```
┌─────────────────────┐
│    Introduction     │
└─────────────────────┘

┌─────────────────────┐
│  Idea with evidence │
└─────────────────────┘

┌─────────────────────┐
│  Idea with evidence │
└─────────────────────┘

┌─────────────────────┐
│  Idea with evidence │
└─────────────────────┘

┌─────────────────────┐
│  Idea with evidence │
└─────────────────────┘

┌─────────────────────┐
│     Conclusion      │
└─────────────────────┘
```

Some points about this approach (good and bad):

- it is logical and structured;
- it can look too much like the essay was written to a formula and doesn't flow;
- use sub-topics as paragraph ideas rather than single points;
- keep your strongest arguments for later paragraphs;
- perhaps use factual ideas first. Win the reader over with facts and then build to an emotional conclusion.

TOPIC 2. DISCURSIVE WRITING

Persuasive planning

The following list will help you to plan your essay:

- Introduction (key facts, overview, line of thought)
- First topic (point(s), evidence, conclusion, persuasive techniques)
- Second topic (point(s), evidence, conclusion, persuasive techniques)
- Third topic (point(s), evidence, conclusion, persuasive techniques)
- Fourth topic (point(s), evidence, conclusion, persuasive techniques)
- Conclusion (go over main points and make overall statement, what persuasive techniques will you use at the end?)

Introduction in Portfolio example - Persuasive

Your introduction should clearly set out the problem. It can also use some overarching facts which let the reader see the scale of the problem. It should also give an outline of the main arguments that you will make but don't overload it with facts.

Here is an example from the essay 'The Jury's Out'

> Example
>
> The Jury's Out
>
> The European Convention on Human Rights Article 6 states that everyone has the right to a fair trial. The definition of a Human Right is a list of entitlements which every human alive should have. A jury is 'A body of people sworn to give a verdict in a legal case on the basis of evidence submitted to them in court'.[1] However, the right to trial by jury is not included in the European Convention on Human Rights, the International Criminal Court or the International Covenant on Civil and Political Rights[2] - so why should trial by jury be classed as serving justice? Dating back to the 13th Century, juries have been at the heart of the judicial system for almost 1000 years.[3] However, I believe that juries are an outdated system which do not provide the guarantee of justice or a verdict based solely on evidence due to the unreliable and unstable nature of juries.[4]
>
> Notes:
>
> [1] The writer clearly identifies the origin of the topic.
> [2] She identifies reasons why something that we believe is necessary is by no means a part of justice systems universally acknowledged as being fair.
> [3] The writer points out why we have such a strong belief in the jury system.
> [4] She finishes with a clear statement of personal conviction.

She uses emotive words like 'outdated' and 'unreliable' to persuade the reader.

You can read the whole essay in the section of Exemplar work.

© HERIOT-WATT UNIVERSITY

Conclusions in Portfolio example - Persuasive

Your conclusion should clearly set out your final views. Go over the main points but don't restate the facts and evidence. Try to make a final new point and perhaps you can do this by looking to the future. Really aim to be at your most persuasive in this section.

Conclusions in Portfolio activity - Persuasive

Here is an example from the essay 'Not on the High Street'.

Not on the High Street

> However, society's attitude isn't going to change on its own. You can't change people's perceptions on the disabled if there is no one willing to listen and stand up for those in our community with a disability. If you are as agitated and passionate on this topic as I am, then set out on what you said you were going to accomplish and get up off that couch. Change starts with you.

Discussion questions

1. How does the writer try to focus on the reader in this last paragraph?
2. How do adjectives like 'agitated' and 'passionate' make the tone persuasive?
3. Comment on the effectiveness of the final sentence.

You can read the whole essay in the section of Exemplar work.

2.4.1 Features of effective persuasive writing

There are many techniques that can be used to convince the reader that you have a strong argument.

Features of effective persuasive writing activity

Q14: Complete the table by matching the techniques listed with their definitions. You can use this as a checklist when you are writing and at the re-drafting stage.

Technique	Definition
	Questions that don't need answered but try to make the reader feel an emotional response
	Building up force using the pattern of three: give three reasons or use three emotive ideas
	Using 'we' to include the audience
	Using 'you' to direct your comments at the reader
	Using words and images which have strong emotional connotations
	Selecting words and phrases to give your writing a dignified tone
	Using numerical information to back up your ideas
	Persuading by telling the reader what to do or think

Techniques

- Statistics
- Rhetorical questions
- Commands
- Three part lists
- Using second person
- Emotive language
- First person plural
- Formal language

> **Persuasion in Portfolio example**
>
> Look at the example below from the essay 'Remembrance'.
>
> > On the other hand, with ex-offenders the charities available seem to be much more effective. For example, the Kenward Trust which runs a programme called 'RESET' aims to help ex-offenders have a place to stay; aid with the mental illnesses; and finally gives them key life skills that would able them to care for their family. Furthermore, another charity, Blue Sky deems very successful as their figures demonstrate that from their help, 75% of the people they assisted have not reoffended. Can we justify a system where people who have served time in prisons be better treated than people that have served their country?
>
> Show where the writer has used:
>
> - Rhetorical question
> - First person plural
> - Statistics
> - Evidence
>
> You can read the whole essay in the section of Exemplar work.

2.5 Planning

The following lists will help you to plan out and check your essays.

For and Against planning

- Introduction (key facts, overview, line of thought)
- First idea against (point, evidence, conclusion)
- Second idea against (point, evidence, conclusion)
- Third idea against (point, evidence, conclusion)
- First idea for (point, evidence, conclusion)
- Second idea for (point, evidence, conclusion)
- Final and main idea for (point, evidence, conclusion)
- Conclusion (go over main points and make overall statement)

TOPIC 2. DISCURSIVE WRITING

Topic based planning

- Introduction (key facts, overview, line of thought)
- First topic (point, evidence from both sides, conclusion)
- Second topic (point, evidence from both sides, conclusion)
- Third topic (point, evidence from both sides, conclusion)
- Fourth topic (point, evidence from both sides, conclusion)
- Conclusion (go over main points and make overall statement)

Persuasive planning

- Introduction (key facts, overview, line of thought)
- First topic (point(s), evidence, conclusion, persuasive techniques)
- Second topic (point(s), evidence, conclusion, persuasive techniques)
- Third topic (point(s), evidence, conclusion, persuasive techniques)
- Fourth topic (point(s), evidence, conclusion, persuasive techniques)
- Conclusion (go over main points and make overall statement, what persuasive techniques will you use at the end?)

Argumentative essay checklist

1. Are you sure there is no plagiarism?
2. Do you have an introduction?
3. Does the introduction clearly explain the topic and your point of view?
4. Does each paragraph have a topic sentence?
5. Does it link?
6. Does the paragraph present both sides? (If not, does the whole essay present both sides?)
7. Is your opinion clear in every paragraph?
8. Does the paragraph use statistics / evidence?
9. Do you have a conclusion that sums up your point of view?
10. Have you written a proper bibliography?
11. Did you reread your essay for errors?
12. Have you used appropriate vocabulary?
13. Is this essay your best work?

Persuasive essay checklist

1. Are you sure there is no plagiarism?
2. Do you have an introduction?
3. Does the introduction clearly explain the topic and your point of view?
4. Does each paragraph have a topic sentence?
5. Does it link?
6. Does the paragraph use several persuasive techniques?
7. Is your opinion clear in every paragraph?
8. Does the paragraph use statistics / evidence?
9. Does your essay build in force as it goes on?
10. Do you have a conclusion that sums up your point of view?
11. Is it persuasive?
12. Have you written a proper bibliography?
13. Did you reread your essay for errors?
14. Have you used appropriate vocabulary?
15. Is this essay your best work?

2.6 Exemplar work

The following pieces of work have been published with the kind permission from students of St Columba's School, Kilmacolm

The Jury's out

Exhibit 13: The Jury's out

Higher Persuasive Essay by Alix Reid, St Columba's School, Kilmacolm

The European Convention on Human Rights Article 6 states that everyone has the right to a fair trial. The definition of a Human Right is a list of entitlements which every human alive should have. A jury is 'A body of people sworn to give a verdict in a legal case on the basis of evidence submitted to them in court'. However, the right to trial by jury is not included in the European Convention on Human Rights, the International Criminal Court or the International Covenant on Civil and Political Rights- so why should trial by jury be classed as serving justice? Dating back to the 13th Century, juries have been at the heart of the judicial system for almost 1000 years. However, I believe that juries are an outdated system which do not provide the guarantee of justice or a verdict based solely on evidence due to the unreliable and unstable nature of juries.

Several countries, including leading European powers, have abolished the jury system in favour of 'bench trials'. A bench trial is a trial by judge instead of using a jury. Examples of countries which use bench trials are Germany and The Netherlands. When compared to the United Kingdom, Germany has half the crime rate and nearly 5000 fewer prisoners in its jails with a larger total population (UK- 64.1 million people, Germany- 82.6 million). The same pattern occurs with The Netherlands, as the UK has a crime rate over 30% higher and 60,000 more prisoners than the Netherlands. Furthermore, I believe that a bench trial would ensure a more accurate percentage of verdicts.

I believe that juries are too expensive for this country to sustain. Juries are unpaid, although expenses can be claimed, ranging from loss of earnings expenses and child minding to travel expenses and even lunch costs. Loss of earnings claims alone can be over £64 per juror per day for the first 5 court days, so in one court loss of earnings claimed in total could reach £960 per day as 15 jurors are used in courts. The total 255 day court use in 1 year (excluding weekends and public holidays) could cost up to £244,800 in jury loss of earning expenses. This is for one court. If juries were scrapped, the costs of wages/work expenses in a year could decrease by over 240% in High Courts and decrease by over 280% in Sheriff Courts based on the figures that in 2013, the salary for high court judges was £174,481 and for sheriff court judges was £129,579. Abolishing juries would save the Government a monumental sum of money per year.

I believe that there is more potential for corruption and intimidation in a jury than when using a single judge. Corruption in a trial includes bribery, threats and illegally influencing the jury. Although rare, there have been some cases of this- for example, no jury was used in the trial of four men accused of armed robbery from Heathrow Airport. Their trial took place but after being stopped multiple times due to intimidation in the jury, they were re-tried without a jury. This serves as evidence that trials without juries can work and are possible. I believe that judges are less likely to be corrupted because they are trained legal professionals who have experience in the judicial system, and would be less likely to be persuaded to become corrupt. There would be no financial benefit as they are already being paid to give verdicts, whereas juries are unpaid and would benefit from more money.

There is no doubt that juries are unable to base a verdict on evidence for several reasons, primarily due to a lack of understanding of the judicial system. Unless juries are given legal training (which would have financial implications for the taxpayer), I believe that they are unreliable. A judge must have a qualification in the law (most commonly a law degree), usually practising for at least five to seven years prior to becoming a judge. When compared to a jury who require no legal training, this seems foolish to use a group of people who potentially have minimal knowledge of the law when instead, a legal professional could solely be used. The complexity of legal cases is part of the legal system where juries fall short of an acceptable standard. Juries have already been abolished for some complex cases because of the 2006 Fraud Act- stating that juries do not have to be used in confusing fraud trials. This proves that the legal system itself admits that juries cannot deliver a fair verdict in complex cases, therefore what guarantee is there that juries provide a fair verdict in other trials? In 2010 the Ministry of Justice surveyed jurors throughout several courts in different regions of the UK. The results were astonishing; in a Nottingham court, the majority of jurors surveyed admitted that the evidence heard was difficult to understand. This is highly unfair on the defendant because their future is supposedly decided on evidence, not the juries' lack of understanding, and proves that juries should be abolished in favour of judges.

Finally, I believe that using a jury creates the possibility of influencing factors other than evidence (such as conscience, emotive evidence or media coverage) to produce a verdict. Juries cannot be relied upon to forget their personal beliefs or media reports on trials. For example, prisoners cannot be a juror for a minimum of 10 years after their release. This is evidence of the legal system itself proving that people have personal views which may change the result of a trial, making it highly unfair. In addition to this, IRA trials held in Northern Ireland did not use a jury. This was on the basis that bias and intimidation were a real threat to the outcome of the trials. Furthermore, the Ministry of Justice report previously mentioned found that some defendants from ethnic minorities may still interpret unfairness when there is a solely white jury. However, media coverage could also influence a jury. The Ministry of Justice report found that 'In high profile cases, 20% of jurors who saw media reports of their case said they found it difficult to put these reports out of their mind while serving as a juror'. This shows that juries cannot be relied upon to provide a fair verdict based solely upon evidence heard in court. A judge will be more likely to base a verdict on evidence as they are an expert and a trained professional in the legal system. A jury is more inclined to look beyond the evidence, feel sympathetic and be influenced by potential media coverage to reach a verdict. That is not a fair trial. I do not believe that a jury can look beyond media coverage to view the defendant as 'innocent until proven guilty', a Human Right of Article 6 itself.

Potential for corruption, complexity of cases and influencing factors other than evidence are all reasons to abolish juries. The United Kingdom's legal system should grasp the example set by Germany and The Netherlands to improve the service of justice. This country cannot risk dangerous criminals being found not guilty, then roaming our precious streets due to an outdated and unfair system. The factors mentioned are adopting an attitude of 'guilty until proven innocent', breaching a Human Right and are therefore not providing fair trials.

Give Without Being Asked

Exhibit 14: Give Without Being Asked

Higher Argumentative Essay by Lucy Grant, St Columba's School, Kilmacolm

For years there has been a dramatic shortage of organ donors in the UK. As of December 2014 there are 6926 people waiting for a transplant. The average waiting time for a kidney is 1,114 days for adults and 354 days for children and about 1,000 people die each year in the UK alone waiting for a transplant. These statistics have left some people in our society questioning the current system for organ donation in the UK including the chief Medical officer who in 2006 expressed his enthusiasm for a well organised and thoroughly explained opt-out system. If an opt-out system were introduced it could be beneficial for those needing transplants, the families of those who have lost their lives and even the government. However the issue with the opt-out system is that it could result in unethical donations and accidental destruction of people's right to freedom. What's more there is no way to be certain that it will have positive effects.

The current system for organ donation is an opt-in system where by people must sign up to register to the ODR (Organ Donation Register) to become an official donor after death. This also applies if someone wishes to be a living donor. An opt-out system would entail that everyone would automatically be assumed an organ donor unless they actively opted-out.

Those in favour believe that one of the main reasons such a small percentage of the population are donors is due to the fact that people simply don't get around to registering or because people do not wish to discuss their death. According to the NHSBT (NHS Blood and transplant) around 90% of the population would agree to donate their organs however only 37% of the population are registered. It can be assumed that that these two figures differ so drastically because many don't find the time to register themselves. The theory then being that if everyone was automatically registered then the full 90% of those willing to donate could be donors. Therefore there would be far more organs available for donation and this would ultimately result in fewer people dying waiting for a transplant which is the most important thing.

On the other hand, this also brings about potential problems with presumed consent. Some people would not have the time to opt-out; the facilities to opt-out may be complex or people may not even fully understand what it is they would be automatically registered to. Other people may be incapable of making such a decision due to mental or physical health. Although this would result in more donors there is every possibility that this could result in the donation of organs that haven't willingly been given. This would most likely be avoidable for nearly every case, but it is a major risk to take as harvesting the organs of someone who did not consent to it would be highly unethical and raises issues regarding violation of human rights.

If the UK were to introduce an opt-out system it would appear to be that we would select a 'soft' opt-out system as we currently have a 'soft' opt-in system. A 'soft' opt-in or opt-out system is where the families are consulted about the donation. They have a say in whether the organs can be harvested or not, even if the deceased has not made their wishes clear. This would mean it is more unlikely that organs will be unwillingly donated and could help avoid these issues. But of course some families may be no more aware of the wishes of the deceased than anyone else and so the risk is still there for some. For those who oppose an opt-out system, the risk that people may have organs unethically donated is not one worth taking.

Furthermore, there is still a lot of debate as to whether an opt-out system is morally correct. Given a utilitarian view the donation of organs would be more beneficial to society and therefore it would seem that organ donation is nothing other than good. However as human beings we are given the right to make decisions for ourselves. The concern is that although people may feel good about going and signing up for organ donation, there may be a certain amount of peer-pressure not to opt-out if presumed consent were introduced. People may feel ashamed of not wanting to donate their organs despite the fact that it is a purely personal decision and it could result in similar abuse to that regarding abortion clinics. This could once again lead to unwilling donations if someone is too afraid to opt-out and therefore introduces many issues with it becoming unethical as well as it potentially causing unnecessary conflict within our society.

Yet it must be asked whether a possibility of unethical donations is worth potentially jeopardising the lives of thousand's being saved. It has become very clear that the number of organ donors must be increased and although as the years go by more and more people are becoming donors there still simply isn't enough capacity. The possibility of unethical donations is there but with so many people dying waiting for organs those in favour of presumed consent point out that it may be worth the risk. There are many potential problems to be taken into account whenever the government creates a new law.

In addition, as an opt-out system does have the potential to increase the number of donors, it could massively decrease the amount of money being spent by the NHS on things such as dialysis and other forms of life support. The current cost for keeping someone on peritoneal dialysis for a year is £17,500 per patient and £35,000 a year for hospital haemodialysis per year. 21,000 people have dialysis each year and 76% of these people are on haemodialysis and 24% on peritoneal dialysis. This means that each year the government is spending around £646,800,000 on dialysis for patients with kidney failure. A transplant only costs £17,000. Since most patients are on dialysis for just over 3 years it would cost the government, assuming they were on haemodialysis, £105,000 before either dying or receiving a transplant. If said person only had to wait for a year for a transplant then this price would drop by £53,000. Therefore, assuming presumed consent would result in more donors the government would be saving a substantial sum of money. This could also have additional benefits as that money could be put back into improving the health care system having an all-round positive effect.

In conclusion, the opt-out system could result in being beneficial to those needing organs, the government and the families of those who have passed. However due to health problems and social situations amongst certain individuals an opt-out system could become highly unethical and therefore there remains a question as to whether an opt-out system would be, as a whole, the best thing for our society.

The ethicality of the use of embryonic stem cells for the treatment of leukaemia

Exhibit 15: The ethicality of the use of embryonic stem cells for the treatment of leukaemia

Higher Argumentative Essay by Iona Grant, St Columba's School, Kilmacolm

There are currently many ethical issues surrounding the use of embryonic stem cells for the treatment of leukaemia. An embryonic stem cell is an undifferentiated cell that is found within a human embryo. To obtain the medically beneficial stem cell, the embryo must be destroyed. An embryonic stem cell can differentiate into any type of cell. Therefore, for the treatment of leukaemia, embryonic stem cells could differentiate into bone marrow cells to help to resume normal cell production to treat living people suffering from leukaemia. In 2011, 8,616 people in the UK were diagnosed with leukaemia and nearly half of those lost their lives.

Leukaemia is cancer of the blood which causes too many white blood cells to be produced which affects the bone marrow. Bone marrow is spongy tissue which is found inside some of your bones such as your hips and thigh bones. Leukaemia causes the bone marrow to produce abnormal white blood cells, or prevents the bone marrow from specialising into red blood cells.

The argument in favour of the use of embryonic stem cells for the treatment of leukaemia argues that the human embryo would be destroyed at a very early stage in its development and is not legally classed as a human. However, opposing the use of embryonic stem cells argue that despite the embryo is only 14 days developed when it is destroyed, it is still a potential life and those who oppose the use of embryonic stem cells do not believe it is morally correct to destroy a human embryo in order to save a living persons' life.

Firstly I will be discussing the arguments in favour of the use of embryonic stem cells. The arguments include, the use of IVF and the fact that many believe anything that can be done to cure cancer, should be done.

During IVF, an egg is surgically removed from the woman's ovaries and fertilised with sperm in the laboratory- the fertilised egg is then returned to the womb for foetal development. However during this process many eggs are fertilised and only the strongest embryos are returned to the womb- the rest are then discarded. This causes many to question why IVF is not viewed as unethical as in both processes embryos are destroyed. However, I disagree with this argument as the treatment of IVF has the aim to create and grow a new baby and to bring a new human with all sorts of potential into our world. Whereas the use of embryonic stem cells for the treatment of leukaemia aim to destroy a human embryo and therefore prevent a new baby to be born into our world in order to save the life of a living human. This also raises the question of who exactly will be receiving the treatment. In our society it is illegal to refuse treatment to anyone with leukaemia or indeed any type of cancer, so does this mean that a human embryo with all sorts of potential is being destroyed to save the life of a criminal? Or does it mean that this embryo will be saving the life of an innocent child?

A second argument in favour of the use of embryonic stem cells is the medical benefits that it will bring to sufferers from leukaemia.

Leukaemia is hard to diagnose at first as in the early stages, there are no symptoms. However in the later stages of this horrifying illness, harsh symptoms start to occur. Some of these symptoms include tiredness, bone and joint pain, excessive bruising, frequent bleeding and malaise. Stem cell transplant would allow sufferers to have higher doses of treatment, so there may be more chance of curing the cancer than with the standard chemotherapy. Nevertheless, although the use of stem cells would increase the statistics of sufferers who receive successful treatment, I do not agree with the destruction of a potential life to save a living human especially when the use of adult stem cells are a possible treatment for leukaemia which does not involve the destruction of a human embryo.

Adult stem cells are cells are found in different tissues and can only specialise into cells from the same tissue. For example, an adult cell extracted from bone marrow can only specialise into a bone marrow cell- it does not have the ability to specialise into any cell in the body unlike embryonic cells. Therefore, people believe that the use of embryonic stem cells are a more convenient and more efficient method of treatment. However, for the treatment of leukaemia, adult stem cells could be extracted from the bone marrow and specialised into bone marrow cells. This could be an effective treatment for leukaemia and would not involve the destruction of an embryo. However as adult stem cells are in short supply and as they are not as easy to manipulate as embryonic stem cells are, scientists believe that embryonic stem cell treatment is more efficient.

Despite the effectiveness of this treatment, there are further arguments as to why embryonic stem cell treatment is morally complex. The development from a fertilized egg into a baby is a continuous process and there is no distinct point in the development when the embryo is classed as a 'human'. A human embryo is a human being in the embryonic stage, just as an infant is a human being in the infant stage. Although an embryo does not *currently* have the characteristics as a living person would, it will *become a person* and should be given the respect, dignity and rights as a living person would.

At fourteen days old the embryo does not have a nervous system and therefore some people do not class the embryo as an actual human. However if we were to judge the moral status of the embryo from its age, then we are making unaccountable decisions about who can be classed as a human. For example, if we were to say that the formation of the nervous system marks the start of personhood, we would equally be saying that a patient who has lost nerve cells in a stroke has become less human which is completely implausible. It is also believed that the use of embryonic stem cells for the treatment of leukaemia is almost a reversed process. Although we are saving a living persons' life who has loved ones and a life, by using embryonic stem cells we are destroying the opportunity for the embryo to develop into a living human and have the same opportunities as the living life has.

To conclude, although all my sympathy goes to those who have had to live with cancer or watch someone suffer from the horrors of it, I do not believe that it is morally correct to destroy the life of developing embryo in order to save the life of another. When there are other potential treatments for example the use of adult stem cells that could be used instead, I don't see why embryos need to be destroyed. Although the embryo is destroyed at an early stage in its development, it has the potential to become a human from the moment it is created and therefore I do not believe it is morally correct to destroy the life of a developing human in order to save the life of a living one.

Not on the High Street

Exhibit 16: Not on the High Street

Higher Persuasive Essay by Rhona MacPhail, St Columba's School, Kilmacolm

On 15th October, the whole of the UK were left dumbfounded and shocked when Lord David Freud of the Conservative party made a comment on the minimum wage for the disabled in our society. He mentioned to a fellow party member at a Conservative Conference the month previously that some disabled workers were *'not worth the full wage'*. This sparked outrage amongst the public creating excessive contempt for the Welfare minister as well as coercion from the Labour Party for him to resign. However, what is fascinating about this dispute is the apparent hypocrisy displayed by the general public, for if discrimination towards the disabled creates such emotional outrage why does it still exist in our local high street, despite our current economically advanced society.

There are currently 12 million people in Britain who have a disability and although I will mainly be focusing on those with an observable physical disability such as wheelchair users, many people who suffer other disabilities; the visually and hearing impaired, are also affected by this inequality in our local high street.

The first issue that is a cause for concern is accessibility, the lesser of two evils. Last year 'DisabledGo' - representatives of the disabled in standing up for their rights - conducted a survey where they investigated the accessibility and equipment for the disabled in local and iconic retailers. The results were shocking;

'They found a fifth of shops had no wheelchair access, only 15% of restaurants and shops had hearing loops and three quarters of restaurants did not cater for those with visual impairments.'

Has our society advanced at all in the last twenty years? The Disability & Discrimination Act was introduced in 1995 stating it is 'unlawful for the disabled to be discriminated against in access to goods, facilities and services.' However as the survey shows we still struggle to provide accessibility and equipment although this law entered the statute books twenty years ago; therefore it appears we are not truly accommodating the needs of the disabled who are legally entitled to our protection.

Lack of accessibility has a much bigger impact than society cares to believe. People don't consider the consequences that it creates for the disabled as well as highlighting society's lack of progress in terms of disabled rights. Since a lack of accessibility to shops can reduce the independence of some of these inspiring individuals, this in turn can create other psychological issues for the disabled person.

Many people, who suffer from a disability, mainly wheelchair users, may lose some of their dignity- since they feel reliant on other people for basic requirements. Respect towards the customer with a disability is lacking if shops do not provide proper facilities and this can lead to the disabled person feeling marginalised and excluded from the mainstream community. Furthermore, this loss of autonomy leaves the disabled person embarrassed and suffering from a feeling of helplessness. Inevitably, since we naturally desire freedom and independence as human beings, this realisation can leave some disabled people feeling useless. How are we to treat the disabled equally when companies aren't even acknowledging them as valued customers? We depreciate the freedom we have in being able to freely enter a shop, browse casually and take enjoyment from these simple outings. Surely we don't have the right to limit the freedom of others and yet when we look at public attitudes we are appalled at what we find - it is not only MPs who are discriminating against those with disabilities.

Let's take a closer look at Public attitudes. Over the last couple of decades our society has become more selfish and self-serving and as a consequence of that the disabled in our midst are suffering. How many of us really think about the plight of the disabled? We certainly know that many iconic retailers on our local high street do not and have appeared to remain ignorant. A recent survey claimed;

'When they asked leading chains directly for more information, only 4% (4.2) of 105 national retailers responded.'

This shows the lack of engagement and concern towards the disabled. It's as if the disabled people's plight has been cast aside by these retailers only interested in making a profit. The 12 million disabled people in Britain mentioned earlier, have an estimated £200 billion spending potential. For many vast and iconic companies this is a valuable source of profit and income therefore why aren't they using this to their advantage? Despite the fact that accessibility in shops has dramatically increased over the years sadly there is still an insufficient amount of retail outlets that have the equipment necessary to meet the requirements of the disabled. And from our survey it can be seen that they do not consider the needs of the disabled as a priority. I comprehend that this is a difficult time financially since we are in the midst of a recession therefore companies do not want to invest in something that won't bring an immediate change in their turnover. How short-sighted and blind has our society become?

Some shocking stories have come to light recently regarding our ignorance surrounding the treatment of the disabled. Last October a middle-aged, blind woman called Maya Makri, attempted to enter a Tesco Express branch in Swiss Cottage, north-west London with her guide dog. Upon entering the establishment, the cashiers and staff told her that animals weren't permitted despite the guide dog being clearly identified with its harness and fluorescent jacket. In spite of telling them that she was registered blind and that her 'pet' was a guide dog she was still confronted and on the receiving end of three shouting and ignorant employees. The mere manner in how they handled the situation shows society's disregard towards the disabled since it was completely unnecessary behaviour and indicates how disabled people are patronised as consumers. This is also an example of the lack of training in staff members to deal with this sort of issue responsibly and respectfully since in a recent survey only a third of retail employees had the training to assist people with disabilities. With this insufficient lack of training it merely proves how employers and public attitudes underpin the lack of impotence to make changes which would be beneficial for the disabled in our present decade.

Therefore, how are we to improve society's attitude and treatment of the disabled in our community - discrimination isn't just limited to our local high street. I understand that it would be very unlikely that we can change the whole world's opinion on those with disabilities overnight. However, there is still plenty of adjustments that can be made to improve their independence and our conduct towards the disabled. The improvements don't need to be vast or immense, a simple, clear policy in the window of a shop or an improvement in training employees in renowned retail outlets is all that's needed. If staff members were able to understand and communicate effectively with the customer by perhaps, by pronouncing words clearly then the disabled customer would notice the effort being made and feel more at ease.

© HERIOT-WATT UNIVERSITY

TOPIC 2. DISCURSIVE WRITING

This surely isn't too much to ask for.

However, society's attitude isn't going to change on its own. You can't change people's perceptions on the disabled if there is no one willing to listen and stand up for those in our community with a disability. If you are as agitated and passionate on this topic as I am, then set out on what you said you were going to accomplish and get up off that couch. Change starts with you.

NATO - Not Another Terrible Organisation

Exhibit 17: NATO - Not Another Terrible Organisation

Higher Persuasive Essay by Alex Schellekens, St Columba's School, Kilmacolm

The North Atlantic Treaty Organisation (NATO) has arguably lost its sense of purpose and direction in recent years. From the beginning of the 21st century, NATO wasn't involved in a single major conflict until the start of the Ukraine crisis occurred in early 2014, which led to many skeptics, such as newspapers like the Guardian and the Telegraph, rightfully questioning the point of its existence. NATO was initially formed in 1949, following on from the conclusion of the First World War as an alliance against the Soviet Union. For the next three decades the Cold War continued and the rivalry between the communist states and the capitalist, democratic, western nations, grew. When the Cold War ended, NATO was defunct but, not to worry, the keen member countries discovered another purpose for this pointless organisation. Nuclear weapons! But sadly, this purpose has been unsuccessful too. Britain should leave NATO due to the inequality that exists among member nations. The fact that our money is wasted regularly and could be better spent on domestic affairs, and because nuclear weapons as an entity are principally wrong as well as also being a waste of money.

There is vast inequality between the member nations that constitute NATO. In order to be part of a successful alliance, there needs to be a balance of give and take from all parties concerned, but this fails to happen in NATO. There are some countries (like the UK) who give more to the organisation then they get out. Furthermore, there has been a bizarre trend that NATO has decided to annex other countries that are unable to give a large financial contribution, and this just adds to the inequality on its already overcrowded rostrum. The USA funded 22.4% of NATO's military budget in 2014, which was twice as much as any other nation. The UK funds 10.4% of the budget and so still plays a vital part in funding NATO as the fourth biggest contributor. Meanwhile, Iceland is one of 14 nations that pay less than 1% of NATO's military budget, but yet reap the benefits of being in an alliance with the USA and having close access to its strong defence system. Obviously, Iceland doesn't have the same size of economy that other NATO members has, but if the organisation was to be truly equal then arguably the budget would be split equally among the members, and no deadwood should be tolerated. Of the 29 member countries, only 3 of them (France, UK, USA) have a nuclear weapons program and only Belgium, Turkey, Germany, Italy and the Netherlands have storage facilities and can store nuclear weapons under NATO's policy of 'nuclear sharing'. This simply proves that the vast majority of countries in NATO are only part of the organisation so that they can be protected in the event of attack by wealthier nations, rather than feeling that they should contribute as well. Furthermore, at the start of this century, the USA set out a guideline that all NATO member countries must spend at least 2% of their GDP on defence. Only four countries currently meet this target, which is ridiculous, and proves how many countries simply aren't willing to follow the guideline on defence spending. This scenario is hugely unfair for the UK who should not have the burden of responsibility of supporting smaller nations when facing difficult economic times ourselves.

The UK spends a lot of money each year on NATO. £5.3 billion to be exact. So what could this extra money be spent on if the UK made the justifiable decision to say 'Bon voyage' to NATO and stopped contributing to the NATO budget? There are many areas of society that would benefit from having extra funds pumped into them, like the state education system, schemes to help unemployment, state welfare, and of course, the saviour that is the NHS.

© HERIOT-WATT UNIVERSITY

TOPIC 2. DISCURSIVE WRITING 459

The list is endless. Last year, the NHS budget was cut by 3.4%, which has led to a decrease in staff wages and a limit in the amount of money at can be spent on updating crucial hospital equipment and purchasing medicines for patients. Furthermore, to add insult to injury, NATO isn't renowned for being frugal with its finances either. How NATO spends its large budget is mainly classified and unknown to the UK. For example, questions concerning 378 NATO investment funds worth £4.5 billion have remained unanswered for decades, and these have never been reviewed or accounted for. This lack of transparency makes it impossible to tell if NATO is using the UK's money wisely, or whether it is being spent on operations and weapon development as is claimed.

NATO has failed to have a positive impact even when attempting to take action on making peace. During the Kosovo conflict in 1999, NATO intervened and deployed military troops and weapons in the area as a method of trying to stop the conflict. The Kosovo conflict would go on for another year, families were torn apart, and the action taken by NATO was not only seen to have not stopped the conflict, but actively seen to have worsened the conflict by arming certain groups with weapons and not others. The NATO officers were seemingly unaware of the deep religious and ethnic tensions there are in that area. Similar failures include wars in Bosnia and Afghanistan, when NATO airstrikes exacerbated violence as opposed to stopping it. Even last year, NATO only succeeded in annoying Russia when interfering in Ukraine, hasn't succeeded in creating peace there, and if anything NATO only encouraged Russia to continue its involvement in helping rebel separatist groups in Ukraine. Considering this, NATO hasn't had much success in reducing conflict, and hasn't provided peace after most of its attempts to stop violence.

NATO's key role is to deal with nuclear weapons, and this leads onto another point entirely; what is the need for nuclear weapons? Do countries need nuclear weapons? Nuclear weapons are probably never going to be used by any country around the globe, regardless of whom NATO sees as its 'enemies' currently. The entire theory of having an organisation solely responsible to dealing with nuclear weapons is flawed for several reasons. Firstly, they cost a lot of money to develop and research effectively and it is estimated that the UK government spends roughly a third of the defence budget (£20 billion) on our nuclear weapons program - Trident. This £20 billion ensures that a submarine carrying a bomb is lurking in the waters, some 25 miles of the coast of Aberdeen in the event of an attack. Does that make you feel safe? Secondly, they only exist to act as a deterrent to supposedly discourage other countries like North Korea or Iran, from setting off theirs. This is something that is impossible to prove whether it is being effective or not. And thirdly, there is a slight flaw in the logic that the west will be able to respond and make use of an alliance like NATO if a nuclear war breaks out. Scientifically, it is widely accepted that if one nuclear bomb went off in the near future, it would destroy all life on earth, such has been the development in the field of nuclear power in the last half a century. Basically, if Kim Jong-Un gets angry and sets off his bombs, we are all doomed. If the UK leaves NATO we would question our desire to keep our big numbers of nuclear weapons and this could potentially save more money in the future that would be better spent on other issues.

Considering Britain's position on the international stage, it's an easy option to think that NATO gives us power. But then, what are the UN, G8 and G20 for? Britain could continue having a limited defence programme, but it's about time Britain learnt to not meddle in Afghanistan's affairs and not continue to feel responsible for tackling rebels abroad. Britain has more than it's own fair share of international power, and the funding required for NATO and defence as a whole is slowly chipping away at our economy and causing us to decline. After all, we won't

© HERIOT-WATT UNIVERSITY

be a major country for much longer if our economy explodes like a nuclear bomb. Britain should leave the other member nations of NATO to stew in their own juice. And stand back, to watch the results.

Remembrance

Exhibit 18: Remembrance

Higher Persuasive Essay by Katya Guyler, St Columba's School, Kilmacolm

We respect the soldiers fighting and dying for us in wars across the world such as Afghanistan and Iran. We honour them in principle with services Remembrance Day Services. Yet, does the government discard their military honour when they return from active service? Is it fair to say that we venerate the soldiers who have fought and died - but forget about the soldiers that have fought and survived by not offering enough help when they come back from the war? In many ways, we treat ex-offenders better than ex-service personnel and, without any aspect of moral judgement of criminals, I find this to be unbalanced.

We must take into account the consequences of lack of help from the government onto the ex-service personnel and what happens as a result of this. Statistics prove that, around three thousand ex-service personnel are on the streets of London; furthermore, in the future this number will apparently rise to five thousand due to government cuts. Additionally, over twenty two ex-service personnel commit suicide each year as a result of no support. In 2013, the number of serving personnel and ex-military personnel committing suicide actually outstripped the number who died in conflict in Afghanistan.

Service in the Armed Forces may, in some cases, also lead to an increased risk of alcohol misuse and mental health difficulties. These include anxiety, depression and post-traumatic stress disorder (PTSD). Therefore, it is likely that those ex-Service personnel who do come into contact with the criminal justice system may be affected by one or more of these vulnerabilities. On returning from prison, ex-offenders often suffer from mental health issues as well. Most commonly, these are anxiety disorders such as panic disorder and agoraphobia (being afraid of places where it might be hard to escape or worrying that there would be no access to help if something went wrong). Finally, research has suggested that ex-Service personnel suffer from more problems surrounding finance, benefit and debt, a lack of employment opportunities and higher rates of homelessness due to a lack of help for their mental illnesses. This makes it harder to make a smooth transition back into normal life.

There are charities and government organisations which aid soldiers returning to normal civilian life. Institutions such as the British Legion and charities like the Soldiers, Sailors, Airmen and Families Association (SSAFA) contribute their services and provide financial and mental support. Apparently, this help is 'lifelong'. However, much evidence proves that this support is not as effective or long-lived as it is portrayed to be. This help stops predominately in the ex-service men's fifties. On average, 44% of ex-service personnel aged fifty to sixty were patrons of a refuge transfer facility. Furthermore, an annual study of homeless ex-service personnel deemed that the majority of the homeless ex-service personnel were mostly aged in their mid-fifties.

On the other hand, with ex-offenders the charities available seem to be much more effective. For example, the Kenward Trust which runs a programme called 'RESET' aims to help ex-offenders have place to stay; aid with the mental illnesses; and finally gives them key life skills that would able them to care for their family. Furthermore, another charity, Blue Sky deems very successful as their figures demonstrate that from their help, 75% of the people they assisted have not reoffended. Can we justify a system where people who have served time in prisons be better treated than people that have served their country?

There are limited attempts to help ex-service personnel. Presently the NHS and the MoD are funding six mental health pilot projects for ex-service personnel across the UK, striving to understand ex-service personnel mental problems thus hopefully improving the standard of help for the ex-service personnel. These projects include: recommendations to public mental health facilities; expert treatment; and housing. I understand that this looks good, yet these are pilots, emphasising that they could be shut down if they are not successful and are also just beginning to address a problem that needed examined decades ago. On the other hand, prisoners are offered treatment with psychologists to help them with the difficulties that caused them to go to prison, including addiction to drugs and alcohol. Moreover, Organisations such as the National Offender Management Service (NOMS) give prisoners places to settle on finishing their sentences. We question why the government would want to put so much effort into helping the people that have committed a crime rather that help the people who are fighting for their country. Why won't our government accept responsibility for ex-service personnel?

In the field of employment there also seems to be more help for ex-prisoners. There are several charities that are available for ex-offenders to make it easy to get jobs for example The Royal London Society, The Princes Trust, Bounce Back and several more which provide the help needed for ex-offenders to find employment. This proves successful, as more and more ex-offenders are getting jobs after they're released. Moreover, the law states that it is illegal to not hire someone because they have been in prison. Nevertheless, the lack of charities to help ex-service personnel to get jobs makes it difficult for them to find employment and not end up homeless. Ex-service personnel face many challenges from returning from war and many find it extremely difficult to find work due to three main aspects: disability; not enough public work experience; and finally difficulties with the switch into normal life.

In conclusion, it is very clear that there needs to be more help offered for the ex-service personnel when they return from war. The government should make it a main priority to make sure that soldiers are always respected - after all they have offered up their lives in sacrifice for their country. Respect should be regardless of whether they died as a result of war, are fighting in war or have survived war.

2.7 Learning points

> **Summary**
>
> In my discursive writing I can:
>
> - provide detail to support my argument;
> - research a topic in detail;
> - express my opinions about a topic;
> - punctuate and paragraph more accurately.
>
> In argumentative writing, I can:
>
> - use a number of techniques to handle more than one side to a topic;
> - structure an essay effectively;
> - use a formal tone to explore a topic.
>
> In persuasive writing, I can:
>
> - use a number of persuasive techniques;
> - engage the reader with my choice of language;
> - express my own opinion clearly.

2.8 End of topic test

End of Topic 2 test — Go online

Q15: What is the word limit for Portfolio essays at Higher?

a) 1500
b) 1300
c) 800

....

Q16: Which two types of writing must your Portfolio have?

a) Discursive writing
b) Critical essay
c) Creative writing
d) Personal reading review

....

Q17: A discursive essay which covers more than one point of view on a topic is called:

a) persuasive.
b) transactional.
c) argumentative.

....

Q18: Which of the following sentences is an example of the error called comma splicing?

a) The internet is everywhere, we can access it twenty four hours per day.
b) With twenty four hour access possible, we can be constantly online.
c) Nevertheless, there is a pressing need for the government to act now.

....

Q19: Can you select topics from other school subjects for a discursive essay?

a) Yes
b) No

....

Q20: Can you use biased sources in your research for a discursive essay?

a) Yes
b) No

Explain why.

....

Q21: What is plagiarism?

....

TOPIC 2. DISCURSIVE WRITING

Q22: Which two of the following is plagiarism?
  a) Quoting from a source document and using quotation marks
  b) Using a paragraph from an older sibling's essay
  c) Copying an effective sentence from a newspaper article

....

Q23: What details about a website need to be in a bibliography? Complete the paragraph using the words listed.

Name of _____ with date of production (if known)
name of _____ and _____ (if known)
full _____
date _____ in square _____

Word list

- accessed
- URL
- article
- website
- brackets
- writer

....

Q24: Which of the following are you allowed help with from a teacher when drafting an essay?
  a) Spelling
  b) Being given a paragraph plan.
  c) Being told how to reword a sentence.
  d) Having a discussion about possible topics.

....

Q25: What is the correct name for the first sentence of a paragraph?

....

Q26: Which of the following linking words would let you change direction in an argument?
  a) Additionally
  b) Alternatively
  c) Subsequently

....

Q27: Put the following three words in order of their connotations:

- Wait
- Procrastinate
- Deliberate

Not on the High Street

Higher Persuasive Essay by Rhona MacPhail, St Columba's School, Kilmacolm

On 15th October, the whole of the UK were left dumbfounded and shocked when Lord David Freud of the Conservative party made a comment on the minimum wage for the disabled in our society. He mentioned to a fellow party member at a Conservative Conference the month previously that some disabled workers were *'not worth the full wage'*.[1] This sparked outrage amongst the public creating excessive contempt for the Welfare minister as well as coercion from the Labour Party for him to resign. However, what is fascinating about this dispute is the apparent hypocrisy displayed by the general public, for if discrimination towards the disabled creates such emotional outrage why does it still exist in our local high street, despite our current economically advanced society.

There are currently 12 million people in Britain who have a disability[2] and although I will mainly be focusing on those with an observable physical disability such as wheelchair users, many people who suffer other disabilities; the visually and hearing impaired, are also affected by this inequality in our local high street.

The first issue that is a cause for concern is accessibility, the lesser of two evils. Last year 'DisabledGo' - representatives of the disabled in standing up for their rights - conducted a survey where they investigated the accessibility and equipment for the disabled in local and iconic retailers. The results were shocking;

'They found a fifth of shops had no wheelchair access, only 15% of restaurants and shops had hearing loops and three quarters of restaurants did not cater for those with visual impairments.'

Has our society advanced at all in the last twenty years?[3] The Disability & Discrimination Act was introduced in 1995 stating it is *'unlawful for the disabled to be discriminated against in access to goods, facilities and services.'*[4] However, as the survey shows we still struggle to provide accessibility and equipment although this law entered the statute books twenty years ago; therefore, it appears we are not truly accommodating the needs of the disabled who are legally entitled to our protection.

Lack of accessibility has a much bigger impact than society cares to believe.[5] People don't consider the consequences that it creates for the disabled as well as highlighting society's lack of progress in terms of disabled rights. Since a lack of accessibility to shops can reduce the independence of some of these inspiring individuals, this in turn can create other psychological issues for the disabled person. Many people, who suffer from a disability, mainly wheelchair users, may lose some of their dignity- since they feel reliant on other people for basic requirements. Respect towards the customer with a disability is lacking if shops do not provide proper facilities and this can lead to the disabled person feeling marginalised and excluded from the mainstream community. Furthermore, this loss of autonomy leaves the disabled person embarrassed and suffering from a feeling

TOPIC 2. DISCURSIVE WRITING

of helplessness.[6] Inevitably, since we naturally desire freedom and independence as human beings, this realisation can leave some disabled people feeling useless. How are we to treat the disabled equally when companies aren't even acknowledging them as valued customers? We depreciate the freedom we have in being able to freely enter a shop, browse casually and take enjoyment from these simple outings. Surely we don't have the right to limit the freedom of others and yet when we look at public attitudes we are appalled at what we find - it is not only MPs who are discriminating against those with disabilities.

Let's take a closer look at Public attitudes. Over the last couple of decades our society has become more selfish and self-serving and as a consequence of that the disabled in our midst are suffering. How many of us really think about the plight of the disabled? We certainly know that many iconic retailers on our local high street do not and have appeared to remain ignorant. A recent survey claimed;

'When they asked leading chains directly for more information, only 4% (4.2) of 105 national retailers responded.'

This shows the lack of engagement and concern towards the disabled. It's as if the disabled people's plight has been cast aside by these retailers only interested in making a profit. The 12 million disabled people in Britain mentioned earlier, have an estimated £200 billion spending potential.[7] For many vast and iconic companies this is a valuable source of profit and income therefore why aren't they using this to their advantage? Despite the fact that accessibility in shops has dramatically increased over the years sadly there is still an insufficient amount of retail outlets that have the equipment necessary to meet the requirements of the disabled. And from our survey it can be seen that they do not consider the needs of the disabled as a priority. I comprehend that this is a difficult time financially since we are in the midst of a recession therefore companies do not want to invest in something that won't bring an immediate change in their turnover. How short-sighted and blind has our society become?

Some shocking stories have come to light recently regarding our ignorance surrounding the treatment of the disabled. Last October a middle-aged, blind woman called Maya Makri, attempted to enter a Tesco Express branch in Swiss Cottage, north-west London with her guide dog. Upon entering the establishment, the cashiers and staff told her that animals weren't permitted despite the guide dog being clearly identified with its harness and fluorescent jacket. In spite of telling them that she was registered blind and that her 'pet' was a guide dog she was still confronted and on the receiving end of three shouting and ignorant employees. The mere manner in how they handled the situation shows society's disregard towards the disabled since it was completely unnecessary behaviour and indicates how disabled people are patronised as consumers.[8] This is also an example of the lack of training in staff members to deal with this sort of issue responsibly and respectfully since in a recent survey only a third of retail employees had the training to assist people with disabilities. With this insufficient lack of training it merely proves how employers and public attitudes underpin the lack of impotence to make changes which would be beneficial for the disabled in our present decade.

Therefore, how are we to improve society's attitude and treatment of the disabled in our community - discrimination isn't just limited to our local high street. I understand that it would be very unlikely that we can change the whole world's opinion on those with

© HERIOT-WATT UNIVERSITY

disabilities overnight. However, there are still plenty of adjustments that can be made to improve their independence and our conduct towards the disabled. The improvements don't need to be vast or immense - a simple, clear policy in the window of a shop or an improvement in training employees in renowned retail outlets is all that's needed. If staff members were able to understand and communicate effectively with the customer by perhaps, by pronouncing words clearly then the disabled customer would notice the effort being made and feel more at ease. This surely isn't too much to ask for.[9]

However, society's attitude isn't going to change on its own. You can't change people's perceptions on the disabled if there is no one willing to listen and stand up for those in our community with a disability. If you are as agitated and passionate on this topic as I am, then set out on what you said you were going to accomplish and get up off that couch. Change starts with you.[10]

Notes:

[1]
[2]
[3]
[4]
[5]
[6]
[7]
[8]
[9]
[10]

Unit 3 Topic 3

Talking: Tips and techniques

Contents

3.1	Introduction	470
3.2	Ideas and content	472
3.3	Language choice	473
3.4	Communicating meaning	474
3.5	Non-verbal communication	475
3.6	Visual aids	476
3.7	Talking from notes	477
3.8	Introductions	478
3.9	Conclusions	478
3.10	Planning	479
3.11	Learning points	480
3.12	End of topic test	481

Prerequisites

If you are approaching Higher after sitting National 5, then you already have many of the skills that you need to produce an effective Talk.

Learning objective

By the end of this topic, you should be able to:

- take part in a group discussion or deliver a detailed and structured presentation which will involve answering questions from the audience. This will ensure that you achieve the Performance - spoken language component.

3.1 Introduction

Giving talks and presentations is a valuable personal skill. There are many situations in the future where you will need to present your ideas formally and to an audience. In English, you will learn how to create and deliver talks. Creating talks will also help you understand many aspects of the course more thoroughly as well as developing your confidence. You also have to take part in talk situations as part of the Performance - spoken language component.

There are four outcomes to achieve in a Higher assessed talk. You need to:

- employ relevant detailed and complex ideas and/or information using a structure appropriate to purpose and audience;
- communicate meaning effectively through the selection and use of detailed and complex spoken language;
- use aspects of non-verbal communication;
- demonstrate listening skills by responding to detailed and complex spoken language.

You might be asked to talk about:

- some aspect of the texts studied in class- perhaps a talk about a theme in a novel, play or poetry;
- some research that you have done into an aspect of classwork;
- your topic for a Portfolio essay (perhaps your discursive essay);
- a personal experience on which you reflect on it;
- a complex subject of personal interest to you.

Whatever the topic, you need to prepare, plan and deliver the talk effectively.

You can see excellent examples of talks at:

- BBC Bitesize National 5 English Talking, which has links to many 'Class Clips' providing great examples of speeches - please see http://www.bbc.co.uk/education/topics/zm4cwmn;
- TED talks, which has great examples of public speaking on a vast range of topics, some of which could even be used as sources of information for your Discursive Essay in your Portfolio - please see https://www.ted.com/talks.

The following list will help you to make notes on the effectiveness of any of these talks. Then, you can build these ideas into the planning of your own talk.

Talk evaluation checklist

Ideas

- Knowledge and understanding of main ideas with detail
- Ideas / opinions and not just facts

Language

- Choice of words
- Rhetorical devices

Communicating meaning

- Visual aids (if any)
- Pace and clarity

Non - verbal communication

- Use eye contact
- Gesture and posture

3.2 Ideas and content

If you choose to create your talk on your Discursive Essay topic, then you can go through the same topic selection process and research methods that you will find in the Scholar resources on these aspects. A topic that is suitable for a Higher Discursive Essay will have the kind of depth and complexity needed to make a good talk as well. (Please see the previous topic in this unit).

Your talk has to be detailed but because it has to be complex don't just present facts, statistics and date details. You will keep the audience more interested by exploring more complicated aspects. For example, if you are creating a biographical talk, don't fill it with details about someone's early life. Look at some of the really interesting parts of his or her life (perhaps controversial elements) and explore them in depth.

Plan and structure your talk in sections. It is important not to wander off topic and only thorough preparation will make sure that you keep on task.

If you are in a group talk situation, you need to take account of other's views. Even in a solo talk, give your audience the chance to express views by asking them questions or inviting them to ask you about your talk.

You also need to link your ideas in a talk. This will help keep it moving. You should use linking and signpost words to let the reader see the shape of your ideas.

Linking ideas   Go online

Effective linkage will lead to a well-structured essay with a clear line of thought. There are different ways of linking ideas.

Q1: Complete the table by matching the words/phrases with the headings.

Adding	Changing direction	Being more specific	Moving on	Reasoning	Summarising
Furthermore	Alternatively	The exact detail of		Subsequently	Finally
In addition to…		In relation to	Even though		Ultimately
	Conversely		Despite	As a result	
Likewise	However	Specifically	Notwithstanding	Therefore	In summary

- On the other hand
- Although
- In conclusion
- Similarly
- In terms of
- Consequently

TOPIC 3. TALKING: TIPS AND TECHNIQUES

3.3 Language choice

There are different purposes to talks. You might be trying to:

- inform;
- entertain;
- persuade.

Your choice of language will be determined by the purpose. If you are trying to inform or persuade, you will probably want to use more formal language but if you are trying to entertain then the option of being less formal is possible.

Features of effective persuasive talking   Go online

There are many techniques that can be used to convince the listener that you have a strong argument.

Q2: Complete the table by matching the techniques listed with their definitions.

Technique	Definition
	Questions that don't need answered but try to make the reader feel an emotional response.
	Building up force using the pattern of three: give three reasons or use three emotive ideas.
	Using 'we' to include the audience.
	Using 'you' to direct your comments at the audience.
	Using words and images which have strong emotional connotations.
	Selecting words and phrases to give your talk a dignified tone.
	Using numerical information to back up your ideas.
	Persuading by telling the audience what to do or think.

- Statistics
- Rhetorical questions
- Commands
- Three part lists
- Using second person
- Emotive language
- First person plural
- Formal language

3.4 Communicating meaning

Apart from getting the wording of your talk right, you have to remember the audience. In order to keep them interested they have to hear you.

There are other aspects that you have to consider when giving a talk.

Pace

You need to get this just right. Going too quickly means the audience can't follow you. This is often a problem when people write their talk out and read it rather than use notes and talk to the audience.

On the other hand, if you fail to prepare or have good notes then you could forget your place and have awkward silences.

A really great talk will vary pace and have short pauses to let the audience consider key points.

Tone

When you study Reading for Understanding, Analysis and Evaluation (RUAE) you will have come across questions asking about the writer's tone. This refers to the writer's attitude to her / his subject and will be reflected in the tone of voice used in a talk.

Q3: Complete the table by matching the appropriate tone with the purpose of the talk.

Tone	Purpose of talk
	A talk explaining UK involvement in NATO.
	A talk to explain why you feel we need an opt-in organ donor system.
	A talk describing a Duke of Edinburgh Award Hike that went wrong and your reflections on it.

- Informative
- Persuasive
- Humourous

The tone of your talk could change during a talk.

TOPIC 3. TALKING: TIPS AND TECHNIQUES 475

Communicating meaning: Talk tone — Go online

Think about a solo talk which explains the pressures of exams.

Q4: Complete the table by matching the tone with the phase of the talk.

Tone	Phase of talk
	Begin with a personal anecdote to get the audience on side.
	Describe the level of pressure that comes from exam system.
	Explain some findings that you have discovered from research- perhaps by psychologists or sociologists.
	Explain to your audience how they could help with their own exam pressures as a conclusion.

- Instructive
- Descriptive
- Chatty/Humourous
- Educational

3.5 Non-verbal communication

The way that a speaker engages with an audience has a significant impact on the effectiveness of the talk.

Eye contact

If you lose eye contact then you lose the interest of the audience. This is another reason for not writing out your talk in full and reading it. Looking up is not enough. Some good tips about eye contact are to think of the audience as having four corners and periodically looking at the person sitting at each corner.

Cover the whole audience with eye-sweeps. A slow and steady approach works best where you slowly move your eye contact across the entire audience.

Talk from *notes* with as few words on them as possible. If you go into a talk with a speech written out, you will read it. For nearly all of the time that you are talking you should be looking at the audience and glancing at notes - not the other way around.

Stance / posture

Not slouching is important and looking like you take your talk seriously will help the audience engage. Really confident speakers may move or change position during a talk.

© HERIOT-WATT UNIVERSITY

Try to look relaxed and put your audience at ease.

Gesture

Depending on the talk and the situation, hand and arm gestures can help emphasise the importance of a part of your talk. A lot of gestures are natural but being nervous can make us keep them in. Think about where gestures could be used and plan their use.

3.6 Visual aids

These can help give the audience something to focus on. Don't have lots of text on them and don't put lots of your speech onto a slide and read it out. Pictures can help engage the audience but talk about the visual aids - not at them. Tell the story behind the picture.

For example, if you were doing a talk on the impact of deforestation, you could have a picture like the one below.

You could use the picture above to explain the:

- scale of damage;
- ecological impact on the soil;
- impact for wildlife on the landscape that has been left.

> **Top tip**
>
> For every image used, think of two or three complex points that you could make to show how the image supports your idea.

3.7 Talking from notes

It is a good idea to write your whole talk out if you are doing a formal solo talk. However, you should not then use this whole talk (which will look like an essay) and read it out.

You won't look at the audience if you do this and your talk will look really forced. Take your fully written talk and reduce it to notes. By rehearsing your talk you will be able to talk from the notes.

> Example
>
> Amazingly[1], people in Britain now spend more time using technology devices than they do sleeping. Research shows that people spend an average of eight hours and 41 minutes a day on media devices[2], compared with a typical night's sleep of eight hours and 21 minutes[3]. P[4]
>
> With younger people[5], the statistics are even more startling. 12-16 year olds were twice as likely to use social media as adults over 30[6]. We seem to be moving into an age where technology is taking over our lives. P
>
> Notes:
> [1] Rehearse so as you get the linkage correct
> [2] Highlight key words and statistics
> [3] Highlight key words and statistics
> [4] Make an indication about where you might pause
> [5] Rehearse so as you get the linkage correct
> [6] Highlight key words and statistics

Could you even use pictures on your notes rather than words? They act as visual reminders but mean that you won't be tempted to read your notes instead of using eye contact with your audience.

3.8 Introductions

A very basic introduction tells the audience what you are talking about and sets out the detail that is going to be in your talk.

> Example Today I am going to be talking about the problems with nuclear waste. I will explain how much nuclear waste is generated and why, despite our best efforts, we cannot really deal with the problem safely.

More stylish introductions will try to get the audience onside. You could:

- ask the audience a question;
- get them to envisage one aspect of your topic that would get them to think;
- don't tell them the topic of your talk in the first sentence. Make them wonder what you are talking about.

> Example Imagine something so dangerous and toxic that it could kill people hundreds of thousands of years from now.

If you get the audience's attention right at the beginning you are on the way to a successful talk.

3.9 Conclusions

A very basic conclusion tells the audience your main ideas and sums up your opinion.

> Example Today I have explained the problems with nuclear waste. I have explained how much nuclear waste is generated and why, despite our best efforts, we have not dealt with the problem safely.

More stylish conclusions will try to get the audience to really think about your topic. You could:

- ask the audience a question;
- get them to envisage one aspect of your topic that would get them to think about how big a problem it is;
- get the audience to think about the future if they don't consider your solutions.

> Example The Pyramids have only lasted three thousand years. How can we possibly make buildings secure for the hundred thousand years that nuclear waste will remain dangerous?

If you keep the audience's attention right to the end you will finish on a climax and make your talk memorable.

3.10 Planning

The following lists will help you to plan out and check your talks.

Talk planning sheet

- Introduction (key facts, overview, line of thought)
- First topic (points to be made, evidence and development of ideas, talk techniques conclusion)
- Second topic (points to be made, evidence and development of ideas, talk techniques conclusion)
- Third topic (points to be made, evidence and development of ideas, talk techniques conclusion)
- Fourth topic (points to be made, evidence and development of ideas, talk techniques conclusion)
- Conclusion (go over main points and make overall statement, remember to thank audience)

Talk preparation / evaluation checklist

Ideas

- Knowledge and understanding of main ideas with detail
- Research
- Ideas / opinions and not just facts

Language

- Choice of words
- Rhetorical devices

Communicating meaning

- Visual aids (if any)
- Pace and clarity

Non - verbal communication

- Use eye contact
- Gesture and posture

© HERIOT-WATT UNIVERSITY

3.11 Learning points

Summary

In preparation for talking, I can:

- provide detail to support my argument;
- research a topic in detail;
- express my opinions about a topic.

In solo talks, I can:

- use a number of techniques to engage the audience;
- consider the tone and pace of my talk;
- use non-verbal communication skills;
- listen and respond to questions.
-

In group discussion, I can:

- contribute ideas of my own;
- listen and respond to others;
- back up my ideas with evidence;
- use non-verbal communication skills.

TOPIC 3. TALKING: TIPS AND TECHNIQUES

3.12 End of topic test

End of Topic 3 test — Go online

Q5: You can use the subject of your discursive essay as the subject for your solo talk.

a) True
b) False

....

Q6: What could be three purposes of solo talks?

a) P_____
b) E_____
c) I_____

....

Q7: Match the following sentences to the correct pronoun in the table.

a) How would you like to be chased and hunted?
b) I think that hunting is immoral.
c) We need to consider how cruel hunting can be.

First person singular	
First person plural	
Second person	

....

Q8: Why would you use statistics in a talk? Think of three reasons.

....

Q9: Which of the following is a command?

a) We have to think carefully about the future.
b) You need to take action now!
c) Why should we put up with this any longer?

....

Q10: What is non-verbal communication?

....

Q11: What is the best way to use a PowerPoint or visual presentation in a talk?

....

Q12: Put the following steps for preparing a talk in the correct order.

a) Make notes.
b) Rehearse
c) Write the talk out in full.

....

Q13: Are you allowed to disagree with others in group discussions?

a) No - the point is to all agree.
b) Yes and make sure that your ideas dominate.
c) Yes but be prepared to have evidence and defend your position.

....

Q14: What are some of the best way to keep your talk flowing?

Complete the table by matching the listed terms with the descriptions for delivering an effective talk.

Term	Description
	Practice in order that you won't forget where you are or what you want to say
	Keep talking but build in small pauses
	Use signpost words and phrases to join your ideas together
	Keeping the talk on subject and not wandering off topic

Terms

- Pace
- Rehearse
- Relevance
- Linkage

Glossary

Alliteration
: use of the same letters or sounds at the start of two or more words

Analyse
: discuss the effect of the use of techniques such as alliteration, imagery, word choice etc.

Assonance
: the repetition of vowel sounds in words close to each other

Characterisation
: the way in which writers portray their characters

Climax
: tension or conflict in a text is at its highest point

Colon
: used to introduce a list or an explanation/expansion of a particular idea

Conflict
: disagreement between characters, or within a character (internal conflict)

Content
: what is included in a text

Dash
: poets use these to create dramatic pauses

Description
: an account of a character's physical appearance, or the setting, or of an incident

Dialogue
: the words the actors speak

Editing
: how scenes and/or camera shots are spliced together to create effect; this can also be referred to as a montage sequence

Effective conclusion
: the final lines of the extract summarise the writer's main points or help us understand the theme more clearly

Enjambment
: where the ending of a particular idea or phrase in a poem can carry over into the next line or stanza

Example
: give a quotation or reference from the text

Exclamation
: are identified by the use of the exclamation mark at the end of the sentence and are used to emphasise the emotion behind what is being said

Explain
: make something clear by describing it in detail

Free verse
: poems written in free verse have no real pattern to them

Ideas
: the main concerns, issues or thoughts explored in the text; the main themes and points raised by the writer

Imagery
: literary devices used by a writer to create pictures and images in the reader/audience's mind

Inversion
: when the normal word order is subverted to place emphasis on a specific word that the poet wishes to highlight to the reader

Key incident(s)
: important episodes which move the plot on, build to a climax, or are important in developing our understanding of character and/or theme

Key scene(s)
: important scenes which move the plot on, build to a climax, or are important in developing our understanding of character and/or theme

Key sequence
: important series of shots or scenes in a film or TV text

Language
: words and rhetoric used by the author to create characters and description

Lighting
: how bright or dark the stage is

List
: items are listed together using commas

Main ideas
: beliefs and concepts conveyed in a text

Main ideas/concerns
: these are the themes and concerns that a writer explores in a text

Metaphor
: a direct comparison between two things, usually things that you wouldn't expect to be compared

Minor sentences
: these are sentences which do not contain a main verb

Mise-en-scène
: props and scenery to create shots and background for a film and TV text

Mood/Atmosphere
: something that a writer creates in a text through the use of techniques

Music/sound
: used to create effects in film and TV texts

Narrative technique
: the way in which the story of the text is told (1st/3rd person narrative)

Narrative voice
: this includes narrative stance (1st/2nd/3rd person) and the use of the active or passive form of the verbs

Onomatopoeia
: when a word describes a sound, for example 'crash', 'bang' or 'crunch'

Parenthesis
: this is when a writer adds extra information to the middle of a sentence or phrase using brackets, commas or dashes.

Pathetic fallacy
: when human emotions are given to the weather in order to convey the mood of a character or a speaker in the poem to the reader

Personification
: human qualities are given to non-human animals or objects

Plot
: what happens in the text in chronological order

Poetic technique
: this term encompasses all the techniques that a writer uses when creating a poem, such as alliteration, rhyme, simile, single sentences

Props
: visual aids to enhance audience understanding

Repetition
: poets often does this to emphasise a particular idea to the reader

Rhyme
: when two words sound similar

Rhyme scheme
: the pattern of rhyme in a poem

Rhythm
: the pattern of syllables in each line of a poem

Selection of material
: examples, quotations, ideas, anecdotes and information that the writer has included for effect

Sentence structure
: often used to create effect: short sentences to create tension, increase pace; lists to emphasise how long something will take

Setting
: this is where and when the event(s) takes place

Short sentences
: often either one word or just a few words

Sibilance
: a special type of alliteration where an 's' sound is repeated

Simile
: compares two things using the 'magic' words 'like' or 'as'

Soliloquy
: a speech performed by an individual, usually showing them thinking out loud

Sonnet
: a 14 line poem written in iambic pentameter with a particular rhyme scheme

Sound
: devices used in poetry to create particular oral effects (alliteration/assonance/onomatopoeia)

Sound effects
: background noises used to create effect

Special effects
: additional effects added to a scene in a film or text

Stage directions
: instructions telling the actors how to move and act; also includes props, stage layout, lighting and sound effects

Stance
: a writer's point of view on a particular topic

Stanza
: verse of poetry

Structure
: the way in which a text's plot is put together

Style
: the writer's use of language to create effect

Symbols
: visual or auditory aids; can also suggest a metaphorical meaning

Synecdoche
: where a part of something is used to refer to the whole

Theme
: the bigger idea that is explored in a text; the overall message created

Tone
: relates to the way in which a line would sound if it was read aloud, often revealing the attitude of the writer towards the subject matter; it is a way we can gauge a writer's thoughts and opinions

Transferred epithet
: when a word that should be used to describe a speaker in a poem or a character is attributed to an object instead

Turning point
: when a significant change takes place regarding the plot or character development

Typography
: the way in which the words in the poem are laid out

Use of camera
: different camera shots used to create effects in film and TV texts

Use of evidence
: statistics, facts and anecdotes used to support or exemplify a writer's point

Word choice
: words are chosen to emphasise particular ideas or evoke certain emotions in the reader

Writer/poet's use of language
: this refers to any techniques used in a poem by the writer

Answers to questions and activities for Unit 1

Topic 1: Reading

Context clues (page 8)

Q1: a) Evil

Q2: b) Reconciliation

Q3: a) Controlling

Q4: a) Bland

Connect to words you know (page 12)

Q5: b) the sending of settlers to establish control of another country.

Q6: a) rising.

Q7: b) a person who gives help.

Q8: b) ruling with absolute power.

Common prefixes (page 13)

Q9:

both	ambi-
two	bi-
bad	dys-
same	homo-
under, too little	hypo-
beside	para-
around	peri-
after	post-
first, chief	prot-
false	pseudo-
across	trans-
three	tri-

ANSWERS: UNIT 1 TOPIC 1

Q10: How many of these words did you come up with? Tick them off your list. If you don't know the meaning of some of these words, work them out, or look them up in a dictionary.

- ambi- (both): ambidextorous, ambiguous, ambivalent...
- bi- (two): biannual, bicycle, bigamy, billion, bipartisan, biped, bipolar, bisexual, biweekly...
- dys- (bad): dysfunctional, dysentery, dyslexia, dystopia, dysphasia, dystrophy...
- homo- (same): homogeneous, homogenise, homosocial, homosexual, homeopathy, homograph, homophone, homonymn, homophone...
- hypo- (under, too little): hypodermic, hypothesis, hypothermia, hypoxia...
- para- (beside): paragraph, paramedic, parabola, parable, parallel...
- peri- (around): perimeter, periscope, peripatetic, periphery, periodontist...
- post- (after): postpone, postdate, postscript, postmeridian, postnatal, postwar...
- prot- (first, chief): protagonist, proton, prototype, protocol, protoplasm...
- pseudo- (false): pseudonym, pseudointellectual, pseudoscience...
- trans- (across): transatlantic, transcontinental, trans fats, transgender, transaction, translator, transcend, transcribe, transducer, transfer...
- tri- (three): triad, triangle, triathlon, tricast, triceps, tricolour, tricorn, tricycle, trident, trilateral, trillion, trilogy, trimester, trinity, trio, triple, tripod...

Common suffixes (page 14)

Q11:

place for	-arium, -orium
state or quality of	-dom
the person affected by an action	-ee
person who does something	-eer
in the style of, resembling	-esque
practice, system or philosophy	-ism
inflammation of	-itis
small	-ling
full of	-ulent

Q12: How many of these words did you come up with? Tick them off your list. If you don't know the meaning of some of these words, work them out, or look them up in a dictionary.

- -arium, -orium (place for): aquarium, planetarium, sanitarium, solarium, terrarium, auditorium, crematorium, emporium, moratorium...
- -dom (state or quality of): freedom, boredom, fandom, kingdom, martyrdom, princedom, wisdom...
- -ee (object of action): addressee, appointee, nominee, abductee, licensee, payee, lessee, employee, mentee, refugee, trainee...
- -eer (person): auctioneer, electioneer, engineer, musketeer, puppeteer, orienteer, overseer...
- -esque (in the style of, resembling): statuesque, grotesque, picturesque, Romanesque, Kafkaesque...
- -ism (doctrine of): capitalism, socialism, communism, patriotism, feminism, nationalism...
- -itis (inflammation of): laryngitis, arthritis, bronchitis, appendicitis, tonsillitis, gingivitis, hepatitis...
- -ling (after): duckling, yearling, suckling, fledgling, sapling, weakling...
- -oid (resembling): humanoid, asteroid, android, paranoid, factoid, planetoid...
- -ulent (full of): turbulent, corpulent, opulent, virulent, succulent, flatulent, fraudulent...

Identifying the word class (page 14)

Q13: a) Noun

Q14: c) Verb

Q15: b) Adjective

Q16: d) Adverb

Q17: c) Verb

Q18: b) Adjective

Q19: d) Adverb

Q20: b) Adjective

Q21: a) Noun

Q22: c) Verb

Alternative words (page 16)

Q23: a) enervated

Q24: a) unruffled

Q25: b) cosseted

Topic 2: Understanding

Which is the topic sentence? (page 22)

Q1: The aim in confining animals indoors was to cut costs —it succeeded. Indoors, one or two workers can 'look after' hundreds of penned or tethered pigs, or a hundred thousand chickens. Great economies were made and thousands of farm workers lost their jobs. This new policy of cheap meat, eggs and cheese for everyone was completely in tune with the national mood, as Britain ripped up its ration books. It was also in tune with nutritional thinking, as nutritionists at that time thought greater consumption of animal protein would remedy all dietary problems.

Q2: So factory farming marched on and became more and more intensive. Where first there were one or two laying hens in a cage, eventually there became five in the same small space. The broiler chicken sheds expanded to cram in vast acres of birds. Many beef cattle were confined in buildings and yards. Until mad cow disease emerged, such animals were fed all kinds of organic matter as cheap food. In the UK dairy cows still spend their summers in the fields, but many of their offspring are reared in the cruelty of intensive veal crate systems.

Q3: The aim of those early advocates of intensive farming was 'fast food' - fast from birth to table - and again, they succeeded. Chicken, once an occasional treat, now the most popular meat in Britain, owes its low price largely to the short life of the bird. Today's broiler chicken has become the fastest growing creature on earth: from egg to take-away in seven weeks. Most farm animals now have less than half of their pre-war lifespan. Either they are worn out from overproduction of eggs or milk, or have been bred and fed to reach edible size in a few short weeks or months.

Q4: But meat, eggs and dairy products have indeed become cheap, affordable even to the poor. All of which made nutritionists exceedingly happy until they discovered that their mid-century predecessors had made a mighty blunder. Before intensive farming brought cheap meat and dairy products to our tables, man obtained most of his calories from cereal crops and vegetables. The meat with which he supplemented this diet had a much lower fat content than intensively produced products. Now, however, degenerative diseases like coronary heart disease and several types of cancer have been linked to our increased consumption of fatty foods. War-time Britons, on their measly ration of meat and one ounce of cheese a week, were much healthier.

Q5: It is also a scientifically proven fact that intensive farming has caused the loss of hedgerows and wildlife sustained by that habitat, has polluted waterways, decimated rural employment and caused the loss of traditional small farms. We need to act in the interests of human health. We need to show humane concern for animals. We need to preserve what remains of the countryside by condemning the practice of intensive farming. We need to return the animals to the fields, and re-adopt the environmentally friendly, humane and healthy system we had and lost: the small mixed farm.

Identifying supporting detail (page 24)

Q6:

The writer describes her experience of visiting an enormous orchard in California	Anecdote
The writer tells us that bees are hired in, that cows never see grass, and how much chickens sell for.	Facts
The writer suggests that the British countryside could soon look like the Central Valley, California.	Speculation
The writer repeats the words of Owen Paterson, the UK environment secretary, a man on local radio, and the British Government.	Quotes
The writer highlights how cheap food has become by telling us 'things that were once delicacies such as smoked salmon, are now as cheap as chips.'	Example
The writer tells us that 'the population of tree sparrows has failed 97%'; '50 billion [animals] are kept permanently indoors'; and 'California's bovine population produces as much sewage as 90 million people'	Statistics
The writer said 'the air can be worse than in Los Angeles'	Comparison

Creating a clear line of argument (page 27)

Q7:

The article employs a chronological structure initially. It begins by looking back to the post-war establishment of factory farming. The use of the past tense, and phrases like 'so factory farming marched on', 'became more and more intensive' and 'eventually there became' present the developments that factory farming has brought about as time has progressed. There is an implicit suggestion that things have grown worse as time has gone on. It ends with the writer's suggestion of what we should do in future.

In the final sentence, the writer advocates a return to 'the environmentally friendly, humane and healthy system we had and lost: the small mixed farm.' This phrase recalls the opening paragraph, in which she described how 'the mixed farm... was replaced by the huge factories we see today', creating a circularity. This structure neatly mirrors the writer's overall argument —that we should return to the way things were 50 years ago.

It could also be argued that the paragraphs are ordered in a climactic hierarchy of importance. They begin with the practical changes factory farming brought: lower production costs, intensive use of space, accelerated growth, consumer affordability. The writer clearly criticises each of these developments in turn. By the penultimate paragraph, though, the writer's criticisms become increasingly damning. As her language becomes more biting, more confrontational, she moves her focus to the morality of intensive farming. In the final paragraph, she delivers her ultimate condemnation: intensive farming must be rejected completely.

Finally, it might be argued there is a ripple effect pattern within the article too. It begins with the farms and animals themselves, moving out to the consumer of cheap food, then to all of society ('we have convinced ourselves...' and 'we need to act...').

ANSWERS: UNIT 1 TOPIC 2

Signpost words (page 29)

Q8:

Adding	Contrasting
and	whereas
also	instead of
as well as	alternatively
moreover	otherwise
too	unlike
furthermore	on the other hand
additionally	conversely

Q9:

Cause and effect	Emphasising
because	above all
so	in particular
since	especially
therefore	significantly
thus	indeed
consequently	notably
hence	in fact

Q10:

Qualifying	Illustrating	Summing up
but	for example	in conclusion
however	for instance	finally
although	such as	last of all
unless	illustrated by	overall
except	as revealed by	in summary
as long as	in the case of	in short
if	in other words	to sum up

© HERIOT-WATT UNIVERSITY

Analysing linking sentences (page 31)

Q11: d) this

Q12: b) British countryside

Q13: c) the way food is produced

Q14: d) powerful forces are pulling us in the opposite direction

Q15: c) such a scene

Q16: d) it is not far-fetched

Answers from page 33.

Q17: Paragraph 1: Intensive farming began enthusiastically 50 years ago.
Paragraph 2: People were initially pleased with the plentiful, cheap food that industrialisation brought.
Paragraph 3: Intensification has developed across all kinds of farming.
Paragraph 4: Fast production is key.
Paragraph 5: Intensive farming has changed our diets for the worse.
Paragraph 6: Intensive farming is immoral.
Paragraph 7: Intensive farming is damaging and must be stopped.

Counting main ideas (page 35)

Q18: There are three main criticisms made: the impact on socialising and bonding in the workplace; the disappearance of shared family viewing; the way it encourages us to binge-watch.
The ideas are structured and separated out by the repeated use of the word 'Gone...'

Q19: There are two main emotions conveyed here: shame and pride.
The paragraph is balanced around the phrase 'Yet, as time passed' which marks the division between the two emotions.

In your own words (1) (page 36)

Q20: Grass and hedgerows are not allowed to grow, and bees are brought in from the other side of the United States.

In your own words (2) (page 37)

Q21: Within the carefully managed orchards, there is an absence of native flora and fauna.

In your own words (3) (page 37)

Q22: Because there is nothing for them to live on, the number of birds is in steep decline.

ANSWERS: UNIT 1 TOPIC 2

End of Topic 2 test 1 (page 38)

Q23: b) False

Q24: b) False

Q25: a) True

Q26: b) False

Q27: a) True

Q28: a) True

Q29: a) She can recall every little detail of her prom

Q30: c) Proms are always a let down

Q31: c) Proms are outdated and artificial

End of Topic 2 test 2 (page 40)

Q32: Proms teach and reinforce unrealistic cultural and social norms.

Q33: Proms rarely live up to expectations in terms of their glamour and pageantry.

Q34: The writer thinks proms are a good way to teach young people that money cannot buy happiness.

Q35: The writer thinks proms —where old-fashioned ideas govern behaviour —are an accurate reflection of adult life.

Topic 3: Analysis

Identify the correct connotations (page 44)

Q1: perfectly aligned

Q2: disturbing

Q3: sterile

Q4: vital

Q5: flaccid

Q6: delicacies

Q7: industrial

Q8: desecration

Q9: widespread

Q10: nightmarish

Q11: nauseating

Q12: towering

Matching neutral and emotive terms (page 50)

Q13:

government	regime
economic savings	cuts
changing	manipulating
freedom fighter	terrorist
injure	main
kill	slaughter
detained	banged up
correctional centre	jail
economic downturn	crash
focused	blinkered
remove	abolish

ANSWERS: UNIT 1 TOPIC 3

Matching emotive words and euphemisms (page 51)

Q14:

cuts	downsizing
war	military intervention
poor	underprivileged
torture	enhanced interrogation
lied	misspoke
drunk	tired and emotional
died	passed away
accidental deaths	collateral damage
fat	big boned
the birds and the bees	sex
unemployed	between jobs

Identifying images (page 52)

Q15:

- 'It may sound like the Garden of Eden but it is a deeply disturbing place' (line 6)
- '... they are pushed so grotesquely beyond their natural limit ...' (lines 14-15)
- '... threatened by a wave of intensification from America.' (line 18)
- 'Choosing to buy fewer imports would reduce the relentless pressure British farmers are under to churn out more for less.' (line 25)
- '... increasingly powerful forces are pulling us in the opposite direction' (lines 28-29)
- 'We have become addicted to cheap meat, fish and dairy products ...' (line 29)
- 'My journey to expose the truth ...' (line 35)
- '... to investigate the dirty secret...' (line 35)
- 'I talked to people on the front line of the global food industry...' (line 37)
- '... treadmill farmers trying to produce more with less' (line 38)
- 'Many had stories about their homes plummeting in value ...' (line 40)

Finding extended images (page 53)

Q16: Often the House of Commons more resembles a three ring circus than a place of serious debate. While the Speaker tries to exert ringmaster-like pressure on the assembled acts, behaviour regularly descends into chaos. Those in the cheap seats jeer and yell, waving papers in the air, and clowning around. The front benches —the party leaders and cabinet ministers —are often seen clapping like performing seals.

Q17: Scotland has long had a reputation as the sickman of Europe. While countries like Denmark, the Netherlands and Iceland are recognised around the world as healthy Northern European countries, Scotland continues to wheeze and creak. And that's with a national health service —usually a marker of a healthy society. It's about time we were written a straight-talking prescription telling us to put down the deep fried Mars Bar, slip on our trainers and get out into the fresh air. Without fundamental change, delivered quickly, Scotland will continue to hobble along behind our contemporaries, coughing and spitting.

Q18: For months afterwards, public opinion on the matter was regularly stoked by inflammatory stories in newspapers and dangerous sparks let loose on social media. Those close to the celebrity tried to extinguish the rumours, denying any inappropriate behaviour. Despite this, they kept reigniting.

Deconstructing images (page 53)

Q19: a) Simile

Q20: a) An orchard

Q21: c) Eden

Q22: b) Metaphor

Q23: a) Intensive farming

Q24: c) A wave

Q25: b) Metaphor

Q26: b) Farmers

Q27: a) Treadmills

Q28: b) Metaphor

Q29: c) Homes

Q30: b) Something falling

Choose the right qualities for the image (page 56)

Q31: a) Relevant

Q32: a) Relevant

Q33: b) Not Relevant

Q34: a) Relevant

Q35: b) Not Relevant

Q36: b) Not Relevant

ANSWERS: UNIT 1 TOPIC 3

Positive and negative tones activity (page 75)

Q72:

Positive	Negative
Intimate	Acerbic
Celebratory	Contemptuous
Happy	Cynical
Grateful	Hectoring
Enthusiastic	Scathing
Lighthearted	Pedantic
Friendly	Menacing
Sympathetic	Accusatory
Optimistic	Outraged
Excited	Pessimistic

Identifying different tones (page 76)

Q73:

The impact of intensive farming certainly deserves some consideration.	Neutral
Intensive farming has brought a new dawn of plenty. Could this be the end of the global food crisis?	Optimistic
One cannot help but be upset by the conditions animals must endure as a result of intensive farming.	Sympathetic
How dare the big agri-businesses try to justify such suffering and cruelty on economic grounds!	Outraged
Long gone are the days when free-range was the norm, and farmers were respected members of the community, not just faceless middle managers in a supply chain.	Nostalgic
Maybe it's time you weighed up the small savings in your shopping basket against the considerable distress factory farmed animals are put through. Maybe it's time you did the right thing, and refused to accept animal cruelty in the a few measly extra pennies in your pocket.	Hectoring
We should loudly applaud the scientific advancements that mean that even in the harshest conditions —flood, drought, pestilence —the boffins have found a way to make secure food sources around the world. In a world of uncertainty, these developments are something to cheer about.	Celebratory

© HERIOT-WATT UNIVERSITY

Identifying language features that create tone (page 78)

Q74:

The impact of intensive farming certainly deserves some consideration.	formal register; statement
Intensive farming has brought a new dawn of plenty. Could this be the end of the global food crisis?	question mark; positive word choice; imagery
One cannot help but be upset by the conditions animals must endure as a result of intensive farming.	emotive word choice; inclusive pronoun
How dare the big agri-businesses try to justify such suffering and cruelty? And on economic grounds!	question mark; exclamation mark; emotive language
Long gone are the days when free-range was the norm, and farmers were respected members of the community, not just faceless middle managers in a supply chain.	contrast; inversion; past tense
Maybe it's time you weighed up the small savings in your shopping basket against the considerable distress factory farmed animals are put through. Maybe it's time you did the right thing, and refused to accept animal cruelty in the a few measly extra pennies in your pocket	contrast; direct address; emotive word choice
We should loudly applaud the scientific advancements that mean that even in the harshest conditions —flood, drought, pestilence —the boffins have found a way to make secure food sources around the world. In a world of uncertainty, these developments are something to cheer about.	positive word choice; list; inclusive pronoun

End of Topic 3 test (page 80)

Q75: Burning bright

Q76: Acuity

Q77: Gruelling

Q78: Ennui

Q79: Script

Q80:

Promise and spectacle	Reality and disappointment
extravagant corsage	inelegant scramble
ballgowns	uncomfortable outfits
fancy cars	papier-mâché
taffeta frocks	chintzy glow
sequined handbags	bad skin
glamour	heartbreak
arriving by helicopter	math teacher is your chaperone

Q81: b) The image suggests the memories are vivid.

Q82: a) The image suggests being enslaved and controlled by money.

Q83: c) The image suggests the total destruction of his desires.

Q84: a) The image suggests behaving in a predetermined manner.

Q85: a) The writer uses a colon to introduce a list of all the specific details she can still remember.

Q86: b) The writer uses a semi-colon to create a contrast, illustrating how her feelings towards her mother's attitude have changed over time.

Q87: a) The writer uses a colon to introduce an explanation of why proms offer a taste of adult life.

Q88: b) Self-deprecating

Q89: a) Cynical

Q90: e) Mocking

Q91: c) Pessimistic

Q92: d) Sarcastic

Topic 4: Evaluation

Evaluating the introduction activity (page 91)

Q1: The repeated use of the personal pronoun 'I' reinforces the anecdote used by the writer as she recounts her visit to Central Valley.

Q2: The use of statistics: 'a million almond trees', '700,000 acres', 'two million dairy cows', 'six billion dollars' worth of milk a year.'

Q3: Use of the word 'vision' suggests not current reality, but a picture being painted about the possibilities that lie in the future; 'may look one day' reinforces this.

Q4: Provides positive word choice and listing: 'sweet air', fields of pomegranate, pistachios, grapes and apricots'

Evaluating supporting detail activity (page 91)

Q5: British farming is already being transformed by processes adopted from America.

Q6:
1. There are fewer bees.
2. Fewer bees negatively affects harvests.
3. Hedgerows, which support many creatures, are also falling in numbers.
4. There is not enough for birds to eat.
5. Some species of birds have almost disappeared.

Q7:
- Using five examples in a row emphasises the number of problems the countryside faces.
- The word choice of 'disappearing' suggests mystery, and that the loss of bees is not yet fully understood; it also suggests the loss is unnatural.
- 'vital habitats' is contrasted with 'sterile' —in other words, life (vital) is contrasted with lack of life (sterile).
- The examples show how different types of wildlife are being affected; this is not just affecting one species.
- Statistics dramatically illustrate how serious the changes in the countryside are.

Q8:

- 'the front line' —imagery suggests that these changes affect people much as a war does.
- 'treadmill farmers' —imagery creates a picture of farmers having to work harder and harder but never making an progress forward.
- 'plummeting' —imagery suggests that those living near to industrial farms are losing huge amounts of money
- The writer also makes it clear that industrial farming negatively affects people who live nearby such facilities, even those who are not involved in the industry.
- The climactic list expresses the idea that intensive farming impacts people in many different ways.

Evaluate the conclusion activity (page 92)

Q9:

- The writer describes the proposal for the mega-dairy in Lincolnshire.
- The writer illustrates that the mindset of some British farmers has changed and they believe animals should be managed differently.
- The writer asserts that British livestock is already being farmed indoors.

Q10: The writer talks about 'mega-dairies' and 'dairies expanding' which connects back to the idea of 'two million dairy cows' and 'six billion dollars' worth of milk a year'.

Q11: 'creep', 'behind closed doors' and 'disappeared' suggest that the changes are secretive and sinister.

Q12:

- The writer suggests that the idea of intensive farming in Britain is 'not far-fetched' —it is rooted in reality; it is not beyond imagination.
- The government appears to support these changes; she uses the present tense when describing the attitude of the government, suggesting it is happening today.

End of Topic 4 test (page 94)

Q13:

- Establishes the core issue that the article is built on: the 'before' and 'after' connected to intensive farming.
- Sets up her belief that intensive farming is a dated concept, using 'The founding fathers ...', '... at the time', '... half a century ago' and 'The post-war government ...'
- Sets up her criticism of intensive farming through the juxtaposition of 'farm' and 'factories'.

Q14:

- It exemplifies the success of the early advocates in producing 'fast food' ('once an occasional treat, now the most popular meat in Britain'; 'from egg to take-away in seven weeks'; 'less than half of their pre-war lifespan'; 'bred and fed to reach edible size a few short weeks or months.').
- It demonstrates the shocking effects of intensive farming ('from egg to take-away in seven weeks'; 'less than half of their pre-war lifespan'; 'bred and fed to reach edible size a few short weeks or months'; 'worn out from overproduction of eggs').

Q15:

- 'scientifically proven' —suggests the veracity and objectivity of her argument.
- list adds to her argument, widening out to include other examples of the damage caused by intensive farming.
- Provides a list of solutions to the problems outlined in the passage.
- Repetition of 'We' suggests the idea of a collective responsibility.
- Repetition of 'We need' to suggest urgency and a call to action.
- Reference to 'small mixed farm' in the final sentence recalls the introduction.
- Positioning of 'small mixed farm' at the end of the passage lends her solution emphasis.

Topic 5: The comparison question

Preparing to answer the comparison question activity (page 97)

Q1:

Paragraph 1:	scale/size/abundance of farm
Paragraph 2:	farm is unnatural
Paragraph 3:	extends idea farm is unnatural with example of cruelty to cows
Paragraph 4:	British farming beginning to change; detrimental impact on nature
Paragraph 5:	Government policy to buy local
Paragraph 6:	Food produced is cheap so desired by consumers; price impacts quality and welfare
Paragraph 7:	International problem; affects more than just farmers
Paragraph 8:	Extends idea farm is unnatural; examples of ugliness, smell, pollution
Paragraph 9:	Continuation of paragraph 8
Paragraph 10:	Change is happening unnoticed, unobserved; idea of conflict

Q2:

Paragraph 1:	intensive agriculture has replaced small-scale farming
Paragraph 2:	intensive farming allows for cheaper food, more readily available produce; impact on workers
Paragraph 3:	system increasingly intensive
Paragraph 4:	production quicker; impact on welfare
Paragraph 5:	cheap produce influenced diet; negatively affected health
Paragraph 6:	intensive farming unethical; justifies cruelty
Paragraph 7:	wider effect on nature; call for change

Identifying areas of agreement and disagreement activity (page 97)

Q3:

1. Abundance/huge scale
2. Influences the consumer
3. Impacts on neighbours/workers
4. Unnatural
5. Causes animal cruelty
6. Impact on the environment
7. Should be resisted

Structuring your answer activity (page 100)

Q4:

- Passage one says that wildlife populations, in particular those of bees and birds, are in steep decline
- Passage two agrees and says that waterways are being polluted as a result of large scale farming.

Q5:

- Passage one says that the farms are enormous, using the example of Central Valley in California where millions of cows are farmed and millions of trees are grown.
- Passage two agrees and says the facilities are huge and, as an example, that a hundred thousand chickens can be farmed in one indoor facility.

Q6:

- Passage one says that intensive farming is not inevitable and that there are other ways to produce food that everyone can afford to buy; she uses Central Valley as a warning to British consumers.
- Passage two agrees and says that there are many things 'We need' to do; she speaks with an urgency and lists all the ways we can resist such change.

Topic 6: Exam skills

Understanding the exam paper activity (page 103)

Q1: a) U

Q2: b) A

Q3: b) A

Q4: a) U

Q5: a) U

Q6: b) A

Q7: a) U

Q8: c) E

Q9: d) C

End of Topic 6 test (page 109)

Q10: b) 30

Q11: c) 90 minutes

Q12: c) Annotating

Q13: a) Skimming

Q14: b) Scanning

Q15: b) False

Q16: a) True

Q17: b) False

Q18: b) False

Q19: b) False

Q20: a) True

Topic 7: Practice Papers

Practice paper 1: Katie Hopkins (page 112)

Q1: *Possible answers include*:

Sentence structure

- *semi-colon* —emphasises the contrast between 'politics' and 'complicated coups';
- ' *...not ...but...* ' —emphasises the contrast between 'complicated coups' and 'bland decisions';
- contrasting alliteration —'*complicated coups*' and '*bland ...beige*' —emphasises the contrast.

Word choice

- '*bland*' suggests boring, humdrum, mundane;
- '*beige*' suggests boring, humdrum, mundane;
- '*meeting rooms*' suggests bureaucratic, paper shuffling, officious, administrative decisions.

Q2: *Possible answers include*:

- she is incredulous or critical etc (1). (No mark for simply 'disagrees').

Sentence structure

- *dash* —introduces an expansion of all the reasons why the decision would not be effective;
- *list* —suggests all the very significant reasons people become refugees;
- '*... never ... do not ... nor do they*' —repeated use of negatives reinforce her dismissal of the decision;
- positioning of '*Nor ...* ' at the start of the sentence —lends emphasise to her rejection of the decision.

Tone

- flippant/sarcastic/dismissive and deliberately incongruous use of 'heard good things about its coastguard services' and/or 'safety features have had their funding cut' —as if the migrants are picking and choosing from a catalogue.

Marks will depend on the quality of comment on appropriate language feature(s).

2 marks may be awarded for reference plus detailed/insightful comment; 1 mark for reference plus more basic comment; 0 marks for reference alone.

ANSWERS: UNIT 1 TOPIC 7

Q3:

a) *Any two of*:
- only thought about in terms of what they add to the financial growth of the country/what they cost the country ('how much they grow the economy or take from it, how much wealth they create in student fees or investment');
- thought to drive down salaries ('what they do to wages');
- their work ethic is seen as damaging / too keen ('pesky hard work');
- seen as a resource to be taken advantage of ('willingness to be exploited');
- seen as a resource to be used when needed and discarded when not ('to attract or repel');
- migration is seen as a political problem to be negotiated ('tango between economic and political expediency');
- migrants are not valued for themselves, as people ('no innate value');
- politicians feel that simply providing refuge has no political currency ('no pride in representing the country that is safe and generous enough to offer a haven');
- migrants are only valued if they have skills or savings (Refugees, arriving with nothing, are worth nothing').

b) *Any two of*:
- *list/parallel structure* —emphasises the relentlessness of our focus on the economic value of migrants;
- *colon* —introduces expansion on the 'innate value' ignored by this 'worldview' i.e. being generous;
- *repetition of 'no/nothing'* —emphasises the paucity/hollowness /negativity of a purely economic view of migrants;
- *short sentence* (*'Refugees... worth nothing'*) —create a blunt, damning tone.

Word choice
- *'something'* suggests a disregard, flippancy;
- contrast (*'attract or repel'... 'economic and political expediency'*) suggests the issue is toyed with; attitude fluctuates; lack of consistency;
- *'safe and generous enough'* implies these qualities should to be aspired to.

Q4: *Glosses of two*:
- whether Katie Hopkins is a 'character' created to shock ('*a construct of its owner*');
- only says what she says in order to create publicity and profit ('*an entertainment turn spun out for money*');
- whether she genuinely holds such deeply unpleasant views ('*a real person with an antisocial personality disorder*').

Q5: *Possible answers include*:

Sentence structure

- '*...no joke ... We are not ... It is not ... I'm not ...*' —succession of negatives/parallel structure emphasise her outright rejection of other arguments;
- '*giving her what she wants*' —inverted commas suggest this is an argument she has heard a lot from other people; she clearly refutes this;
- '*It is not a joke when people start talking like this.*'/'*It is not a free speech issue*' —short sentences act as clear and forceful rebuttals to counterclaims that Hopkins should be allowed to say what she likes;
- '*I'm not saying ... : I'm saying ...*' —balanced structure created by colon presents declaratively what her argument is not, and then what it is;
- '*Articulate ... Stop .... Start*' —command structure —her demand that this is what we must do;
- parenthesis —'..., *the human empathy*, ...' —inserts what she feels is most important;
- '*Stop ... Start*' —parallel structure to make clear what must come to an end and what we must begin doing.

Word choice

- '*no joke*' —no time to laugh about it, must be taken seriously now;
- '*make manifest*' —suggests loud and clear, spread widely, spoken about everywhere;
- '*disgust*' —suggests horror, revulsion, antipathy;
- '*fight her*' —suggests tackling the issue, not allowing her to get away with it, forcing the issue;
- '*Articulate*' —suggests intelligent discussion, debate, progressive thinking;
- '*fellowship*' —suggests togetherness, joint purpose, a common goal;
- '*human empathy*' —fundamental compassion, something utterly intrinsic to the human condition;
- '*important*' —significant, they matter, worth discussing;
- '*everybody's life*' —suggests all human life is valuable, everyone matters, all should be cared for;
- '*cherishable*' —dear, valuable, important;
- '*anything*' —suggests everything/everyone is valued, everything/everyone should be included, no parameters to the way we value life.

ANSWERS: UNIT 1 TOPIC 7

Q6: *Possible answers include:*

Tone

- uncertainty, doubt, helplessness, confusion, guilt (1).

Sentence structure

- *series of questions* suggest she doesn't know how to respond to Hopkins' outburst, and/or the bigger issue of the migrant crisis;
- *repetition of 'Are we ...'* suggests she doesn't know how to respond to Hopkins' outburst, and/or the bigger issue of the migrant crisis;
- *repetition of 'so much ...'* suggests feeling overwhelmed by the issue;
- *repetition/parallel structure of 'I didn't ... I've never'* suggest introspective guilt at her lack of action;
- *listing* —all the things she could have done but failed to do;
- *series of statements followed by a question* suggests her inaction prevents from having any authority on the matter. Climactic positioning of final question emphasises this.

Word choice

- *'luxurious'* suggests indulgent, selfish, self-gratification;
- *'meaningless'* suggests empty, pointless, vacuous, purposeless;
- *'ding-dong'* suggests superficial argument, not serious, flippant;
- *'manufacture'* suggests artificial, generated, created;
- *'so far removed'* suggests disconnected, at a safe distance, to not understand, no true sense of something;
- *'real peril'* suggests genuine threat, danger to life and limb;
- *'fresh loss'* suggests very recent, too early to make sense of;
- *'collective guilt'* suggests common responsibility, shared sense of impotence;
- *'even'* intensifies how little she did, that the simplest thing was not attempted;
- *'solidarity'* suggests on the same side, shared goals, common cause, common humanity;
- *'beaten up'* suggests suffering, injustice, thuggery.

Contrast

- *'manufactured conflict ... real peril'* suggests the difference between superficial, vacuous arguments stirred up at home and the genuine danger others are in.

Imagery

- *'feeding off ...'* —thriving or being nourished by the arguments; parasitic; exploitative;
- *'ding-dong'* —senseless toing and froing of the argument; empty sounds;
- *'manufacture conflict'* —the argument as a product, made to entertain/for money.

© HERIOT-WATT UNIVERSITY

Q7:

- They are easy to talk about (1);
- but almost impossible to live up to through our actions (1).

Q8: *Possible answers include*:

Ideas

- the writer responds clearly to those who suggest we should stay quiet in the face of provocation;
- she provides the words that she knows we have to live up to, no matter how hard that might be —referencing the previous paragraph;
- she links back to the title and the earlier reference to Rwanda where the world stood back and allowed dreadful things to happen;
- she refers again to the idea that all lives are valuable;
- she admits that even when we can only do a little —in reference to her sense of confusion and impotence about how to really respond —we should still do it;
- she answers the question about whether silence is the only respectful response;
- the final sentence is effectively a call to arms to speak out about the situation —which is what the article as a whole is doing.

Language

Sentence structure

- *'Because...'* —starts the sentence with the connective as she begins to ramp up her powerful reasons for speaking out, links back directly to the previous questions;
- repetition of *'people knew...'* —asserts we already know right from wrong, we already know what we need to do, perhaps we just need to be reminded. Also suggests the number of awful events we have silently witnessed already.

Word choice

- *'barbarous'* —suggests savage, brutal, inhumane;
- *'outraged'* —suggests driven to fury, provoked desperate anger;
- *'the conscience of mankind'* —suggests the most essential and human part of us, what separates us from animals;
- *'innate dignity'* —suggests intrinsic goodness, honesty, self-worth;
- *'human family'* —suggests connectedness, sense of shared humanity;
- *'all members'* —suggests equality, fraternity, valuing all equally.

Tone

- elevated quality of the final paragraph —a rallying call; has moved out from the argument about Hopkins and looks philosophically at the situation;
- restatements of certainty; again confident of what must be done in contrast to the paragraph immediately before which is full of questions.

ANSWERS: UNIT 1 TOPIC 7

Q9:

	AREA OF AGREEMENT	PASSAGE ONE	PASSAGE TWO
1	The scale of the migrant crisis	• only 28 out of a possible 700 were saved from the latest sinking	• lists the hundreds who have died between Africa and Italy
2	That migrants have many good reasons for seeking refuge	• Refugees will continue to seek refuge despite cuts to rescue boats, because they are fleeing from terrible conditions in their own countries	• those killed in the Med are fleeing 'war, poverty, or Isis, or violence' • Nobody would attempt the crossing unless the alternative was worse
3	Migrants are viewed in economic terms	• Refugees have no worth besides their impact on the economy	• Asylum seekers are forbidden to work, and given meagre state benefits
4	Migrants are dehumanised	• Katie Hopkins descriptions of migrants as cockroaches • The similarities with language used during the Rwandan genocide	• guards at asylum centres treat migrant inmates appallingly • the benefits given to asylum seekers force them to choose between hygiene and food • Asylum seekers are forced to present evidence of their case that is demeaning and deeply personal

© HERIOT-WATT UNIVERSITY

	AREA OF AGREEMENT	PASSAGE ONE	PASSAGE TWO
5	Governments behave based on their own self-interest	• Political parties are not interested in doing the right thing, only managing the problem	• The 'Mare Nostrum' rescue service was suspended because governments were unwilling to be seen by their anti-immigration citizens as supporting migrants • Claims governments followed public attitude that sees dead refugees as more acceptable than allowing immigrants into their country • Labour used a pledge about curbing immigration as a marketing slogan
6	Katie Hopkins is not the main problem	• We should blame the media outlets that employ Hopkins and give her a voice	• Hopkins' words have not physically caused harm, but politicians have (by cutting 'Mare Nostrum') • The hatred directed at Hopkins should be focused on the government
7	There is complacency / More must be done to help	• People are distracted from the real issue by the debate over how best to respond to Hopkins • Writer questions her own inaction in the face of the crisis	• Nobody protested when abuse of asylum seekers was reported at Yarls Wood

Practice paper 2: Attention and distraction (page 117)

Q10:
- Making money (1);
- from attracting/distracting people for a short time (1).

Q11: *Possible answers include*:

Word Choice

- *'threatening'* suggests learning is in danger, peril, jeopardy;
- *'edutainment'* implies a dilution of intellectual rigour;
- *'celebrating performance and storytelling (over factual accuracy)'* suggests the glorification of superficiality;
- *'invites us'* suggests a knowing encouragement; deliberate solicitation;
- *'actually'* suggests that watching is more important, and dwelling on selecting a movie is trivia;
- *'infinite'* suggests an unending array of distractions;
- *'cascade'* suggests a deluge, torrent, capable of drowning us; one video leads to another endlessly;
- *'procrastinate in style'* uggests the glamourising/glorification of laziness.

Sentence Structure

- *'edutainment'* —inverted commas creates critical/mocking tone;
- *'TED talks are threatening... Netflix invites us... Youtube provides...'* —parallel structure suggests the number and/or intensity of distractions vying for our attention;
- *'learning/edutainment... performance and storytelling/factual accuracy... selecting/actually watching'* —series of contrasts emphasises the (number of) negative changes caused by technology, away from the meaningful towards the frivolous.

Q12: *Possible answers include*:

Us

- there is a surplus of sensory information (*'information over-load... non-stop media bombardment'*); (1)
- being distracted damages us (*'distraction is destruction'*); (1)
- we must teach ourselves to ignore our surroundings (*'what's adaptive today is the ability to ignore our distracting environments'*); (1)
- focussing takes effort (*'the only recipe for focus is discipline and self-control'*). (1)

Our evolutionary ancestors

- there was less information competing for their attention; (1)
- being distracted by their surroundings was advantageous (*'rewarded for absorbing as much of their sensory surroundings as they possibly could'*); (1
- paying attention to surroundings helped them evolve (*'what's adaptive today...'*). (1)

Q13: *Possible answers include:*
- *'information overload'* suggests information has become a burden too great to cope with;
- *'(non-stop media) bombardment'* suggests that we are defenceless against the information that is constantly assailing us;
- *'distraction is destruction'* suggests that distractions cause us irreparable damage;
- *'the only recipe for focus is discipline and control'* suggests we need a plan or strategy to combat distraction;
- *'the distraction economy'* suggests that distraction has become something to be traded, or sold to the highest bidder;
- *'real war'* suggests a battle is being fought between advertisers and consumers;
- *'if attention is the new currency'* suggests attention has no value but its potential monetary worth to advertisers.

Q14:
- *'attention is the new currency of the digital economy'* links back to the preceding paragraph and the theory of an *'attention economy'* (1); *'what are consumers getting in return'* introduces the next paragraph which answers the question by describing the erosion of our attention spans and behaviour like ADHD. (1)

or

- Marks a shift from focusing on the advertisers and online companies discussed in the previous paragraphs (1), towards the impact on consumers/people. (1)

or

- Moves from focusing on the wider economical/technological context (1), to look at the physical/psychological human impact. (1)

Q15: *Glosses of three:*
- causes a self-fulfilling spiral whereby distractions create short attention spans, which are then catered to with yet more distractions (*'producing a vicious circle'*); (1)
- has a damaging effect on how we behave, making it difficult to moderate our concentration (*'causes ADHD-like behaviours, such as impulsivity and boredom'*); (1)
- takes up more of our time and focus than we can afford (*'creates a poverty of attention'*); (1)
- prevents us from fully taking advantage of the benefits of technology (*'instead of reaping the benefits of the digital revolution...'*); (1)
- prevents us from discerning useful information from useless information, thus inhibiting learning (*'...we are intellectually deprived by our inability to filter out sensory junk in order to translate information into knowledge'*); (1)
- makes it possible to access a huge amount of information (*'we are collectively wiser, in that we can retrieve all the wisdom of the world in a few minutes'*); (1)
- robs us of the means and/or inclination to take advantage of the information available (*'but individually more ignorant, because we lack the time, self-control, or curiosity to do it'*). (1)

© HERIOT-WATT UNIVERSITY

Q16: *Possible answers include*:

Word Choice

- *'consumed/consumes'* suggests being destroyed (as by fire or disease);
- *'degradation'* suggests an irreparable breaking down, erosion;
- *'deprived'* suggests an unnatural deficit is being created;
- *'wealth/poverty'* contrast emphasises the inverse correlation between information and attention;
- *'reaping the benefits/deprived'* contrast emphasises we are experiencing the opposite of what we should expect;
- *'wisdom of the world/individually more ignorant'* contrast/alliteration emphasises the trade-off leaves us personally less intelligent.

Imagery

- *'bombardment'* suggests an assault, attack, war;
- *'digital withdrawal'* suggests an addiction to digital distractions, like a drug;
- *'wealth of information... poverty of attention'* metaphor emphasises the cost of increasing access to information technology;
- *'(sensory) junk'* suggests worthless clutter, bad for our health (cf. 'junk food').

Sentence Structure

- *'Hence'/ 'Thus' / 'As a result'* at start of consecutive sentences, implies an inevitability, or progression of unforeseen consequences;
- Parenthesis (*',in that...,'*) qualifies the idea that we are wiser;
- Balanced sentences (*'reaping... deprived'*; *'collectively wiser... individually more ignorant'*) draws attention to how the problems outweigh the (potential) benefits;
- Tricolon/list (*'lack the time, self-control, or curiosity'*) emphasises how much our lack of attention strips us of.

Q17:

- Prioritising immediate, quick thinking (1) over careful, deep thought. (1)

Q18: *Possible answers include*:

- '*Some scientists*' and the use of quotation from Professor David Meyer and tech writer Linda Stone mirrors the use of professional opinion cited throughout the article / lends authenticity to the writer's argument and reaffirms his stance;
- the analogy between distraction and the tobacco industry neatly summarises the key idea of the passage —that the distraction economy is a growing problem;
- writer strikes a balanced tone ('*some scientists. . . although this may be an overstatement. . .* ');
- emphatic language ('*clear. . . dramatically*') lends weight to the writer's main idea;
- the quoted oxymoron ('*continuous partial attention*') echoes the many contrasts and parallels built up throughout the passage (abundance of information/deficit of attention; wealth/poverty; attention/distraction; intelligence/ignorance);
- direct address to reader ('*Thank you for giving me yours*') leaves the reader considering their own attention in relation to the article's points;
- oxymoron and meta-textual direct address to the reader both create a humorous/light-hearted conclusion to a passage that has otherwise been relatively serious.

ANSWERS: UNIT 1 TOPIC 7

Q19:

	AREA OF AGREEMENT	PASSAGE ONE	PASSAGE TWO
1	There are an increasing number of distractions designed to catch our attention	• Examples of Facebook, Tinder, Buzzfeed, TED Talks, email, Spotify, text messaging, WhatsApp • Statistics show we are using technology for many hours every day, often on multiple screens at a time • 'non-stop media bombardment'	• example of Dunkin' Donuts aromatizer on bus • description of airport and hotel crammed with adverts
2	Our attention is valuable	• 'attention is valuable' • 'attention is limited and precious' • Michael Goldhaber's definition of the 'attention economy' • Tiziana Terranova's explanation of how increasing scarcity makes it increasingly valuable	• idea that attention should be protected like water or area; an 'attentional commons' • calls our attention a 'limited resource' • compares the exploitation of attention to the 'transfer of wealth'
3	Companies are exploiting our attention for their own gain	• 'marketers are at last coming to terms with the attention economy: the battle for monetising ephemeral interests' • says companies are fighting to catch customers' attention 'even for a few seconds'	• describes the exploitation of attention as an act of commercial greed; comparison with dumping toxic chemicals • says 'attention has been monetized' • calls advertisers 'attention-colonizers' • suggests that silence to think can only be afforded by the wealthy; example of airport business lounge

© HERIOT-WATT UNIVERSITY

	AREA OF AGREEMENT	PASSAGE ONE	PASSAGE TWO
4	We can become addicted to distraction	• explanation of the 'vicious cycle' • examples of ADHD-like symptoms during 'digital withdrawal' when separated from technology for a long time • causes physiological changes to the brain	• suggests that distractions cannot be ignored because our brains are wired to pay attention • reference to slot machine study;
5	We need to fight distraction and train our attention to be more focused	• calls it a 'crisis' • says 'distraction is destruction' • describes a 'war' over concentration • comparison with evolutionary ancestors who needed to pay attention to everything around them suggests that we need 'discipline and self-control' to do the opposite	• also calls it a 'crisis of attention' • calls for 'attentional commons' • says that we need 'self-discipline' to master technology's distractions • makes a plea to those with influence over designing public space • final sentence: 'we may have to fight hard to keep things that way, though'
6	The situation is perhaps not as grave as some might suggest	• 'Some scientists take a fatalistic outlook on this...' • 'although this may be an overstatement...'	• Writer says he is not calling for 'draconian regulations'; nor does Crawford's book. • In the final paragraph, the writer notices there are many places unaffected by intrusive distractions.

Practice paper 3: Food and diets (page 123)

Q20:

- The people he spoke to refused to believe Scottish food could be good; (1)
- he had just come from a Scottish restaurant serving delicious food. (1)

Q21: *Any two of*:

- use of humour engages the reader's interest; (1)
- establishes an upbeat tone, reflecting the article's title; (1)
- establishes a personal, informal tone continued throughout the passage; (1)
- anecdote establishes idea of a 'debate/argument' around food/eating, mirrored later in the passage by the debate around clean eating; (1)
- introduces the idea that people are willing to make pronouncements about food despite being ill-informed (*'an interrogation led, I later learned, by those that had never visited my country'*) returned to later in the article (Belle Gibson/Hemsley sisters). (1)

Q22: *Possible answers include:*

Word choice

- *'honoured'* —held in high regard, worshipped;
- *'celebrated'* —widely admired, publicised, revered, held in high regard;
- *'feted'* —widely acclaimed, publicised, talked about;
- *'latest'* —implies there have been many already;
- alliteration (*'processed... prohibited; sugars... shunned; gluten... grains gone'*) —catchy, slogan-like, mantra-like;
- *'inspired'* —suggests people have been motivated and engaged;
- *'mode'* —a fashion or fad;
- *'goddesses'* —idolised, worshipped, revered;
- *'bestselling'* —commercially popular;
- *'advancing'* —evolving, growing, continuing into the future;
- *'aesthetic'* —beautiful, admired, pleasurable;
- *'adored'* —love, respect, worship, veneration;
- alliteration (*'aesthetic adored by A-list actors, feted by the fashionistas'*) —emphasises the extent of the popularity.

Imagery

- *'wield (the greatest power)'* —suggests influence, supremacy, authority;
- *'love affair'* —suggests obsession, adoration, infatuation;
- *'sent down from Olympus... mere mortals... goddesses'* —suggests something divine, spiritual, mythic, all-powerful, sublime.

Sentence Structure

- Tricolon/list ('food, cooking and the chef'; 'honoured, celebrated and feted') —emphasises the extent of the popularity/praise;
- Tricolon/list/parallel structure ('processed foods... grains gone') —suggests the principles of clean eating have been embraced;
- Inversion —emphasises the continuing success of the Helmsley sisters in the past (*'behind them'*) and future (*'starting this week... advancing'*).

ANSWERS: UNIT 1 TOPIC 7

Q23: *Glosses of three*:

- it fails to live up to its promise; is misleading (*'gives false hope'*);
- it has become dogmatic (*'wellness evangelism'*);
- it is often based on testimony rather than evidence (*'evangelism/bad science'*);
- it can lead to bad/dangerous advice (*'please be cautious'*);
- it can be physically damaging (*'your health is too precious to lose'*);
- it is a craze/fashion (*'fad'*);
- it may based on unproven ideas (*'conjecture'*);
- it is poorly researched, not founded on valid principles (*'bad science'*).

Q24:

- *'The woman that bakes might have a point'* links back to Ruby Tandoh's warning about those who make claims about wellness (1); and looks forward to the example of Belle Gibson's dubious claims. (1)

or

- Marks a shift from looking at the popularity of food and fads (1) to the consequences and dangers. (1)

or

- Marks change in tone, from light-hearted (1), to serious and cautionary. (1)

or

- Moves from quoting/describing others (1) to personal opinion/exhortation. (1)

Q25: *Possible answers include*:

Word choice

- *'sizeable (minority)'* —suggests a significant number of men are affected;
- *'blighted'* —a plague, disease, affliction;
- *'dysfunctional relationship'* —damaged, dangerous, unable to live normally;
- *'overcome'* —suggests the condition is a hurdle or obstacle;
- *'(never fully free themselves of its) shackles'* —permanently imprisoned, limited, confined by their condition;
- contrast between what food should be (*'fundamentally fulfilling... paramount of pleasures'*) and the reality for many (*'stick to beat... eating disorders... blighted... dysfunctional... shackles... lifelong challenge'*).

Imagery

- *'a stick that some folk beat themselves with'* —food has become a weapon, torture device, source of suffering.

Sentence structure

- climactic sequence of statistics —highlights extent/rapid rise of eating disorders;
- parenthesis —adds conjecture that problem may really be even bigger than officially reported.

ANSWERS: UNIT 1 TOPIC 7

Q26: *Possible answers include:*

Tone

- disbelief, consternation, outrage, incredulity, bewilderment, indignation, confusion.

Sentence structure

- alliteration ('*profound pressure/eternal expectation/constant comparison*') —emphasises the level/variety of scrutiny that young women are under;
- intensifying adjectives ('*profound... eternal... constant*') —emphasises the enormity of the pressure that young women are under;
- list ('*the profound pressure, the eternal expectation, the constant comparison*') —emphasises the level/variety of scrutiny that young women are under;
- minor sentences ('*Six. Fat.*') —the abrupt nature of the sentence structure emphasise his shock;
- juxtaposition ('*Six. Fat*') —the absurdity of the situation/the age of the girls and their concerns about their weight is made clear;
- (rhetorical) question ('*Where is that coming from?*') —underlines his bewilderment.

Word choice

- '*profound*' suggests significant, deep rooted, overwhelming;
- '*eternal*' suggests age-old, permanent, endless;
- '*constant*' suggests no pause, no respite ever;
- '*contend*' suggests doing battle, having to juggle, having to triumph over.

Q27:

- It brings happiness ('*food is joy*');
- it is integral to our lives; it is central to many of life's milestones ('*we raise families... we fall in love... we enact business... we build out lives around food*').

© HERIOT-WATT UNIVERSITY

Q28: *Possible answers include:*

- short sentences ('*I'm all for healthy eating*'... '*But food is joy*') —emphasise the writer's impartial, even-handed approach to the issue.
- repeated use of statements —lends rhetorical emphasis; creates assertive tone;
- contrast/parallel structure/balanced sentence —lends emphasis;
- alliteration ('*food fads... detriment and damage*') —emphasises his central argument;
- makes use of alliteration, a prominent feature of the whole passage;
- emotive language ('*indulge... detriment and damage... visited upon so many*') —concludes the passage with a strong persuasive appeal;
- moves from personal/singular ('*I'm*') to wider/plural perspective ('*We*');
- climactic structure, ending with his most important point that food fads are dangerous.

Q29:

	AREA OF AGREEMENT	PASSAGE ONE	PASSAGE TWO
1	The widespread popularity of food/food fads	• sales of cookbooks, influence of bloggers, number of cookery programmes • Hemsley sisters' success	• Amanda Bacon's food diary went viral • the number of food diaries and lifestyle magazines • popularity of Buzzfeed articles and Deliciously Ella cookbooks about 'clean eating'
2	The poor quality of advice about healthy eating	• Australian guru's dubious claim to have cured cancer being investigated • Ruby Tandoh's criticism of the Hemsleys • There's a lack of scientific evidence supporting fads	• food websites and magazines encourage bad eating habits ('guidebooks for disordered eating') • Disputes suggestion that gluten-free/dairy-free, juice fasts have any nutritional benefit for most people
3	The health dangers of fads	• Australian guru's dubious claim to have cured cancer being investigated • Rising numbers of eating disorders	• diet advice often leaves one hungry • gluten-free has no health benefits for non-coeliacs • 'detoxing is a myth' • people are misdiagnosing themselves with dairy intolerance

ANSWERS: UNIT 1 TOPIC 7

	AREA OF AGREEMENT	PASSAGE ONE	PASSAGE TWO
4	The psychological impact of food fads	<ul><li>negative impact on self esteem and body image of girls as young as six</li><li>Rising numbers of eating disorders</li><li>causes physiological changes to the brain</li><li>food fads have already damaged many people</li></ul>	<ul><li>food fads encourage us to pursue something unattainable</li><li>fads damage our perception of food</li><li>'clean eating' creates a fear around other foods that can actually be healthy</li></ul>
5	Food should be enjoyable / enjoyed in moderation	<ul><li>encourages healthy eating</li><li>supports making our diets more 'balanced and nutritious'</li></ul>	<ul><li>encourages Amanda Bacon to do whatever she needs to 'stay alive and feel sane'</li></ul>

© HERIOT-WATT UNIVERSITY

Answers to questions and activities for Unit 2

Topic 1: Scottish Texts: Prose

Understanding and analysing characterisation (page 137)

Q1: b) excited.

Q2: unresponsive

Q3: b) remorseless.

Q4: b) Disgust

Q5: b) To emphasise how violently aggressive he is.

Q6: a) violent and threatening

Q7: a) arrogant.

Q8: a) It suggests how deeply he feels he needs to mock the other.

Q9: a) desperate and terrified.

Q10: c) a crushing fear.

Q11: a) Ghostly and deathly.

Q12: b) evil.

Q13: a) That the man is utterly evil.

Q14: a) poor.

Q15: b) Repetition

Key events (Precursor to themes) (page 143)

Q16:

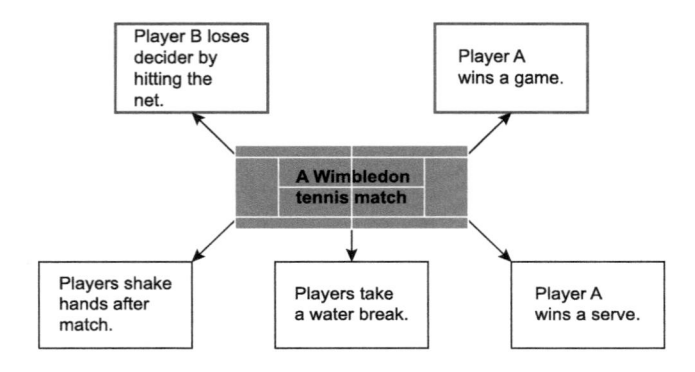

- A Wimbledon tennis match
  - Player B loses decider by hitting the net.
  - Player A wins a game.
  - Players shake hands after match.
  - Players take a water break.
  - Player A wins a serve.

ANSWERS: UNIT 2 TOPIC 1

Understanding setting (page 145)

Q17: c) love.

Q18: '... soft peach glow...'

Q19: b) identity.

Q20: '... his reflection wobbled in the windows of the building, giving only a vague impression of who he was.'

Q21: d) materialism.

Q22: a) To highlight the character's shallow motives.

Answers from page 148.

Q23: a) Triumphant and majestic

Answers from page 149.

Q24: a) terrifying that even the trees (which don't have breath to hold) were frightened into silence.

© HERIOT-WATT UNIVERSITY

End of Topic 1 test (page 151)

Q25: b) False

Q26: a) True

Q27: b) False

Q28: b) False

Q29: a) True

Q30: a) True

Q31: b) False

Q32: a) True

Q33: a) True

Q34: b) False

Q35: c) Vicious

Q36: c) Happy

Q37: a) Frightening

Q38: a) Evil

Q39: b) Kingly

Q40: c) Intimidating

Q41: b) Invisible

Q42: a) Selfish

Q43: a) Dangerous

Q44: b) Focussed

Q45: b) 10 out of 20

Q46: b) helps the author to convey their overall message.

Q47: b) setting.

Q48: c) work out meaning.

Q49: a) convey effect.

Q50: a) connotations

Q51: a) character, theme, setting and key events.

Q52: b) word

Q53: a) realism and help us to relate to a character.

Q54: b) can be extended to run through the novel.

ANSWERS: UNIT 2 TOPIC 2

Topic 2: Scottish Texts: Drama

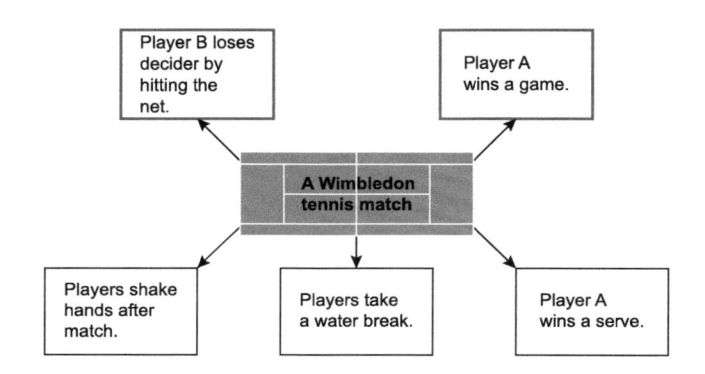

Understanding and analysing characterisation (page 160)

Q1: c) worried.

Q2: 'Abruptly', 'halt' and slowly'.

Q3: a) Alliteration

Q4: a) distracted.

Q5: a) He is secretly in love with her.

Q6: a) vengeful.

Q7: c) brave and strong.

Q8: 'Damn', 'vulture', 'black', 'hell'.

Q9: b) Death

Q10: b) arrogant and haughty.

Q11: c) Sibilant

Q12: b) wise.

Q13: b) Juxtaposition

Q14: a) Violent and merciless

Q15: a) Dangerous

Key events (Precursor to themes) (page 165)

Q16:

- Player B loses decider by hitting the net.
- Player A wins a game.
- A Wimbledon tennis match
- Players shake hands after match.
- Players take a water break.
- Player A wins a serve.

© HERIOT-WATT UNIVERSITY

Understanding setting (page 167)

Q17: a) isolation.

Q18: c) community.

Q19: b) natural beauty.

Answers from page 169.

Q20: b) That the amount of misfortune suffered seems endless.

Answers from page 170.

Q21: a) He doesn't really want to do it.

End of Topic 2 test (page 171)

Q22: b) False

Q23: a) True

Q24: b) False

Q25: b) False

Q26: a) True

Q27: a) True

Q28: b) False

Q29: a) True

Q30: a) True

Q31: a) True

Q32: a) True

Q33: b) False

Q34: a) True

Q35: a) True

Q36: b) False

ANSWERS: UNIT 2 TOPIC 2

Q37: c) Mysterious

Q38: a) Dangerous

Q39: c) Mysterious

Q40: b) Villainous

Q41: a) Dangerous

Q42: b) 10 out of 20

Q43: b) unique and vivid ways.

Q44: b) by understanding the different elements used within a character, the audience will be able to enhance their overall understanding of the text.

Q45: a) setting.

Q46: c) and when the action takes place so that we can work out meaning and theme.

Q47: a) a variety of different techniques, from soliloquy, stage directions to dialogue and props.

Q48: a) connotations

Q49: a) character, theme, setting and key events.

Q50: a) can be extended to run through the text.

Topic 3: Scottish Texts: Poetry

Form and structure: Petrarchan sonnet annotation (page 183)

Q1:

> A My letters! all dead paper, mute and white!
> B And yet they seem alive and quivering
> B Against my tremulous hands which loose the string
> A And let them drop down on my knee tonight.[1]
> A This said—he wished to have me in his sight
> B Once, as a friend: this fixed a day in spring
> B To come and touch my hand . . . a simple thing,
> A Yes I wept for it—this . . . the paper's light . . .[2]
> C Said, Dear, I love thee; and I sank and quailed
> D As if God's future thundered on my past.
> C This said, I am thine—and so its ink has paled
> D With lying at my heart that beat too fast.
> C And this . . . O Love, thy words have ill availed
> D If, what this said, I dared repeat at last![3]
>
> Elizabeth Barrett Browning
>
> * Volta: In the octave the poet focuses on her excitement at reading over the letters, whereas in the sestet she more fully reflects on the love between her and her lover.
>
> Notes:
>
> [1] In the first quatrain (the first *ABBA*) the poet describes settling down to read a bunch of old letters from a lover.
> [2] She reflects on the writer of the letters and their courting (the second *ABBA*).
> [3] In the sestet (*CDCDCD*) she changes focus to reflect more on the loves she feels for him and declares the depth of feeling she has for him.

ANSWERS: UNIT 2 TOPIC 3

Form and structure: Shakespearean sonnet annotation (page 185)

Q2:

> A Full many a glorious morning have I seen
> B Flatter the mountain-tops with sovereign eye,
> A Kissing with golden face the meadows green,
> B Gilding pale streams with heavenly alchemy;[1]
> C Anon permit the basest clouds to ride
> D With ugly rack on his celestial face,
> C And from the forlorn world his visage hide,
> D Stealing unseen to west with this disgrace:[2]
> E Even so my sun one early morn did shine
> F With all triumphant splendor on my brow;
> E But out! alack! he was but one hour mine,
> F The region cloud hath mask'd him from me now.[3]
> G Yet him for this my love no whit disdaineth;
> G Suns of the world may stain when heaven's sun staineth.[4]
>
> Notes:
> [1] In the first quatrain (ABAB) Shakespeare describes a beautiful summer's morning where the sun is shining brightly and how this makes us feel joyful.
> [2] In the second quatrain (CDCD) he describes a gloomy, cloudy morning and how that can provoke feelings of pessimism and despair.
> [3] Shakespeare builds to a climax in the third quatrain (EFEF) by using these two descriptions as a metaphor for the difference he feels when his lover is there and then gone.
> [4] In the rhyming couplet (GG) Shakespeare's solution to these feelings of pity and sadness in the absence of his lover is to realise that disappointment is part of life and that we must reconcile ourselves with this thought.

Theme: Poetry excerpts (page 188)

Q3: b) Fate

Q4: c) Religious hypocrisy

Q5: b) Realising our own faults

Q6: b) Enduring love

Q7: a) Unconditional love

© HERIOT-WATT UNIVERSITY

Theme: Explanations (page 190)

Q8:

Poem	Theme	Evidence	Explanation
'Holy Willie's Prayer'	Religious hypocrisy	At times I'm fash'd wi' fleshly lust;	Burns uses the word 'lust' to hint at Holy Willie's feelings of sexual desire and, in doing so, Burns shows that he is capable of sin, just like those he condemns, highlighting the hypocrisy that he sees inherent within the Calvinist faith.
'Address to the Deil'	Religion	Auld Hornie, Satan, Nick, or Clootie,	Burns uses a list of nicknames to refer to the Devil, immediately undermining his power and position. This shows him to be a character whose evil and intimidating characteristic have been exaggerated by the Calvinist faith.
'A Man's a Man For a' That'	Social justice	The coward slave - we pass him by,	By making reference to the ideas of passing by a beggar in the street, Burns highlights the need for equality amongst society: he does not think we should ignore those less fortunate than ourselves, but extend our help to them in the name of humanity.
'A Poet's Welcome to His Love-Begotten Daughter'	Unconditional Love	'...mishanter fa' me, If thoughts o' thee, or yet thy mamie, Shall ever daunton me or awe me, '	Burns calls upon misfortune to enter his life if he is ever embarrassed or ashamed of his daughter, or even the mother of his child. The baby may be born out of wedlock, but Burns is fully committed to being a father and loves this child in spite of the situation surrounding its birth.

Sound: Devices (page 194)

Q9: a) Alliteration

Q10: d) Sibilance

Q11: a) Alliteration

Q12: b) Assonance

Q13: c) Onomatopoeia

Q14: a) Alliteration

ANSWERS: UNIT 2 TOPIC 3

Sound: Explanations (page 196)

Q15: a) Burns uses alliteration to bring our attention to the way the alcohol tasted to Tam. He suggests that the beer was being drunk easily by Tam, emphasising the excessive way he is drinking, showing Tam to be a character of little self-restraint.

Q16: c) Burns uses sibilance to imitate the hushed voices of both Tam and the landlady, showing how they are whispering to each other. This suggests that what they are saying is salacious in some way, highlighting the inappropriate nature of their dialogue, which has been exacerbated by alcohol.

Q17: b) Burns uses assonance to mimic the wind blowing: the repeated vowel sounds slow the rhythm and reflect the continuous force of the wind. This highlights to the reader the severity of the storm and the danger it poses to anyone who has to go out in it.

Q18: a) Onomatopoeia is used to the constant drumming of the rain falling outside the pub, highlighting the ferocity of the storm and creating a sense of foreboding about what will happen to Tam.

Imagery: Identification (page 198)

Q19: Similes

- 'like a red, red rose' - the poet compares his love to a rose that is blooming during the height of summer, emphasising the growth of his love for this person.
- 'like the melodie' - here the poet compares the feelings of love he has to a song, something which is joyous and appealing that brings happiness to him.

Metaphors

- 'Till a' the seas gang dry' - the seas will not literally dry up so the metaphor implies that the love he feels for her will never dissipate.
- 'While the sands o' life shall run' - the poet imagines existence and time being measured by a sand timer, showing how the love he feels will last until the end of time.
- 'Tho' it were ten thousand mile' - at this point the poet and his love are parting, but he uses the metaphor of 'ten thousand mile' to show how he will do whatever he need to get back to her.

© HERIOT-WATT UNIVERSITY

Imagery: Analysis (page 200)

Q20:

Tam o' Shanter			
Technique	Evidence	Root	Extension
Metaphors	Tam had got planted unco right	• Fixed position • Occupying a particular place • Interred in the ground	This suggests that Tam is comfortable and relaxed, that he is rooted to the spot and unwilling to move.
Simile	Tam lo'ed him like a vera brither	• Male sibling • Kinsman • Blood relation	This emphasises the closeness of the two friends and create a convivial mood between them.
Metaphor	'Nae man can tether time or tide;'	• Tide: unstoppable rise and fall of the ocean • Time: measurements that chart existence • Tether: to control or stop	In comparing feeling of satisfaction to our inability to control time and the tides of the sea, Burns is emphasising the fleeting nature of gratification.
Simile	'Or like the rainbow's lovely form/Evanishing amid the storm'	• Arc of seven different colours in the sky caused by rain and sunshine during a storm.	Just as rainbows are an attractive sight but disappear quickly, so too does the feeling of enjoyment that may be derived from something.

Word choice: Missing words (page 203)

Q21: c) panic's

Q22: a) damned

Q23: c) divinely

Q24: b) bonie

ANSWERS: UNIT 2 TOPIC 3

Word choice: Analysis (page 205)

Q25:

Robert Burns			
Word choice	Denotation	Connotation	Link to theme
Panic's	Uncontrollable fear/anxiety	• Out of control • Wild behaviour • Hysterical	By describing the mouse as feeling panicked, Burns recognises that it feels fear and highlights the disruptive presence of man on the natural world. In some ways he sympathises with the mouse, understanding its plight as running parallel to that of the poor during Burns' era. The humanity Burns shows the mouse is something which he wishes that mankind could show to each other.
Damned	Condemned by God to hell	• Evil • Cursed • Doomed • Lost	Burns uses the word 'damned' to describe those that, according to Calvinism, are not predestined to go to heaven and, therefore, will end up in hell, regardless of their actions when on Earth. This links to the theme of religious hypocrisy as Burns is being ironic in using rhetoric that the Calvinists would use to describe those who they believe to be less worthy than themselves.
Divinely	Something which is God-like	• Exquisite • Attractive • Reverential • Magnificent	Burns uses the word 'divinely' to describe the ease with which the beer is being drunk by Tam. It gives the beer an almost reverential quality, showing how Tam thinks of the alcohol as being tempting, but also something which is beneficial. This creates a sense of irony as we know the alcohol will lead Tam to trouble.

© HERIOT-WATT UNIVERSITY

Word choice	Denotation	Connotation	Link to theme
Bonie	Attractive	• Beautiful • Charming • Engaging	The poet uses the Scots word to describe his baby daughter, clearly expressing his affection for her. This child is clearly very special to him and, unlike the rest of society, he does not view it as something he should be embarrassed by. This links to his criticism of society by highlighting the lack of humanity they express towards something so beautiful and innocent.

Sentence structure: Identification (page 209)

Q26: Repetition:

- Tho' ye come here a wee unsought *for*,
- And tho' your comin' I hae fought *for*,
- Yet, by my faith, ye're no unwrought *for*,

Enjambment:

- Or if I blush when thou shalt ca' me
  Tyta or daddie.
- An auld wife's tongue's a feckless matter
  To gie ane fash.

Exclamation:

- Welcome!
- That I shall swear!

Listing:

- bonie, sweet, wee

Parenthesis:

- by my faith

ANSWERS: UNIT 2 TOPIC 3

Sentence structure: Mind maps (page 211)

Q27:

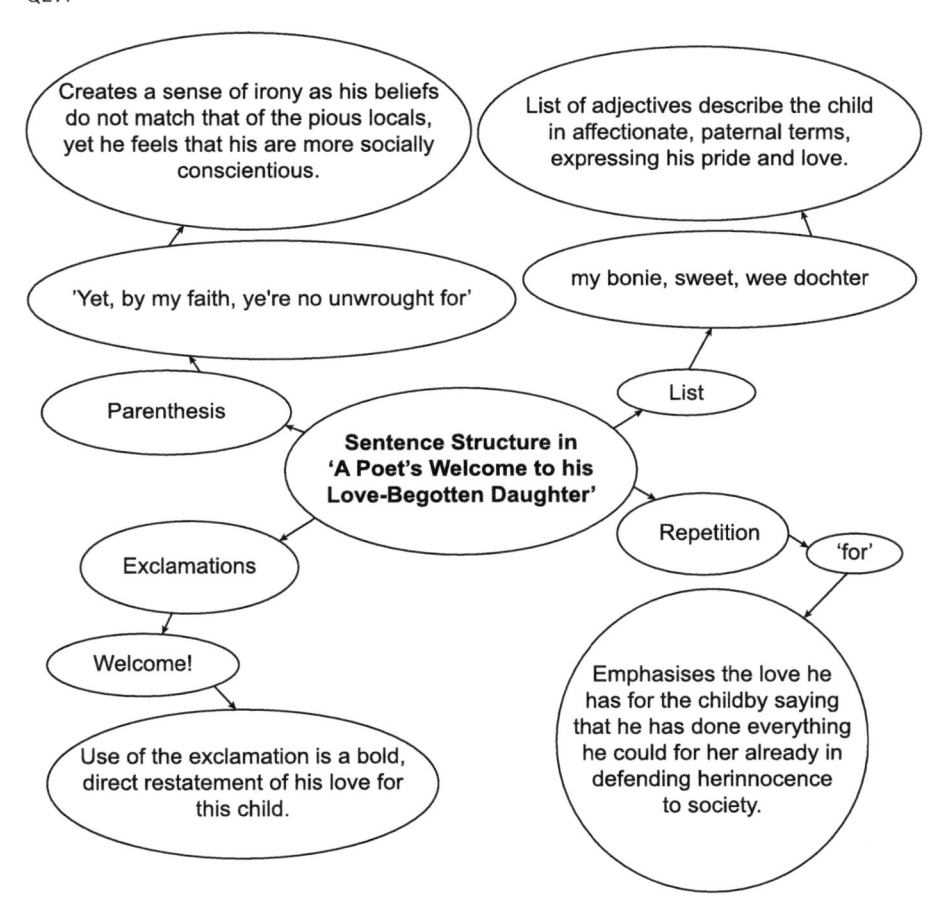

Sentence Structure in 'A Poet's Welcome to his Love-Begotten Daughter'

- **Parenthesis**: 'Yet, by my faith, ye're no unwrought for'
  - Creates a sense of irony as his beliefs do not match that of the pious locals, yet he feels that his are more socially conscientious.

- **List**: my bonie, sweet, wee dochter
  - List of adjectives describe the child in affectionate, paternal terms, expressing his pride and love.

- **Exclamations**: Welcome!
  - Use of the exclamation is a bold, direct restatement of his love for this child.

- **Repetition**: 'for'
  - Emphasises the love he has for the child by saying that he has done everything he could for her already in defending her innocence to society.

End of Topic 3 test (page 213)

Q28: b) Rhythm

Q29: a) Sibilance

Q30: b) Onomatopoeia

Q31: c) Metaphor

Q32: b) Transferred epithet

Q33: a) Inversion

Q34: b) Free verse

Q35: c) Minor

Q36: a) Parenthesis

Q37: a) Synecdoche

Q38: a) Metaphor and word choice

Q39: b) Alliteration and word choice

Q40: a) List

Q41: c) Simile

Q42: c) Metaphor

Q43: b) Onomatopoeia

Q44: b) Personification

Q45: b) List

Topic 4: Scottish Texts: Exam techniques

Key vocabulary: Exam techniques definitions (page 221)

Q1:

Something that a writer creates in a text through the use of techniques.	Mood/atmosphere
Discuss the effect of the use of poetic techniques such as alliteration, imagery, word choice.	Analyse
Refers to any techniques used in a poem by the writer.	Writer/poet's use of language
The final lines of the poem summarise the writer's main points or help us understand the theme more clearly.	Effective conclusion
This term encompasses all the techniques that a writer uses when creating a poem, such as alliteration, rhyme, simile, single sentences.	Poetic technique
These are the themes and concerns that a writer explores in a text.	Main ideas/concerns

End of Topic 4 test (page 238)

Q2: A is the better answer. It provides two quotations, each of which is discussed fully. The candidate identifies techniques exploited by Burns in each of the quotations and discusses the impact and effect of them. In answer B, the analysis is very thin and superficial. It is an example of a more basic comment.

Q3: B is the better response to the question. In this answer there is detailed and insightful analysis of the quotations, often choosing two or three techniques to discuss. In addition, the candidate also links the discussion of techniques to the themes of the poem, as well as the question. Although answer A does discuss the effect of some of the techniques used, it is more basic and does not full explain how they create pity for the mouse.

Q4: A is the better response to the question. It is more analytical than answer B. It focuses on evidence in the poem and explains how it creates the contrast between the speaker and the mouse, rather than just state what the contrast is, which is what answer B does. Answer A also explains the answer more thoroughly, making the comments detailed and insightful.

Topic 5: Critical Essay

Key vocabulary: Definitions (page 248)

Q1: b) Setting

Q2: a) Plot

Q3: c) Theme

Q4: a) Conflict

Q5: b) Climax

Q6: a) Description

Q7: c) Characterisation

Q8: a) Key incident(s)

Q9: b) Narrative technique

Q10: a) Language

Q11: a) Use of evidence

Q12: c) Stance

Q13: b) Selection of material

Q14: a) Style

Q15: c) Ideas

Q16: b) Structure

Q17: a) Theme

Q18: c) Rhythm

Q19: a) Imagery

Q20: c) Sound

Q21: c) Key sequence

Q22: a) Dialogue

Q23: b) Mise-en-scene

Q24: a) Editing

Q25: a) Special effects

ANSWERS: UNIT 2 TOPIC 5

Preparation: Activity (page 263)

Q26: c) Analysis
Q27: d) Link to overarching topics
Q28: a) Context
Q29: b) Understanding
Q30: a) Context
Q31: c) Analysis
Q32: d) Link to overarching topics
Q33: d) Link to overarching topics
Q34: b) Understanding

Q35: d) Link to overarching topics
Q36: c) Analysis
Q37: b) Understanding
Q38: b) Understanding
Q39: d) Link to overarching topics
Q40: c) Analysis
Q41: c) Analysis
Q42: a) Context
Q43: d) Link to overarching topics
Q44: b) Understanding

Q45: c) Analysis
Q46: d) Link to overarching topics
Q47: c) Analysis
Q48: a) Context
Q49: c) Analysis
Q50: b) Understanding
Q51: c) Analysis

Q52: c) Analysis
Q53: b) Understanding

Q54: c) Analysis
Q55: a) Context
Q56: d) Link to overarching topics
Q57: c) Analysis
Q58: c) Analysis
Q59: d) Link to overarching topics
Q60: c) Analysis
Q61: d) Link to overarching topics

Q62: c) Analysis
Q63: b) Understanding
Q64: c) Analysis
Q65: d) Link to overarching topics
Q66: c) Analysis
Q67: a) Description
Q68: c) Analysis
Q69: b) Understanding
Q70: c) Analysis
Q71: d) Link to overarching topics
Q72: c) Analysis

ANSWERS: UNIT 2 TOPIC 5

Criteria: Explanations (page 280)

Q73:

Understanding	Appertains to what you know about the text in terms of plot, character, setting and theme. You must show understanding of the following: 1. The text. 2. The themes and main ideas. 3. The question.
Analysis	When analysing a text in your essay, you must discuss how a writer or director uses techniques and stylistic devices to create meaning and effect.
Evaluation	When you evaluate a text in a critical essay you must show how the evidence/quotation you have discussed links to the question you are answering.
Technical accuracy	This area covers the following: 1. Spelling 2. Grammar 3. Sentence construction 4. Punctuation 5. Structure 6. Paragraphing

Criteria: True and false (page 281)

Q74: a) True

Q75: a) True

Q76: b) False

Q77: b) False

Q78: b) False

Q79: a) True

Q80: a) True

Q81: b) False

Criteria: Descriptors (page 282)

Q82: b) secure.

Q83: c) clear.

Q84: c) clearly structured and expressed.

Q85: d) adequate.

Q86: b) engaged.

The question: Past paper questions (page 289)

Q87: Choose a play in which a *major character's actions influence the emotions of others*.
[Briefly explain how the dramatist presents these emotions and actions] and [discuss how this contributes to your understanding of the play as a whole].

Q88: Choose a play which *explores an important issue or issues within society*.
[Briefly describe what happens in this scene] then, by referring to dramatic techniques, [go on to explain why the scene is important to the play as a whole].

Q89: Choose a novel or short story in which the *method of narration is important*.
[Outline briefly the writer's method of narration] and [explain why you feel this method makes such a major contribution to your understanding of the text as a whole].

Q90: Choose a novel or short story in which there is a *moment of significance for one of the characters*.
[Explain briefly what the significant moment is] and [discuss, with reference to appropriate techniques, its significance to the text as a whole].

Q91: Choose a non-fiction text which *recreates a moment in time*.
[Discuss how the description effectively recreates this moment] and [show how important this is to your appreciation of the text as a whole].

Q92: Choose a non-fiction text which is *structured in a particularly effective way*.
[Explain how the structure enhances the impact of the writer's message].

Q93: Choose a poem which *takes as its starting point a memorable experience*.
[Discuss how the poet's presentation of the experience helps you to appreciate its significance].

Q94: Choose a poem which *encourages you to think differently or to understand something in a new way*.
[Discuss how the poet's ideas and techniques led you to change your thinking or understanding].

Q95: Choose a film or television drama in which the *setting in time or place is important*.
[Explain how the film or programme makers use media techniques effectively to create this setting].

Q96: Choose a film or television drama where the *hero is not completely good and/or the villain is not completely bad*.
[Explain how the film or programme makers use media techniques to develop the hero and/or villain].

ANSWERS: UNIT 2 TOPIC 5

Analysis: Quotations and references (page 296)

Q97: b) Shakespeare uses the words 'free' and 'open' to show how Othello is a very trusting character. He is not naturally suspicious of others, something that Iago intends to fully exploit. In addition, Iago uses the word 'honest', which is something he is described as by Othello, highlighting Othello's gullibility.

Q98: a) Jenkins uses the word 'melancholy' to describe the way in which Neil feels when he remembers his past love. This shows a softer, more vulnerable side to Neil which contrasts with the tetchy and grumpy character the reader has become accustomed to.

Q99: b) By using the word 'quaint', Marvell implies that the speaker views the addressee's attitude as old-fashioned and conservative. He then uses a metaphor to warn against the destructive nature of time: by using 'dust', Marvell makes reference to the idea that soon she will die and will regret her decision.

Q100: a) Swift uses the word 'papists' to refer to the Catholic population of Ireland at the time. This derogatory term reflects the anti-Catholic feelings that existed in Ireland at the time and, by using it, Swift highlights the bigotry present within society and the prejudice with which the poor were met with. This is further emphasised by describing them as 'enemies', showing the hostility that existed towards the poor at the time.

Q101: b) Using this shot focuses the audience's attention on Norman's face. He is staring directly in to the camera as if he is directly addressing them as an individual. The menacing stare is almost defiant: he does not care if the audience judge him for his evil deeds.

Structure: Introduction (page 299)

Q102:

- Author: 'Robin Jenkins'
- Title: 'The Cone Gatherers'
- Reference to the question: 'skilfully constructs he conflict between Calum and Duror in order to parody the story of Christ'.
- Reference to the theme: 'perennial fight between good and evil'.
- Outline of what will be discussed in the essay: 'to show how the conflict that exists between the two characters develops and can only be resolved through the sacrificial killing of Calum by Duror'.

© HERIOT-WATT UNIVERSITY

Structure: Main paragraphs (page 303)

Q103:

1. Othello regains some of his honourable and heroic character in the closing lines of the play.
2. He is completely devastated after Iago's evil plot has been revealed and he has mistakenly murdered his wife:
3. Of one that loved not wisely, but too well.
   Of one not easily jealous, but being wrought,
   Perplexed in the extreme.
4. Through using the word 'wisely', Shakespeare shows that Othello has come to understand his mistake: he recognises that his jealousy was driven by his love for Desdemona, which clouded his judgement and ability to look objectively at the situation. He acknowledges the lack of jealousy within his character, but knows that he was manipulated to feel that way, placing some of the blame with Iago. In describing himself as 'perplexed', Shakespeare conveys to the audience Othello's acceptance of the tyrannical way in which he behaved, expressing regret with regards to his actions.
5. Othello wants his story to be a warning to others and urges those around him to tell it as cautionary tale as he recognises how easily he was manipulated and how devastating the consequences were. In killing himself, he dies with honour, not allowing himself to be disgraced upon his return to Venice. His suicide is his own decision, taking the control and power away from Iago and restoring some of the audience's respect for him.

Q104:

1. The depth of Duror's hatred for Calum is fully exposed in the Deer Drive.
2. He mercilessly slaughters the deer in front of Calum with no regard for his feelings:
3. 'rushing upon the stricken deer and the frantic hunchback, he threw the latter off with furious force, and then, seizing the former's head with one hand cut its throat savagely with the other. Blood spouted.'
4. Jenkins uses words like 'rushing' and 'frantic' to convey the chaos of the scene. Duror leaps on the opportunity to violently and unrestrainedly kill the deer, in order to agitate and frighten Calum. The short sentence 'Blood spouted' adds to the horrific description of the scene, emphasising the brutality and cruelty that Duror is capable of. It foreshadows Calum's death: the deer is sacrificed by Duror to satiate his hatred of Calum, much like Calum will be killed in order to cleanse the wood of the evil represented by Duror.
5. The killing of the deer exposes Duror's lack of compassion towards Calum: he subjects Calum to this level of violence in the full knowledge that it will have a devastating effect on Calum.

Q105:

1. Marvell uses increasingly violent imagery in order to convey the devastating effects of the passing of time.
2. The speaker calls upon the addressee to join him in thwarting time by taking advantage of the time they do have:
3. And now, like am'rous birds of prey,
   Rather at once our time devour,
4. Marvell uses a simile to describe the speaker and the object of his desire: he compares them to 'birds of prey', placing them in the role of hunters. Birds of prey are violent creatures that prey on smaller animals, and this suggests that the couple must be more powerful and commanding in their attitude to time. He continues this imagery by using the word 'devour', linking to the carpe diem theme: 'devour' has connotations of being overwhelmed and the couple must make the most of the time they have together before it inevitably runs out.
5. The poet is able to convey to us, through imagery, the importance of using our time wisely: he cleverly conveys the destructive power of time as something we can overcome by being proactive and enjoying the time we have to its fullest.

Q106:

1. Swift continues to expose the prejudice against the poor at the time by giving reasons as to why his proposal is valid.
2. In his third point, the speaker uses statistics and facts to outline the benefits that his proposal will bring to the community:
3. Thirdly, Whereas the maintenance of an hundred thousand children, from two years old and upward, cannot be computed at less than ten shillings a-piece per annum, the nation's stock will be thereby increased fifty thousand pounds per annum, beside the profit of a new dish introduced to the tables of all gentlemen of fortune in the kingdom.
4. The speaker refers to 'an hundred thousand' poor children being on the streets in Ireland, but there is little evidence to compound this statement. It is clear that Swift is using hyperbole in order to exaggerate the extent of the problem, mimicking the overly dramatic response of the upper classes to the poor. The speaker then claims that Ireland's GDP will increase by 'fifty thousand pounds a year', a sum based on the hypothesised numbers with no substantial evidence to back them up. Although this number would have seem impressive at the time, Swift employs hyperbole once more in order to entice the upper classes as he knows that their weakness is money and profit, not the care and well-being of other human beings.
5. Through the use of hyperbole to create humour, Swift skilfully exposes the discrimination that the poor in Ireland are met with and shows those more affluent members of society to be lacking in compassion for others less fortunate than themselves.

Q107:

1. From the opening credits alone, it is clear the Hitchcock intends to subvert all the audience's expectations.
2. Hitchcock immediately unsettles the audience and makes them feel tense.
3. In the opening credits there is loud string music played staccato and the screen in split into bars that move frantically across the screen.
4. The music is repetitive and short in length, foreshadowing the way in which Marion will be slashed later in the film. The sound is unpleasant chaotic, adding to the sense that this will not be a relaxing film to watch and that the audience will spend most of their time on edge. This is further emphasised by the bars that whizz across the scene with no apparent pattern. This reflects the mental breakdown of Norman: his ability to think logically has been completely disturbed. This echoes the feeling of the audience in response to the opening credits: the unstable and disordered movement of the bars points toward the dual personality of Norman.
5. The sound and the graphics on screen point towards instability, which is something that Hitchcock builds throughout the entire film, keeping the audience in suspense.

ANSWERS: UNIT 2 TOPIC 5

End of Topic 5 test (page 308)

Q108: c) understanding

Q109: a) analysing

Q110: b) evaluate

Q111: b) two

Q112: a) a focus

Q113: b) structure

Q114: c) micro

Q115: c) central concerns

Q116: b) topic

Q117: b) main paragraphs

Answers to questions and activities for Unit 3

Topic 1: Creative writing

Answers from page 327.

Q1: b) As he crashed into the room, he tripped over the table.

The comma splice questions (page 327)

Q2: "We need to go soon," Jane pleaded.

Q3: The river Nile, the longest in Africa, brought more dangers to his adventure.

Q4: As he left for school, he snatched his bag, his coat and a soggy piece of toast.

Q5: Following the path carefully, he entered the shelter of the silent forest.

Answers from page 333.

Q6:

Positive	Negative
Hope of rescue	Destruction
Protection	Pain

Creating characters activity (page 335)

Q7:

Technique	Advantages	Disadvantages
Using someone that you know	You understand this person and know all their habits / mannerisms	You might forget that the reader does not know this person
Using a famous person- perhaps from history	You will realise that the reader will know this person	You might not know enough about them to make them realistic
Creating a character from looking at pictures	You can visualise the person	In your story, you might not create enough of a personality for them
Basing them on characters that you have read or seen in film/television	You have a lot of ideas about the character	The characters are not yours and only copies of another writer's ideas

ANSWERS: UNIT 3 TOPIC 1

Punctuation of speech (page 343)

Q8: "Hand me that screwdriver," he demanded.

Q9: I heard a distant voice scream, "It was you."

Q10: "How did you discover the body?" he asked.

Themes in Portfolio (page 351)

Q11:

Story	Theme
'Olivia's Choice'	Family strife and coping with death.
'The Apple Incarnate'	Obsession and self-destruction.
'Shipwrecked'	Dealing with rejection and self-doubt.
'Magnum Opiate'	We get inside the mind of a conspiracy theorist.

Narrative voice in Portfolio activity: Olivia's Choice (page 353)

Expected answer

I thought back to the first day I ran away. A decision quickly made in haste, out of frustration at someone my father loved, but someone I didn't. I couldn't understand how he could move on when I couldn't, and why he would want to. All my anger about my mother's death I took out on her, and now only realising now how unfair that was. I remember the moment when I left the front door knowing I wasn't coming back - yet I so deeply wanted to. The air smelt cleaner than it did before and the outdoors more welcoming. I walked over to somewhere I called my second home, somewhere frightening to others yet for myself a place of tranquillity. I sat beside her grave and talked with her - "I'm sorry I let you down". I didn't need to tell her how upset I was - she could see it.

Story structure (page 355)

Q12:

Story structure	Description
Set-up	You set up the story by introducing the main character
Conflict	You introduce a problem or a challenge for the character
Climax	The problem develops and it reaches a worst moment
Resolution	The problem is concluded. The character has learned what they need to

© HERIOT-WATT UNIVERSITY

Conflict in Portfolio examples: Olivia's Choice (page 359)

Expected answer

> I had been living like this for seven days now. It may not seem long, but after counting every hour, every minute, and every second; it felt like an eternity. I was my own prisoner, but ironically I held the key to my escape. However my freedom would mean going back[1] and I didn't know if I was ready to leave my self-inflicted cell just yet.[2] I knew he would be worried and I knew he wanted me back but I didn't know if I could let go of the past and what the future would bring. Sitting alone staring into the darkness my stomach growling, twisted in pain from hunger was my choice. How could this be right?
>
> I don't think I had come to terms with losing her. I don't think I ever would but I had to find a way of living, I had to find a way of living without her and for myself, something she had always insisted on. My mother had only been gone a year and it all just seemed too soon, too sudden, too new.[3] I couldn't accept the change, I didn't want to - all I wanted to be wrapped in the blanket of her arms, to hear her voice and to feel her warmth yet that was nothing but a distant memory.
>
> Notes:
>
> [1] Perhaps here where there is a conflict with the past.
> [2] Perhaps the introduction to possible different outcomes.
> [3] Perhaps here where she has a conflict of feelings about change.

Conflict in Portfolio examples: Magnum Opiate (page 360)

Expected answer

> The dust smeared the car windows and the thin tyres seemed to accentuate every bloody bump they hit on the bare dirt road. He began to realise where he really was headed for - forget the 'artists' - metaphorically. This was the one story that really mattered, the magnum opus, his very own evidence to prove that behind all the dormant years scripting ads for lousy catering companies he was actually a competent and rather gifted collector of information.[1] He thought of the irony that would ensue. All the papers that previously rejected his stories, laughed at his inaudible evidence tapes of countless 'artists' and even went as far to declare him deluded and bearing the same mindset as the 'artists' themselves. But alas, here he was basking in the glory of an overheated Honda hatchback heading into God knows where to catch the mad fools in their artistic act. It was priceless, reminding him of his watch - beautifully handmade but utterly worthless and to be honest, when he really thought about it, lacking in any aesthetic appeal.
>
> Although his thoughts were that of a content disposition, even against the discomfort of the cardboard backseat he crumpled over, they were quickly shot down as the taxi came to an alarming brake stop in the middle of the dirt road. He rose quickly from his slouch to observe the surroundings outside the window caked in the midday heat. There was no house here. It wasn't even an 'artistic' illusion. It was gravel followed by gravel and a little bit of sand.

© HERIOT-WATT UNIVERSITY

ANSWERS: UNIT 3 TOPIC 1

> Emptiness. Why had we stopped? He had heard the 'artists' (he was quite happy at how well he had continued this odious analogy of 'artists'; it was one of the few humorous things he had left) hid their....ehm... art well but this level of isolation was laughable, in a horribly self-loathing kind of way. He rubbed his eyes and leaned forward to confront the driver but was set aback upon witnessing the small hairy man hunched over the wheel and bleeding. [2] He himself, hated the sight of blood and started to feel sickness in the dusty sauna of the harboured Honda. Panting melodramatically, he let himself out of his door - it's not like the dead taxi driver was going to do it - and fell back into the barren, sandy waste in a state of shock.
>
> Notes:
>
> [1] His past - behind all the dormant years scripting ads for lousy catering companies he was actually a competent and rather gifted collector of information.
> [2] Physical - He rubbed his eyes and leaned forward to confront the driver but was set aback upon witnessing the small hairy man hunched over the wheel and bleeding.

Resolution in Portfolio example: The Apple Incarnate (page 364)

Expected answer

- *Words / ideas that suggest he is now content*
- *Words / phrases which contain unpleasant ideas of images of pain*

A foggy night. He rose, wounded but awake from them. This *familiar serenity*. Ephemeral. He walked doggedly around the twisted metropolis. The sky looked kaleidoscopically pained and he too felt the air awakening. They'd be back out soon. But he was so *cosily nestled* in this small pocket of thoughtlessness, he decided he'd walk on. For the bright magenta light of the motel was bound *to welcome him back to his place of sanctuary* - the *home of resting* off his latest mess and avoiding them until the urge for repetition took over.

Story structure (page 367)

Q13:

Story structure	Description
Set-up	You set up the story by introducing the main character
Conflict	You introduce a problem or a challenge for the character
Climax	The problem develops and it reaches a worst moment
Resolution	The problem is concluded. The character has learned what they need to

Set-up in Portfolio activity: Bursting the Bubble (page 370)

Expected answer

Expected	Experienced
Similarly affluent	Traumatised
Big houses	Utter loathing
Fancy cars	Despicable village

Conflict in Portfolio Example: All Children are Artists (page 371)

Expected answer

> Thinking back to when I was five, I learned how to add numbers together and one afternoon we got to colour in and I made a tower with the Jenga blocks. I really loved school. Ignorance is bliss, right? I have tried to remember at which point I was educated beyond ignorance[1], at which point the blissful bubble of colouring in, Golden Time and playing games pretending we were anything and everything, popped and left a hollow filled with Past Papers and late nights fuelled by caffeine desperately trying to finish the thousand or so words that are[2] "...Due first period tomorrow, mum!"[3] It doesn't really matter when I finish whatever homework I'm trying to complete though. I'll stay up late pretending that I won't be woken up at 6.15 by an alarm[4] so loud it causes me pain, and struggle through another exhausting day, tired as always. Primary school seems like a distant bliss[5], waking up half an hour before going to school for a fun-filled day and finishing homework by four o'clock.
>
> Notes:
>
> [1] Conflict with self over different feelings as she gets older
> [2] Conflict with self over behaviour
> [3] Conflict with mother
> [4] Conflict with self over behaviour
> [5] Conflict with self over different feelings as she gets older

ANSWERS: UNIT 3 TOPIC 1

Conflict in Portfolio Example: Crossing the divide (page 372)

Expected answer

- Comfortable and familiar
- *Unsettling*

As we stepped off the short plane journey from Glasgow, we were greeted by the same weather as home. The short bus journey into the city was just like home. As we reached the city, it seemed like any other British city I had ever been to. But as we left the bus station and strolled past the Europa hotel (*Europe's most bombed hotel*), and down the pedestrian lane adjacent to the court house, *closed to traffic because of a persistent stream of bombs*, everything seemed normal. The people were fresh faced and friendly, never shying away from a polite nod as you passed them in the street. Everyone seemed to be living in perfect harmony. However as my trip progressed, *I learned that harmony is a word that should never be used when describing Belfast.*

We spent the next few days seeing the very tourist-orientated side of Belfast, the side of the city that they wanted you to see. We marvelled at how wonderful the Titanic was and were ushered round 'Belfast's very own leaning tower of Pisa'. All very nice and, well, touristy. It wasn't until our third and final day that I started to get a *true indication of what Belfast was really like*, not what it was supposed to be like, when I visited the Crumlin Road Jail (Or 'the Crum' as it had been nicknamed by the tourist board) there was the *odd inscription on the wall, or mark on the floor that hinted at the deep divisions in the city.*

As we walked into the prisoner's registration area, there were *cubicles where they were stripped and put into their prison clothes.* As I look into each of the cubicles, I noticed that each one was marked at least 20 times with either 'IRA' or 'UVF'. It seemed like every prisoner had a political preference, and *I found it unthinkable that the divisions in the city weren't just limited to the streets, but even the prisons had to be completely divided.* How they could keep people imprisoned alongside the very people they were imprisoned for trying to kill was beyond me.

Climax in Portfolio activity: Journeying (page 373)

Q14:

Distant sirens
Observes the woman hiding
Writer thinks of her own comforts
Writer speculates on the woman's life
The police arrive

© HERIOT-WATT UNIVERSITY

Reflection in Portfolio activity: In the Grand Scheme of Things (page 378)

Expected answer

> We all have these funny aspirations[1] and desires for things in our lives, something as simple as a good job or a nice car; personally I like clothes and appreciate a good quality leather. However these things are only material, one thing you cannot be taught in a classroom is that the only way you can be happy is to stop trying to be. Life has a habit of throwing events at us we cannot prepare for in a classroom or with a university degree. We must to an extent try to grasp the true feeling of living and being alive and cherish it while we can. We find it in that awkward moment when you laugh at your own fake laugh and end up crying, that moment when you lose your concentration and rub conditioner all over your face.[2] You can't recreate these moments; somehow getting conditioner in your eye wouldn't be as funny if you deliberately put it there. Constantly striving for new goals and aspirations will mean if we don't already appreciate what we have in that moment, as said by Omar Khayyam "Be happy for this moment. This moment is your life."[3]
>
> Notes:
> [1] Thinks of engaging the reader- appealing to things common to many people
> [2] Thinks of engaging the reader- appealing to things common to many people
> [3] Uses quotation from a famous writer to summarise her feelings

End of Topic 1 test (page 408)

Q15: a) The time / era that the story takes place, and
c) The place where the action happens

Q16: Details from their life which are needed for the story but don't happen during the timeframe of the plot.

Q17: You cannot develop more characters in 1000 word limit.

Q18: b) "This is the last time we will meet," she asserted.

Q19: She pondered, "When will this ever end?"

Q20: a) To help create a character's personality, and
c) To use dialect

Q21: c) Sneered

Q22: c) Use gestures and actions to make the reader work out how a character is feeling.

Q23:

a)	You change time - 'Later that day...' 'A few moments later...' You can use changes in time to structure a story or a personal essay.
d)	You want to create a dramatic moment- perhaps with a single sentence paragraph.
e)	You introduce a new character and describe them in some detail.
g)	A new person begins to speak.
h)	You change place - think of it like changing the scene that you would like the reader to visualise.

Q24: b) Stream of consciousness

Q25:

Third Person Objective	The narrator can only relate to the reader what is seen or heard. The narrator does not tell us what the character is thinking.
Third Person Omniscient	The narrator knows everything and can choose to tell us how characters are thinking.
Third Person Limited	The narrative voice is third person but focusses on a single character and tells the story from their point of view.

Q26: b) The story can go to places without the main character being present

Q27:
1. Set-up.
2. Conflict.
3. Climax.
4. Resolution.

Q28: c) Comparing how the writer feels now compared to the time when the action took place.

Q29: a) True

Q30: a) True

ANSWERS: UNIT 3 TOPIC 2

Topic 2: Discursive writing

Topic choice (page 414)

Q1:

Topic	Comment
Drugs in sport.	A vague topic and it covers too many areas.
Evaluating proposals to close a local hospital.	It is topical and because it is in the area where you live you will see campaigns on both sides often.
The death penalty.	There is no topic to study. No-one is seriously considering reintroducing this.
Does the government spend enough on public sports facilities?	You can use a range of health statistics and public funding statistics to explore the topic. By describing facilities in your own area you could localise the topic.

Fewer or less? (page 425)

Q2: a) fewer

Q3: b) less

Q4: a) fewer

Q5: b) less

Statistics in Portfolio activity: The Jury's Out (page 426)

Q6:

Statistic	Impact
£244,800	Proves how much is wasted on expenses
£129,579	Provides the salary for a judge- implies that more judges could be paid rather than juries
15 jurors	Implies the size of jury in relation to one accused
Decrease by 280%	Shows the extent of reduced costs

Answers from page 429.

Q7: b) Unless the First Minister changes her mind, the policy will continue as planned.

© HERIOT-WATT UNIVERSITY

Linking ideas (page 431)

Q8:

Adding	Changing direction	Being more specific	Moving on	Reasoning	Summarising
Furthermore	Alternatively	In terms of	Although	Subsequently	Finally
In addition to...	On the other hand	In relation to	Even though	Consequently	Ultimately
Similarly	Conversely	In terms of	Despite	As a result	In conclusion
Likewise	However	Specifically	Notwithstanding	Therefore	In summary

Linking in Portfolio example: Remembrance (page 432)

Expected answer

> Service in the Armed Forces may, in some cases, also lead to an increased risk of alcohol misuse and mental health difficulties. These include[1] anxiety, depression and post-traumatic stress disorder (PTSD). Therefore[2], it is likely that those ex-Service personnel who do come into contact with the criminal justice system may be affected by one or more of these vulnerabilities. On returning from prison, ex-offenders often suffer from mental health issues as well. Most commonly, these are anxiety disorders such as panic disorder and agoraphobia (being afraid of places where it might be hard to escape or worrying that there would be no access to help if something went wrong). Finally[3], research has suggested that ex-Service personnel suffer from more problems surrounding finance, benefit and debt, a lack of employment opportunities and higher rates of homelessness due to a lack of help for their mental illnesses. This makes it harder to make a smooth transition back into normal life.
>
> Notes:
>
> [1] presents a range of ideas to exemplify the topic sentence
> [2] explains the reasoning of the next step of the argument
> [3] explains a last step. Note how the argument is supported by two sentences

ANSWERS: UNIT 3 TOPIC 2

Vocabulary activity (page 434)

Expected answer

Word	Connotations	Impact
Surrendered	Suggests defeat	A word which suggests that they have been beaten- forced to change
Changed	More neutral	Neutral- more even handed
Reconsidered	Suggests control and foresight	Suggests that the policy was an active decision

Word choice in Portfolio example (page 434)

Q9: There is vast inequality between the member nations that constitute NATO.

Q10: A jury is more inclined to look beyond the evidence, feel sympathetic and be influenced by potential media coverage to reach a verdict.

Q11: However, the issue with the opt-out system is that it could result in unethical donations and accidental destruction of people's right to freedom.

Argumentative writing activity: Give Without Being Asked (page 436)

Q12:

> Furthermore, there is still a lot of debate as to whether an opt-out system is morally correct. Given a utilitarian view the donation of organs would be more beneficial to society and therefore it would seem that organ donation is nothing other than good.[1] However as human beings we are given the right to make decisions for ourselves. The concern is that although people may feel good about going and signing up for organ donation, there may be a certain amount of peer-pressure not to opt-out if presumed consent were introduced. People may feel ashamed of not wanting to donate their organs despite the fact that it is a purely personal decision and it could result in similar abuse to that regarding abortion clinics. This could once again lead to unwilling donations if someone is too afraid to opt-out and therefore introduces many issues with it becoming unethical as well as it potentially causing unnecessary conflict within our society.[2]
>
> Notes:
> [1] Argument for
> [2] Argument against

© HERIOT-WATT UNIVERSITY

Conclusions in Portfolio example - Argumentative (page 439)

Expected answer

> The ethicality of the use of embryonic stem cells for the treatment of leukaemia
>
> To conclude, although all my sympathy goes to those who have had to live with cancer or watch someone suffer from the horrors of it, [1] I do not believe that it is morally correct to destroy the life of developing embryo in order to save the life of another.[2] When there are other potential treatments for example the use of adult stem cells that could be used instead, I don't see why embryos need to be destroyed. Although the embryo is destroyed at an early stage in its development, it has the potential to become a human from the moment it is created and therefore[3] I do not believe it is morally correct to destroy the life of a developing human in order to save the life of a living one.[4]
>
> Notes:
> [1] The acknowledgement of other's arguments.
> [2] The writer's own views.
> [3] This sentence develops and explains the scale of the problem.
> [4] The writer's own views.

Argumentative writing: Techniques (page 440)

Q13:

Technique	Definition
comparison	Showing how one situation is like another
contrast	Showing how one situation is like another but with some differences
confirmation	Stating how valid your argument is or showing complexity of your argument
refutation	Denying the validity of opponents' arguments
counter-argument	An alternative argument
proof	Using hard evidence to back up your point
disproof	Using hard evidence to prove the opposing argument wrong

ANSWERS: UNIT 3 TOPIC 2

Argument handling in Portfolio activity (page 441)

Expected answer

> **The ethicality of the use of embryonic stem cells for the treatment of leukaemia**
>
> Firstly, I will be discussing the arguments in favour of the use of embryonic stem cells. The arguments include, the use of IVF and the fact that many believe anything that can be done to cure cancer, should be done.
>
> During IVF, an egg is surgically removed from the woman's ovaries and fertilised with sperm in the laboratory- the fertilised egg is then returned to the womb for foetal development. However, during this process many eggs are fertilised and only the strongest embryos are returned to the womb- the rest are then discarded. This causes many to question why IVF is not viewed as unethical as in both processes embryos are destroyed.[1] However, I disagree with this argument as the treatment of IVF has the aim to create and grow a new baby and to bring a new human with all sorts of potential into our world. Whereas the use of embryonic stem cells for the treatment of leukaemia aim to destroy a human embryo and therefore prevent a new baby to be born into our world in order to save the life of a living human.[2] This also raises the question of who exactly will be receiving the treatment. In our society it is illegal to refuse treatment to anyone with leukaemia or indeed any type of cancer, so does this mean that a human embryo with all sorts of potential is being destroyed to save the life of a criminal? Or does it mean that this embryo will be saving the life of an innocent child?[3]
>
> Notes:
>   [1] Confirmation
>   [2] Contrast
>   [3] Comparison

© HERIOT-WATT UNIVERSITY

Features of effective persuasive writing activity (page 445)

Q14:

Technique	Definition
Rhetorical questions	Questions that don't need answered but try to make the reader feel an emotional response
Three part lists	Building up force using the pattern of three: give three reasons or use three emotive ideas
First person plural	Using 'we' to include the audience
Using second person	Using 'you' to direct your comments at the reader
Emotive language	Using words and images which have strong emotional connotations
Formal language	Selecting words and phrases to give your writing a dignified tone
Statistics	Using numerical information to back up your ideas
Commands	Persuading by telling the reader what to do or think

Persuasion in Portfolio example (page 446)

Expected answer

> Remembrance
>
> On the other hand, with ex-offenders the charities available seem to be much more effective. For example, the Kenward Trust which runs a programme called 'RESET'[1] aims to help ex-offenders have a place to stay; aid with the mental illnesses; and finally gives them key life skills that would able them to care for their family. Furthermore, another charity, Blue Sky deems very successful as their figures demonstrate that from their help, 75% of the people[2] they assisted have not reoffended. Can we[3] justify a system where people who have served time in prisons be better treated than people that have served their country?[4]
>
> Notes:
> [1] Evidence
> [2] Statistics
> [3] First person plural
> [4] Rhetorical question

ANSWERS: UNIT 3 TOPIC 2

End of Topic 2 test (page 464)

Q15: b) 1300

Q16: a) Discursive writing, and
c) Creative writing

Q17: c) argumentative.

Q18: a) The internet is everywhere, we can access it twenty four hours per day.

Q19: a) Yes

Q20: a) Yes, but you need to realise that it is biased and you can balance research by looking for other points of view.

Q21: Copying someone else's work and passing it off as your own.

Q22: b) Using a paragraph from an older sibling's essay, and
c) Copying an effective sentence from a newspaper article

Q23:
Name of website with date of production (if known)

name of article and writer (if known)

full URL

[date accessed in square brackets]

Q24: d) Having a discussion about possible topics.

Q25: Topic sentence

Q26: b) Alternatively

Q27:

Positive	Deliberate
Neutral	Wait
Negative	Procrastinate

Q28:

Contrast	Showing how one situation is like another but with some differences
Refutation	Denying the validity of opponents' arguments
Counter-argument	An alternative argument

© HERIOT-WATT UNIVERSITY

Q29:

Not on the High Street

Higher Persuasive Essay by Rhona MacPhail, St Columba's School, Kilmacolm

On 15th October, the whole of the UK were left dumbfounded and shocked when Lord David Freud of the Conservative party made a comment on the minimum wage for the disabled in our society. He mentioned to a fellow party member at a Conservative Conference the month previously that some disabled workers were *'not worth the full wage'*.[1] This sparked outrage amongst the public creating excessive contempt for the Welfare minister as well as coercion from the Labour Party for him to resign. However, what is fascinating about this dispute is the apparent hypocrisy displayed by the general public, for if discrimination towards the disabled creates such emotional outrage why does it still exist in our local high street, despite our current economically advanced society.

There are currently 12 million people in Britain who have a disability[2] and although I will mainly be focusing on those with an observable physical disability such as wheelchair users, many people who suffer other disabilities; the visually and hearing impaired, are also affected by this inequality in our local high street.

'They found a fifth of shops had no wheelchair access, only 15% of restaurants and shops had hearing loops and three quarters of restaurants did not cater for those with visual impairments.'

Has our society advanced at all in the last twenty years?[3] The Disability & Discrimination Act was introduced in 1995 stating it is 'unlawful for the disabled to be discriminated against in access to goods, facilities and services.'[4] However, as the survey shows we still struggle to provide accessibility and equipment although this law entered the statute books twenty years ago; therefore, it appears we are not truly accommodating the needs of the disabled who are legally entitled to our protection.

Lack of accessibility has a much bigger impact than society cares to believe.[5] People don't consider the consequences that it creates for the disabled as well as highlighting society's lack of progress in terms of disabled rights. Since a lack of accessibility to shops can reduce the independence of some of these inspiring individuals, this in turn can create other psychological issues for the disabled person. Many people, who suffer from a disability, mainly wheelchair users, may lose some of their dignity- since they feel reliant on other people for basic requirements. Respect towards the customer with a disability is lacking if shops do not provide proper facilities and this can lead to the disabled person feeling marginalised and excluded from the mainstream community. Furthermore, this loss of autonomy leaves the disabled person embarrassed and suffering from a feeling of helplessness.[6] Inevitably, since we naturally desire freedom and independence as human beings, this realisation can leave some disabled people feeling useless. How are we to treat the disabled equally when companies aren't even acknowledging them as valued customers? We depreciate the freedom we have in being able to freely enter a shop, browse casually and take enjoyment from these simple outings. Surely we don't have the right to limit the freedom of others and yet when we look at public attitudes we are appalled at what we find - it is not only MPs who are discriminating against those with disabilities.

Let's take a closer look at Public attitudes. Over the last couple of decades our society has become more selfish and self-serving and as a consequence of that the disabled in our midst are suffering. How many of us really think about the plight of the disabled? We certainly know that many iconic retailers on our local high street do not and have appeared to remain ignorant. A recent survey claimed;

'When they asked leading chains directly for more information, only 4% (4.2) of 105 national retailers responded.'

This shows the lack of engagement and concern towards the disabled. It's as if the disabled people's plight has been cast aside by these retailers only interested in making a profit. The 12 million disabled people in Britain mentioned earlier, have an estimated £200 billion spending potential.[7] For many vast and iconic companies this is a valuable source of profit and income therefore why aren't they using this to their advantage? Despite the fact that accessibility in shops has dramatically increased over the years sadly there is still an insufficient amount of retail outlets that have the equipment necessary to meet the requirements of the disabled. And from our survey it can be seen that they do not consider the needs of the disabled as a priority. I comprehend that this is a difficult time financially since we are in the midst of a recession therefore companies do not want to invest in something that won't bring an immediate change in their turnover. How short-sighted and blind has our society become?

Some shocking stories have come to light recently regarding our ignorance surrounding the treatment of the disabled. Last October a middle-aged, blind woman called Maya Makri, attempted to enter a Tesco Express branch in Swiss Cottage, north-west London with her guide dog. Upon entering the establishment, the cashiers and staff told her that animals weren't permitted despite the guide dog being clearly identified with its harness and fluorescent jacket. In spite of telling them that she was registered blind and that her 'pet' was a guide dog she was still confronted and on the receiving end of three shouting and ignorant employees. The mere manner in how they handled the situation shows society's disregard towards the disabled since it was completely unnecessary behaviour and indicates how disabled people are patronised as consumers.[8] This is also an example of the lack of training in staff members to deal with this sort of issue responsibly and respectfully since in a recent survey only a third of retail employees had the training to assist people with disabilities. With this insufficient lack of training it merely proves how employers and public attitudes underpin the lack of impotence to make changes which would be beneficial for the disabled in our present decade.

Therefore, how are we to improve society's attitude and treatment of the disabled in our community - discrimination isn't just limited to our local high street. I understand that it would be very unlikely that we can change the whole world's opinion on those with disabilities overnight. However, there are still plenty of adjustments that can be made to improve their independence and our conduct towards the disabled. The improvements don't need to be vast or immense - a simple, clear policy in the window of a shop or an improvement in training employees in renowned retail outlets is all that's needed. If staff members were able to understand and communicate effectively with the customer by perhaps, by pronouncing words clearly then the disabled customer would notice the effort being made and feel more at ease. This surely isn't too much to ask for.[9]

However, society's attitude isn't going to change on its own. You can't change people's perceptions on the disabled if there is no one willing to listen and stand up for those in our community with a disability. If you are as agitated and passionate on this topic as I am, then set out on what you said you were going to accomplish and get up off that couch. Change starts with you.[10]

Notes:
- [1] Uses a quotation to show level of discrimination (f)
- [2] Use of statistics to prove own argument (b)
- [3] Rhetorical question (a)
- [4] Quotes legislation directly (d)
- [5] Effective linking topic sentence (c)
- [6] Dignified vocabulary (g)
- [7] Proof that the problem affects many people (h)
- [8] Use of anecdote (i)
- [9] A paragraph that presents simple, first step solutions (j)
- [10] Uses second person to address the reader (e)

ANSWERS: UNIT 3 TOPIC 3

Topic 3: Talking: Tips and techniques

Linking ideas (page 472)

Q1:

Adding	Changing direction	Being more specific	Moving on	Reasoning	Summarising
Furthermore	Alternatively	The exact detail of	Although	Subsequently	Finally
In addition to...	On the other hand	In relation to	Even though	Consequently	Ultimately
Similarly	Conversely	In terms of	Despite	As a result	In conclusion
Likewise	However	Specifically	Notwithstanding	Therefore	In summary

Features of effective persuasive talking (page 473)

Q2:

Technique	Definition
Rhetorical questions	Questions that don't need answered but try to make the reader feel an emotional response.
Three part lists	Building up force using the pattern of three: give three reasons or use three emotive ideas.
First person plural	Using 'we' to include the audience.
Using second person	Using 'you' to direct your comments at the audience.
Emotive language	Using words and images which have strong emotional connotations.
Formal language	Selecting words and phrases to give your talk a dignified tone.
Statistics	Using numerical information to back up your ideas.
Commands	Persuading by telling the audience what to do or think.

© HERIOT-WATT UNIVERSITY

Answers from page 474.

Q3:

Tone	Purpose of talk
Informative	A talk explaining UK involvement in NATO.
Persuasive	A talk to explain why you feel we need an opt-in organ donor system.
Humourous	A talk describing a Duke of Edinburgh Award Hike that went wrong and your reflections on it.

Communicating meaning: Talk tone (page 475)

Q4:

Tone	Phase of talk
Chatty/humourous	Begin with a personal anecdote to get the audience on side.
Descriptive	Describe the level of pressure that comes from exam system.
Educational	Explain some findings that you have discovered from research- perhaps by psychologists or sociologists.
Instructive	Explain to your audience how they could help with their own exam pressures as a conclusion.

End of Topic 3 test (page 481)

Q5: a) True

Q6:
- a) Persuade
- b) Entertain
- c) Inform

Q7:

First person singular	I think that hunting is immoral.
First person plural	We need to consider how cruel hunting can be.
Second person	How would you like to be chased and hunted?

ANSWERS: UNIT 3 TOPIC 3

Q8: Any three from:
- to back up your ideas;
- to persuade the audience;
- to show that you have done research;
- to inform.

Q9: b) You need to take action now!

Q10: The way in which we get the audience interested by means other than words.

Q11: Put key ideas or graphics on it.

Q12:
1. Write the talk out in full.
2. Make notes.
3. Rehearse

Q13: c) Yes but be prepared to have evidence and defend your position.

Q14:

Term	Description
Rehearse	Practice in order that you won't forget where you are or what you want to say
Pace	Keep talking but build in small pauses
Linkage	Use signpost words and phrases to join your ideas together
Relevance	Keeping the talk on subject and not wandering off topic